THE NEW NATURE OF MAPS

Published in cooperation with the
Center for American Places

SANTA FE, NEW MEXICO, AND HARRISONBURG, VIRGINIA

J. B. HARLEY

The New Nature of Maps

Essays in the History of Cartography

EDITED BY

Paul Laxton

INTRODUCTION BY

J. H. Andrews

The Johns Hopkins University Press

BALTIMORE AND LONDON

© 2001 *The Johns Hopkins University Press*
All rights reserved. Published 2001
Printed in the United States of America on acid-free paper
9 8 7 6 5 4 3 2 1   ·

The Johns Hopkins University Press
2715 North Charles Street
Baltimore, Maryland 21218-4363
www.press.jhu.edu

Library of Congress Cataloging-in-Publication Data will be found at the
end of this book.

A catalog record for this book is available from the British Library.

ISBN 0-8018-6566-2

CONTENTS

ILLUSTRATIONS

𝓑rian Harley died in Milwaukee in 1991, aged fifty-nine and at the height of his scholarly career.[1] Among the several manuscripts and publishing projects he left unfinished or in the hands of editors was a proposal for a book of his own published or forthcoming essays to be called *The New Nature of Maps*.[2] It has fallen to me to see it through to press. That has involved difficult decisions; Harley did not leave notes for the substantial introductory essay that he had envisaged, nor was it clear how and to what extent the articles in the collection were to be edited. Had he intended to reduce repetition, to restore editorial cuts, or to offer reflections on the articles with the benefit of hindsight? Given the particular appeal of this work to those interested in Harley's writings for their wider methodological or philosophical importance, there was also the challenge of providing a complete and accurate list of his publications.[3]

This volume is not intended as a memorial: Brian Harley's life as a scholar and teacher has been marked both in obituaries and in a collection of appreciative essays by his colleagues first presented at a meeting in the Royal Geographical Society in London on 17 March 1992.[4] While a full record of Harley's work is included, these, we must presume, are the articles that he thought best exemplified his philosophy of cartographic history and the meaning of maps. That philosophy has been influential beyond the confines of map history, and Harley has had an enthusiastic following. His ideas continue to excite students from a variety of disciplines, some of whom clearly idolize him.[5] On the other hand, some of his followers elevate him to "personality" status in a way that would probably have amused but embarrassed him.[6]

These essays will survive as important statements in map history, but all fields of enquiry move on, and a critical evaluation is now both necessary and healthy. I took the view that such an evaluation in the form of an introductory essay, far from being disrespectful to Brian Harley, would set up within a single volume a debate about his ideas. I have no doubt that he would have been the first to approve; vigorous intellectual discourse was in his bones. John Andrews taught at Trinity College Dublin from 1954 to 1990, establishing a reputation as the foremost authority on Irish maps and one of the few academic geographers in the British Isles with an international reputation in map history. He and Harley were friends, corresponding and exchanging ideas for many years, but they did not formally collaborate on any publications.[7] Most of their exchanges predated Harley's move to the United States, and Harley became less inclined to seek Andrews's opinion in the late 1980s, though Andrews was an editorial advisor to the *History of Cartography.* So John Andrews is particularly well placed to present an objective view (*dispassionate,* as readers will soon appreciate, would be the wrong adjective in this context) of Harley's work. He was therefore invited to produce a shortened version of the Trinity College occasional paper in which he set out his critique of Harley's map philosophy.[8]

Andrews's assessment is sometimes stringent, especially in regard to some aspects of Harley's ideological assumptions. Harley was well aware of these misgivings, and yet Andrews was the first of five scholars he named as potential referees in his submission to the Johns Hopkins University Press.[9] It is neither appropriate nor necessary in this short preface to gloss what John Andrews presents with admirable clarity, except perhaps to urge those who have embraced Harley's theoretical papers with a less than critical eye to read Andrews's essay with the same open-mindedness as its author displays to his subject. Above all, it is important that Brian Harley's philosophy of maps does not become an unquestioned orthodoxy or, worse, a catechism.[10] Some may find Andrews simply out of tune with the postmodern temperament and an uncomfortable intrusion. I can only say that the juxtaposition of his essay and the papers that Brian Harley selected to represent his own view of the new nature of maps is deliberate; this volume is not a panegyric or Harleyfest. It is, I hope, the start of a reassessment and perhaps a restatement of the themes, maybe in a different key.

The text of Harley's essays is reproduced here in its original form without editorial intervention. Bibliographical apparatus has been standardized; a handful of minor corrections have been made, some captions to illustrations expanded, references to works not yet in print when Harley wrote have been completed, and appropriate cross references have been given. Two bibliographies are provided, both of which are of interest to those wishing to understand Harley's ideas in their widest context.[11]

A consolidated bibliography has been compiled of all works cited in the seven articles reproduced here, by no means a trivial task since Harley's notes are little essays in themselves, and he had the admirable habit, editors permitting, of citing not only the works in question but where he found them cited or quoted. The bibliography, which omits the few references to Harley's own publications, is of considerable interest in itself. Of the nearly 500 works cited in the seven articles reproduced here, only fifty-three appear in more than one article, and only ten in three or more. Harley always resisted the pernicious habit of citing works just to reassure the sort of reader inclined to check the citations before addressing the text. Works are cited to give readers authority or information about a particular argument, not to provide an introductory bibliography on every uncontentious comment in the text or to satisfy the voracious appetites of citation indexers. Thus his citations are a very real insight into his intellectual journey. Harley was also meticulous in acknowledging his debts to the many scholars across a variety of disciplines from whom he collected ideas and references. His natural eclecticism was one of the foundations of his creativity.

A complete list of Harley's own publications, compiled by Matthew Edney, is also provided. It repays study and reveals several facets of Harley's research and the way he chose to disseminate his thoughts and findings. He made vigorous use of local journals and popular collectors' magazines, as well as commentaries accompanying facsimiles, to develop ideas. There is a lesson here for those who endorse the modern heresy that there is a natural pecking order for journals and publishers which, irrespective of content, confers status on authors. Indeed, Harley's early publication record would probably count for little in the hysterical climate of performance indicators that pervades universities today. Yet Brian Harley was curiously ambivalent about local details: he loved places (the 1987 essay on his favorite map, the Ordnance Survey six-inch sheet for Newton Abbot, his home for nearly twenty-two years, is testimony to that) but was reluctant to spend time on what one might call the "analysis" of early maps; and although he was an occasional expert witness in legal cases involving map evidence for rights of way—the ultimate test of a map specialist in local detail—in his research he liked to work in partnerships and have others deal with the local detail while he handled the larger picture.[12] Many of Harley's pieces on individual map makers, map collectors, or particular maps were quite short, sometimes no longer than 2,000 words of text, albeit with copious illustrations. He used them, though, to convey ideas of wider significance than the titles might suggest. There are incentives to publishing in journals that pay fees, but Harley had a practical view that, in addition to the opportunity for generous illustration, requiring modest length and little or no attention to notes and citations, such outlets also allowed him to reach a wider audience whose knowledge of maps was sometimes as extensive, and certainly as valid, as that of academic map historians. The trick was to say something significant in the fluent style at which he excelled, without patronizing the reader. These writings are never remotely vacuous; Brian couldn't stand padding.

Harley's bibliography also shows a journey through seven main topics: the historical geography of England, English county maps, English maps and atlases more widely, the mapping of America, the Ordnance Survey (both through its history as an institution and through its maps reissued in facsimile), the philosophy of map history (emerging in the 1980s), and the great project, conceived with David Woodward, of the University of Chicago Press's *History of Cartography*.[13] The temptation to see these broad topics as planned stages should be resisted: Harley followed his nose (that is, he was opportunistic in the proper sense), and, like many—perhaps most—scholars, his intellectual journey was a combination of discovering things that fascinated him, planning finite projects, and answering calls from colleagues and publishers. Even in the latter stages of his life, as the *History of Cartography* got under way, it is unlikely that he had what would be called an intellectual agenda. This point is important for those who would wish to evaluate his work; Harley *reacted* to the map history that he encountered. Being a learner and borrower from other disciplines, as well as a fighter with a personal and political ideology that made him wish to shock, he quickly identified his targets: narrow and sloppy thinking and the sort of map history that failed to acknowledge political and cultural realities. In short, Harley's best-known theoretical writings are not philosophical statements or commandments presented on tablets of stone but passionate debates intended to galvanize his readers.[14]

In some sense these essays must stand proxy for Harley's unpublished "The Map as Ideology," the chef-d'oeuvre of his ideological preoccupations in the 1980s. "Ideology" was one of the islands in the archipelago of current and planned writings mapped out on the floor of his study in Milwaukee. All the chapters in the present volume, which was a response to a request from George F. Thompson, an editor for the Johns Hopkins University Press, were written after the drafts of "The Map as Ideology." Harley had long been keen to get back to that book, the drafts of which were completed in June 1984. It is perhaps worth relating the story of that project and its relationship to the present work. According to a draft preface dated July 1984, "The Map as Ideology," described as an essay, was conceived at a meeting of the advisors for the *History of Cartography* held over a convivial lunch in Chicago in November 1983. The geographer Paul Wheatley asked whether there had ever been a Marxist interpretation of cartography. Harley, in a preface full of carefully worded disclaimers, insisted that what he had written was not "an attempt to undertake such a radical reinterpretation of the history of the map." More modestly, he wrote, "by linking the idea of maps as a living graphic 'language' with aspects of the key Marxian concept of ideology, it seeks to illustrate the possibility of writing a social history of the map rather than one which is mainly antiquarian, bibliographical or technical in its emphasis."[15]

That was probably no more than a realistic alternative to the "radical reinterpretation" raised by Wheatley's question. In January 1984 Harley presented "the outline argument" at Ruskin College, Oxford, where he received warm encouragement from a lively discussion, and from Raphael Samuel in particular, to publish the lectures as "a short book."[16] The result was the draft of "The Map as Ideology," which Harley described as an "essay . . . a preliminary sketch towards an ideological history of the map". By 1986 Harley had conceived a new and expanded outline, now entitled "The Map as Ideology: Knowledge and Power in the History of Cartography"; he seemed uncertain as to whether it was an improvement but was "glad to have waited" rather than having gone into print.[17] Unhappily, he turned to other tasks and waited too long. His readers will have to be content with the essays in this present book in place of the magnum opus.

Brian Harley's approach is not without its critics in the map fraternity, for whom philosophy and ideology are only at best subconsciously acknowledged. Barbara Belyea took him to task for his handling of philosophical sources, and a wide-ranging critique comes from cartographic historian John Andrews, whose arguments readers can judge for themselves herein.[18] On the whole, though, dissenting voices have been mute. Harley's work continues to excite great interest among geographers, historians, and the substantial number of cultural and literary historians currently exploring the relationship between maps, literature, and the visual arts. It is difficult to measure the extent to which his publications inform current research and writing, for there are no citation indexes to dissertations, theses, monographs, and collected works. However, judging by the narrower criterion of bibliographical references in journals, he continues to be widely read.[19] Harley was not, of course, the first to draw attention to the obvious point that maps can tell lies, but he did break new ground by treating their hidden agendas as an integral part of maps as texts, as recoverable experience. To do this he took arguments to extremes, often coming dangerously close to promoting conspiracy theories. One might see Harley's intellectual life as a constant tension between his natural inclination to be an inquisitive and troublesome thorn in the flesh to establishments and established ideas and his intellectual discipline, which made him ever conscious of the need to seek evidence and to appeal to reason. Jeremy Black's recent study of the way historical atlases have both reflected the historical climate of their times and created history in their own image very naturally takes its cue from Brian Harley.[20]

Brian loved to provoke an argument but was often less sure of his ground than sometimes appears from his text. Nevertheless, as John Andrews insists, "Harley must be assumed to have meant what he said," and the key texts Harley himself selected, brought together here for the first time, are presumably as open to deconstruction and interpretation as the maps he writes about.[21] It would, we may be sure, have been his hope that students would approach these essays in a lively, critical, and, above all, informed frame of mind. If they do, the future of map history will be exciting.

It is one of the regrettable ironies of modern geography that the production and study of maps should have become not just a distinct specialty but also in many respects altogether detached from academic geography. Harley may have regretted that schism (he did more than anyone to combat it by dragging cartography away from its narrow technical confines), but at the same time all his instincts rebelled against the boundaries between disciplines. His work, and its legacy in the *History of Cartography,* which continues under David

Woodward's editorship, will be regarded as significant in geography, to which Brian was committed intellectually and institutionally all his adult life. As his collaborator on the *History* recalled, Harley would often refer to the history of cartography, doubtless fully conscious of the appropriateness of the metaphor, as "a field where the vineyard is large, and the labourers few."[22] Few laborers have wielded a sharper pruning hook than Brian Harley.

BRINGING THIS BOOK to publication has been a protracted and sometimes difficult process and has only been achieved with the help of several scholars, librarians, and others. I am grateful to all of them. Essential help in procuring illustrations has been given by Jovanka Ristic, Yolanda Theunissen, Carolyn Travers, and Ronald Grim. Matthew Edney has clarified many points of detail. George Thompson and Randall Jones patiently urged the project along and kept communication alive between Liverpool, England, and Harrisonburg, Virginia, when my energy flagged. My thanks to Ellen Goldlust-Gingrich, who wrote the index. My faith in publishers has been restored by the unfailingly perceptive and efficient copyediting of Celestia Ward. Roger Kain, Catherine Delano Smith, and David Woodward commented on the preface, as did John Andrews, whose contribution in agreeing to provide the Introduction speaks for itself. Above all, for their constant guidance, support, and practical assistance in the preparation of this book, I am grateful to Catherine Delano Smith and David Woodward, both of whose associations with Brian Harley and his ideas go far deeper than a short acknowledgment can express.

THE NEW NATURE OF MAPS

Introduction

Meaning, Knowledge, and Power
in the Map Philosophy of J. B. Harley

J. H. ANDREWS

*I*t was in 1980, after a long and highly productive apprenticeship as a map historian, that Brian Harley began publishing separate essays on what might be called cartographic philosophy.[1] His immediate purpose was to establish theoretical foundations for a definitive history of cartography undertaken in coeditorship with David Woodward, but contrary to his original expectations he remained philosophically active long after the plan of the history had been decided and many of its contributors briefed.[2] By the time he died, in December 1991, Harley had written and prepared for publication more than twenty essays on different aspects of this new preoccupation. There is evidence that as the series unfolded he gave up certain of his earlier doctrines or at least attached less importance to them: it is notable, for instance, that shortly before his death, when planning to republish some of these writings, he chose none that had appeared before 1988.[3] Yet despite a considerable change of emphasis and some occasional disharmonies, none of the later essays expressly repudiates any of the earlier ones, and it seems justifiable to treat the whole sequence nonhistorically, as a set of propositions that may be either true or false. The significance of these propositions as stages in their author's intellectual development will be left for others to explore.

All Harley's writing in this genre is fluent, zestful, and compulsively readable, but what gives his philosophical judgements their authority is the combination of a close familiarity with innumerable maps of all kinds, a seemingly total knowledge of cartographic literature, and an unrivaled firsthand experience of map-historical research and writing. He was also widely read in several academic subjects not generally associated with cartography, including art history, literary criticism, and the philosophy of history, and he gathered ideas from (to quote one of his own lists) information-theory, linguistics, semiotics, structuralism, phenomenology, developmental theory, hermeneutics, iconology, Marxism, and ideology. Outside the academic arena, no reference to maps in fiction or poetry seems to have escaped him. Indeed he gives the impression of having spent a lifetime in a library with open access to every book ever published and an army of research assistants at his service. The result is a bumper harvest of concepts and theories, some of them couched in a new quasitechnical terminology and others using old terms reanimated with novel but usually unstated definitions. The invocation of names like Panofsky, Foucault, and Derrida gave notice that Harley was not alone in his new intellectual stance. (Whether these pundits would have approved his use of their ideas is another matter, though in the present context perhaps not a very interesting one.)[4] The common denominator in his treatment of other disciplines is a quick responsiveness to radical ideas. While hardly ever quoting Marx or Marxist catchwords—even *capitalism* is a rarity[5]—he shows consistent hostility towards authoritarianism, militarism, colonialism, and corporatism, as well as towards various forms of "centrism," especially the ethno- and Euro- varieties.

The peculiar quality of Harley's achievement may best be appreciated by inventing a game for map historians: Tabulate the specialized vocabularies of cartography, philosophy, and the aggregate of all other academic subjects in three columns. Choose one term at random from each column. Whoever combines these terms into the most arresting and plausible short sentence wins the round. I am not suggesting that Harley ever actually played this game, but had he done so he would certainly have beaten all comers. His judgements are seldom totally incomprehensible or self-evidently false, but they are often gnomic and idiosyncratically expressed. Many of his bolder statements occur in two forms, strong and weak, roughly corresponding to the difference between *all* and *some.* This makes his ideas hard to summarize and even harder to criticize; it would be agreeable—and in my opinion ultimately profitable—to set aside the strong versions as deliberately and challengingly overstated while accepting the weak as records of genuine belief. However, experience with other authors and their *oeuvres* has shown this policy to be misguided. In all but extreme cases, Harley must be assumed to have meant what he said.

The Problem of Self-reference

Harley considers most map makers to be less objective than they think they are. Can the same judgement be applied to him?[6] Just as a government-supported cartographer may draw maps that favor the political status quo, so from similar motives a university-supported historian might invent theories that make himself look clever and original. Conceivably, then, map scholars in institutions of higher learning feel such pressure to innovate that they some-times do so not from conviction but simply to impress a peer group or an employer. According to Harley, by the 1960s interest in maps and map history was on the wane among his fellow geographers, some of whom had taken to comparing cartographic history with philately in its allegedly uncritical con-cern for the differentiating and listing of material objects. Strong intellectual reinforcements were needed if the subject was to grow with the vigor befitting a university discipline.[7] (Harley's belief in historiographical "growth" is an evolutionary doctrine that he was reluctant to see applied to the map-making process itself.)[8] Sure enough, advanced ideas about map history began to emerge soon afterwards in the world of university education, many of them emanating from Harley himself. Yet this was a trend that found little favor among those who were mainly concerned with maps as artifacts, such as li-brarians, archivists, dealers, and collectors, and who had hitherto been equally active in the pursuit of cartographic history. This last group could make some claim to the status of impartial jury. Unlike the professional cartographers of Harley's acquaintance, the artifact specialists had no motive for opposing his philosophy; but neither—unlike the university intellectuals—did they have any motive for promoting it.

Two commentators, Richard Helgerson and Robert Baldwin, have threat-ened Harley with semipersonal arguments on the level of the foregoing dis-cussion. For some reason, perhaps tactical rather than intellectual, neither of these attacks was pressed home. Helgerson touches on the career-building motive but quickly adds the rather vague qualification that individual be-havior in this field cannot be separated from a social framework—to which it can surely be replied that social groups as well as individuals may practice the kind of self-advancement now under consideration, in this case by building entire professions rather than personal careers.[9] Baldwin claims to be deterred by the thought that opponents of deconstruction (then Harley's latest philo-sophical interest) cannot deconstruct a deconstructionist without thereby embracing the very philosophy that they seek to subvert.[10] This argument seems excessively self-regarding. If a deconstructionist's theories have the ef-fect of deconstructing himself, he does not need opponents, only spectators. In the last resort, however, these *ad hominem* criticisms have probably missed the point. We cannot disprove an author's statements about subjects other than himself by analyzing his personal psychology or defining his social position. Ulterior motives may make him less self-critical, and his theories therefore less likely to be valid; but the theories still have to be refuted in the ordinary way.

Cartographic Positivism

Before examining Harley's own ideas, we should identify the attitude, described by him as "positivism," that he claims to be bringing under critical scrutiny. His opponents are said to maintain that cartography can be, and usually is, objective, detached, neutral (in all disputes except that between truth and falsehood), and transparent—four terms which in this context probably mean much the same. Also, cartography is or can be exact and accurate. It can progress, and often has progressed, towards greater accuracy. The accuracy of maps consists of mirroring their subject matter. Harley's word, *mirror*, presents a difficulty, because it is hard to imagine any so-called positivist using it in this sense: what might be said is that accuracy depends on the degree of resemblance between two sets of space relations, one within the map itself and the other on the surface being mapped.[11] Whether the foregoing characteristics are sufficient to make cartography a "science" is an issue that (despite Harley's interest in it) may be left to civil servants and educational administrators. Nor will detailed consideration be given to Harley's judgements on the moral integrity of the map-making profession.[12] The standpoint adopted here is that of a map historian interested in philosophical questions, not that of a present-day cartographer or patron of cartographers.

According to Harley, most practicing map makers are positivists. Some readers may want proof of this. Before about 1930, cartographers made few general pronouncements of any kind about their subject, and even after that time it is hard to discover the stridency, hysteria, ideological fervor, and vigilantism that Harley claims to find (though, unusually for him, without quoting examples) in cartographic discourse.[13] However, positivism in some sense does seem an appropriate doctrine for practicing cartographers, whatever its limitations on a purely philosophical plane.

Harley does not reject cartographic positivism in its entirety. At one point he denies that maps in themselves can be true or false but immediately adds the proviso "except in the narrowest Euclidean sense."[14] He expands this phrase by admitting that an accurate road map will help a traveler reach his destination.[15] This is surely a major concession. Harley does not disagree with what cartographers say about the part of cartography that interests them. His point is that there are other aspects of the subject to which these opinions are irrelevant. Cartographers, he seems to think, are less tolerant in this respect than he is. They not only ignore the nonpositivistic element in their subject but also refuse to accept its existence. His own belief, in its stronger form, is that "an alternative epistemology, rooted in social theory rather than in scientific positivism, is *more* [not *equally*] appropriate to the history of cartography" and that "it is better to begin from the premise that cartography is *seldom* [not *not always*] what cartographers say it is."[16] In the weaker version of this view, the two epistemologies are of comparable value, one supplementing the other rather than supplanting it.[17]

A similar variation in levels of intellectual tolerance is suggested by the terminology of different varieties of history. In the historiography of many activities or artifacts, it is common to distinguish technical or business preoccupations from an attitude more concerned with social issues. It is probably the case that, in practice, each of these two approaches (not necessarily the only two available) has its own scholarly personnel, its own literature, and its own readers. However, social and professional specialists are in no sense enemies or competitors. Their disciplines are bound to overlap and interact; but in historical writing about the motor car, for instance, a publisher might well try to avoid confusion by putting the word *social* on the cover of any book that deals mainly with drive-in movies, traffic wardens, personalized registration numbers, Breathalyzers, car-bombs, joy-riding, and the decline of the village shop. Sometimes Harley advocates "a social history of cartography," apparently in this spirit of live-and-let-live multilateralism.[18] On other occasions he seems to see map history as a single arena within which a specified group of people—himself and his readers—are advised to move or shift in a "social" direction.[19]

However it is classified, Harley's nonpositivist alternative entails looking not through the map at the world it depicts but inwards or backwards to its maker and outwards or forwards to its readers. The cartographer has figured in many map philosophies, notably in the so-called communication model,[20] as a mind that registers impressions from the external world and translates them into graphic form. Harley rejects this individualistic view, even if (perhaps especially if) the individuals in question can be presented as figures of special merit or influence.[21] For him, the cartographer belongs not to a particular professional community but to society in its broadest sense. He even *defines* a map as "a social construction."[22]

In a long view of intellectual history, Harley can here be seen as heir to a tradition which developed from Kant through Hegel and Marx and rejects the premise of antecedent skepticism associated with the philosophy of René Descartes. In a Cartesian scenario, Robinson Crusoe could have been shipwrecked in infancy, survived to the age of reason without ever meeting Man Friday, and invented the art of cartography as a personal database to help him learn the layout of his island. An unfashionable figure in modern philosophy, Crusoe may be allowed an occasional comeback.[23] Cartographic philosophers should certainly remember him when they read that the map is a "socially constituted image"[24] or "inherently political."[25] They might then become aware that map making, in Harley's eyes an essentially interactive exercise, is easier for a one-man community than, say, starting a family, voting in an election, serving on a jury, or betting in a game of chance. Harley's task, an orthodox cartographic historian might suppose, is to determine how maps produced in a social setting necessarily differ from Crusoe's. In fact, Harley never frames the question in these terms, but his answer would probably distinguish different kinds of meaning and knowledge expressed in a "social" map and different forms of power exercised by it. These topics are the main concern of the present essay.

Levels of Meaning

Meaning in the sense of purpose or intention has been crucial to positivist map historiography at least since James Williamson insisted more than seventy years ago that "it is impossible to be dogmatic about the evidence of maps unless we know more than we commonly do about the intention and circumstances of those who drew them."[26] Harley took up the subject of the cartographer's intentions at a time when he was especially concerned with maps as sources for orthodox historical geography, but more than one postmodern preoccupation is foreshadowed in these early comments.[27] Intentions provide the kind of noncartographic context he was later to see as indispensable for any map-historical study. Like other kinds of meaning, they may be avowed or unavowed, conscious or unconscious, "internal" or "external" (a distinction explained later in this essay), single or multiple. Moreover, the philosophical possibilities of purposiveness should not be despised: one could, for example, debate the status of a map that is drawn with the sole purpose of proving that not every map is drawn with a purpose. In later life, however, Harley's interpretation of *meaning* was rather different, being concerned with significance rather than purpose and resting on a framework devised for art history by Erwin Panofsky.[28]

Panofsky's meanings are of three kinds. Primary elements appear in cartography as conventional signs and, more specifically, as the kind of point-symbol used for trees, mountains, settlements and the like.[29] Their equivalents in verbal language are common nouns, and like common nouns (which after all include such words as *centaur* and *phoenix*) they stake no kind of ontological claim when considered in isolation.[30] On a map, however, such symbols participate in indicative statements. These statements, we may note in passing, are far from being exclusively spatial: a sixteenth-century map containing a point-symbol surmounted by a double cross states by implication that some members of the human race may be classified as archbishops, an assertion which, whatever its philosophical significance, can hardly be dismissed as "narrowly Euclidean" but which nevertheless makes its own bid to rank as either true or false.

Later Harley applies his doctrine of silence (of which there is more below) to primary meanings: a village symbol, he claims, is "silent" to the extent that it ignores the individuality of particular villages.[31] The same argument embraces certain kinds of thematic cartography, because choropleth and isopleth maps suppress the numerical differences between areas or points belonging to the same statistical class.[32] To individualize the content of every location on every map is the cartographic equivalent of replacing all common nouns by proper nouns. This process would play havoc with verbal language, but some approach to it might be achieved in visual communication by replacing maps with air photographs. At times Harley lays so much emphasis on the weaknesses of cartography that he seems almost ready to welcome this solution, but elsewhere his faith in topographical (if not thematic) maps is made encouragingly clear.[33] Incidentally, he is wrong to give the impression that the world as mapped must appear more homogeneous than the world of common sense.[34] This may well be true of so-called general reference maps, but thematic cartography embraces many spatial variations—in atmospheric pressure, for instance—that are detectable only by scientific instruments beyond the limits of normal sensory experience. Certainly the range of soils apparent to an untrained eye in real fields and gardens can never match the chromatic splendors of a typical soil map.

Of Panofsky's secondary meaning, Harley (collaborating with M. J. Blakemore) writes: "This level of meaning Panofsky suggests is apprehended by 'realising that a male figure with a knife represents St Bartholomew' or 'that a group of figures seated at a dinner table in a certain arrangement and in certain poses represents the Last Supper.'"[35] For these second-level scriptural referents, Blakemore and Harley substitute the cartographical example of the Mediterranean Sea. A simpler case would be the appearance on a small-scale map of a single settlement. The real town of Bath in the real county of Somerset might be part of the second-level meaning conveyed by a map, its representation having some affinity in verbal language with a proper noun. A first-level counterpart would be some phrase in which all the nouns are common, such as "a spa town associated with buns and wheel-chairs." Whether this distinction matches what Blakemore and Harley have in mind is not very important, as second-level meanings play little part in their treatment of maps.

The third kind of meaning in Panofsky's system is intrinsic, latent or iconological. For Harley this category is much more interesting: it embraces mainly values, ideologies, and myths and is comparable with the similar meanings that he believes to be conveyed by art, poetry, music, and architecture. Perhaps it is at this point that the idea of rhetoric can best be introduced. Harley describes cartography as "inherently rhetorical."[36] The speaking or writing of any declarative statement whatever may indeed qualify as rhetorical in one of the word's dictionary senses, namely that of seeking to persuade or influence, though to confer a necessarily rhetorical status on "It's raining" or "There's someone at the door" can add little to anyone's understanding. It must also be allowed that many ordinary sentences can become rhetorical if uttered in suitable circumstances, a familiar case in point being the "rhetorical question." For most writers, however, and in most cases, rhetoric depends on some distinctive feature of style or vocabulary. Harley would almost certainly agree, to judge from his own references to the rhetorician's "common devices" and to rhetoric as an "ancient art," neither of which seems a very appropriate phrase for the whole faculty of human speech.[37] On this interpretation, it is natural to begin by assuming that verbal and cartographic languages probably resemble each other in being rhetorical and nonrhetorical to about the same extent. However, what Harley seems to be proposing is the much more dubious thesis that *every* map includes elements which, if translated into verbal form, would be recognized by anyone with common sense as rhetorical. Some possible examples of map rhetoric will be considered below.

Harley's symbolic meanings are expressible in verbal language as short, abstract phrases, some of which may be roughly classified as follows.[38] (1) Power relationships: empire, monarchy,[39] seigneurial authority, mercantile wealth, proprietorship, the power of cities. (2) Types of social group, real or unreal: the ideal city, the county community, the political state, the nation. (*Class* may be placed in either or both of these categories or somewhere between them.) (3) Characteristics of such groups: antiquity, fame, and celebration of cities. (4) States of mind: patriotism, "pride, attitudes towards landscape and discovery of nature."[40] (5) Systems of belief, for example, science, cosmographies, and religious systems. This list was devised especially for Tudor maps of England, but in keeping with his emphasis on rhetoric Harley believes all maps of every place and period to carry some comparable message outside the ambit of traditional geography. Rather than admit that a map may be meaningless in this sense, he would accept a category of "undecidable" meanings.[41] This gives the cynic a pointer towards a Harleian-positivist reconciliation: all maps have "intrinsic" meanings, it might be half-seriously suggested, but by an unlucky turn of fate none of those meanings is capable of being ascertained.

The Total Image

Admitting for the sake of argument that at least some meanings are decidable, just how do we set about deciding them? On Panofsky's first and second levels there are recognized codes, which are either spelled out by the cartographer (typically in a marginal key) or capable of being learned inductively, as Harley and others have learned those used in early Ordnance Survey maps.[42]

Few maps supply a key to their third-level meanings, and it is hard to see any iconological equivalent of "the ground." Two independent observers can agree on the first-level meaning of a symbol by inspecting the correlative location in the landscape and identifying what is actually there. There is nowhere they can go to verify the presence of the abstract ideas allegedly embodied in the map through any process as convincing as sensory observation. The most we can expect in this case is an analogy with other art forms whose practitioners have been more communicative,[43] which soon leads to a distinction between a map's cartographic and noncartographic properties. The latter include (1) the materials composing the map, particularly as they relate to its physical strength and durability;[44] (2) its associated decorative embellishments; (3) written inscriptions in its margin, on its reverse, or on the pages with which it is bound in a book or atlas;[45] (4) references to it in other documents, including pictures; and (5) its location, especially if this is more or less permanent.[46]

Inscriptions and documentary references have the advantage of being verbally explicit, but unfortunately they seldom mention concepts like class or empire. They also share one handicap with the other noncartographic attributes noted above. Harley strenuously denies that decoration is only a "marginal exercise" and insists that "both decorative and geographical images on a map are unified parts of a total image."[47] He later writes of having "rehabilitated" marginal decoration to the center of the map.[48] It is odd that, far from deconstructing cartography, he is here reversing a process of deconstruction carried out by those orthodox historians who had treated substance and ornament as separable categories. It is hard not to sympathize with the proponents of orthodoxy in this case. Geographical and ornamental elements in the same map have often originated with different individuals;[49] and the map compiler may well have felt as little empathy with the cartouche designer as a modern literary author feels with the picture editor who chooses illustrations for his article. This disharmony is well exemplified by Christopher Saxton's map of England and Wales (1583), where the strapwork decoration cuts across rivers, a coastline, and a town symbol in flagrant defiance of any "unification"-principle suggested by a phrase like "total image."[50]

However, such details are not crucial to the present discussion. The heart of the matter is that if, in a nonphilosophical moment, Harley had found an improbably innocent reader applying a pair of dividers to the length or breadth of a cherub or goddess, his remonstrations would surely have included the words "Cherubs are not part of the map!" or some similar expression. Once this point is granted, we are free to argue that it is the margin, and not the map (as we may now insist on calling it) that incorporates the third-level meaning. In fact it is presumably the failure of the map to incorporate this meaning that justifies the addition of the marginalia. Many cartographic historians will probably continue to see map decoration as a subject comparable with judges' wigs and gowns in a history of the law—relevant, certainly, and neglected by previous writers, but hardly worth "rehabilitating to" a central position.

Marginal decoration raises a more general problem, which can best be introduced by a comparison of maps and books. Consider any familiar work of literature that has been frequently republished without verbal alteration, and imagine every one of its English-language editions brought together in the same room. What common feature transcends all their differences of shape, size, color, physical composition, and typography? The answer is the text—or at least that would have been the answer before writers like Harley started describing buildings and landscapes as texts. Tinted end-papers and ten-point Baskerville type would hardly be considered "integral" to the meaning of *A Christmas Carol* or *Alice in Wonderland.* Can there be a cartographic text in any sense that is analogous to an author's words considered independently of their physical form? For maps that retain their interest over a long period, it may be difficult to reject this possibility out of hand. Simple copying, plagiaristic or otherwise, is not the issue here. What concerns us is rather the old estate map that is redrawn for legal purposes in the style of a later generation but with no change of content.[51] A similar case would be the copying and restyling of early maps (before the advent of photography) to illustrate an antiquarian publication or the inclusion for comparative purposes of a seventeenth-century town plan alongside a Victorian representation of the same city.[52] In such cases, the distinction between form and substance would have been regarded as enforceable by all concerned. Admittedly the analogy between maps and books may not be quite exact: there are good reasons for a cartographer to show more interest in the minutiae of engraving than an author would in letterpress printing. Yet the parallel is close enough to arouse suspicions about Harley's concept of the total image.

The Geographical Image

For these reasons, it is regrettable that in illustrating cartographic symbolism Harley should place so much reliance on what would traditionally be regarded as extraneous features.[53] Within the body of the map, most of his criteria seem reducible to the single notion of visual prominence. They may be listed as follows.

(1) Size. This has two aspects: (a) The larger the scale, the more prominent the subject. Thus Europe is favored in the equatorial case of Mercator's projection because its linear scale on this projection is larger than that of the tropics.[54] (b) Irrespective of scale, conventional signs may be large or small. Harley's example is the cartographer's endorsement of class and status divisions through variously sized symbols representing settlements of different legal, administrative, or ecclesiastical rank, regardless of the area occupied by these settlements on the ground.[55]

(2) Centrality. Whatever the scale, a cartographer will often put his own homeland in the middle of a map.[56] Harley sees this as a sign of ethnocentricity.

(3) Color. Harley's references to this subject are brief but characteristic. He notes the "appeal" and "emotiveness" of colors and deplores the Eurocentricity involved in the use of brown for land surfaces. He picks up imperialistic vibrations in a pink tint and quotes G. K. Chesterton on the cartographic redness of the British Empire. He does not repeat George Orwell's dictum that every nation colors itself red on its own maps, perhaps because there are too many exceptions to it.[57]

(4) Script. Inscriptions may be longer or shorter, larger or smaller, more or less colorful, more or less marginal; to that extent they have already been dealt with under the three previous headings. But, except in the case of place-names, prominence is more likely to be part of a word's meaning than a function of its visible form. An obvious example is the verbal identification of favored social classes, as when cartographic settlement classifications reflect the difference between nobility and gentry or between archbishops and bishops, rather than total populations or numbers of buildings. Ethnocentricity finds scribal expression in names like *Nigger Canyon* and *Squaw Hump* or (less offensive, but still presumably anathema to strict moralists) *Waterloo Bridge* and *Blenheim Palace*. And even enlightened substitutes—*Brother Canyon* and *Sister Hump*, say—would still reveal a chauvinistic preference for the English language.[58]

(5) Other cartographic properties. Harley writes:

> A map which lacks any decorative features or even caption and explanation can nevertheless stand on its own as a symbol of political authority. . . . Far from being incompatible with symbolic power, more precise measurement intensified it. Accuracy became a new talisman of authority. For example, an accurate outline map of a nation, such as Cassini provided for Louis XIV, was no less a patriotic allegory than an inaccurate one.[59]

Again,

> In "plain" scientific maps, science itself becomes the metaphor. . . . Accuracy and austerity of design are now the new talismans of authority. . . . The topography as shown in maps, increasingly detailed and planimetrically accurate, has become a metaphor for a utilitarian philosophy and its will to power. . . . Precision of instrument and technique merely serves to reinforce the image, with its encrustation of myth, as a selective perspective on the world.[60]

Here it is the very lack of visual prominence that carries meaning.[61] The properties that Harley finds symbolic in this connection are evidently any that distinguish, say, an English one-inch Ordnance Survey sheet from an Elizabethan county map. The features in question mark the progress of applied science in general and the rise of a utilitarian philosophy; they also point towards the kind of governmental apparatus needed to produce extensive large-scale maps of nineteenth-century quality.

(6) Silence. This is the most original and provocative of all the vehicles for meaning. The empty spaces on a map are "positive statements, and not merely passive gaps in the flow of language."[62] Here Harley makes a point of opposing silences to "blank spaces." Admittedly the two features look alike, but the difference between them seems genuine enough and reassuringly capable of being stated in non-Harleian language. Three kinds of proposition appear to be involved here. First, space can be described as blank when a cartographer is using it to record his ignorance. Second, there is what may be called negative space, which can be translated into any one of the "audible" sentences "this is not a town," "this is not a river," and so on until the visible thematic content of the map has been exhausted. Finally, what Harley calls silence involves a deliberate withholding of information, and his claim to positivity can just about be validated if the omission of x is taken to mean "x has certain properties that render it unsuitable for inclusion in this map."

Silence can be brought under the heading of size if symbols at the bottom of a graded series are conceived as shrinking to invisibility, for example by making towns rather than villages (or villages rather than farms) the lowest level of a settlement hierarchy, but in most cases silence forms a category of its own, heavily fraught with ideological significance. Thus subordinate ethnic groups can be silenced by ignoring their distinctive monuments, and subordinate religions can be deleted by imposing the symbolism of one religion on another, as when a cross is used to represent a mosque.[63] A more important kind of silence occurs when cartographers ignore topics unpopular with the governing class, such as poverty, pollution, and traffic congestion.[64] Cartouches may be as pointedly silent as any other part of a map, for instance when members of the working class are excluded from the marginal views in English Georgian county atlases.[65]

The Cartographic Proposition

So much for Harley's views on intrinsic meaning. Without necessarily endorsing the Panofskyan terminology, we can agree that such meanings do exist. That Saxton's maps are expressions of territorial pride, for instance, is an idea at least as old as the irredeemably pre-postmodernist map historian Edward Lynam—a fact that Harley, with characteristic vigilance and honesty, was quick to notice and acknowledge.[66] It is the method by which third-level hypotheses are validated that seems questionable, and under this heading there are two problems that require discussion. One is how to identify the objects of intrinsic meaning, the other is how to decide what is being said about these objects.

Harley's identifications are easily challenged. For example the community favored by being centrally placed on a map need not be an ethnic group. If the center of a map must be equated with people, they are people linked by proximity, not necessarily by race or culture. And from a Cartesian standpoint, a map may be regarded not as ethno- but as egocentric, like those in which the Ordnance Survey offers to place an individual customer's home at the center—though, unlike the cartographers of Harley's argument, the Ordnance Survey does not tell its clients that this arrangement has been "divinely appointed."[67] Similarly, an equatorial Mercator projection seems to favor Arctic North Americans and Asians more than any Europeans apart from

Lapps. Whatever the projection, Harley associates "Enlightenment" world maps with "the manifest destiny of European overseas conquest and colonisation," but this alleged link would at once reveal its weakness if the cartographer were identifiable as belonging to some non-imperialistically minded nation like the Swiss or Poles.[68] In the same period, it is not clear why strange-looking men and animals in remote countries should symbolize "the acquisition of overseas territory" when such oddities were equally common before the age of empire in medieval *mappaemundi*.[69] And how can an imperialistic message be conveyed by making Africans look either excessively European or excessively non-European—and also conveyed, to judge from Harley's doctrine of silences, by omitting the Africans altogether?[70] In Europe, can estates, waterways, and political boundaries really be said to typify the cartography of nation-states as opposed to that of multinational empires?[71] And in North America is it not strange that availability for European settlement should be signaled both by evidence of civilization such as roads and courthouses and also by large tracts of empty wilderness?[72]

On the topographical scale there are similar problems. A hierarchy of settlement symbols may say more about the physical character of buildings than about the social status of their occupants. Thus Harley finds social favoritism in the use of larger symbols for castles than for villages even where the villages cover more ground,[73] but castles can be seen and identified from longer distances, and visibility has always been an important practical consideration in the choice of detail for topographical maps.[74] In towns and other areas of close settlement, this ground-covering paradox becomes inoperative: a cartographer's neglect of lanes and alleyways,[75] for instance, may owe more to scale constraints than to social prejudice and may even depend on his socially "value-free" judgements about the magnitude of traffic flows. Then in Harley's discussion of marginalia it seems odd for state power to be symbolized by both the use and nonuse of decorative embellishment. Finally, not all the features of a modern topographical map can be linked with a utilitarian philosophy: such maps have sometimes been more accurate than is required by any practical need.[76]

The doctrine of silence is no more straightforward. Even on Panofsky's relatively unproblematic first level, blank and negative spaces are not always easily distinguished from silence or from each other. On the third level, the difficulty seems insuperable. Take the emptiness of the west in eighteenth-century maps of North America. Does the cartographer mean "Here is an area I know nothing about" or "What disqualifies this area from appearing on my map is the fact that its inhabitants are non-Europeans whom my countrymen are about to dispossess"? Harley naturally chooses the second interpretation, but he fails to say what makes it preferable to the first.[77] Behind this example lies the broader question: What is a map keeping quiet about? In general terms we can only reply "everything in the world except its own subject matter," but this is not an answer that gives much support to Harley's argument. Nor can the difficulty be removed by restricting the silences of map-philosophical discourse to those that common sense would find it reasonable and practicable to break. For instance, early-twentieth-century stud farms could easily have been distinguished on a large- or medium-scale Ordnance Survey map, where their characteristic field boundaries would make them a useful landmark for the traveler, but their absence can hardly be seen as proof of hippophobia among the Survey's senior staff, especially when these men—if typical of British army officers—are likely to have taken some pleasure in equestrian pursuits.

There is no doubt that maps can be rendered seriously and reprehensibly deceptive by practicing "economy with the truth": an English county cartographer who marks nine out of ten parish churches, for example, might fairly be criticized for his exclusion of the missing 10 percent. At the same time, a topographical map can show Stonehenge without implicitly promising total coverage of ancient stone circles in general. It needs little reflection on such issues to confirm that the most obvious reason for what looks like cartographic silence is shortage of space. Even the most skilled and scholarly map maker would find it hard to meet Harley's implicit demand that "the history of the landscape" should somehow be squeezed into "an ordinary road atlas."[78] Any cartographic scholar who tries to formulate general principles about the "pragmatics" of keeping silent (a task that has yet received little attention) will have to ask what map makers and map readers may reasonably expect from each other, and this in turn raises the question of what they actually do expect. Harley's treatment of map silences makes no contribution to this problem. It may even have done harm by helping to obscure the borderline between selectivity and inaccuracy.[79] At this point we may pause to emphasize a difference fundamental to clear thinking about all forms of communication. The communicator's selection process has its own psychology, its own sociology, and no doubt its own ethics. The fact remains, however, that we do not become liars by failing to give an exhaustive account of the universe every time we open our mouths. If map historians are deluded into thinking that no cartographer can ever tell the truth, they may well give up the search for truth themselves. From here it is only a short step to the active propagation of falsehood.[80]

The second general problem posed by cartographic iconology is in some respects more interesting. A general feature of symbolism is to be dominated by concepts to the exclusion of propositions. Harley's table of Tudor meanings is not unusual in this respect. It resembles the entries in a dictionary of symbolism in which a plough stands for fertilization, a bottle for salvation, a stork for filial piety, and so on.[81] Here is a significant difference between Panofsky's third level and what Harley calls the Euclidean aspect of map-communication. In traditional map reading the cartographer's task is to supply not concepts but facts; his symbols are bound into propositional form by the space relations on the map surface. Third-level symbolism possesses no such network of built-in relationships, which means that the structural or "landscape" element in Harley's "invisible landscape of ideas" must be rejected even if we accept the existence of the ideas as individual entities.[82] So, to continue the grammatical analogy, having identified the theme of a map as, say, "empire," we still have to provide this subject with a predicate—a difficult task when the language of iconology seems to be devoid of verbs.

In reply to this argument it might be contended that on its third level of meaning the map is not a statement or proposition but a gesture—of celebration, glorification, or "privileging." On this subject Harley speaks with two voices. At one point, as we have seen, he denies that maps can, in third-level terms, be either true or false.[83] But in another formulation all maps are said to "state an argument about the world and they are propositional in nature."[84] On the second hypothesis, what proposition is expressed by a map that symbolizes empire? That empires exist? That the notion of empire is in some way important or consequential? That imperialism—or at least one individual empire—is a good thing? In most of the cases he discusses, Harley would undoubtedly choose the last of these interpretations: for him maps underwrite the status quo and can be held to function in both modes,[85] performative as well as declarative, thus evading or postponing the issue of proposition versus gesture, which some people will regard as not very important anyway except to students of language and logic.

The weakness of the celebratory approach or its propositional equivalent is that there seem to be so many exceptions to it. Consider for instance Harley's comment that the North Carolina state highway map "idolises our love affair with the automobile."[86] On the plan of a hospital the various wards and departments may be at least as prominent as the roads on a road map. Do hospital plans idolize our love affair with injury and illness? An example more central to map history is the broad stream of nineteenth-century European thematic cartography devoted, often at state expense, to the mapping of poverty, crime, poor housing, illiteracy, and disease.[87] Perhaps an ingenious celebratory theorist could find some way of presenting such ostensibly self-critical endeavors as favorable to the status quo. As it happens the effort is not worth making, for Harley has already sold the pass by admitting the major exception that was noticed earlier in this essay. Many cartographers showed North America as misleadingly empty, he argues, not because they wished to perpetuate a contemporary state of affairs by having it remain empty but rather in hopeful anticipation of European settlement.[88] The force of the status-quo argument thus depends on which continent is being mapped.

If a map may express either approval (for a European nation state) or disapproval (for a near-empty American continent) how can we tell the difference? This question will arise again in due course, but in the meantime there is no help to be had from methods of portraying geographical reality: on the contrary, one of Harley's complaints about early maps of North America is that they treat the landscape as if it were part of Europe.[89] This difficulty might perhaps be met by reprieving the "total image" and even investing it with propositional status so as to assert, at first sight not very helpfully, that it is appropriate for such and such a map to be accompanied by such and such marginal features. For the sake of argument, expensive and ostensibly purposeless decoration can be accepted as signaling approval—of something or other—though even this hypothesis is implausible unless the ornament reaches a certain standard of ostentation: small amounts of conventional embellishment may accompany a negative moral judgement, as in Victorian prison architecture. Disapproval might be effectively shown by a marginal display featuring skeletons, devils, gibbets, poison bottles, and instruments of torture,[90] but within the body of the map few kinds of geographical symbolism are self-evidently moralistic. Before the advent of political correctness, grey darkening to black on a choropleth map might have seemed an appropriate color scheme for representing degrees of, say, illiteracy. Otherwise, the only obvious sign for evaluative status is an eye-catching red. This color has already been noticed as a self-congratulatory feature of political maps, but its significance is by no means patently obvious: in the Book of Isaiah scarlet is a mark not of virtue but of sin, and, within a single cartographic genre, "the best routes colored red" on one map are negated by "inferior roads red" on another.[91] It is hard to resist the conclusion that any moralist with a deeply felt message would do well to express himself in words rather than maps.

One element inadequately represented in Harley's analysis is the kind of cartography that would win his own approval.[92] If a coalition of Diggers, Levellers, and other radical groups had come to power in the seventeenth century, for example, what sort of maps would they have encouraged? Would they have reduced the English cartographer's customary emphasis on local-government boundaries, agreeing with Harley that these features "express beliefs" of the nobility and gentry?[93] And how would they have done cartographic justice to the small, scattered dwellings of the rural poor without doing more than justice to the large and space-consuming habitations of the rich? Perhaps they would have refrained from drawing any maps until all the big houses had been pulled down. Or possibly it would have been enough to write the seventeenth-century equivalent of "future state-controlled workers' rest-home" beside the symbol previously used for castles and mansions. The cartographic problem posed by the poor throughout the history of map making is simply that there are so many of them: their dwellings cannot be shown individually at the kind of scale that topographical-map readers (of any income level) are likely to find helpful. Harley does little to address this problem. He just insists that a neutral map is politically impossible. Yet if such a map is in any case technically impossible, his assertion loses much of its bite.

Knowledge and Power

Harley's use of the word *knowledge* requires comparatively little comment. His characterization of maps as a form of cognition is satisfactory on a common-sense level,[94] but in philosophical discussion knowledge may best be defined as belief that is both true and "warranted" (lucky guesses are not knowledge), and belief requires a map user as well as a map.[95] Some readers may feel uneasy at the thought of ethical propositions being true or false, but from Harley's standpoint there is no difficulty here. If a map asserts that the status quo is good, and the status quo is actually evil, then the map is to that extent incorrect and those who accept its moral judgements are not knowledgeable but ignorant—though they may still learn something from it in a "Euclidean" sense, of course.

More interesting psychologically in this connection is the ordinary geographical substance of a map. Running through Harley's later work is an undercurrent of philosophical idealism or phenomenalism which almost breaks the surface in an instinct to distance himself from truth, reality, and other such ideas by segregating their names between quotation marks.[96] In deconstructing the map, he undertakes to "break the assumed link between reality and representation."[97] Also relevant at this point is the emphasis placed on art-history, literary criticism, architecture, and music in the discussion of "texts." All four of these activities are concerned in some sense and in varying degrees with fiction. Despite his enthusiasm for interdisciplinary relationships, Harley seldom draws analogies from avowedly nonfictional forms of communication such as "straight" history, biography, and his own subject of geography. So when he describes how the world is disciplined, normalized, or structured by cartography,[98] is "the world" here to be interpreted in some figurative sense or are we to suppose that cartographers create noncartographic reality as well as representing it? The latter interpretation would put Harley in the presumably small group of map historians who regard California as a seventeenth-century island that later became attached to the mainland. In fact, his idealist tinge is probably just a rhetorical device recalling modern and postmodern applications of the word *inventing* to entities like America or Shakespeare. After all, he does concede that "it would be unacceptable for a social history of cartography to adopt the view that nothing lies outside the text."[99] Nevertheless, deprecatory quotation marks around "truth," "fact" and "reality" remain a good rough-and-ready index of a writer's capacity for self-refutation.

In Harley's last writings the emphasis shifts from meaning to power. A typical passage runs: "Cartographers manufacture power. They create a spatial panopticon. It is a power embedded in the map text. We can talk about the power of the map just as we already talk about the power of the word or about the book as a force for change. In this sense maps have politics. It is a power that intersects and is embedded in knowledge. It is universal."[100] The idea that all knowledge confers power is simply wrong: a man pushed over a high cliff gains no power from the knowledge that he will soon be hitting the ground. Just as Harley has not proved that all maps pass moral judgements, so he has not proved that all maps perform actions. As before, each group of cases must be considered on its merits, and Harley at least takes a step in the right direction by separating external from internal power.[101]

The locus of power is now defined in relation to the map-making community so that, roughly speaking, *external* means the power of noncartographers over cartographers, and *internal* means the power of cartographers over non-cartographers. No one will deny the existence of either variety of power. However, Harley prefers to blur his own distinction by claiming, for his chosen historical period, that in the exercise of internal power cartographers were "responding to the dictates of external power."[102] Both kinds of power can be expected to produce the same results, in other words. This is not a point to be labored, because in general Harley prefers to turn the spotlight on a later link in the chain of cause and effect, so that the executant of power becomes not the map maker but the map itself: that is the burden of the quotation that begins the previous paragraph and also the burden of the protest attributed to a would-be scientific cartographer—"I only draw the map. I'm not responsible for how it's used or *what it does.*"[103] For maps-in-action thus conceived, it will be more convenient to classify power alternatively as instrumental, psychological, moral, and metaphysical, though no special virtue is claimed for these categories outside the framework of the ensuing discussion.

At first sight, instrumental power offers few difficulties. Maps are universally admitted to help those who exercise power as it is normally understood, for instance in waging war, levying taxes, enforcing law and order, administering justice, and managing landed property. Harley's writings abound with examples of this relationship, and so do those of most other map historians. It is only the degree of potency that needs to be disputed. When Harley writes that "to map the land was to own it," few readers will wish to infer that every piece of real estate in North America belongs or should belong to the descendants of a land surveyor.[104] Many will be equally reluctant to make cartography "as much" a weapon of imperialism as artillery.[105] At this point, unintentionally, Harley evokes a vision of twentieth-century statesmen classifying "strategic materials" as a prelude to imposing trade sanctions on a recalcitrant foreigner. Clearly different products are "strategic" to varying degrees, with nuclear weapons at one extreme and foodstuffs at or near the other. While a map might perhaps be rolled up and used as a blowpipe for shooting poisonous darts, it cannot be placed on the same high level of purpose-built destructiveness as a mortar or field-gun. The truth is that maps, like unarmed vehicles, occupy an intermediate position in this respect. How far along the scale a substance becomes "inherently political" is a matter of taste. No inanimate object can be activated to produce material effects except within a causal framework, which in this case must include someone to read the map and someone to pull the trigger. The lower down the table of destructiveness, the more complex must be the causal aggregate and the less capacity for harm can be convincingly attributed to any one of its "strategic" components. If maps exercise instrumental power, it is only in a sense too dangerously loose to be acceptable among careful writers.[106]

Before leaving instrumental power, we may note in passing that Harley's views on this subject might be more effective if accompanied by a historian's version of "control experiments" investigating human ability to act without cartographic assistance. Boundary-making provides an obvious case in point. Maps have undeniably been used for this purpose, as Harley demonstrates,[107] but many boundaries originated before maps became available.[108] Even after the advent of accurate large-scale cartography, delimitation often took the unadventurous form of endowing old boundaries with new functions. Likewise, maps are not essential to the taxing of landed property, improbable as this may seem to nonhistorians.[109] The question prompted by these reflections is, What are the most complicated kinds of spatial thinking achieved by cartographically illiterate individuals or communities? Here is one kind of cartographic silence that no map historian appears to have investigated.[110] But at least it is clear that maps are no more a necessary condition of power-enforcement than they are a sufficient condition.

The term *psychological* can justly be applied to map-power in a nonaffective sense, denoting for instance the ability to show that Italy is shaped like a boot. This is probably what traditional writers mean by describing maps as "a very powerful tool."[111] In the Harleian system, however, psychology is a matter of attitudes and emotions. For example, by dehumanizing a landscape, maps make it easier for military commanders or civil administrators to escape the pangs of conscience when inflicting cruelty or hardship on the inhabitants of the mapped area.[112] Harley might have added that in this context every cartographic symbol is a euphemism and differs from verbal euphemisms by being untranslatable into plain language. A writer can choose between "become a fatal casualty" and "be blown to pieces," but a colored rectangle on a battle plan cannot so easily be made to resemble a group of flesh-and-blood soldiers. However, this too is not a point to linger on: no positivist cartographic historian would deny that maps may exert something of the psychological power unanimously accorded to books, plays, films, and television programs, though it might be hard to find an example as influential as the Bible or the Communist Manifesto.

The only reason for making moral power a separate category is to find temporary accommodation for Harley's concept of "legitimizing."[113] Anyone can pass a moral judgement; but to impose the attribute of rightness on a situation that was previously wrong or neutral and which in other respects remains unchanged is a power more suitable for study by theologians than philosophers, let alone cartographers. The truth is that *legitimize* in Harley's writings invariably carries the meaning "hope to legitimize" or "seem to legitimize," so that the power involved here is not truly moral but psychological. As already suggested, whether maps really are more persuasive on this level than other media is open to doubt. At any rate, they do not persuade the map-philosophers, and to assume that other readers are more gullible than we are comes perilously near to elitism.

Finally there is the power exercised by maps over the real world—if not over the coastline of California then at least over certain immaterial features such as legal boundaries and place-names. Though often considered together, the two last-mentioned cases are clearly distinct. The boundaries now at issue are not those created by politicians or civil servants, as in Harley's examples. They are made after these authorities have already defined a boundary by a verbal statement or a small-scale map statement that the practical surveyor finds too vague to be translated into one particular line on the ground.[114] The surveyor is then forced to act as his own interpreter. If his decision satisfies the interested parties, the result can count as genuine cartographic world-making, at any rate when his boundary is physically marked in the landscape.

Notice boards and street signs are less convincing "reifications" than boundaries, while spoken nomenclature is least convincing of all, for names give the impression of being "reified" only if they are widely known—and not always then. Yet Harley writes, of Columbus and other early explorers in America, that "their toponymic actions meant that the worlds that they brushed against were never quite the same."[115] The comparatively nonviolent words *brushed against* are significant. They suggest changes caused by the act of mapping itself rather than by the processes of conquest and occupation that may follow, and they also seem to acknowledge that much of the naming done by travelers and map makers has had no effect on the usage preferred by indigenous populations. "Brushing against" at any rate gives a quite different impression from the more robust phrase, "the taking away of a name," which Harley uses elsewhere, but "taking away" presents difficulties of its own by ignoring the possibility of toponymic aliases and assuming that a new name must somehow destroy all earlier names. In reality there is ample room for peaceful coexistence in this field: *Edinbourg* on some maps does not preclude the occurrence of *Edinburgh* on others any more than *Germany* is incompatible with *Deutschland*.[116] Of course, through all this discussion it remains possible for a name with emotive overtones to influence a map reader's attitudes, but here as in so many other cases the power is psychological rather than metaphysical.

As a subject for analysis, power has much in common with Panofskyan meaning. In both cases the map admits alternative interpretations but does little or nothing to help us choose between them. To reconsider some of the power categories listed above, if a map can disapprove as well as approve, so it can criminalize as well as legitimize. A cartographic euphemism can also work both ways. In a regrettably chauvinistic judgement, Jean-Jacques Rousseau condemned European philosophers who "will love the Tartars to avoid loving their neighbour," and indeed some map users (unlike Harley's desensitized military commanders) might have more sympathy with the object of a remote and anonymous symbolism than with people they feel they already know by personal acquaintance only too well.[117]

Cartography can likewise act against governments as well as for them. A record of strong points is also a record of targets, and in the interpretation of a political map my enemy's enemy becomes my friend. In principle, Harley would not disagree. He is even willing to recognize a "cartography of protest," though he cites few maps that fit this description from earlier than the 1980s,[118] and as a matter of historical fact he sees the map as authoritarian rather than revolutionary.[119] To make a map required material resources that governments were more likely to command than rebels. This opinion may be valid for accurate surveys of a large area at the behest of a postmedieval state machine, but rebellions have often been supported by foreign powers with their own map-making capacity. The maps of some potential freedom fighters—indigenous Americans, for instance—have needed no elaborate state apparatus. Within Europe, there are few modern revolutionary movements whose leaders have been too poor to buy a map. In the Irish Troubles of 1918–20, for example, the official one-inch and half-inch Ordnance Survey maps seem to have been as familiar to the insurgents as to the British army.[120] Harley does have a strong case in that governments often operate at a distance while rebels usually fight on their own ground, thus allowing maps to help tilt the balance in favor of centralized power. Yet there is nothing inherently absurd about the idea of a small, compact sovereign state being threatened by a world-wide network of map-using criminals. Not a very likely scenario in practice, perhaps; but the question that counts here is whether the criminals' maps would necessarily look different from anyone else's.

Text and Context

Among the most memorable features of Harley's writing is his fondness for words like *all, every, no, never, inherent, quintessential, universal, ubiquity,* and *rule.*[121] Thus it is not just some but all maps that include a hidden component of symbols, ideas, and even fictions transcending what is merely physical or technical. In another dimension of generality, it is not just some particular place that these ideas relate to but the whole world and indeed the whole universe. Similarly, all maps are social, presumably in that they concern people in groups rather than as individuals; they are also all political, presumably in the sense that they are social on a scale at which government institutions can be expected to recognize their existence in some way. Another universal characteristic of cartography is not only to express social and political conflicts but also to take sides in them: thus every map is also ideological, deploying thoughts as weapons in a confrontation which itself arises from essentially nonintellectual causes. And of course every map is rhetorical. Harley's *laws* (a term he never uses, it is fair to add) are propounded too often to be dismissed as carelessly exaggerated statements of less comprehensive beliefs. On the contrary, he more than once outflanks this line of defense by explicitly opposing his own universalist opinions to the less radical view that political commitment is a property of some maps but not all.[122]

A skeptic might well ask how generalizations of this kind can be justified except by inspecting every map ever produced and then demonstrating that no example has been overlooked. However, a comforting if problematic feature of Harley's work is that in his "weaker" moments such claims are moderated by being confined to a majority of possible instances, perhaps only to a minority.[123] The change can be disconcertingly abrupt. Advance and retreat may even fall within a single sentence, as when "all maps" appear as carriers of a meaning which "in many cases" mediates some social purpose or value,[124] though more often the rules and exceptions are some distance apart. On one occasion generality collapses into the irreducibly particular when Harley suggests, as a possible reply to criticism, that "our map of theory would be redrawn for each cartographic event"—a statement that seems to take empiricism as far as it can possibly go.[125]

The principle involved in these provisoes and qualifications is that each map must be seen within one or more specific contexts.[126] It may then be found to transmit different meanings, to confer power on opposing interests, or to provide evidence for incompatible historical theories.[127] Once universality is abandoned (a major withdrawal), "contextualizing" looks like a counter to many of the arguments deployed in earlier sections of this essay; but its effectiveness remains a matter for debate. To begin with, *context* cannot refer simply to spatio-temporal adjacency within a single flow of communication, as the original literary or linguistic meaning of the word might seem to require: in that sense a map would have no context unless it formed part of some larger graphic or literary composition. Harley's contexts are social or political rather than linguistic, but that does not make them any easier to define. "Placing" a map in its broader historical environment can be accepted as a worthwhile exercise. The resulting amalgam forms an agreeable object of contemplation, inducing the same mental response as a play performed with costumes and sets appropriate to its period. Some of Harley's mentors seem to regard such perceptions as sufficient to constitute an act of understanding. He himself appropriates the phrase "new ways of seeing," as well as several of the metaphors that go with it.[128] Elsewhere his language becomes more particularized:

> Any self-respecting history must systematically embrace the structures or contexts within which individuals acted to produce their maps. This "contextualisation of representation" is a thread that runs through a wide spectrum of historical scholarship. For instance, iconology seeks to place the image or text into the matrix of thought of the society that created it; realism, as understood by historians of science, assumes that there are unseen forces that both influence, and are influenced by, the actions of individuals; structuration theory is concerned with reciprocal interaction of agents and structures in society.[129]

Here "matrix of thought" clearly belongs with the ways-of-seeing package, but words like *created, forces, influenced, interaction*, and *agents* strike a more positive—and no doubt positivist—note: to understand the cartographer's achievement, they suggest, it must be linked with adjoining events by relationships that in the last analysis can only be those of cause and effect. On this point, the foregoing quotation seems to show Harley in sympathy, at least for the moment, with both realists and structuration theorists. In other essays he himself defines context as a set of interactive forces (he even underlines the word *interactive*) and writes of causal arrows flowing into and out of the map.[130] This interpretation blends smoothly into Harley's general approach. The overlap between causality and power has already been discussed. A map's context may also form part of its meaning to the extent that in ordinary language a cause can mean its effect (e.g., "Those clouds mean rain") and an effect can mean its cause (e.g., "What is the meaning of this outrage?"). The difficulty is that the links in question are so seldom available for scrutiny. We cannot get inside a dead cartographer's mind; nor is he or she likely to have left a signed statement saying "This map is meant to promote the oppression of the working class." More often the only way to interpret a map is to formulate a hypothesis about it.

Few map historians of an earlier generation would take issue with the preceding paragraph. It is in characterizing the map's external relationships that we are led back to debatable ground. At first sight, context as defined above would seem to include an almost inexhaustible variety of circumstances: for instance, if there are more villages than a map can accommodate at its chosen scale, exactly what causes the cartographer to include village A and omit village B? To a map historian the answer will be worth knowing, however trivial it may seem to anyone else. But Harley's contexts turn out to be "universally" or "ubiquitously" political.[131] True, he makes no such sweepingly unqualified assertion about the exact nature of the politics at issue. He does, however, give the impression that in the history of *most* maps two and not more than two groups of people stand opposed in one of "the larger battles that constitute our world."[132] They may be governors (of either church or state) against governed, Europeans against non-Europeans, colonizers against colonized, rich against poor, or in general strong against weak. In all these confrontations the map is wielded as an instrument of power by one side over the other. This then is Harley's hypothesis. Is it "relevant"? And has he proved it?

A gap between haves and have-nots has admittedly been part of world history for much and perhaps all of its duration, and most of what Harley says about maps could equally well be applied to works of art in general or to the written word. Indeed his historical contexts amount to little more than a description of the human predicament; this is what makes them of so little use. No doubt most men enjoy exercising power over one another; but historians might just as well be told to remember that most map-users are endowed with color vision and have difficulty handling sheets of paper more than sixty inches wide. The background is too broad and too remote from its foreground to be capable of projecting any real explanatory force: the reader in his intellectual nakedness asks for a suit of clothes, only to find himself presented with a marquee-sized tent. Harley's explanations start so far outside the map before beginning to move inwards that sometimes they never reach their goal.[133]

It may just be bad luck that when Harley's theories hit cartographic bedrock the results are often unsatisfying and sometimes factually incorrect. What he might usefully have done is propose some general method of inquiry, especially as it is so difficult to deduce any such method from his chosen examples, numerous though they are. The problems may be illustrated schematically by using H for a hypothesis about contextual relationships and p for a proposition describing a map. Let H_1 and H_2 be incompatible and assume both p_1 and p_2 to be true. It is then inconclusive to cite p_1 as evidence for H_1 if the logical relation of p_2 to H_2 is the same as that of p_1 to H_1. Here H_1 might be Harley's doctrine of the status-quo while p_2 would cover the kind of "self-critical" cartography associated with Victorian reform movements. Again, a proposition p may be consistent with a hypothesis H, but it can hardly do much to support that hypothesis if not-p is also consistent with H, which is what happens when both decoration and the absence of decoration are adduced as evidence for authoritarian map rhetoric. Similarly—and this is perhaps the commonest of the fallacies we are dealing with—no benefit comes from p being consistent with H_1 if it is equally consistent with H_2: an example is to interpret large map symbols as signs of social prominence rather than signs of visual prominence. The weakness in all these cases lies in ignoring possibilities unfavorable to the author's preconceived theory.

A notable feature of Harley's explanations, then, is how much of their weight is borne by his contexts and how little—sometimes none—by the maps themselves. To vary the metaphor, he shows cartographic historians as essentially importers of ideas but seldom if ever as exporters. To vary it again, he leads cartography into the intellectual mainstream of his time, only to see its essence unrecognizably diluted. Some of his colleagues have welcomed this trend. Why should anyone regret it? The answer must inevitably seem narrow, unaccommodating, and even bigoted, as it depends on a kind of professional and academic boundary demarcation that most scholars in their enlightened moments would profess to deplore. It may be posed as another question: in an age of specialization, how many spheres of historical judgement can be commanded by any one person? The obvious response is that surely no individual should be barred from the discussion of rhetoric, ideology, etc., by virtue of not possessing the appropriate university degrees.[134] Rhetoricians may be left to pass their own judgement on this point. What about cartographic history? For Harley, this was a scholarly subject in its own right, a subject that he did more than any other writer to define and promote.[135] To be what we might call a resident practitioner of the map-historical discipline, and not just an occasional visitor, requires a knowledge of quasitechnical subjects in which philosophers, sociologists, and literary theorists are unlikely to have received much training. Examples are geometry, metrology, terrestrial magnetism, physiography, hydrology, historical geography, semiology (of a sort), calligraphy, draftsmanship, and printing. It is by meeting at least some of these requirements that academic geographers like Harley have made their contribution to the history of maps, and it is notable that many of the "socially rooted" studies that he has welcomed have been isolated ventures into map history by scholars whose main interest was evidently elsewhere.[136] Of course Harley himself, as an orthodox map scholar, had paid his dues many times over. It would be presumptuous and impertinent to complain that in his later writings he was no longer exploiting his cartographic qualifications to the full and that at times he was even turning his back on them. Still, we can object when he urges map scholars in general to "move" or "shift" in the same direction, especially when so much work remains to be done in the history of map making as a profession. Should every trained engineer be discoursing on traffic wardens and Breathalyzers if all around us there are cars that fail to start?

The fact remains that on a "weak" interpretation Harley's essays may yet prove to be ahead of their time. His predecessors and contemporaries have known perfectly well that cartography works against a background of capitalism, elitism, nationalism, imperialism, and religious prejudice. Few of them would be surprised if privilege and victimization were found to lie behind the making of Micronesian stick charts and prehistoric European rock drawings. And not one of them would feel a thrill of discovery to read that most sixteenth-century cartographers were interested in religion and that no eighteenth-century English county map is known to have used a distinctive color for areas of avoidable poverty. But as society changes, the world that Harley wrote about will no doubt gradually grow stranger, and the trend of his thinking will begin to seem less unoriginal. When young map historians start asking "Daddy, what is class?" Harley's arguments will come into their own.

To what extent the arguments in question can influence the way maps are analyzed in the immediate future remains to be seen. At an earlier stage of his philosophical development, Harley suggested that "any theory of maps, once proved to contain even a grain or two of truth, may help to guide the historian of cartography in structuring his research."[137] It would be unfair to seize on the alarmingly modest phrase "a grain or two" as a stick to beat the philosophical Harley. The subject at issue now is the structuring of research in a more conventional sense. Yet it is research, as things turned out, that has so far done most to set the positivist and social epistemologies apart. As both R. A. Skelton and David Woodward make clear,[138] positivist historians have plenty to do when confronted with a previously unknown map. Besides establishing its date and authorship, they can analyze material form, method of drawing or reproduction, use of inks or paints, projection, graticule, scale, units of measurement, linework, extent of generalization, choice of symbols, stylistic affinities, sources of information, method of survey, influence on other maps, archival history, distribution, and use. What can the nonpositivist scholar do except say, "Just as I thought: more glorification of state power," before or after taking Skelton's and Woodward's advice? This, roughly speaking, is just what several recent writers have done.[139] It is what Harley himself has done in his capacity as coeditor of a monumental history of cartography.[140] Commended on occasion for an ability to lay out research agendas,[141] he provides no list of tasks for postmodern or post-postmodern map historians, and there seems to be no evidence that he believed the time was ripe for doing so. Of course, his untimely death has done much to weaken this criticism. For the full Harleian agenda, and the research based on it, we must depend upon a later generation.

HARLEY'S PHILOSOPHICAL WRITINGS deserve praise as a stimulus to thought in readers who might otherwise have remained unselfconsciously empirical. His allusions and citations provide an extraordinarily comprehensive guide to parallel literature in many disciplines. For the more traditionally minded cartographic historian, his abundant and wide-ranging illustrations amply demonstrate the influence of social and political factors on the way maps have been devised, produced, and used. He has subjected the "technocratic" claims of modern cartography to the kind of critical onslaught that outsiders are always glad to see leveled at any entrenched professional group. Not least important, in each of these activities he has found new ways of taking pleasure in the map itself. The writings considered here will survive as tokens of intellectual light-footedness and literary skill. All this can be gratefully acknowledged without accepting either their methods or their conclusions. And it remains possible that some other map scholar of powerful intellect will one day restate Harley's case with enough rigor and precision to convince the silent majority of his colleagues. This essay may be read as an appeal for volunteers.

CHAPTER ONE

Text and Contexts in the Interpretation of Early Maps

This chapter originally appeared as "Introduction: Text and Contexts in the Interpretation of Early Maps," in David Buisseret, ed., *From Sea Charts to Satellite Images: Interpreting North American History through Maps* (Chicago: University of Chicago Press, 1990), 3–15. It introduced a set of twelve essays on selected types of American maps.

Old maps are slippery witnesses. But where would historians be without them?

—J. H. PARRY, 1976

*A*mong the many classes of documents regularly used by historians, maps are well known but less well understood. We could compile an anthology of statements that categorize maps not only as "slippery" (the adjective used by the distinguished historian J. H. Parry), but also as "dangerous" or "unreliable." Historians have tended to relegate maps—along with paintings, photographs, and other nonverbal sources—to a lower division of evidence than the written word.[1] Much historical research and writing is undertaken without systematic recourse to contemporary maps. Moreover, even where maps are admitted as documents, they are regarded as useful principally for a narrow range of selected historical questions. It is widely acknowledged, for instance, that maps are valuable for such topics in United States history as its discovery, exploration, territorial expansion, and town planning. Less frequently are they considered as offering crucial insights into processes of social history. When a historian reaches for a map, it is usually to answer a fairly narrow question about location or topography and less often to illuminate cultural history or the social values of a particular period or place. Why should maps have suffered such neglect?

Part of the answer, as already noted, lies in the attitudes of historians. Writing about the history of maps per se has been at best a marginal interest for mainstream historians: when, we may ask, did an article about cartography last appear in *The American Historical Review?* Yet part of the problem also lies with those who call themselves historians of cartography. In describing the bibliographical and technical complexity of maps, they have failed to communicate an understanding of their social nature. In the light of these tendencies, the answer to the question "What is a map?" is a vital preliminary to the fruitful interrogation of maps as historical documents.

Mirror or Text?

The usual perception of the nature of maps is that they are a mirror, a graphic representation, of some aspect of the real world. The definitions set out in various dictionaries and glossaries of cartography confirm this view.[2] Within the constraints of survey techniques, the skill of the cartographer, and the code of conventional signs, the role of a map is to present a factual statement about geographical reality. Although cartographers write about the art as well as the science of map making, science has overshadowed the competition between the two approaches. The corollary is that when historians assess maps, their interpretive strategies are molded by this idea of what maps are claimed to be. In our own Western culture, at least since the Enlightenment, cartography has been defined as a factual science. The premise is that a map should offer a transparent window on the world. A good map is an accurate map. Where a map fails to deal with reality adequately on a factual scale, it gets a black mark. Maps are ranked according to their correspondence with topographical truth. Inaccuracy, we are told, is a cartographic crime.

This value judgment is often translated into the way we read old maps. It promotes a mode of interpretation that emphasizes the factual or literal statements maps make about an empirical reality. Whether depicting the Caribbean landfall of a sixteenth-century navigator or the relict features of some ghost town from a nineteenth-century mining boom, the map is judged in terms of the positioning of its coordinates, the shape of its outlines, or the reliability of features measured in the landscape. It is used purely and simply as a quarry of facts in the reconstruction of the past. I am not suggesting that we downgrade this historical application of old maps. As an index to the location of things, processes, and events in the past maps are a unique form of documentation. Locating human actions in space remains the greatest intellectual achievement of the map as a form of knowledge.

There is, however, an alternative answer to the question "What is a map?" For historians an equally appropriate definition of a map is "a social construction of the world expressed through the medium of cartography." Far from holding up a simple mirror of nature that is true or false, maps redescribe the world—like any other document—in terms of relations of power and of cultural practices, preferences, and priorities. What we read on a map is as much related to an invisible social world and to ideology as it is to phenomena seen and measured in the landscape. Maps always show more than an un-mediated sum of a set of techniques. The apparent duplicity of maps—their "slipperiness"—is not some idiosyncratic deviation from an illusory perfect map. Rather it lies at the heart of cartographic representation. Herein lies a historical opportunity. The fascination of maps as humanly created docu-ments is found not merely in the extent to which they are objective or accu-rate. It also lies in their inherent ambivalence and in our ability to tease out new meanings, hidden agendas, and contrasting world views from between the lines on the image.

In introducing ways of interpreting the maps of America, I propose a different interpretative metaphor. They will be discussed as text rather than as a mirror of nature. Maps are text in the same senses that other nonverbal sign systems—paintings, prints, theater, films, television, music—are texts. Maps also share many common concerns with the study of the book, exhibiting a textual function in the world and being "subject to bibliographical control, interpretation, and historical analysis."[3] Maps are a graphic language to be decoded. They are a construction of reality, images laden with intentions and consequences that can be studied in the societies of their time. Like books, they are also the products of both individual minds and the wider cultural values in particular societies.

Signs, Symbols, and Rhetoric

Like all other texts, maps use signs to represent the world. When these become fixed in a map genre, we define them as conventional signs. Maps do not possess a grammar in the mode of written language, but they are none-theless deliberately designed texts, created by the application of principles and techniques and developed as formal systems of communication by map makers. In modern cartography strenuous efforts have been made to stan-dardize these rules of map composition. Textbooks and models tell us how the world should "best" be graphically represented in terms of lines, colors, sym-bols, and topography.[4] For some of the older maps that are described below there were also rule books for their construction and design, and vocabularies of different signs. Such works can act as a grammar or dictionary in learning to read or translate the map text.

The symbolic dimension of maps also links them to other texts. Modern cartographers usually regard their maps as factual statements written in the language of mathematics, but they are always metaphors or symbols of the world. A mode of interpreting such symbolic layers of meaning by employing iconographical principles will be discussed below.

Maps are also inherently rhetorical images. It is commonplace to say that cartography is an art of persuasion. What goes against modern wisdom is to suggest that *all* maps are rhetorical. Today's map makers distinguish maps that are impartial or objective from other maps used for propaganda or advertising that become "rhetorical" in a pejorative sense. Cartographers also concede that they employ rhetorical devices in the form of embellishment or ornament, but they maintain that beneath this cosmetic skin is always the bedrock of truthful science. What I am suggesting is that rhetoric permeates all layers of the map. As images of the world, maps are never neutral or value-free or ever completely scientific. Each map argues its own particular case. The thematic maps discussed by Karrow and Grim,[5] for example, are especially rhetorical. They are part of a persuasive discourse, and they intend to convince. Theirs is not an innocent reality dictated by the intrinsic truth of the data; they are engaging in the ancient art of rhetoric. Most maps speak to targeted audiences, and most employ invocations of authority, especially those produced by government, and they appeal to readerships in different ways. The study of the history of cartographic representation, when employed as an aid to the interpretation of maps as historical documents, is also a history of the use of the different rhetorical codes employed by map makers.[6]

The Cartographer's Context

The basic rule of historical method is that documents can only be interpreted in their context. The rule applies equally to maps, which must be returned to the past and situated squarely in their proper period and place. The readers of this book may be disappointed to learn how little contextualization of maps there is in the literature of the history of cartography. Connoisseurs' books on maps, for example, are oblivious of the social reality beyond the decorative price tag. Technical specialists in the history of maps, those trained as cartographers, seldom step beyond the workshop door and into the outside world. Context is simplistically portrayed as "general historical background." What is lacking is a grasp of context as a complex set of interactive forces—a dialogue with the text—in which context is central to the interpretative strategy. We tend to regard context as "out there" and the maps we are studying as "inside." Only when we knock down this barrier—this false dichotomy between an externalist and an internalist approach to historical interpretation—can map and context be studied in an undivided terrain. To achieve this it is necessary to distinguish between three aspects of context that intersect the reading of maps as texts.[7] The three aspects of context in my argument will be (1) the context of the cartographer, (2) the contexts of other maps, and (3) the context of society.

The context of the cartographer is best represented in the literature of early map interpretation. It is almost sixty years since the historian J. A. Williamson wrote, "It is impossible to be dogmatic about the evidence of maps unless we know more than we commonly do about the intention and circumstances of those who drew them."[8] This simple dictum—enshrining the why, who, and how approach to maps—is a good starting point. Yet the relationship between the maker and map is far from straightforward. It is neither a simple question of establishing authorship—as with books and documents—nor of determining the intention of the map maker.

With respect to authorship, if we exclude manuscript maps that are unambiguously identified and have a known provenance, the historian is frequently confronted with disentangling multiple authorship. Most maps are the product of a division of labor. As we enter the long transition from the manuscript age to the age of printing, the cartographic division of labor is accentuated, the author becomes a shadowy figure, and the translation from mapped reality to map is more complex. The question arises, "To what extent was a particular map the work of a surveyor, an editor, a draftsman, or an engraver?" Who has determined its form and content? As we concern ourselves with different craftsmen, Williamson's question about circumstances becomes more difficult to resolve. The relationship between the facts of the map makers' lives and what appears in the map is correspondingly fragmented. Within the frame of one map there may be several texts—"an intertextuality"—that has to be uncovered in the interpretative process.

More than many other texts, maps are thus mediated by a series of technical activities, each performed by a different "author." R. A. Skelton once wrote: "As bibliography to literary criticism, or as diplomatic to the interpretation of medieval documents, so is the technical analysis of early maps to the studies they serve."[9] It is this requirement—reconstructing the technical contexts of map making—that places a heavy demand on the ancillary skills of the historian. The student of early maps may have to become an expert on the histories of different types of maps,[10] be well versed in navigation and survey-ing techniques,[11] be familiar with the processes by which maps were com-piled, drafted, engraved, printed, or colored, and know something about the practices of the book and map trades. Every map is the product of several processes involving different individuals, techniques, and tools.[12] To under-stand them, we need to deploy specialist knowledge from subjects as diverse as bibliography and paleography, the history of geometry and magnetic declina-tions, the development of artistic conventions, emblems and heraldry, and the physical properties of paper and watermarks. The pertinent literature is like-wise scattered in a large number of disciplines and modern languages,[13] strad-dling the history of science and the history of technology as well as the humanities and social sciences. But how the author or authors of a map made it in a technical sense is always a first step in interpretation.

Establishing the map maker's intention is similarly less straightforward than might appear at first sight. Every map codifies more than one perspective on the world. As an expression of intention, function remains a key to reading historical maps, but such purposes were often loosely defined, or the map was directed at more than one kind of user. While we may accept, for example, that fire-insurance maps have a single use, many other groups of maps were designed for a variety of purposes. Such multiple aims complicate the assess-ment of maps as historical documents. Topographical maps or city maps and plans were made to fulfill several needs at once. They were designed as admin-istrative or jurisdictional records, for defense, for economic development, or perhaps as general works of topographical reference. The simple link between function and content breaks down. It is inadequate, for example, to define a topographical survey as merely producing a "map showing detailed features of the landscape." Topographical map series were often of military origin, and they emphasized features of strategic significance. In the United States, even after the Geological Survey assumed control of the national topographical survey in 1879, maps were still expected to serve logistical military purposes as well as geological and other civilian functions. Even today we can detect traces of the military mind in the woodland density categories of USGS maps that are still classified in relation to the ease with which infantry can move through the countryside.[14] In many nineteenth-century topographical maps, with military needs in mind, relief was similarly emphasized at the expense of cultural detail.

Intention thus cannot be fully reconstructed through the actions of individual map makers. A simple intention may still be found in individual manuscript maps, but there are also broader aspects of human agency that impinge on interpretation. Cartographic intention was seldom merely a question of an individual's training, skill, available instruments, or of the time and money needed to complete the job properly. Cartographers were rarely independent decision makers or free of financial, military, or political constraints. Above the workshop there is always the patron, and consequently the map is imbued with social as well as technical dimensions. We might do well to adapt to cartography the words of Michael Baxandall on fifteenth-century Italian painting. Such art was always

> the deposit of a social relationship. On one side there was a painter who made the picture, or at least supervised its making. On the other side there was somebody else who asked him to make it, provided funds for him to make it and, after he had made it, reckoned on using it in some way or other. Both parties worked within institutions and conventions—commercial, religious, perceptual, in the widest sense social—that were different from ours and influenced the forms of what they together made.[15]

In much of history, the cartographer was a puppet dressed in a technical language, but the strings were pulled by others.

The role of patronage varies considerably in the maps of America. With earlier manuscript maps, such as those of the age of European exploration, patrons were powerful individuals—kings or queens, princes or popes. By the nineteenth century, however, American map makers were increasingly dragooned by larger institutions such as the General Land Office and the United States Geological Survey. Personal map-making skills were subordinated not only to sets of standard instructions designed to make whole classes of maps uniform but also to state and federal politics. With political influence in mind, we should be chary of interpreting the official topographic surveys of the United States as "standard" historical documents. It has been said that "the geodetic and topographic surveys conducted by the federal government throughout the nineteenth century evolved as byproducts of ad hoc Congressional legislation and the personal intervention of civil servants, and not as a result of a national policy for map making."[16] Both the geographical order in which surveys were conducted and the content of the maps were influenced by the need to map first areas with valuable mineral deposits. Policy concerns as much as the skills of individual map makers gave rise to the diverse images of the American landscape preserved in the national series of topographical maps.

In qualifying the limits of the individual cartographer's influence, I am not denying that "map makers are human."[17] Unusual personal skill as well as idiosyncrasy still flourishes in the interstices of institutional practice. In the maps of the township and range system, for example, "possibilities of error, omission, personal bias and even misrepresentations abounded."[18] Even in today's machine-generated maps and aerial images, historians should remain alert to deviant ways in which individual technicians may have inscribed their routine tasks. This may be more difficult to detect behind the assertive rhetoric of computer technology, but again the standard historical record does not exist.

Similar observations may be made about commercial mapping. This forms an important part of the cartographic historical record in the United States,[19] but it also shows conflicts of interest. The market place usually constrains the free play of cartographic standards. One text we always read in these maps is a financial balance sheet. "Where the detective hunts for fingerprints," it has been remarked, "we must look for profit if we are to understand the basic mechanism of early map publishing. . . . No salesman ever tells the whole truth and it would be an unwary historian who took land sale maps for a true cartographic record."[20] Moreover, as the size of map businesses increases and print runs grow longer, cartography acquires a corporate image. The patron is now a larger public or perhaps a special interest group, such as the consumers of highway maps, who look over the cartographer's shoulder to influence what is being mapped.

The Context of Other Maps

A major interpretative question to be asked of any map concerns its relationship to other maps. The inquiry has to be focused in different ways. For example, we could ask: (1) What is the relationship of the content of a single

map (or some feature within it) to other contemporary maps of the same area?
(2) What is the relationship of such a map to maps by the same cartographer
or map-producing agency? (3) What is its relationship to other maps in the
same cartographic genre (of one bird's-eye view, for instance, to other North
American bird's-eye views)? (4) Or what is the relationship of a map to the
wider cartographic output of an age? The questions vary but their importance
is universal. No map is hermetically closed upon itself nor can it answer all the
questions it raises. Sooner or later early map interpretation becomes an exercise in comparative cartography.[21] The cartographic characteristics of the
larger family may enable anonymous maps to be identified, unusual signs or
conventions interpreted, or inferences made about the parameters of accuracy.
Our confidence in a map document may be increased (or diminished) when it
exhibits the proven characteristics of a larger group.

In this part of contextual study a corpus of related maps is built around the
single map. Just as in the analysis of literary texts the unity or identity of a
corpus of texts has to be constructed,[22] so too in early map interpretation we
can follow definite procedures. These can be applied to a group of maps of the
same period, but, equally, the depiction of an area or feature can be traced on a
series of maps through time. Three approaches will be noted below, and they
may be used either separately or in combination in evaluating a single map
within the larger group.

The comparative study of linear topographical features on maps (such as
coastlines, river networks, or a system of trails and highways) is a well-tried
technique. Outlines are reduced to common scale and are then compared
visually. Examples appear in the classic nineteenth-century studies of early
maps,[23] and the method can also be adapted to the digital analysis of linear
features by computer.[24] A recent application of the older method is to the
Spanish and French mapping of the Gulf of Mexico in the sixteenth and
seventeenth centuries.[25] After "photocopying, assembling, and examining a
great many maps" it was possible,[26] on the basis of salient features in coastal
outlines, to identify five main phases of map making. Through the use of this
comparative classification, individual maps were then assigned to stages of
development and their origin, sources, and topographical reliability were
assessed from the characteristics of the larger group.

But if every map has a genetic fingerprint that the method helps to identify,
caution must also be exercised. The study of outlines may fall short of provid-

ing conclusive evidence of provenance. There are many pitfalls. R. A. Skelton has written that "visual impressions suggesting affinity or development of the outline in two maps may be misleading if we do not take into account the license in drawing or interpretation that the cartographer might allow."[27] Or again, there may be technical variations influencing the shape of map outlines or their graticules of latitude and longitude. Maps are easily corrupted in the process of copying, or they may derive from surveying or navigation techniques that have been obscured in the process of compilation. Before the nineteenth century, maps were frequently aligned toward magnetic rather than true north. Magnetic declination varied locally and changed through time so that map makers were unable, in the absence of systematic observations, to correct for this factor. It remains a critical source of error in the comparison of outlines.[28]

A second aspect of the comparative analysis of early maps involves the study of place-names or toponymy. Like outlines, place-names offer a way of constructing genealogies and source profiles for previously scattered maps. Indeed, the two methods are often used in conjunction, as in the classic studies of the early cartography of the Atlantic coast of Canada.[29] Yet the cross-tabulation of the names on a series of maps as a means of classification or of establishing the interrelationships of the group must also be approached with caution.[30] In initial periods of exploration, Europeans of different nationality would have heard names from the mouths of Native American speakers of a variety of languages, and they would have attempted to record them in accordance with their own sound system, in far from standardized spellings. Even where European names were applied to North American geography, there was ample scope for corruption in the processes of translating and editing them: the names attest to carelessness, misreading, or misunderstanding by successive generations of cartographers who had no firsthand knowledge of the places or languages involved. Of names on the maps of the sixteenth-century Dieppe school of cartographers,[31] for example, it is said that "no two Dieppe cartographers coincide completely in the number of names they record, while spelling varies widely and even the positioning of names is not always consistent."[32] Not surprisingly, place-names have sometimes been used uncritically for purposes of comparing maps.[33] The sound practice is to confine the analysis to only those names unambiguously common to a number of maps.

The third method for comparative cartography—carto-bibliography—has the largest literature. Not only have the definition and finer points of the method been extensively discussed,[34] but its practice is fully represented in a series of fundamental works on early American cartography.[35] The aim of carto-bibliography is to bring together a series of maps printed from the same printing surface. It applies equally to the woodcut, copperplate, lithographic, or other map-printing processes.[36] By this method a sequence of geographical and other changes in related maps can be reconstructed. This in turn allows the publication history of the maps of an area to be pieced together. It also allows the single map to be dated and slotted into this sequence, and the extent of geographical revision between states or editions of maps to be detected. Maps are often representations of time as much as space. As Skelton puts it, we discover how "matter from various horizons of time or intellectual development" is incorporated into their images. And we learn that "the search for the ultimate source may lead us back through many stages of revision or adaptation, derivation or transcription, compilation."[37] Carto-bibliography is thus a basic tool of the map historian. Either as a technique or as a means of measuring the channels and rate of diffusion of geographical knowledge (thereby linking maps to the context of society), its insights are indispensible.

The Context of Society

The third context of cartography is that of society. If the map maker is the individual agent, then society is the broader structure. Interpretation—reading the cartographic text—involves a dialogue between these two contexts. The framework of definite historical circumstances and conditions produces a map that is inescapably a social and cultural document. Every map is linked to the social order of a particular period and place. Every map is cultural because it manifests intellectual processes defined as artistic or scientific as they work to produce a distinctive type of knowledge. There is no neat causal arrow that flows from society into the map, but rather causal arrows that flow in both directions. Maps are not outside society: they are part of it as constitutive elements within the wider world. It is the web of interrelationships, stretching both inside and beyond the map document, that the historian attempts to read. In exploring this reflexivity, two strategies might be used to survey the context of society in the maps of America.

The Rules of Cartography

The first strategy is to attempt to identify "the rules of the social order" within the map.[38] Every map manifests two sets of rules. First, there are the cartographers' rules, and we have seen how these operate in the technical practices of map making. The second set can be traced from society into the map, where they influence the categories of knowledge. The map becomes a "signifying system" through which "a social order is communicated, reproduced, experienced, and explored."[39] Maps do not simply reproduce a topographical reality; they also interpret it.

The rules of the social order are sometimes visible, even self-evident, within a group of maps. Alternatively, they are sometimes hidden within the mode of representation. Among the category of "visible society," we may place the North American bird's-eye views of towns and cities, the city maps and plans, and the county maps and atlases. They are all cultural texts taking possession of the land.[40] All proclaim a social gospel and serve to reinforce it. Bird's-eye views of towns, for instance, "sing the national anthem of peace and prosperity, of movement and openness, of calm and order, and of destinies to be fulfilled."[41] The map wears its heart on its sleeve and it comes alive in a context of frontier ethics and patriotism as topography is decoded from the emphatically rhetorical style of the image.

Where the social rules of cartography are concealed from view, a hidden agenda has to be teased out from between the lines on the map. Such a map is duplicitous, and a different strategy is called for. Instead of picking up social messages that the map emphasizes, we must search for what it de-emphasizes; not so much what the map shows, as what it omits. Interpretation becomes a search for silences,[42] or it may be helpful to "deconstruct" the map to reveal how the social order creates tensions within its content.[43] Among the maps that could be so elucidated are some of the eighteenth-century large-scale maps, the topographic surveys of the United States, and the aerial images. Here technology has suppressed social relations. Because they appear to be accurate or objective, such maps are often viewed as nonproblematic documents. A satellite image or a topographical map made by "scientific" methods, so it is believed, has a moral and ethical neutrality. It is a factual and straightforward document. So long as we recognize *technical* limitation, the pathway of interpretation is secure.

Such assumptions are false. Representation is never neutral, and science is still a humanly constructed reality. The large-scale maps of eastern North America in the mid–eighteenth century illustrate this contention. At first sight they meet the goals of Enlightenment cartography. They are built on geodetic measurements; they begin to show "cartographic mastery" over the landscapes of eastern North America; and they suppress some of the more overtly fanciful, mythic, and pictorial elements of earlier maps. Take a closer look, however, and they also signal the territorial imperatives of an aggressive English overseas expansion.[44] Colonialism is first signposted in the map margins. Titles make increasing reference to empire and to the possession and bounding of territory; dedications define the social rank of colonial governors; and cartouches, with a parade of national flags, coats of arms, or crowns set above subservient Indians, define the power relations in colonial life.[45] But the contours of colonial society can also be read between the lines of the maps. Cartography has become preeminently a record of colonial self-interest. It is an unconscious portrait of how successfully a European colonial society had reproduced itself in the New World, and the maps grant reassurance to settlers by reproducing the symbolic authority and place-names of the Old World. Moreover, as the frontier moved west, the traces of an Indian past were dropped from the image. Many eighteenth-century map makers preferred blank spaces to a relict Indian geography.[46] I do not suggest that the omissions—the "rules of absence"—were deliberately enforced in the manner of a technical specification. But even where they were taken for granted, or only subconsciously implemented, to grasp them helps us to interrogate early maps.

The Meaning of Maps

Another interpretative strategy applies the iconographical methods of art history to maps. Iconography is defined as "that branch of the history of art which concerns itself with the subject matter or meaning of works of art."[47] The question "What did the map mean to the society that first made and used it?" is of crucial interpretive importance. Maps become a source to reveal the philosophical, political, or religious outlook of a period, or what is sometimes called the spirit of the age. An iconographical interpretation can be used to complement the rules-of-society approach. While the latter reveals the tendencies of knowledge in maps—its hierarchies, inclusions, and exclusions—

the former examines how the social rules were translated into the cartographic idiom in terms of signs, styles, and the expressive vocabularies of cartography.

The essence of iconographical analysis is that it seeks to uncover different layers of meaning within the image. Panofsky suggested that in any painting we encounter (1) a primary or natural subject matter consisting of individual artistic motifs; (2) a secondary or conventional subject matter that is defined in terms of the identity of the whole painting as a representation of a specific allegory or event (he gave the example of a painting of the Last Supper); and (3) a symbolic layer of meaning that often has an ideological connotation. This does not offer a neat formula for early map interpretation, but it may be ventured that the levels of meaning in a map are similar to those in a painting.[48] These parallel levels in the two forms of representation are summarized in Table 1.

First, at the level 1, the individual signs, symbols, or decorative emblems on a map are made equivalent to the individual artistic motifs. While the full meaning of any single sign may become apparent only when viewed in the mosaic of other signs in the map as a whole, for some interpretative purposes it may be necessary to evaluate the content and meaning of individual signs (for example, as well as establishing its cultural meaning, we may need to know how far the sign for the depiction of a church or a house on an early map is reliable from the architectural point of view).

Second, the identity of the real place represented on a map is assumed to be the equivalent of Panofsky's level 2 or second stage in interpretation. Its apprehension involves a recognition that a particular map is that of a plantation in South Carolina, of Boston, or of California. It is at this level—that of the real place—that maps have been most used by historians. Moreover, it is for evaluating the real places in maps that most interpretive techniques, whether devoted to their planimetric accuracy or to their content, have been developed. There are numerous exemplars for this type of topographical scholarship.[49]

The third interpretive level in a map is the symbolic stratum. Until recent years, apart from the contributions of a handful of art historians,[50] this hermeneutic dimension of early cartography was neglected. Only recently has interpretation moved to embrace a symbolic and ideological reading of early maps. Here we accept that maps act as a visual metaphor for values enshrined in the places they represent. The maps of America are always laden with such

TABLE I
Iconographical Parallels in Art and Cartography

Art (Panofsky's terms are used)	Cartography (suggested cartographic parallel)
1. Primary or natural subject matter: artistic motifs	Individual conventional signs
2. Secondary or conventional subject matter	Topographical identity in maps: the specific place
3. Intrinsic meaning or content	Symbolic meaning in maps: ideologies of space

cultural values and significance, plotting a social topology with its own cultur-ally asserted domain. Maps always represent more than a physical image of place. A town plan or bird's-eye view is a legible emblem or icon of commu-nity. It inscribes values on civic space, emphasizing the sites of religious belief, ceremony, pageant, ritual, and authority. Or in the nineteenth-century county and historical atlases, there is more on the maps than an inert record of a vanished topography. What we read is a metaphorical discourse, as thick as any written text, about immigrant rural pride, about Utopias glimpsed, about order and prosperity in the landscape. Such maps praise possession of the land, enshrine property demarcations, and memorialize farm buildings and the names of property holders. Through both word and image they appealed to the industry and patriotism of the new Americans. And the longer we look the more symbolic cartography becomes. Thus a Rand McNally highway map speaks to the American love affair with the automobile, and even the seem-ingly earthy maps of the United States Geological Survey are a symbolic assertion of the changing perceptions and priorities of society rather than just maps of objects in the landscape. In such ways, "maps speak, albeit softly, of subtle value judgments."[51] To read the map properly the historian must al-ways excavate beneath the terrain of its surface geography.

Conclusion

By accepting maps as fundamental documents for the study of American past, we begin to appreciate how frequently maps intersect major historical pro-cesses. From territorial treaties to town planning, and from railroads to the rectangular grid, they underlie the making of modern America.[52] But if this is an immense practical contribution, neither should we ignore the historical influence of real maps upon the more elusive cognitive maps held by genera-tions of Americans since the sixteenth century. In addition to regarding the map as a topographical source, we are becoming aware of a cartographic power that is embedded in its discourse.[53] The power of the map, an act of control over the image of the world, is like the power of print in general.[54] Since the age of Columbus, maps have helped to create some of the most pervasive stereotypes of our world.

How the historian uses a map also depends on the context of the individual scholar. Insights are determined not only by the intrinsic qualities of a particular map but also by the historical investigation in hand, by its objectives, by its research methods, and by all the other evidence that can be brought to bear on its problems. Just as there are innumerable maps of America for the historian to consult, so there is an equally unlimited list of research topics for which maps may be appropriate. It has not been my intention to play down the technical aspects of early map interpretation, but in view of the fact that these already have an extensive literature, it seemed important to take this opportunity to sketch in a broader framework within which they can be deployed. The three contexts of cartography that have been outlined are never mutually exclusive but are subtly and often inextricably interwoven. Maps, once we learn how to read them, can become uniquely rewarding texts for the historian.

CHAPTER TWO

Maps, Knowledge, and Power

This chapter originally appeared in Denis Cosgrove and Stephen Daniels, eds., *The Iconography of Landscape: Essays on the Symbolic Representation, Design and Use of Past Environments,* Cambridge Studies in Historical Geography, 9 (Cambridge: Cambridge University Press, 1988), 277–312.

Give me a map; then let me see how much
Is left for me to conquer all the world, . . .
Here I began to march towards Persia,
Along Armenia and the Caspian Sea,
And thence unto Bithynia, where I took
the Turk and his great empress prisoners.
Then marched I into Egypt and Arabia,
And here, not far from Alexandria
Whereas the Terrene and the Red Sea meet,
Being distant less than full a hundred leagues
I meant to cut a channel to them both
That men might quickly sail to India.
From thence to Nubia near Borno lake,
And so along the Ethiopian sea,
Cutting the tropic line of Capricorn,
I conquered all as far as Zanzibar.

— CHRISTOPHER MARLOWE,
Tamburlaine, Part 2 (V.iii.123–39)

$\mathcal{A}$ book about geographical imagery which did not encompass the map would be like *Hamlet* without the Prince.[1] Yet although maps have long been central to the discourse of geography they are seldom read as "thick" texts or as a socially constructed form of knowledge. "Map interpretation" usually implies a search for "geographical features" depicted on maps without conveying how as a manipulated form of knowledge maps have helped to fashion those features.[2] It is true that in political geography and the history of geographical thought the link is increasingly being made between maps and power—especially in periods of colonial history[3]—but the particular role of maps, as images with historically specific codes, remains largely undifferentiated from the wider geographical discourse in which they are often embedded. What is lacking is a sense of what Carl Sauer understood as the eloquence of maps.[4] How then can we make maps "speak" about the social worlds of the past?

Theoretical Perspectives

My aim here is to explore the discourse of maps in the context of political power, and my approach is broadly iconological. Maps will be regarded as part of the broader family of value-laden images.[5] Maps cease to be understood primarily as inert records of morphological landscapes or passive reflections of the world of objects, but are regarded as refracted images contributing to dialogue in a socially constructed world. We thus move the reading of maps away from the canons of traditional cartographical criticism with its string of binary oppositions between maps that are "true and false," "accurate and inaccurate," "objective and subjective," "literal and symbolic," or that are based on "scientific integrity" as opposed to "ideological distortion." Maps are never value-free images; except in the narrowest Euclidean sense they are not in themselves either true or false. Both in the selectivity of their content and in their signs and styles of representation maps are a way of conceiving, articulating, and structuring the human world which is biased towards, promoted by, and exerts influence upon particular sets of social relations.[6] By accepting such premises it becomes easier to see how appropriate they are to manipulation by the powerful in society.

Across this broad conceptual landscape I shall pinpoint three eminences from which to trace some of the more specific ideological contours of maps. From the first I view maps as a kind of language[7] (whether this is taken metaphorically or literally is not vital to the argument).[8] The idea of a cartographic language is also preferred to an approach derived directly from semiotics which, while having attracted some cartographers,[9] is too blunt a tool for specific historical enquiry. The notion of language more easily translates into historical practice. It not only helps us to see maps as reciprocal images used to mediate different views of the world but it also prompts a search for evidence about aspects such as the codes and context of cartography as well as its content in a traditional sense. A language—or perhaps more aptly a "literature" of maps—similarly urges us to pursue questions about changing readerships for maps, about levels of carto-literacy, conditions of authorship, aspects of secrecy and censorship, and also about the nature of the political statements which are made by maps.

In addition, literary criticism can help us to identify the particular form of cartographic "discourse" which lies at the heart of this essay. Discourse has been defined as concerning "those aspects of a text which are appraisive, evaluative, persuasive, or rhetorical, as opposed to those which simply name, locate, and recount."[10] While it will be shown that "simply" naming or locating a feature on a map is often of political significance, it nevertheless can be accepted that a similar cleavage exists within maps. They are a class of rhetorical images and are bound by rules which govern their codes and modes of social production, exchange, and use just as surely as any other discursive form. This, in turn can lead us to a better appreciation of the mechanisms by which maps—like books—became a political force in society.[11]

A second theoretical vantage point is derived from Panofsky's formulation of iconology.[12] Attempts have already been made to equate Panofsky's levels of interpretation in painting with similar levels discernible in maps.[13] For maps, iconology can be used to identify not only a "surface" or literal level of meaning but also a "deeper" level, usually associated with the symbolic dimension in the act of sending or receiving a message. A map can carry in its image such symbolism as may be associated with the particular area, geographical feature, city, or place which it represents.[14] It is often on this symbolic level that political power is most effectively reproduced, communicated, and experienced through maps.

The third perspective is gained from the sociology of knowledge. It has already been proposed that map knowledge is a social product,[15] and it is to clarify this proposition that two sets of ideas have been brought to bear upon the empirical examples in this essay. The first set is derived from Michel Foucault, who, while his observations on geography and maps were cursory,[16] nevertheless provides a useful model for the history of map knowledge in his critique of historiography: "the quest for truth was not an objective and neutral activity but was intimately related to the 'will to power' of the truth-seeker. Knowledge was thus a form of power, a way of presenting one's own values in the guise of scientific disinterestedness."[17]

Cartography, too, can be "a form of knowledge and a form of power." Just as "the historian paints the landscape of the past in the colours of the present,"[18] so the surveyor, whether consciously or otherwise, replicates not just the "environment" in some abstract sense but equally the territorial imperatives of a particular political system. Whether a map is produced under the banner of cartographic science—as most official maps have been—or whether it is an overt propaganda exercise, it cannot escape involvement in the processes by which power is deployed. Some of the practical implications of maps may also fall into the category of what Foucault has defined as acts of "surveillance,"[19] notably those connected with warfare, political propaganda, boundary making, or the preservation of law and order.

Foucault is not alone in making the connection between power and knowledge. Anthony Giddens, too, in theorizing about how social systems have become "embedded" in time and space (while not mentioning maps explicitly) refers to "authoritative resources" (as distinguished from material resources) controlled by the state: "storage of authoritative resources involves above all *the retention and control of information or knowledge.* There can be no doubt that the decisive development here is the invention of writing and notation."[20] Maps were a similar invention in the control of space and facilitated the geographical expansion of social systems, "an undergirding medium of state power." As a means of surveillance they involve both "the collation of information relevant to state control of the conduct of its subject population" and "the direct supervision of that conduct."[21] In modern times the greater the administrative complexity of the state—and the more pervasive its territorial and social ambitions—then the greater its appetite for maps.

What is useful about these ideas is that they help us to envisage cartographic images in terms of their political influence in society. The mere fact that for centuries maps have been projected as "scientific" images—and are still placed by philosophers and semioticians in that category[22]—makes this task more difficult. Dialectical relationships between image and power cannot be excavated with the procedures used to recover the "hard" topographical knowledge in maps and there is no litmus test of their ideological tendencies.[23] Maps as "knowledge as power" are explored here under three headings: the universality of political contexts in the history of mapping; the way in which the exercise of power structures the content of maps; and how cartographic communication at a symbolic level can reinforce that exercise through map knowledge.

Political Contexts for Maps

Tsar. My son, what so engrosses you? What's this?
Fyodor. A map of Muscovy; our royal kingdom
   From end to end. Look, father,

Moscow's here
Here Novgorod, there Astrakhan.
The sea there,
Here is the virgin forestland of Perm,
And there Siberia.
Tsar. And what may this be,
A winding pattern tracing?
Fyodor. It's the Volga.
Tsar. How splendid! The delicious fruit of learning!
Thus at a glance as from a cloud to scan
Our whole domain: its boundaries, towns, rivers.
—Alexander Pushkin, *Boris Godunov*

In any iconological study it is only through context that meaning and influence can properly be unraveled. Such contexts may be defined as the circumstances in which maps were made and used. They are analogous to the "speech situation" in linguistic study[24] and involve reconstructions of the physical and social settings for the production and consumption of maps, the events leading up to these actions, the identity of map makers and map users, and their perceptions of the act of making and using maps in a socially constructed world. Such details can tell us not only about the motives behind cartographic events but also what effect maps may have had and the significance of the information they communicate in human terms.

Even a cursory inspection of the history of mapping will reveal the extent to which political, religious, or social power produce the context of cartography. This has become clear, for example, from a detailed study of cartography in prehistoric, ancient and medieval Europe, and the Mediterranean. Throughout the period, "mapmaking was one of the specialised intellectual weapons by which power could be gained, administered, given legitimacy, and codified."[25] Moreover, this knowledge was concentrated in relatively few hands and "maps were associated with the religious elite of dynastic Egypt and of Christian medieval Europe; with the intellectual elite of Greece and Rome; and with the mercantile elite of the city-states of the Mediterranean world during the late Middle Ages."[26]

Nor was the world of ancient and medieval Europe exceptional in these respects. Cartography, whatever other cultural significance may have been attached to it, was always a "science of princes." In the Islamic world, it was the caliphs in the period of classical Arab geography, the Sultans in the Ottoman Empire, and the Mogul emperors in India who are known to have patronized map making and to have used maps for military, political, religious, and propaganda purposes.[27] In ancient China, detailed terrestrial maps were likewise made expressly in accordance with the policies of the rulers of successive dynasties and served as bureaucratic and military tools and as spatial emblems of imperial destiny.[28] In early modern Europe, from Italy to the Netherlands and from Scandinavia to Portugal, absolute monarchs and statesmen were everywhere aware of the value of maps in defense and warfare, in internal administration linked to the growth of centralized government, and as territorial propaganda in the legitimation of national identities. Writers such as Castiglione, Elyot, and Machiavelli advocated the use of maps by generals and statesmen.[29] With national topographic surveys in Europe from the eighteenth century onwards, cartography's role in the transaction of power relations usually favored social elites.

The specific functions of maps in the exercise of power also confirm the ubiquity of these political contexts on a continuum of geographical scales. These range from global empire building, to the preservation of the nation state, to the local assertion of individual property rights. In each of these contexts the dimensions of polity and territory were fused in images which— just as surely as legal charters and patents—were part of the intellectual apparatus of power.

Maps and Empire

As much as guns and warships, maps have been the weapons of imperialism. Insofar as maps were used in colonial promotion, and lands claimed on paper before they were effectively occupied, maps anticipated empire. Surveyors marched alongside soldiers, initially mapping for reconnaissance, then for general information, and eventually as a tool of pacification, civilization, and exploitation in the defined colonies. But there is more to this than the drawing of boundaries for the practical political or military containment of subject populations. Maps were used to legitimize the reality of conquest and empire. They helped create myths which would assist in the maintenance of the territorial status quo. As communicators of an imperial message, they have been used as

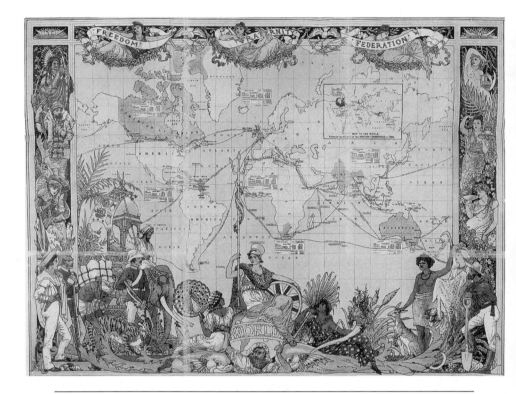

Figure 1. *Imperial Federation—Map of the World Showing the Extent of the British Empire in 1886* was first published as a supplement to the *Graphic* newspaper, 24 July 1886. Mercator's projection, a pink tint for empire territory, and decorative emblems showing Britannia seated on the world are used to articulate the message of the "New Imperialism." By permission of the British Library.

an aggressive complement to the rhetoric of speeches, newspapers, and written texts, or to the histories and popular songs extolling the virtues of empire.[30]

In these imperial contexts, maps regularly supported the direct execution of territorial power. The grids laid out by the Roman *agrimensores*, made functional in centuriation, were an expression of power "rolled out relentlessly in all directions . . . homogenizing everything in its path,"[31] just as the United States rectangular land survey created "Order upon the Land" in more senses than merely the replication of a classical design.[32] The rediscovery of the Ptolemaic system of coordinate geometry in the fifteenth century was a critical cartographic event privileging a "Euclidean syntax" which structured European territorial control.[33] Indeed, the graphic nature of the map gave its imperial users an arbitrary power that was easily divorced from the social responsibilities and consequences of its exercise. The world could be carved up on paper. Pope Alexander VI thus demarcated the Spanish and Portuguese possessions in the New World.[34] In the partitioning of North America, itself "part of a vast European process and experiment, an ongoing development of worldwide imperialism," the "very lines on the map exhibited this imperial power and process because they had been imposed on the continent with little reference to indigenous peoples, and indeed in many places with little reference to the land itself. The invaders parceled the continent among themselves in designs reflective of their own complex rivalries and relative power."[35] In the nineteenth century, as maps became further institutionalized and linked to the growth of geography as a discipline, their power effects are again manifest in the continuing tide of European imperialism. The scramble for Africa, in which the European powers fragmented the identity of indigenous territorial organization, has become almost a textbook example of these effects.[36] And in our own century, in the British partition of India in 1947, we can see how the stroke of a pen across a map could determine the lives and deaths of millions of people.[37] There are innumerable contexts in which maps became the currency of political "bargains," leases, partitions, sales, and treaties struck over colonial territory and, once made permanent in the image, these maps more than often acquired the force of law in the landscape.

Maps and the Nation-State

The history of the map is inextricably linked to the rise of the nation-state in the modern world. Many of the printed maps of Europe emphasized the estates, waterways, and political boundaries that constituted the politico-economic dimensions of European geography.[38] Early political theorists commended maps to statesmen who in turn were among their first systematic collectors.[39] The state became—and has remained—a principal patron of cartographic activity in many countries.[40]

Yet while the state was prepared to finance mapping, either directly through its exchequer or indirectly through commercial privilege, it often insisted that such knowledge was privileged. In western Europe the history of cartographic secrecy, albeit often ineffective, can be traced back to the sixteenth-century Spanish and Portuguese policy of *siglio*.[41] It was the practice to monopolize knowledge, "to use geographic documents as an economic resource, much as craft mysteries were secreted and used."[42]

A major example of the interaction between maps and state polity is found in the history of military technology. In military eyes, maps have always been regarded as a sensitive sort of knowledge, and policies of secrecy and censorship abound as much today in the "hidden" specifications of defence and official map-making agencies as in the campaign headquarters of the past.[43] At a practical level, military maps are a small but vital cog in the technical infrastructure of the army in the field. As the techniques of warfare were transformed from siege tactics to more mobile strategies, especially from the eighteenth century onwards, so too were the maps associated with them transformed.[44] Even in these active contexts, however, there were subtler historical processes at work. Map knowledge allows the conduct of warfare by remote control so that, we may speculate, killing is that more easily contemplated.[45] Military maps not only facilitate the technical conduct of warfare, but also palliate the sense of guilt which arises from its conduct: the silent lines of the paper landscape foster the notion of socially empty space.

Not all military maps are silent; many stridently proclaim military victory. Just as there were military parades, songs, and poems, so too, at least from the fifteenth century onwards in Europe, there have been battle plans designed to commemorate the sacred places of national glory.[46]

Maps and Property Rights

Cadastral or estate maps showing the ownership of property reveal the role of mapping in the history of agrarian class relations. Here the map may be regarded as a means by which either the state or individual landlords could more effectively control a tenant or peasant population.[47] In Roman society the codified practices of the *agrimensores* may be interpreted not just as technical manuals of land division in a theoretical sense but also as a social apparatus for legally regulating appropriated lands and for exacting taxation.[48] The maps themselves, whether cast in bronze or chipped in stone, were designed to make more permanent a social order in which there were freemen and slaves and for which the territorial division of land was the basis of status.[49] In early modern Europe, too, though the sociological context of mapping was different, some of the same forces were at work. The extent to which the map-

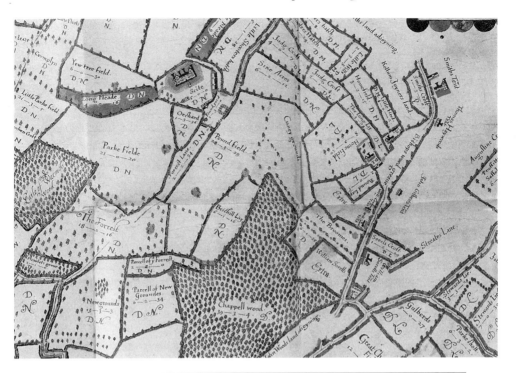

Figure 2. Large-scale estate maps, and the written cadastres they accompanied, became a tool in the rise of agrarian capitalism in England from the sixteenth century. In this portion of Samuel Walker's map of the estate of Garnetts, Essex (1622), details of ownership (DN = Edward Naylor's desmesne, DL = Richard Lavender's desmesne, etc.), precise delineation, and accurate measurement (in acres, roods, perches) translate property rights into a tangible and legally binding image. The original is at a scale of about twenty inches to one mile. This reproduction is approximately 1.0 by 0.7 miles. By permission of the British Library (Additional Manuscripts 41848).

ping of local rural areas was locked into the process of litigation can leave us in no doubt about its socio-legal context and as a means by which conflict between lords and peasants over private rights in land could be more effectively pursued.[50] Maps fitted as easily into the culture of landed society as they had into the courtly diplomacies and the military maneuvers of European nation-states in the Renaissance.

In similar terms maps can be seen to be embedded in some of the long-term structural changes of the transition from feudalism to capitalism. The world economy and its new geographical division of labor was produced with the aid of geographical documents including maps.[51] Accurate, large-scale plans were a means by which land could be more efficiently exploited, by which rent rolls could be increased, and by which legal obligations could be enforced or tenures modified. Supplementing older, written surveys, the map served as a graphic inventory, a codification of information about ownership, tenancy, rentable values, cropping practice, and agricultural potential, enabling capitalist landowners to see their estates as a whole and better to control them.[52] Seeing was believing in relation to the territorial hierarchies expressed in maps. Whether in the general history of agricultural improvement, of enclosure, of the draining or embankment of fens and marshes, or of the reclamation of hill and moor, the surveyor ever more frequently walks at the side of the landlord in spreading capitalist forms of agriculture.[53]

Maps impinged invisibly on the daily lives of ordinary people. Just as the clock, as a graphic symbol of centralized political authority, brought "time discipline" into the rhythms of industrial workers,[54] so too the lines on maps, dictators of a new agrarian topography, introduced a dimension of "space discipline." In European peasant societies, former commons were now subdivided and allotted, with the help of maps, and in the "wilderness" of former Indian lands in North America, boundary lines on the map were a medium of appropriation which those unlearned in geometrical survey methods found impossible to challenge. Maps entered the law, were attached to ordinances, acquired an aureole of science, and helped create an ethic and virtue of ever more precise definition. Tracings on maps excluded as much as they enclosed. They fixed territorial relativities according to the lottery of birth, the accidents of discovery, or, increasingly, the mechanism of the world market.

Map Content in the Transaction of Power

> "Is that the same map?" Jincey asked. She pointed to the large map of the world that hung, rolled up for the summer, above the blackboard behind Miss Dove. "Is China still orange?" "It is a new map," Miss Dove said. "China is purple." "I liked the old map," Jincey said. "I like the old world." "Cartography is a fluid art," said Miss Dove.   —Frances Gray Patton, *Good Morning, Miss Dove*

Cartographers and map historians have long been aware of tendencies in the content of their maps that they call "bias," "distortion," "deviance," or the "abuse" of sound cartographic principles. But little space in cartographic literature is devoted to the political implications of these terms and what they represent, and even less to their social consequences. Such "bias" or "distortion" is generally measured against a yardstick of "objectivity," itself derived from cartographic procedure. Only in deliberately distorted maps, for example in advertising or propaganda, are the consequences discussed.[55] "Professional" cartography of the Ordnance Survey, the USGS, Bartholomew or Rand McNally or their predecessors would be regarded as largely free from such politically polluted imagery. That maps can produce a truly "scientific" image of the world, in which factual information is represented without favor, is a view well embedded in our cultural mythology. To acknowledge that all cartography is "an intricate, controlled fiction"[56] does not prevent our retaining a distinction between those presentations of map content which are deliberately induced by cartographic artifice and those in which the structuring content of the image is unexamined.

Deliberate Distortions of Map Content

Deliberate distortions of map content for political purposes can be traced throughout the history of maps, and the cartographer has never been an independent artist, craftsman, or technician. Behind the map maker lies a set of power relations, creating its own specification. Whether imposed by an individual patron, by state bureaucracy, or the market, these rules can be reconstructed both from the content of maps and from the mode of cartographic representation. By adapting individual projections, by manipulating scale, by over-enlarging or moving signs or typography, or by using emotive colors, makers of propaganda maps have generally been the advocates of a one-sided view of geopolitical relationships. Such maps have been part of the currency of international psychological warfare long before their use by Nazi geopoliticians. The religious wars of seventeenth-century Europe and the Cold War of the twentieth century have been fought as much in the contents of propaganda maps as through any other medium.[57]

Apparently objective maps are also characterized by persistent manipulation of content. "Cartographic censorship" implies deliberate misrepresentation designed to mislead potential users of the map, usually those regarded as opponents of the territorial status quo. We should not confuse this with deletions or additions resulting from technical error or incompetence or made

Figure 3. Even simple thematic maps can carry subtle propaganda messages. This school atlas map, from *Geschichtsatlas für die deutsch Jungen* (Julius Belz, 3d ed., 1935), represents Germanic elements in Europe and (inset) overseas but omits a key to the values of the three sizes of symbol. While the distribution pattern is realistic, German minorities in European countries were usually very much smaller (under 4% of total population) than the use of ranked symbols suggests. By the permission of the British Library (Maps 30.b.25).

necessary by scale or function. Cartographic censorship removes from maps features which, *other things being equal,* we might expect to find on them. Naturally this is less noticeable than blatant distortion. It is justified on grounds of "national security," "political expediency," or "commercial necessity" and is still widely practiced. The censored image marks the boundaries of permissible discourse and deliberate omissions discourage "the clarification of social alternatives," making it "difficult for the dispossessed to locate the source of their unease, let alone to remedy it."[58]

The commonest justification for cartographic censorship has probably always been military. In its most wholesale form it has involved prohibiting the publication of surveys.[59] On the other hand settlement details on eighteenth-century maps were left unrevised by Frederick the Great to deceive a potential enemy, just as it has been inferred that the towns on some Russian maps were deliberately relocated in incorrect positions in the 1960s to prevent strategic measurements being taken from them by enemy powers.[60] Since the nineteenth century, too, it has been almost universal practice to "cleanse" systematically evidence of sensitive military installations from official series of topographical maps.[61] The practice now extends to other features where their inclusion would be potentially embarrassing to the government of the day, for example, nuclear waste dumps are omitted from official USGS topographical maps.

Deliberate falsification of map content has been associated with political considerations other than the purely military. Boundaries on maps have been subject to graphic gerrymandering. This arises both from attempts to assert historical claims to national territory,[62] and from the predictive art of using maps to project and to legitimate future territorial ambitions.[63] For example, disputed boundaries, whether shown on official maps, in atlases, or in more ephemeral images such as postage stamps, have been either included or suppressed according to the current political preference.[64] Nor do these practices apply solely to political boundaries on maps. It is well documented how the geographies of language, "race," and religion have been portrayed to accord with dominant beliefs.[65] There are the numerous cases where indigenous place-names of minority groups are suppressed on topographical maps in favor of the standard toponymy of the controlling group.[66]

"Unconscious" Distortions of Map Content

Of equal interest to the student of cartographic iconology is the subtle process by which the content of maps is influenced by the values of the map-producing society. Any social history of maps must be concerned with these hidden rules of cartographic imagery and with their accidental consequences.[67] Three aspects of these hidden structures—relating to map geometry, to "silences" in the content of maps, and to hierarchical tendencies in cartographic representation will be discussed.

Subliminal Geometry

The geometrical structure of maps—their graphic design in relation to the location on which they are centred or to the projection which determines their transformational relationship to the earth[68]—is an element which can magnify the political impact of an image even where no conscious distortion is intended. A universal feature of early world maps, for example, is the way they have been persistently centred on the "navel of the world," as this has been perceived by different societies. This "*omphalos* syndrome,"[69] where a people believe themselves to be divinely appointed to the center of the universe, can be traced in maps widely separated in time and space, such as those from ancient Mesopotamia with Babylon at its center, maps of the Chinese universe centred on China, Greek maps centered on Delphi, Islamic maps centered on Mecca, and those Christian world maps in which Jerusalem is placed as the "true" center of the world.[70] The effect of such "positional enhancing"[71] geometry on the social consciousness of space is difficult to gauge and it would be wrong to suggest that common design features necessarily contributed to identical world views. At the very least, however, such maps tend to focus the viewer's attention upon the center, and thus to promote the development of "exclusive, inward-directed worldviews, each with its separate cult center safely buffered within territories populated only by true believers."[72]

A similarly ethnocentric view may have been induced by some of the formal map projections of the European Renaissance. In this case, too, a map "structures the geography it depicts according to a set of beliefs about the way the world should be, and presents this construction as truth."[73] In the well-known example of Mercator's projection it is doubtful if Mercator himself—who designed the map with navigators in mind to show true compass directions—would have been aware of the extent to which his map would eventually come to project an image so strongly reinforcing the Europeans' view of their own world hegemony. Yet the simple fact that Europe is at the center of the world on this projection, and that the area of the land masses are so distorted that two-thirds of the earth's surface appears to lie in high latitudes, must have contributed much to a European sense of superiority. Indeed, insofar as the "white colonialist states" appear on the map relatively larger than they are while "the colonies" inhabited by colored peoples are shown "too small" suggests how it can be read and acted upon as a geopolitical prophecy.[74]

The Silence on Maps

The notion of "silences" on maps is central to any argument about the influence of their hidden political messages. It is asserted here that maps—just as much as examples of literature or the spoken word—exert a social influence through their omissions as much as by the features they depict and emphasize.

So forceful are the political undercurrents in these silences that it is sometimes difficult to explain them solely by recourse to other historical or technical factors. In seventeenth-century Ireland, for example, the fact that surveyors working for English proprietors sometimes excluded the cabins of the native Irish from their otherwise "accurate" maps is not just a question of scale and of the topographical prominence of such houses, but rather of the religious tensions and class relations in the Irish countryside.[75] Much the same could be said about omissions on printed county surveys of eighteenth-century England: the exclusion of smaller rural cottages may be a response as much to the ideal world of the map makers' landed clients as to the dictates of cartographic scale.[76] On many early town plans a map maker may have unconsciously ignored the alleys and courtyards of the poor in deference to the principal thoroughfares, public buildings, and residences of the merchant class in his conscious promotion of civic pride or vaunting commercial success.[77] Such ideological filtering is a universal process. In colonial mapping, as in eighteenth-century North America, silences on maps may also be regarded as discrimination against native peoples. A map such as Fry and Jefferson's of Virginia (1751) suggests that the Europeans had always lived there: where "Indian nations" are depicted on it, it is more as a signpost to future colonial expansion than as a recognition of their ethnic integrity.[78] In this way, throughout the long age of exploration, European maps gave a one-sided view of ethnic encounters and supported Europe's God-given right to territorial appropriation. European atlases, too, while codifying a much wider range of geographical knowledge, also promoted a Eurocentric, imperialist vision, including as they did a bias towards domestic space which sharpened Euro-

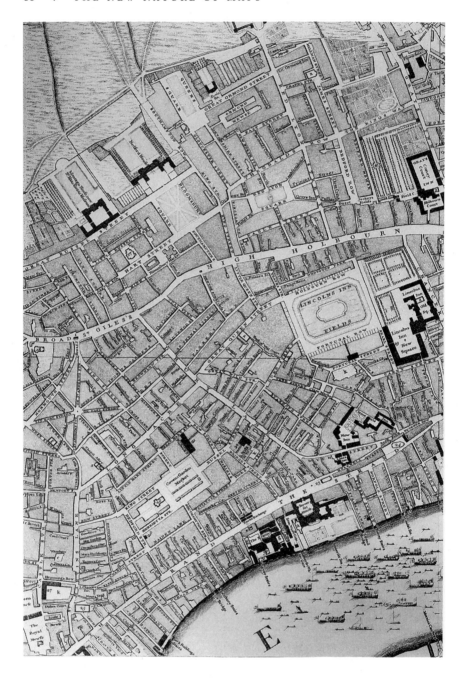

peans' perception of their cultural superiority in the world system.[79] Silences on maps—often becoming part of wider cultural stereotypes—thus came to enshrine self-fulfilling prophecies about the geography of power.

Representational Hierarchies

The role of the map as a form of social proclamation is further strengthened by the systems of classification and modes of representation—the so-called conventional or cartographic signs[80]—which have been adopted for landscape features. It has long been one of the map maker's rules that the signs for towns and villages—whether depicted iconically or by abstract devices—are shown proportionally to the rank of the places concerned. Yet the resulting visual hierarchy of signs in early modern maps is often a replica of the legal, feudal, and ecclesiastical stratifications. Indeed, the concept of a tiered territorial society was by no means lost on contemporary map makers. Mercator, for example, had hoped in his 1595 atlas to show "an exact enumeration and designation of the seats of princes and nobles."[81] Like other map makers before him, he designed a set of settlement signs which, just as truly as the grids which have already been discussed, reify an ordering of the space represented on the map by making it visible. On other maps, towns occupy spaces on the map— even allowing for cartographic convention—far in excess of their sizes on the ground.[82] Castle signs, too, signifying feudal rank and military might, are sometimes larger than signs for villages, despite the lesser area they occupied on the ground. Coats of arms—badges of territorial possession—were used to locate the *caput* of a lordship while the tenurially dependent settlements within the feudal order were allocated inferior signs irrespective of their population or area size. This was particularly common on maps of German territory formerly within the Holy Roman Empire. Such maps pay considerable attention to the geography of ecclesiastic power. The primary message was often

FACING PAGE

Figure 4. Silences on maps: Detail of John Rocque's *A Plan of the Cities of London and Westminster* (1775) showing the built-up area west of the City of London and the prestigious new green field developments of Bloomsbury. While districts to the north of Covent Garden and around Broad Street and St Giles were rapidly becoming slums, the cartographer has produced an idealized view of the city which emphasizes the gracious rurality of the main squares but fails to convey urban squalor. By permission of the British Library (Grace Collection, port. 3:107).

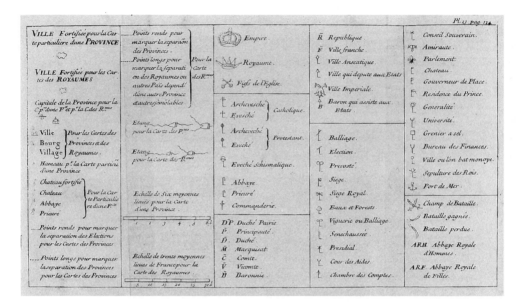

Figure 5. Social hierarchies confirmed in cartographic signs: Plate 14 from M. Buchotte, *Les Règles du dessein et du lavis* (Paris, 1721). By permission of the British Library (Printed Books, 57.c.21).

that of the ubiquity of the church. Whether in "infidel" territory held by the Turk, in lands under the sway of the Papacy, in areas dominated by protestants in general, or by particular sects such as the Hussites, maps communicated the extensiveness of the temporal estate within the spiritual landscape. As a secondary message, not only do these maps heighten the perception of the power of the church as an institution within society as a whole, but they also record the spatial hierarchies and conflicting denominations within the church itself. On the former point, we may note that on Boazio's map of Ireland (1599), an exaggerated pictorial sign for "a Bishopes towne" is placed at the head of its key,[83] just as on the regional maps of Reformation England the signs for church towers and spires often rose far above the requirement of a notional vertical scale. On the matter of hierarchy, individual signs for archbishoprics and bishoprics, in arrays of single or double crosses, or croziers, mitres, and variations in ecclesiastical headgear, testify to the social organization of religion.[84] Here again, the selective magnifications of cartographic signs were closely linked to the shifting allegiances of opposing faiths. They survive as expressions of the religious battlegrounds of early modern Europe.

But if map signs sometimes reacted to changing religious circumstances they also tended to favor the status quo, legitimizing the hierarchies established on earlier maps. They were a socially conservative vocabulary. In France, for example, map makers, as servants of the crown, inscribed images as a form of state propaganda, emphasizing the administrative mechanisms of its centralized bureaucracy and depicting aspects of the legal code of the *ancien régime.*[85] In 1721, when Bouchotte codified the signs to be used on regional maps (*cartes particulières*), for the territories which gave holders their titles, no less than seven of these are listed (*Duché Pairie, Principauté, Duché, Marquisat, Comté, Vîcomté, Baronnie*) as well as five ecclesiastical ranks (archbishopric, bishopric, abbey, priory, *commanderie*).[86]

The Cartographic Symbolism of Power

> The earth is a place on which England is found,
> And you find it however you twirl the globe round;
> For the spots are all red and the rest is all grey,
> And that is the meaning of Empire Day.
> —G. K. Chesterton, "Songs of Education: 11 Geography,"
> *The Collected Poems of G. K. Chesterton*

In the articulation of power the symbolic level is often paramount in cartographic communication and it is in this mode that maps are at their most rhetorical and persuasive. We may consider the symbolic significance of the group of maps found within paintings, where maps are *embedded in the discourse of the painting*. Alternatively we may assess how artistic emblems—which may not be cartographic in character but whose meaning can be iconographically identified from a wider repertoire of images within a culture—function as signs in decorative maps where they are *embedded in the discourse of the map*. Having linked the meaning of particular emblems with the territory represented on the map, we may consider how nondecorative maps may equally symbolize cultural and political values.

Maps in Painting

The use by artists of globes and maps as emblems with their own specific symbolism can be traced back to the classical world. As a politically laden sign

Figure 6. The map as territorial symbol: in this painting of Thomas, 14th Earl of Arundel, and his wife Alethea (by or after Van Dyck, ca. 1635), the Earl points to a colonial venture in the island of Madagascar which he was promoting. Reproduced by kind permission of His Grace The Duke of Norfolk. Photograph, Courtauld Institute of Art.

the globe or orb has frequently symbolized sovereignty over the world.[87] From Roman times onwards—on coins and in manuscripts—a globe or orb was held in the hand of an emperor or king. In the Christian era, now surmounted by a cross, the orb became one of the insignia of the Holy Roman Emperors and, in religious painting, it was frequently depicted held by Christ as *Salvator Mundi,* or by God the Father as *Creator Mundi.*[88] Such meanings were carried forward in the arts of the Renaissance. By the sixteenth century, globes, which like maps had become more commonplace in a print culture,[89] were now shown as part of the regalia of authority in portraits of kings, ambassadors, statesmen, and nobles. But now they were primarily intended to convey the extent of the territorial powers, ambitions, and enterprises of their bearers. These paintings proclaimed the divine right of political control, the emblem of the globe indicating the worldwide scale on which it could be exercised and for which it was desired.[90]

Maps in painting have functioned as territorial symbols. The map mural cycles of the Italian Renaissance, for example, may be interpreted as visual summa of contemporary knowledge, power, and prestige, some of it religious but most of it secular.[91] In portraits of emperors, monarchs, statesmen, general, and popes, maps also appear as a graphic shorthand for the social and territorial power they were expected to wield. It is apt that Elizabeth I stands on a map of sixteenth-century England; that Louis XIV is portrayed being presented with a map of his kingdom by Cassini;[92] that Pope Pius IV views the survey and draining of the Pontine marshes;[93] and that Napoleon is frequently shown with maps in his possession, whether on horseback, when campaigning, or seated and discussing proposed or achieved conquest.[94] Even when the medium changes from paint to photography and film the potent symbolism of the map remains, as the makers of films about Napoleon or Hitler readily grasped.[95] In newspapers, on television screens, and in innumerable political cartoons, military leaders are frequently shown in front of maps to confirm or reassure their viewers about the writ of power over the territory in the map. Map motifs continue to be accepted as geopolitical signs in contemporary society.

The Ideology of Cartographic Decoration

Since the Renaissance, map images have rarely stood alone as discrete geographical statements, but have been accompanied by a wide range of decorative emblems.[96] From Jonathan Swift onwards these elements have been dismissed as largely incidental to the purposes of cartographic communication.[97] Decorative title pages, lettering, cartouches, vignettes, dedications, compass roses, and borders, all of which may incorporate motifs from the wider vocabulary of artistic expression, helped to strengthen and focus the political meanings of the maps on which they appeared. Viewed thus, the notion of cartographic decoration as a marginal exercise in aesthetics is superannuated.

Such a symbolic role for decoration can be traced through much of the history of European cartography. The frontispieces and title pages of many atlases, for example, explicitly define by means of widely understood emblems both the ideological significance and the practical scope of the maps they contain.[98] Monumental arches are an expression of power; the globe and the armillary sphere are associated with royal dedications; portraits of kings and queens and depictions of royal coats of arms are incorporated into the design; royal emblems such as the fleur-de-lis or the imperial eagle also triggered

THEA
TRVM
ORBIS
TERRA
RVM

Opus nunc denuò ab ipso Auctore recognitum, multisque locis castigatum, & quamplurimis nouis Tabulis atque Commentarijs auctum.

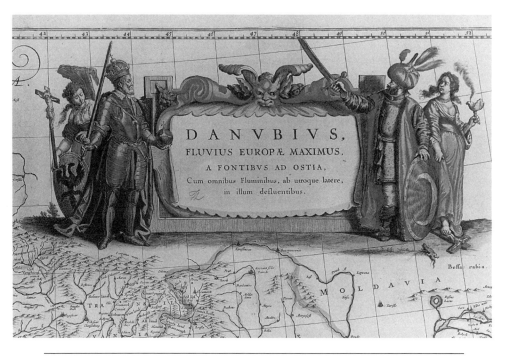

Figure 8. Religious and territorial conflict is epitomized in the cartouche to the map of the Danube in *Mayor o Geographia Blaviana,* vol. 3: *Alemania* (Amsterdam, 1662). Here, the Holy Roman Emperor (left), vested with emblems of power and the Christian faith, confronts the infidel Sultan, enemy of Christendom and spoiler of the cross. From the American Geographical Society Collection, University of Wisconsin-Milwaukee Library.

political as well as more mundane geographical thoughts about the space mapped. The figures most frequently personified are those of nobles, bishops, wealthy merchants, and gentry. On English estate maps, microcosmic symbols of landed wealth, it is the coats of arms, the country house, and the hunting activity of the proprietors which are represented.[99] To own the map was to own the land.

In atlases and wall maps decoration serves to symbolize the acquisition of overseas territory. European navigators—portrayed with their cartographic

FACING PAGE

Figure 7. Atlas title page as geopolitical affirmation: in that of the 1573 edition of Abraham Ortelius's *Theatrum Orbis Terrarum,* Europe, personified as ruler of the world, is enthroned above the other three continents. From the American Geographical Society Collection, University of Wisconsin-Milwaukee Library.

trade symbol of compasses or dividers in hand[100]—pore earnestly over *terrae incognitae* as if already grasping them before their acts of "discovery," conquest, exploration, and exploitation have begun. Indeed, it is on the maps of these overseas empires that we find some of the most striking examples of ideological reinforcement through decoration. Whether we are looking at the French explorer's maps of South America in the sixteenth century[101] or nineteenth-century British maps of African territories, decoration plays a part in attaching a series of racial stereotypes and prejudices to the areas being represented. This is manifestly so with Africa. The decoration on maps produced in Europe disseminated the image of the Dark Continent. Some of the motifs employed suggest that Europeans found it hard to accept that African humanity *was* different. Thus, in the margins of many maps African faces stare out with European features. African men were given "ideal" physiques and poses found in the iconography of figures in classical Greece and Rome; and African rulers—in obedience to the assumption that the political systems of Europe were universal—were usually depicted on maps as "kings."

In other cases the symbols of "otherness" assumed the form of a bizarre racism. Natives are shown riding an ostrich or a crocodile, engaged in cannibal practices, located in captions as "wild men," or, as on one French map of the eighteenth century, include "a race of men and women with tails." Female sexuality in depictions of African women and allegories for America and the other continents is often explicit for the benefit of male-dominated European societies.[102] Nor are the symbols of European power ever far from African space. European ships, castles, forts, and soldierly figures in European uniforms are deployed on maps in coastal regions; African "kings" are subject to European authority; and allegorical angels, the Bible, or the cross, bring to the "barbarous" Africans the benefits of Christianity as part of a colonial package of enlightenment. Sometimes, too, cartouches and vignettes symbolize the colonial authority of individual nations: on a French map of 1708, black Africans are shown with a lion below the arms of France.[103]

Cartographic "Fact" as Symbol

It is a short step to move back from these examples of artistic expression to consider another aspect of "real" maps. Having viewed maps in metaphorical contexts, it is easier to realize how a map which lacks any decorative features or even caption and explanation can nevertheless stand on its own as a symbol of political authority. Such maps are characterized by a "symbolic realism," so that what appears at first sight to be cartographic "fact" may also be a cartographic symbol. It is this duality of the map which encompasses much cartographic discourse and is a principal reason why maps so often constitute a political act or statement.

Once the ubiquity of symbolism is acknowledged, the traditional discontinuity accepted by map historians, between a "decorative" phase and a "scientific" phase of mapping, can be recognized as a myth.[104] Far from being incompatible with symbolic power, more precise measurement intensified it. Accuracy became a new talisman of authority. For example, an accurate outline map of a nation, such as Cassini provided for Louis XIV, was no less a patriotic allegory than an inaccurate one, while the "plain" maps of the Holy Land included in Protestant Bibles in the sixteenth century, in part to validate the literal truth of the text, were as much an essay in sacred symbolism as were more pictorial representations of the region.[105]

These are not exceptional examples of the historical role of measured maps in the making of myth and tradition.[106] Estate maps, though derived from instrumental survey, symbolized a social structure based on landed property; county and regional maps, though founded on triangulation, articulated local values and rights; maps of nation-states, though constructed along arcs of the meridian, were still a symbolic shorthand for a complex of nationalist ideas; world maps, though increasingly drawn on mathematically defined projections, nevertheless gave a spiralling twist to the manifest destiny of European overseas conquest and colonization. Even celestial maps, though observed with ever more powerful telescopes, contained images of constellations which sensed the religious wars and the political dynasties of the territorial world.[107] It is premature to suggest that within almost every map there is a political symbol but at least there appears to be a prima facie case for such a generalization.

Conclusion: Cartographic Discourse and Ideology

I have sought to show how a history of maps, in common with that of other culture symbols, may be interpreted as a form of discourse. While theoretical insights may be derived, for example, from literary criticism, art history, and sociology, we still have to grapple with maps as unique systems of signs, whose

Figure 9. Maps came to serve as surrogate images for the nation-state itself. In this engraving from *The Polish Campaign* (vol. 1, London, 1863), the partition of Poland in 1772 is signified by the tearing of the map. The act is witnessed with distress by its onlookers (from left: Catherine the Great, Empress Maria Theresa, Joseph II of Austria, and Frederick II of Prussia), while an angel, representing the Catholic Church, turns away in horror and sounds a trumpet in alarm. From the American Geographical Society Collection, University of Wisconsin-Milwaukee Library.

codes may be at once iconic, linguistic, numerical, and temporal, and as a spatial form of knowledge. It has not proved difficult to make a general case for the mediating role of maps in political thought and action nor to glimpse their power effects. Through both their content and their modes of representation, the making and using of maps has been pervaded by ideology. Yet these mechanisms can only be understood in specific historical situations. The concluding generalizations must accordingly be read as preliminary ideas for a wider investigation.

The way in which maps have become part of a wider political sign system has been largely directed by their associations with elite or powerful groups and individuals and this has promoted an uneven dialogue through maps. The ideological arrows have tended to fly largely in one direction, from the powerful to the weaker in society. The social history of maps, unlike that of literature, art, or music, appears to have few genuinely popular, alternative, or subversive modes of expression. Maps are preeminently a language of power, not of protest. Though we have entered the age of mass communication by maps, the means of cartographic production, whether commercial or official, is still largely controlled by dominant groups. Indeed, computer technology has increased this concentration of media power. Cartography remains a teleological discourse, reifying power, reinforcing the status quo, and freezing social interaction within charted lines.[108]

The cartographic processes by which power is enforced, reproduced, reinforced, and stereotyped consist of both deliberate and "practical" acts of surveillance and less conscious cognitive adjustments by map makers and map users to dominant values and beliefs. The practical actions undertaken with maps: warfare, boundary making, propaganda, or the preservation of law and order, are documented throughout the history of maps. On the other hand, the undeclared processes of domination through maps are more subtle and elusive. These provide the "hidden rules" of cartographic discourse whose contours can be traced in the subliminal geometries, the silences, and the representational hierarchies of maps. The influence of the map is channeled as much through its representational force as a symbol as through its overt representations. The iconology of the map in the symbolic treatment of power is a neglected aspect of cartographic history. In grasping its importance we move away from a history of maps as a record of the cartographer's intention and technical acts to one which locates the cartographic image in a social world.

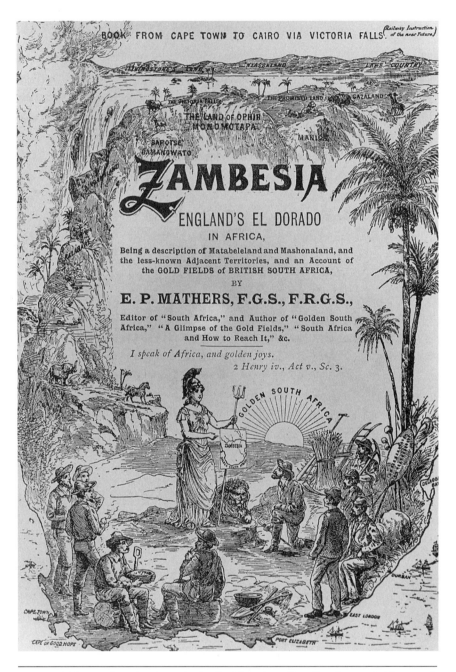

Figure 10. Title page from *Zambesia, England's El Dorado in Africa* (London, 1891). The scene is set on an outline map of southern Africa. Britannia, displaying a map of Zambesia, entices white colonists to take advantage of the economic wealth of the country while the indigenous African population is excluded from the stage. From the American Geographical Society Collection, University of Wisconsin-Milwaukee Library.

Maps as an impersonal type of knowledge tend to "desocialize" the territory they represent. They foster the notion of a socially empty space. The abstract quality of the map, embodied as much in the lines of a fifteenth-century Ptolemaic projection as in the contemporary images of computer cartography, lessens the burden of conscience about people in the landscape. Decisions about the exercise of power are removed from the realm of immediate face-to-face contacts.

These ideas remain to be explored in specific historical contexts. Like the historian, the map maker has always played a rhetorical role in defining the configurations of power in society as well as recording their manifestations in the visible landscape. Any cartographic history which ignores the political significance of representation relegates itself to an "ahistorical" history.

CHAPTER THREE

Silences and Secrecy

The Hidden Agenda of Cartography in Early Modern Europe

This chapter originally appeared in *Imago Mundi* 40 (1988): 57–76.

On a visit to Leningrad some years ago I consulted a map to find out where I was, but I could not make it out. From where I stood, I could see several enormous churches, yet there was no trace of them on my map. When finally an interpreter came to help me, he said: "We don't show churches on our maps." Contradicting him, I pointed to one that was very clearly marked. "That is a museum," he said, "not what we call a 'living church.' It is only 'living churches' we don't show."

It then occurred to me that this was not the first time I had been given a map which failed to show many things I could see right in front of my eyes. All through school and university I had been given maps of life and knowledge on which there was hardly a trace of many of the things that I most cared about and that seemed to me to be of the greatest possible importance to the conduct of my life. I remembered that for many years my perplexity had been complete; and no interpreter had come along to help me. It remained complete until I ceased to suspect the sanity of my perceptions and began, instead, to suspect the soundness of the maps.
                                        —E. F. SCHUMACHER,
            "On Philosophical Maps," *A Guide for the Perplexed*

*T*he present paper picks up a theme explored more fully in the context of the ideological dimensions of cartography.[1] It is concerned with the dialogue that arises from the intentional or unintentional suppression of knowledge in maps. It is based on a theory of cartographic silence. My reading of the map is not a technical one (this already has a voluminous literature) but a political one. The aim in this paper is to probe those silences which arise from deliberate policies of secrecy and censorship and to examine the more indeterminate silences rooted in often hidden procedures or rules. These rules, it can be argued, are a sort of subconscious *mentalité* that mediates the knowledge contained in maps in order to maintain the political status quo and the power of the state. Although much of what is said here applies to all periods, including the present,[2] the focus is on early modern Europe. Maps from the sixteenth century onwards offer particularly clear opportunities for the exploration of a new perspective on the changing and reciprocal relation-ships between the rise of the nation-state and the expansion of cartography.[3] The establishment of stability and durability, the primary tasks of each and every nation-state,[4] in early modern Europe as at other times, provides the background to this essay. In outlining, first, the theoretical framework, it will be argued that cartography was primarily a form of political discourse[5] concerned with the acquisition and maintenance of power. Examples drawn from the maps themselves will then be used in support of this argument.

Theories about Silences in Maps

Mapping in the nation-states of early modern Europe offers examples of many types of cartographic silence. As in the history of cartography as a whole it would be possible to construct a broader typology of silences. Silences are contributed by many agents in the map-making process, through the stages of data gathering to those of compilation, editing, drafting, printing, and publication.[6] In assessing silences we must be aware not only of the geographical limits to knowledge but also of the technological constraints to representation, and of the silences in the historical record owing to the destruction of evidence. In the present essay, however, I am not concerned with those silences which arise from geographical ignorance, lack of data, error, the limitations of scale, deliberate design or other aspects of specification and technical limitation.[7] I am dealing here with political silences. An adequate theory concerning the political silences in maps is thus central both to my interpretation of the nature of state cartography and to the ways in which maps were used to maintain and legitimize state power. My theoretical position is derived from two directions. The first concerns a philosophical and, more particularly, a phenomenological, understanding of silences.[8] The second concerns the sociology of power and the idea that knowledge is power.

From the philosophers we learn that silence is a phenomenon "encountered in every segment of human experience in which utterance takes place."[9] We learn, too, that utterance is defined as "any performance employing systematically related signs, sounds, gestures, or marks having recognizable meanings to express thoughts, feelings, states of affairs" and that the "deployment of any sort of language is counted . . . as an utterance."[10] This means that although most obvious are the silences which occur in speech and music, they also occur in nonperforming arts such as painting and sculpture.[11] In this way, the concept of silences is also applicable to maps. To ignore or downgrade these silences—as both the history of cartography and cartography have done—is to close up an important avenue of historical exploration, one in which maps can be seen to engage both the imagination and the social preconceptions of their readers.[12]

Thus we learn that that which is absent from maps is as much a proper field for enquiry as that which is present. A second insight derived from the philosophical direction is that silences should be regarded as positive statements and not as merely passive gaps in the flow of language. So, allowing for those gaps on the map which make the pattern of lines and points a comprehensible image, we should be prepared to regard silences on maps as something more than the mere absence of something else. I am deliberately insisting on the term *silences* in the context of maps, rather than the somewhat negative *blank spaces* of the older literature,[13] for the reason that silence should be seen as an "active human performance."[14] Silence can reveal as much as it conceals and, from acting as independent and intentional statements, silences on maps may sometimes become the determinate part of the cartographic message. So, just as in verbal communication the silence is more than the mere correlate of what is sounded, in the case of a map the silence is not merely the opposite of what is depicted. The white spaces which abound on the maps of early modern Europe, for example, cannot be explained simply by positing "fact" against "no fact." Silence and utterance are not alternatives but constituent parts of map language, each necessary for the understanding of the other. A cartographic interpretation of silences on a map departs, then, from the premise that silence elucidates and is likely to be as culturally specific as any other aspect of the map's language.[15]

My second insight comes from sociology. This helps us gain a historical understanding of cartographic silence. It involves seeing cartography as a form of knowledge and that knowledge as discourse. In this light, maps are interpreted as socially constructed perspectives on the world rather than as the "neutral" or "value-free" representations that, some historians insist, define the rise of state cartography in early modern Europe. This myth of a measurement-based "objectivity" in maps has yet to be stripped away: the application of the sociological concept of "power-knowledge" to the history of cartography is another step in that process.[16]

From the sociological literature on the nature of knowledge, I have drawn in this essay on the ideas of Michel Foucault[17] to help interpret the categories of cartographic silence—the intentional and the unintentional—identified below. Two sets of ideas in particular seem of direct relevance: the idea of power-knowledge (*pouvoir savoir*) and the concept of an *episteme*.

1. Foucault constantly stresses the relationship between power and knowledge. For him, this serves to frame the instances of deliberate secrecy and censorship. He writes that:

> We should admit . . . that power produces knowledge (and not simply by encouraging it because it serves power or by applying it because it is useful); that power and knowledge directly imply one another; that there is no power relation without the correlative constitution of a field of knowledge, nor any knowledge that does not presuppose and constitute at the same time power relations.[18]

While the universality of these assertions may be rejected, it is easier to accept the implication that the map was an instrument of power and that much of the instrumentality of maps in early modern Europe was concerned with power in one form or another. Foucault seems to have accepted the map as a tool of state measurement, enquiry, examination, and coercion.[19] In his view, cartographers provide the state with a mass of information which the state, from its strategic position, is able to exploit. Moreover, the state was also frequently able to impose its own rules upon this cartographic knowledge, giving rise to the silences that are induced by those occasions of deliberate secrecy and censorship that recur so often in the history of European state mapping. Elsewhere, Foucault goes on to note that the production of discourse in every society "is at once controlled, selected, organised and redistributed according to a certain number of procedures."[20] In the case of cartography, these procedures involved external controls, internal rules, and the regulation of access to knowledge. Thus a state gains power over knowledge.

2. The second set of Foucault's ideas, the *episteme,* helps us interrogate the unintentional silences on maps (the residual "blank spaces" of the older cartographic literature). As already noted, these silences are "active performances" in terms of their social and political impact and their effects on consciousness. They are, moreover, a feature of all discourse,[21] part of the cultural codes which underlie all forms of knowledge and which structure "its language, its perceptual schemata, its exchanges, its techniques, its values, the hierarchy of its practices."[22] As far as early European maps are concerned, we

find that these silences are best understood in terms of "historical *a priori*" which "in a given period, delimits . . . the totality of experience of a field of knowledge."[23] These historical *a priori* form what Foucault once termed an *episteme:*[24] like all other knowledge, cartographic knowledge is similarly de-limited, so that while some information is included on the maps, other aspects of life and landscape are excluded according to the *episteme.*

Thus equipped with these philosophical and sociological insights into the meanings communicated by the "blank spaces" on maps, it seems to me we are in a better position to attempt to unearth the history of those meanings. We may be better equipped, too, to unravel those systems of "nonformal" knowledge that suffused everyday cartographic practice in early modern Europe, as it does still.

Secrecy and Censorship: The Intentional Silences in Maps

By the sixteenth century literary censorship of various kinds was a common aspect of European culture as the emergent nations struggled as much for self-definition as for physical territory.[25] It will be shown here how the production of cartographic knowledge was similarly controled, selected, organized, and redistributed according to definite procedures. Even in many ancient and traditional societies maps were frequently regarded as privileged knowledge, with access given only to those authorized by the state or its ruler.[26] By the early modern period, cartographic secrecy (maintained by what may be defined as rules of exclusion and prohibition) was clearly widespread and the "official" cartography of this period furnishes a classic case of "power-knowledge."[27] At the very time maps were being transformed by mathematical techniques, they were also being appropriated as an intellectual weapon of the state system. If their study had become, by the end of the sixteenth century, the "science of princes," it was because maps were by then recognized as a visual language communicating proprietorial or territorial rights in both practical and sym-bolic senses.[28] In cartographic terms, however, the exercise of such power could be negative and restrictive. The map image itself was becoming in-creasingly subject to concealment, censorship, sometimes to abstraction or falsification. It is these deliberate manipulations, willed by individuals, groups, or institutions,[29] that give rise to our category of intentional silences.

Of course, we have to reconcile, map by map, the study of these intended cartographic silences with the complexity of different historical events. The immediate circumstances which led princes, both secular and ecclesiastical, and their advisors, to control cartography by means of censorship and secrecy spanned a wide range of their vital interests. These could be military, commercial, or religious. So, for example, on Jesuit Matteo Ricci's world map published at Peking in 1602, the sacred places of Christianity are suitably annotated while those of Islam appear without comment, the reason for Ricci's silence being that he knew "the Chinese would be unlikely to be drawn to the religion he was preaching if they knew that deep fissures of belief existed in the Western world from which that religion came."[30] Reflecting different ways of sharing power within nation-states in sixteenth- and seventeenth-century Europe, the manner in which control over maps and their content was effected also varied. In some states, control centered on the crown and a group of close advisors. In other cases, it was delegated to a bureaucratic institution. In either case, the effects were complex, even paradoxical, while elsewhere policies of secrecy were inconsistently applied. On the maps of sixteenth- and seventeenth-century Europe these aspects of national secrecy are manifested in various ways. Here we shall consider just two ways; first, examples of strategic secrecy; and second, cases of commercial secrecy.

Strategic Secrecy

Some of the most clear-cut cases of an increasing state concern with the control and restriction of map knowledge are associated with military or strategic considerations. In Europe in the sixteenth and seventeenth centuries hardly a year passed without some war being fought. Maps were an object of military intelligence; statesmen and princes collected maps to plan, or, later, to commemorate battles; military textbooks advocated the use of maps. Strategic reasons for keeping map knowledge a secret included the need for confidentiality about the offensive and defensive operations of state armies, the wish to disguise the thrust of external colonization, and the need to stifle opposition within domestic populations when developing administrative and judicial systems as well as the more obvious need to conceal detailed knowledge about fortifications.[31]

But besides these understandable and practical bases for military secrecy, an increasing number of states adopted a more custodial attitude towards maps of their cities and territories in general independent of such strategic considerations. The Dutch merchant Isaac Massa, for example, who was living in Muscovy in the late-sixteenth century, found it difficult to obtain maps of both Moscow and the Siberian territory only because it would have been a capital offense to supply him with such maps.[32] In the same century, the *Bol'shoy Chertyozh* map (which shows the whole of the Muscovite state) seems to have been drafted in only one copy and to have remained wholly unknown to Western European map makers.[33] Similar policies have been common throughout Europe and can be found, for example, in Prussia in the sixteenth and seventeenth centuries;[34] in late-sixteenth-century Italy (map of the Kingdom of Naples);[35] in sixteenth-century Spain (the "Escorial atlas");[36] in seventeenth-century Switzerland (Hans Conrad Gyger's map of the Canton of Zurich).[37] Herein lies one of the paradoxes of map history. Just as the printing press was facilitating the much wider dissemination of survey data, and just as regional topographical maps were being made for the first time, so, some states and their princes were determinedly keeping their maps secret through prohibiting their publication.

Why did some states insist upon cartographic secrecy while others allowed the publication of their earliest national surveys? One reason, it may be suggested, is that strong monarchies may have perceived less need for secrecy than did the weak and threatened. Certainly, in strongly centralized Elizabethan England, surviving documents imply few doubts about the wisdom of publishing Saxton's survey.[38] From the 1570s Saxton's maps were seen by statesmen such as Burghley as an aid to national administration and defense although a few may have taken a different view.[39] Of seventeenth-century France, too, it has been observed how "maps seem to have functioned in untroubled support of a strongly centralized monarchic regime."[40] But such an argument fails to explain all. On the contrary, some of these maps became double-edged weapons. Once generally available, they were used to support other sides in political power struggles. In England, for example, Saxton's maps did not (as had been intended) serve solely to strengthen the power of the monarchy. Once published and in circulation, they would surely also have been a contributory factor in the growth of the strong sense of provincial identity and independence which was so successfully articulated against the crown in the Civil War.[41] Likewise, it has been remarked that in the Low Countries the widespread use of maps went hand-in-hand with the nascent bourgeois republicanism of the seventeenth century.[42] With such complex, and sometimes contradictory, aspects in mind we can perhaps begin to glimpse how, for the cautious monarchy determined to preserve its power, map secrecy came to be regarded as a prudent policy of good government.

Commercial Secrecy

The rise of map secrecy in early modern Europe was also associated with a second theater of geographical activity—that of commerce and the rise of monopoly capitalism. In a period when the foundations of the European world economy and its overseas empires were being laid,[43] absolute monarchs were often also "merchant kings," pursing economic objectives through the trade monopolies opened up by their navigations.[44] As in the case of the nation-state, the essence of empire is control. For such commercial monopolies to survive and for the policies of *mare clausum* to be implemented, there had to be a monopoly of the knowledge which enabled the new lands and the routes to and from them to be mapped. Arguably, the process of monopolization of map knowledge paralleled the secreting and use of craft mysteries in the control of medieval guilds.[45]

The mechanism by which vital cartographic information from nascent overseas empires was censored, regulated, and secreted varied considerably. In some countries, it was an ad hoc process linked to individual voyages. This seems to have been the case in England, where contemporary writers on the navigations were aware of the practice of censorship[46] and knew that new knowledge was controlled in a few powerful hands, those of the sovereign, an inner circle of ministers, or the principal merchants and navigators involved with a venture. For example, the sketch maps and drawings brought back by Drake's voyage round the world (1577–80) became secret documents. Drake had been given express orders that "none shall make any charts or descriptions of the said voyage," a prohibition of publication that was to remain in force until 1588 (figure 11).[47]

Much more elaborate were the bureaucratic systems set up by the crowns of both Portugal and Spain to regulate the overseas trade and the knowledge on which it depended. Maps quickly became key documents in the launching of the Luso-Hispanic empires. While both the extent to which the Portuguese policy of secrecy actually existed and its effectiveness have been the subject of heated debate,[48] the evidence does suggest the length to which a self-

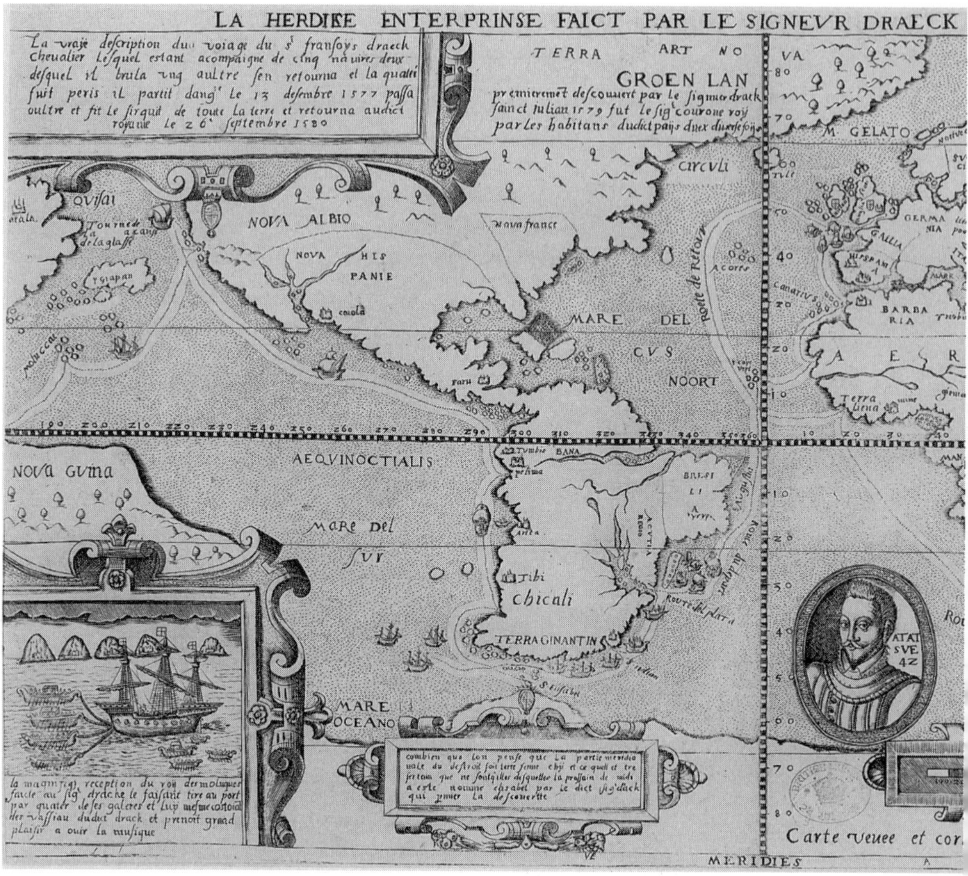

Figure 11. Part of the world map by Nicola van Sype, showing Drake's circumnavigation and engraved and published at Antwerp, ca. 1583, was probably an unauthorized copy, made from a secret English original and smuggled out of the country. By permission of the British Library (Maps C2.a.7).

interested and powerful monarchy might go to control and suppress sensitive maps. For instance, the penalty for pilots giving or selling charts to foreigners was to be death.[49] Measures were taken, late in the fifteenth century, by John II of Portugal (1481–95) to exclude foreigners, especially Genoese and Florentines, from all Portuguese territory, while the Cortes of 1481, in relation to the West African navigation, is said to have "demanded severe measures for maintaining the secret of the discovered lands. The documents were sequestered; to record new lands on the maps was forbidden; the nautical works became secret books; prohibitory tales were spread; and the navigators forced to keep the oath of silence."[50]

By the beginning of the sixteenth century, Portuguese controls on cartographic knowledge had been further tightened by the establishment of a "hydrographical repository" within the "Storehouse of Guinea and the Indies" (*Armazem da Guine e Indias*).[51] This clearly exercised censorship functions. A royal charter of 13 November 1504 prohibited the making of globes and forbade nautical charts to depict the West Africa coast beyond the river Congo. Charts not complying with this provision were required to be taken to an officer of the hydrographical repository to be cleansed of such details. Moreover, such an organization made it possible to insist that nautical charts issued before a voyage were handed back on its completion while the duty of another official was to screen intended recipients lest there might be objections to their handling of charts.[52] Contemporaries alleged the deliberate falsification of charts: it is easy to see how it could have come about in both Portugal and Spain.[53]

The objectives of state control of overseas cartographic knowledge and the regulating mechanisms in Spain were much the same as in Portugal. The Castilian court had set up a special institution in the first decade of the sixteenth century called the *Casa de Contratación* (colonial office in control of shipping, commerce and finance, probably based on the Portuguese model), to oversee exploration and to house, in secrecy, documents of discovery.[54] By 1508 a special geographical and cosmographical department had been created within the *Casa*. It was here that a master world map, the *Padrón Real*, was kept up-to-date by trained chartmakers.[55] The *Casa*'s many provisions included the instructions that

> Pilots were not to be permitted to make use of any other maps than this, and they were directed, upon finding new islands or lands, new ports or bays, or any other thing—currents or tides, headland or mountains—which might serve the purpose of subsequent identification of localities, to enter the same in the copy of the *Padrón Real* which they carried, reporting all entries made on return, but nothing should be inserted that was not properly attested and sworn to.[56]

The situation in both Portugal and Spain early in the sixteenth century suggests that the rulers of the nation-states of Europe, together with their rising bourgeois merchant classes, were not slow in discovering the value of centralized control in trying to ensure the confidentiality of geographical knowledge about the New World. Rivals of Portugal and Spain copied their navigational institutions. The hydrographic office established at Amsterdam, after the organization of the Dutch merchant companies into the United East India Company in 1602, paralleled the *Casa da Contratación* in a number of ways, including the institutionalization of a secret cartography.[57] Each chart maker in the Dutch East India Company

> was . . . obliged to ensure that the logs from arriving vessels were delivered in good order, and did not fall into the wrong hands. He had to file them in a special room in East India House and had also to keep proper records. Every six months he had to account for all the improvements he had made in the charts and rutters. The chartmaker was sworn not to disclose any information about his activities to persons not in the employ of the company. He was not allowed to publish, directly or indirectly, any of the company's material without the company's knowledge and comment, and every newly appointed chart-maker had to swear before the mayor of Amsterdam that he would obey these instructions.[58]

The Dutch East Company had become, in effect, the state's surrogate organ, acting as a ministry with particular responsibility for the eastern colonies. Its map policy was especially cautious when the handing out of charts of newly explored regions was in question. The practice was to supply pilots with these in manuscript and as required, and to check their return at the end of a voyage. Company officials, such as Plancius and later, Blaeu, were expected to exercise tight control, even to the point of censoring maps intended for publication. Consequently, maps associated with important voyages, such as those of Tasman to Australia, were effectively being kept secret (figure 12).[59]

Nor were the Dutch monopoly companies alone in adopting such restrictive cartographic practices. In seventeenth-century England, after the Restoration, as trading companies became increasingly monopolistic in structure so they also tended to act as a brake on map publication, if not map making itself.[60] Once the Hudson's Bay Company (founded in 1670) had acquired its territorial monopoly, its substantial archive—including all the maps—remained all but closed until the late-eighteenth century because of the Company's restrictive policies.[61] These policies meant in practice that the Company "did not allow details of the geographic pattern of riverways, lakes, and

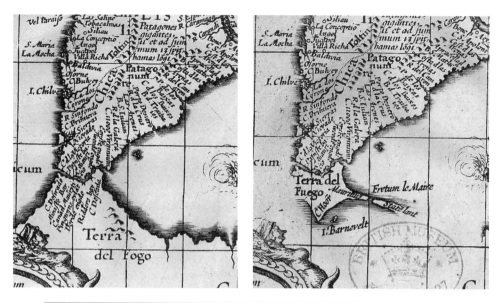

Figure 12. Tierra del Fuego on two states of Willem Janzoon Blaeu's *Nova Orbis Terra* (left, 1606/1617; right, after 1618). Knowledge, available in 1617, on the Straits of Magellan from le Maire's voyage was censored for commercial reasons until after 1618 (see Tony Campbell in note 59). By permission of the British Library (Maps 920 [262] and Maps 188.j.l[i]).

the terrain to become known" for the simple reason that "such geographic data were considered crucial to the formulation and operation of its trading policies, and thus were commercial secrets."[62] Particularly interesting is the way the English parliament reacted when faced with these policies. Even when opportunities presented themselves to legislate against these practices it was unable to assert itself as the disinterested patron of a "scientific" knowledge expressed through geographical maps.[63]

Thus the forces impinging upon the cartography of early modern Europe were much more complex than the initially simple notion of power-knowledge allows for. A number of characteristics can be observed. For instance, while it can be claimed that secrecy has been endemic in the history of maps and map making as well as in the activities of monopoly capitalism, there has been nothing neat or predictable in the timing or the geographical pattern of its imposition. We find that some periods are characterized by "high security" while in others this has been allowed to slip. When the world limits of the Spanish and Portuguese empires were being demarcated, between about 1515 and 1529, control over secrecy was rigorously enforced but later in

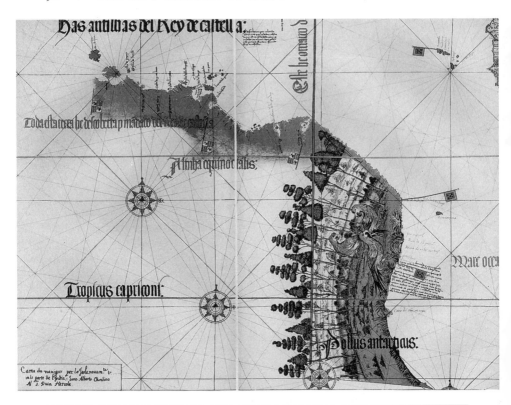

Figure 13. Brazil on the Cantino Chart, 1502. Anxiety about the Italian spice trade led the Duke of Ferrara to obtain by bribery this map of the "islands recently discovered in the . . . Indies" from a Portuguese original in Lisbon, from H. Harrisse's facsimile in *Recueil de voyages et de documents pour servir à L'Histoire de la Géographie No 3 Les Corte-Real et leurs voyages au Nouveau-Monde* (Paris 1883). By permission of the British Library (Maps 7.e.8).

the century laxity crept in (figure 13). Another point is the way state policies have been inconsistent. Despite Spain's usual preoccupation with secrecy and control, cartographic caution was thrown to the winds when Charles V of Spain wished to impress foreign crowns with propaganda maps showing the territorial extent of Spanish influence.[64] Nor were the manipulations of one state always meekly accepted by its rivals. These sought to obtain maps as much by espionage,[65] theft, and piracy as by direct observation and their own survey. So, Walter Raleigh's collection of New World maps, which had come mainly from Spanish sources, included "a secret mappe of those partes made in Mexico . . . for the King of Spaine."[66] Moreover, the strictest policies of cartographic secrecy could be undermined by the ease with which cosmographers and pilots, taking with them their specialist cartographic knowledge, entered the service of rival crowns. There are well-known cases of Portuguese pilots being lured into the more lucrative service of Spain, France, or England while cartographers such as Cabot, Ribeiro, and Rotz are known to have been the agents by which once-confidential maps were given wider currency. Even the *Padrón* of Spanish navigation did not remain secret for ever and its contents were eventually published. Finally, and yet more remarkable, perhaps, were the occasions when ideological conflicts about secrecy emerged in the very institutions set up to enforce it. It has been shown, for example, how there was a protracted debate and even litigation within the *Casa da Contratación* over the role of patriotism in scientific argument and the role of secrecy in the growth of knowledge.[67] In view of all this, we have to conclude that access to knowledge must be regarded as one of the more complex socio-legal dimensions that structured the development of cartography in early modern Europe.

Epistemological or Unintentional Silences on Maps

A second category of silence on maps is the unintentional silence. This is a silence that does not seem to have been "explicitly commanded" by the cartographic patrons of early modern Europe yet that was nonetheless instrumental in the diffusion of state power.[68] What commanded the unintentional silence was "the play of rules which determines within a culture the appearance and disappearance of statements"[69] on maps. So our concern here is with the absence or presence of categories of cartographic detail that cannot be explained by reference to either secrecy or technical factors but by "historical rules" that are not merely theoretical but observable in forms which varied according to the particular "social, economic, geographic or linguistic zone" within which a map originated.[70] These "rules" help to fashion two sets of discourse, the scientific, and the political-social, whose function is to structure the framework within which cartographic knowledge is created.

The Scientific Discourse in Maps

Already in the Renaissance, two "scientific" characteristics, the "universal science of measurement and order" and the principle of classification or ordered tabulation,[71] were important underpinnings of map content. From then on, increasingly precise instruments of survey and techniques of mapping contributed to the "science of measurement" while the way in which cartographic signs were classified and ordered (i.e., set out in tabulated characteristic sheets)[72] points to the adoption of the principle of classification. As scientific progress and increasing technical accuracy marched ahead, few doubts were expressed. State cartography was thus, in the sixteenth century, well on the way to becoming a scientific and technological discourse. Contained within it was the unwritten assumption of an objective world in which the new techniques, being repeatable and transmissible, were always able to be successful in measuring or describing accurately.[73] Today, many historians still accept this model of scientific progress as the standard interpretation of the rise of state cartography.[74] Yet of equal interest are the silences on those allegedly "objective" products of state mapping. My contention is that while measurement and classification may have fostered objectivity within the terms of reference of the cultural *episteme,* in other respects the maps still remain a subjective perspective on the world of that culture. Standardization, with its Euclidian emphasis on space as uniform and continuous, generates the silences of uniformity. For instance, in many of the topographical atlases of early modern Europe, especially those of the seventeenth century, but even in Mercator's and Saxton's, much of the character and individuality of local places is absent from the map. Behind the facade of a few standard signs on these atlases, the outline of one town looks much the same as that of the next; the villages are more nearly identical and are arranged in a neat taxonomic hierarchy;[75] woodland is aggregated into a few types; even rivers and streams become reduced into a mere token of reality; objects outside the surveyor's classification of "reality" are excluded. The epistemological force of scientific procedures was, moreover, intensified by their further standardization through map printing—the innovation which saw the start of "the technologizing of the map"—so that the map images acquire a tidiness and inevitability lacking in the manuscript age.[76] The net result was that the cartographic landscapes of Europe became more generalized, more abstract, and less differentiated in the mode of their representation. Their silences are those of the unique.

It is generally accepted that mapping is an activity designed to promote state efficiency and that with good maps the writ of centralized power can be made to run more uniformly over a country as a whole. But we need to ask "Why was it that it had to be scientific mapping that made this task easier?" If we leave aside all the logistical arguments that have been marshaled in favor of maps—and clearly they persuaded a considerable investment by the rulers of early modern Europe—then there is another side to the explanation: the silences in maps act to legitimize and neutralize arbitrary actions in the consciousness of their originators. In other words, the lack of qualitative differentiation in maps structured by the scientific *episteme* serves to dehumanize the landscape. Such maps convey knowledge where the subject is kept at bay.[77] Space becomes more important than place: if places look alike they can be treated alike. Thus, with the progress of scientific mapping, space became all too easily a socially empty commodity, a geometrical landscape of cold, non-human facts.

The Political and Social Discourse in Maps

But not all is explained in this way.[78] The paradox is that the socially empty spaces on the map were not without social consequences. Yet other threads weave through map imagery. In particular, there are those of political consciousness, mediated through patronage,[79] and those of religious values or of social or ethnic attitudes. With the help of these epistemological insights, we can listen to the other silences in our maps.

Political discourse is grounded in an assumption of the legitimacy of an existing political status quo and its values. Its utterances through maps as elsewhere, are intended, consciously or unconsciously, to prolong, to preserve, and to develop the "truths" and achievements initiated by the founding fathers of that political system or modified by their successors. However, it can be argued that this cognitive infrastructure itself determines the nature of the technical specification of maps and provides the rules of what is included and excluded on a map. It can also be suggested that political discourse is responsible for differential emphases, through selection and generalization, which privilege some aspects of "reality" while others are silenced. Individual cartographers would not have been in the position to control or balance these nuances, even had they been aware of them.

Examples of many different sorts of political and social silences can be found on maps from the early modern period. One category is the toponymic silence. Conquering states impose a silence on minority or subject populations through their manipulation of place-names. Whole strata of ethnic identity are swept from the map in what amount to acts of cultural genocide.

While such manipulations are, at one level, the result of deliberate censorship or policies of acculturation,[80] at another—the epistemological—level, they also can be seen as representing the unconscious rejection of these "other"[81] people by those belonging to the politically more powerful groups.

A similar reading can be made of the silences found in the keys to cartographic signs included on some maps in early modern Europe. On Mercator's map of Europe dated 1554, for example, the map maker chose to identify four ecclesiastical ranks—the Vatican (*Pontifex Romanus*), the patriarchal sees (*patriarchales*), the archiepiscopal sees (*archiepiscopales*), and bishoprics (*episcopales*)—while remaining silent about the four or five ranks of secular status also differentiated and shown on the maps.[82] By implication, the political power acknowledged here is the ecclesiastical one; small settlements (villages) at the bottom of the ecclesiastical hierarchy are of no consequence. Silence thus becomes an "active performance" giving affirmative support to the political status quo.

In yet another group of examples, we can detect how maps were implicated in a discourse of promise—their silences reciprocating eschatological dimensions in the sacred books of particular sects or religions. Thus, in the depiction of the Holy Land inspired by Luther and Calvin, in which a *geographia sacra* was combined with geographical realism (the latter reflecting the scientific discourse in maps), it is events of the Old Testament and the Protestant message of "Salvation History," epitomized by the Exodus route, which are emphasized.[83] Left silent are the history and sites of New Testament lore which feature so prominently in the *mappaemundi* of the Catholic Middle Ages.[84]

The content and publication of maps may thus be structured by the religious schisms and ideological battles of early modern Europe. The publication of books of town plans of Italy, for example, may have been inhibited in some areas by the aversion of Calvinists to representations of Catholic Rome. Similarly, it may be significant that the ecclesiastic rank of settlements is indicated more frequently on maps of regions south of the Alps (or on the maps of cartographers from countries in which the Roman Catholic Church remained in power, such as Italy, Spain, and France) than in the Protestant regions to the north. In contrast, maps containing information about the different sects and adherences of European Christians were more common north of the Alps, where they reflected the religious turmoil of the Reformation, about which maps from the Catholic heartlands of Italy, France, and Spain remained silent.[85] Sectarian splits are sometimes discernible in maps whose authors were hotly partisan to one doctrine, for instance through the map's silence about the churches and settlements of the other[86] (figure 14). On yet other maps, including portolan charts, lands which the Ottomans had conquered were shown as if still in Christian hands, while Jerusalem was often depicted as Christian on some of the maps of the Middle Ages long after its fall to Islam.[87]

The first problem encountered in attempting to integrate the silences in European maps that might have arisen from contemporary perceptions of class or race is the tendency to assume that these perceptions would have been identical amongst all Europeans and throughout the sixteenth or seventeenth century. Even so, it is reasonable to suggest that there was a common conceptual base to European society of the time. For instance, social status and the nature of men's occupation were matters of deep concern both in feudal central Europe and amongst the rising middle ranks or *grande bourgeoisie* of other states which would have influenced map knowledge. Witness the careful ranking of the costumed figures that so often compose the marginal decoration of late-sixteenth- and seventeenth-century maps such as those of Speed and Blaeu, for instance.[88] While those social distinctions are easily discerned, others may be more subliminal. But the same sort of social taxonomy seems to have underlain the silence in European cartography about the majority social class. For map makers, their patrons, and their readers, the underclass did not exist and had no geography, still less was it composed of individuals. Instead, what we see singled out on these maps are people privileged by the right to wear a crown or a mitre or to bear a coat of arms or a crozier. The peasantry, the landless laborers, or the urban poor had no place in the social hierarchy and, equally, as a cartographically disenfranchised group, they had no right to representation on the map. Credentials of social status, which gave an individual the right to hold land, also conferred the right to appropriate the most prominent signs in the map maker's repertoire. The largest (and most eye-catching) pictorial signs on the map turn out to be those associated with feudal, military, legal, or ecclesiastical status. A peasant village, lacking strong overlordship or church patronage, recedes into the near-silence of an abstract dot or sign. Moreover, these European notions of status were carried into the New World. They are discernible on, in particular, maps of regions where the

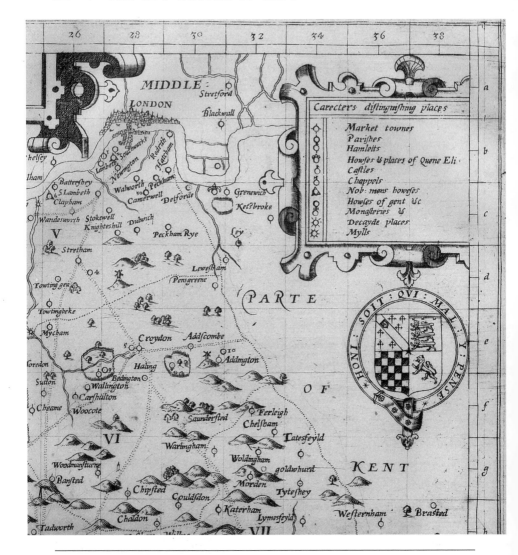

Figure 14. Part of John Norden's *Surrey*, 1594. It has been argued that Norden, being anti-Catholic, omitted "Bishops sees" from his map. The only one of his maps to show them, *Middlesex,* 1593, marks them by a star rather than a Papists' cross. "Chappels" (chapels-of-ease) make their appearance, reflecting Norden's attention to ecclesiastical detail. By permission of the British Library (Maps C2cc7).

European culture encountered the Indian culture. They are found, for instance, on maps showing the early English settlement of Virginia. Here the distinction between Indians of the "better sort" and the common Indian people, frequently made by contemporary writers,[89] is conveyed (as on European maps) by representations of individuals from the privileged upper stratum of Indian society—a Powahatan, Pocahontas, or Susquehanna chief, for example—while the ordinary men and women are shown massed anonymously at their feet and, by implication, at their command. Likewise, European hierarchies are found in the settlement signs of maps of the New World. For the two hundred or so Indian settlements that are depicted on John Smith's map of Virginia (1612), a careful distinction is made between "Kings Houses" (drawn with a visually prominant sign), and "ordinary Houses" (marked by a relatively insignificant sign), and chief Powhatan's settlement (given the largest sign of all).[90]

Another type of silence found on maps of the New World arises from the tendency to obliterate the uniqueness of the American landscape in favor of a stereotype, a tendency that is more difficult to explain. It could be, of course, simply the result of a lack of information. Faced with empty spaces on the sketches and drafts they were given as models, European engravers would have filled these with the only landscape conventions familiar to them. Alternatively, the stereotype of the American landscape can be seen as a deliberate act of colonial promotion, designed to make the new lands more attractive to settlers or to tempt proprietors and potential investors.[91] But we may also seek explanations of these silences in another direction, at the structural level of Foucault's *epistemes*. Thus, they would be manifestations of yet another way European scientific values were reflected in Renaissance cartography through, especially, measurement and simple landscape classification. So, we could be witnessing here, once again, the unconscious transposition into American geography of European values and preferences, this time in relation to the landscape. Maps such as those of John Smith (*Lord Baltimore's Map*, 1635) or William Wood (*The South Part of New England*, 1634),[92] seem to show us an already tamed wilderness, one that has been rendered more acceptable to English eyes (figure 15). There may be a parallel here to the way Theodore de Bry and his assistants transformed John White's paintings of Indians in the Roanoke Colony. We have been told how de Bry "retained White's meticulous attention to detail in dress, hair style, and body decoration, but changed the

Figure 15. Captain John Smith's map of Virginia. William Hole's engraving constructs a landscape with hills, rivers, woods and settlements recognizable to eyes familiar with the English county maps of the period. With the royal coat of arms inserted as an emblem of colonial possession beneath the title scroll we see the beginning of a cartographic discourse which ends with maps silent about Indian rights to the territory. The 1625 edition is shown here. By permission of the British Library (Maps 75005 [9]).

faces, postures, and bodies of the Indians in dramatic ways" and how their "faces were sweetened, softened, and Europeanized" so that, with their "new high foreheads, puckered mouths and ringleted hair they resemble the classical figures in the German engraving tradition."[93] So, too, it seems to have been with the landscape in some of the earliest and most influential printed maps of the regions of North America. In essence, these maps depict a European landscape in European engraving style but far from being actual portraits of America, they really show landscapes whose advent Europe desired and they remain silent about the true America. This sort of cartographic silence becomes an affirmative ideological act. It serves to prepare the way for European settlement. Potential settlers see, on the map, few obstacles that are insurmountable. Least of all does the map reflect the presence of indigenous peoples and their imprint on the land: "It is as if America were a stage tableau, with the arrival of Europeans as the raising of the curtain and the beginning of action."[94] In short, such maps are ethnocentric images, and part of the apparatus of cultural colonialism. It is not only that they offer a promise of free and apparently virgin land—an empty space for Europeans to partition and fill— but that the image offered is of a landscape in which the Indian is silent[95] or is relegated, by means of the map's marginal decoration, to the status of a naked cannibal.[96] Through these silences, the map becomes a license for the appropriation of the territory depicted. It is yet another means by which to insist upon the inherent superiority of European technologies and European ways of life.

Conclusions

This essay was designed to illustrate the potential for a history of maps of ideas derived from outside our subject. It has been primarily a theoretical exploration. It should be made clear, however, that neither concepts such as that of power-knowledge nor that of the *episteme* can offer "provable" generalizations which can be neatly plugged into the "facts" for this or that map culture. My argument stems from a humanistic standpoint, that it is the role of theory to reveal the complexity of the world rather than to reduce it to the simpler models of the social scientist. Thus, our first conclusion is that, while initially simple and familiar, the notions of power-knowledge and of cartography as a discourse of power with social effects are immensely complex once we start to relate them to specific historical contexts. Faced with a particular map, it is often hard to tell from the historical context whether its silences are the result of deliberate acts of censorship, unintentional epistemological silence, or a mixture of both, or perhaps merely a function of the slowness with which cartographers revised their maps to accord with the realities of the world. The relationships between maps and power, and between maps and other forms of knowledge, were constantly changing. The contribution of cartography in the maintenance of authority throughout the sixteenth and seventeenth centuries was never a constant factor. The complexities were recognized by Helgerson, who pointed out that maps could never be ideologically neutral, whatever their use or the consequences of their use and that they could never be "mere tools" whether of monarchic centralism or any other organization of power. They inevitably entered, he said, "into systems of relations with other representational practices and, in so doing, altered the meaning and authority of all the others."[97] It is this constantly shifting terrain between maps and other forms of power-knowledge which still has to be charted within the history of cartography.

A second conclusion is that we are on much surer ground when it comes to the importance of silences. Assuming the world to be a place where human choice is exercised, the absence of something must be seen to be as worthy of historical investigation as is its presence. So it is with cartography. Recently it has been suggested that "the map that is not made . . . warrants as much attention as the map that is made."[98] This aphorism can be extended both into the history of map production and into the history of the representational silences in particular maps. We have been able to show, from particular maps, that deliberate acts of censorship and secrecy in the past have indeed resulted in detectable cartographic and historical consequences. But the same is true of the epistemological silences, the "unthought" elements in discourse.[99] These are also affirmative statements, and they also have ideological consequences for the societies in question. Such silences also help in the reproduction, the reinforcement, and the legitimation of cultural and political values. Finding them expressed geographically on maps points to their universality. There is no such thing as an empty space on a map. Revealed by a careful study of the cartographic unconscious and its social foundations, these hidden agenda have much to offer historians of cartography in coming to an understanding of how maps have been—and still are—a force in society.

The third, and final, conclusion concerns the nature of cartography itself as a form of knowledge. Cartographers may continue to masquerade their products solely in terms of the application of a technical specification—survey instruments, scale, generalization, design, printing, and so forth—but an integral place in the historical interpretation of maps must also be demanded for the cultural choices that were taken for granted in particular societies. Indeed, maps are being read as literary texts[100] rather than as a mechanical replication of technical processes, by an increasing number of scholars. Such an approach has much to commend it, not least as applied to maps of the early modern period.[101] Maps are, in the apt phrase of one cartographer, best viewed as "a controlled fiction."[102] This textual viewpoint—reading the map as rhetoric—has important implications for alternative ways in which maps can be used to understand the past. The more we think about the universality of secrecy, of censorship and silence in maps, and the more we continue to reflect upon the epistemological codes of map knowledge, the less convinced we become the map knowledge can be regarded as "objective" or "value-free." Maps became part of "an increasing repertoire of power techniques"[103] and it is a major error to conflate the history of maps with the history of measurement. The essential paradox has been missed. As cartography became more "objective" through the state's patronage, so it was also imprisoned by a different subjectivity, that inherent in its replication of the state's dominant ideology. The old question of whether particular maps are true or false has not been my concern in this paper. On the contrary, this question has to be downgraded if it is accepted—as I have tried to argue here—that maps are perspectives on the world at the time of their making. My aim in this essay has been to initiate the interrogation of maps as *actions* rather than as impassive descriptions and to persuade historians of cartography to ask the crucial question "What are the 'truth effects' " of the knowledge that is conveyed in maps,[104] both of its more emphatic utterances, and also of its equally emphatic silences?

CHAPTER FOUR

Power and Legitimation in the English Geographical Atlases of the Eighteenth Century

This chapter originally appeared in John A. Wolter and Ronald E. Grim, eds., *Images of the World: The Atlas through History* (New York: McGraw-Hill for the Library of Congress, 1997), 161–204.

... power does not merely impinge on science and scientific knowledge from without. Power relations permeate the most ordinary activities in scientific research. Scientific knowledge arises out of these power relations rather than in opposition to them. Knowledge is power, and power knowledge.

—JOSEPH ROUSE,
Knowledge and Power: Toward a Political Philosophy of Science
(Ithaca: Cornell University Press, 1987), 24

A publication of the Center for the Book in the Library of Congress is an appropriate place to explore the history of the geographical atlas in its wider political, social, and cultural context. Both the specific topic I have selected to write about—the way social power intersects cartographic knowledge—and the approach I have adopted—drawing from social theory and the philosophy of science to interrogate my evidence—is in sympathy with the spirit of *L'histoire du livre.* Indeed, it will be recalled that in *The Coming of the Book,*[1] often regarded as the seminal text of a new historicism in bibliographical interpretation, one of the objectives of Lucien Febvre and Henri-Jean Martin was to establish the role in society of the "Book as a Force for Change."[2] While the analysis of power has not been an explicit concern in the new historical bibliography—for example, the word does not appear in the index of Elizabeth L. Eisenstein's classic study of *The Printing Press as an Agent of Change*[3]—there are recent signs of a new radical awareness. Thus D. F. McKenzie was able to speak in 1985 not only of "bibliography and the sociology of texts," but also to extend his argument to "nonbook texts," including maps, and above all to recognize that maps "may . . . express ideological meanings" and "function as potent tools for political control."[4] It is equally hard to conceive of a study of the atlas which does not come to terms in some way with the power relations within cartography which do much to structure both its form and its historical significance as a graphic text. The old aphorism that knowledge is power will accordingly be explored in the context of the English geographical atlases of the eighteenth century.

This essay does not seek to make a general case for the effects of power in cartography[5] but to examine how the structure of social power in a particular historical society influenced the production of knowledge and its mode of representation in the geographical atlases produced in England in the eighteenth century. The argument will be presented in three stages. First, the nature of power as it affected the geographical knowledge contained in atlases will be scrutinized and a new distinction drawn between internal and external power within cartography. Then, the patrons of atlas making—the holders of power in English society—will be identified and the links established between them and the small group of craftsmen who produced the geographical atlases. Finally, the influence of power on cartographic representation in the atlases is examined and suggestions made as to how the atlases may have influenced aspects of group consciousness, or *mentalité,* in eighteenth-century England. It will be argued that while the atlas makers were attempting to produce scientific maps of *territorial* space, they were also ineluctably generating images of *social* space which, far from being value-free or objective images from the so-called Age of Reason, were subjective, partisan, and rhetorical delineations. Yet it was through these partisan, social configurations, as much as through any factual representation of landscape, that the atlases became a force in history.

External and Internal Power in Cartography

I owe my understanding of the distinction between external and internal power to Joseph Rouse's recent book on *Knowledge and Power.*[6] I have freely adopted his discussion of science in general to the particular case of cartographic knowledge, but the argument requires some initial generalizations about its workings in cartography. External power is often written about by historians of cartography. Individuals, such as a monarch or a minister of the Crown, state institutions, and the institutionalized Church, employ power to initiate a program of mapping for administrative or military purposes.[7] The annals of atlas making alone contain numerous such instances. Political activities, involving what Foucault called the exercise of "juridical power,"[8] have always exerted a marked influence on the organization and practice of cartography. Moreover, as well as in the matter of state sponsorship—in setting up national surveys, for example—juridical power was also used to impede the dissemination of cartographic knowledge. Policies of censorship or secrecy are woven into the history of atlas making as frequently as in that of other forms of cartographic activity.[9] In all these contexts external power is that which was usually centralized, and thus imposed from above. It was usually manifest in acts of deliberate policy. It was exercised discontinuously to meet particular needs and situations. At the same time, it was directed towards particular map makers and to the creation of particular cartographic products.

In contrast, the idea of a power internal to cartography stresses that power is not separate from knowledge. It is an integral part of the practices that create knowledge and of the way maps—as a particular form of knowledge—work in society. It is universal, being found wherever maps are made, but equally it creates a local knowledge dependent on context. The focus of inquiry, therefore, shifts from the place of cartography in a juridical system of power to the political effects of what cartographers do when they make maps.[10] We find that cartographers cease to be "nonpolitical agents" in society, above or beyond politics. Inasmuch as power traverses the everyday workshop practices of map making, the atlas maker—albeit often unwittingly—was inevitably concerned with the manufacture of power. The key to this internal power lies in the nature of the cartographic processes. Compilation, generalization, classification, formation into hierarchies, and standardization of geographic data, far from being mere neutral technical activities, involve power-knowledge relations at work. Just as the disciplinary institutions described by Foucault—prisons, schools, armies, factories—serve to normalize human beings,[11] so too the workshop of the map maker can be seen as normalizing the phenomena of place and territory in creating a sketch of a made world that society desired. The power of the surveyor and the map maker was not generally directly exercised over individuals but over the knowledge of the world made available to people in general.[12]

Internal power is thus clearly different from external power in form and nature. Internal power is local and decentralized rather than being centralized and concentrated; it suffuses the practices of all cartographic workshops rather than being targeted only at the projects of state patronage. As it acts through the cartographic workshop, internal power is not necessarily consciously exercised; its practice is taken for granted, unlike the deliberate acts of externally applied power. Yet these differences between internal and external power do not obscure the fact that power relations penetrate the interstices of cartographic practice and representation. Maps may be read as texts of power-knowledge no less than other fabricated systems of signs.

The trade practices of the English atlas maker can be fitted into this interpretation of power-knowledge. By the eighteenth century, the internal logic of printed cartography—what we are defining here as its internal power—was already well established. Indeed, printed maps share the wider characteristics of the "logic of print" which Marshall McLuhan long ago identified as abstraction, uniformity, repeatability, visuality, and quantification.[13] The consequence of these tendencies was that the technology of map making "began to shape mental structures, imparting a sense of the world as a set of abstract ideas rather than immediate facts, a fixed point of view organizing all subject matter into an equivalent of perspective in painting, the visual homogenization of experience."[14] If we substitute *place* for *experience,* we can begin to see how the workshop practices of cartography may have acted in a similar way. The approach to training draftsmen and engravers, by means of apprenticeship and the performance of repetitive tasks, by means of a division of labor in the workshop, by the use of standard tools and techniques, and through the circulation of practical manuals, can all be interpreted as procedures to secure a standardized knowledge.[15] Standardization became the golden calf of printed cartography. It was the means by which order was instilled into geography. Rules, specifications, techniques, and regular arrays of conventional signs were tools of normalization. The map maker used these to reinvent or redescribe reality in the process of making the world known to society. He produced an artificially simplified world. The images which made the esoteric exoteric carried the potential to constrain the way people thought and acted.

The external-internal distinction reveals some distinctive configurations of power in the atlas trade of eighteenth-century England. For a society in which political power was concentrated in relatively few hands, external power was remarkably diffused when applied to cartography. In particular, the notion of a cartography controlled externally from above does not ring true in this historical context. Direct state power exerted relatively little influence on either the form or content of the English atlases. In this matter, we may draw a general comparison with Enlightenment France in the same period where the government, beginning with Louis XIV and Colbert, used its power to shape institutions to undertake national mapping for military, political, and practical purposes.[16] In England, however, public-sector geographical mapping (as opposed to military surveys) did not get underway until the second half of the eighteenth century despite the auspicious start made by Saxton's atlas some two centuries earlier. Even when a start was made, it was at first confined to general surveys of the North American colonies,[17] and even after the establishment of the Ordnance Survey in 1791, public sector maps were not published until the following century.[18]

Instead, such official power as impinged upon the atlas trade in eighteenth-century England was of an informal and irregular nature. It was imposed through the market and rather than setting up institutions to make maps, the English authorities turned to private map makers, sometimes even to organize surveys. John Cary's relationship with the post office in the late eighteenth century—which resulted in the detailed depiction of roads in his maps[19]—provides a good example of such an arrangement. So too, especially in relation to maps of North America, do some of the sheet and atlas maps prepared for publication in the 1760s by Thomas Jefferys, Geographer to the King. It is possible that Jefferys enjoyed a special relationship with the Board of Trade and Plantations and the Admiralty, and Skelton has suggested that Jefferys may have "enjoyed semiofficial standing which gave him access to public documents and map-drafts for engraving and publication."[20] Yet, if this was so, the arrangements must have been of an ad hoc nature; Jefferys did not acquire a monopoly of those cartographic raw materials that government departments wished to see in print for practical or propaganda reasons.[21] The contacts were casual and apparently noncontractual. Moreover, once the drafts had reached the map makers' workshop, the state discreetly withdrew, retaining a nominal patronage (statements such as "By Authority" appear in the titles of some maps) but leaving the atlas maker free to determine the final content, the design, and the distribution of the work.

If the state held the reins of cartographic power lightly in eighteenth-century England, then the same was even more true of the principal patrons of the geographical atlases—the nobility and gentry who will be identified below. There is no evidence that any individual patron or group of readers tried to exert direct power on the business of atlas making. No patron instructed the cartographers to make a particular type of atlas, nor did they determine its contents. The formats adopted by atlas makers and the subjects they chose to map seem to have been arrived at through a combination of tradition, the possession of existing copperplates for printing, market opportunity, and what can be seen as only an unwritten social consensus between patron and map maker as to what the maps might show. In short, the eighteenth-century English atlases were far from a standard type of knowledge. As is usual with European atlases since the sixteenth century, the balance between maps and text could vary markedly, size and scale also varied considerably, and even single maps within an atlas "could have a quite unique and individual bibliographical history."[22] The group of folio atlases of the Americas, for instance, published by map sellers such as Jefferys, Faden, and Sayer, were composite works, put together from stocks of preexisting maps (see figure 16.)[23]

The distinction between external and internal power should not be drawn too sharply. In exercising internal power, cartographers were responding to the dictates of external power even where it appears to be weak, and the process of legitimation, in particular, entails a conjunction of powers. Nevertheless, the particular nature of external power in eighteenth-century English atlas making suggests that a direct causality in its operation was not a precondition for power relationships to arise in the atlases. Rather it is that the weakness of direct causality enables us to see more clearly the force of internal power in everyday cartographic practice.

What we uncover, as already noted, is a set of well-established customary processes of standardization and normalization. By the eighteenth century it was these codes that structured the internal power of the English atlas maps. Standard map signs, a clear idea of what was normal content for atlas maps, an acceptable design, and an awareness of the market, were so enshrined in craft practices and advertised in widely circulating models of what an atlas should look like, that they represent nothing less than a received geography of power. New surveys and raw material arriving in the workshop were processed in the light of the logic of this defined canon. They were accorded, unchallenged, the standard treatment and—not surprisingly—emerged as standardized new maps.

The origin of these graphic stereotypes can be traced back to the sixteenth century, when the epistemological principles of measurement and classification were first indoctrinated into English atlas making.[24] By the eighteenth century, the descendants of these first stereotypes were as much the product of social as of technical factors. Map makers were guided by a broad consensus

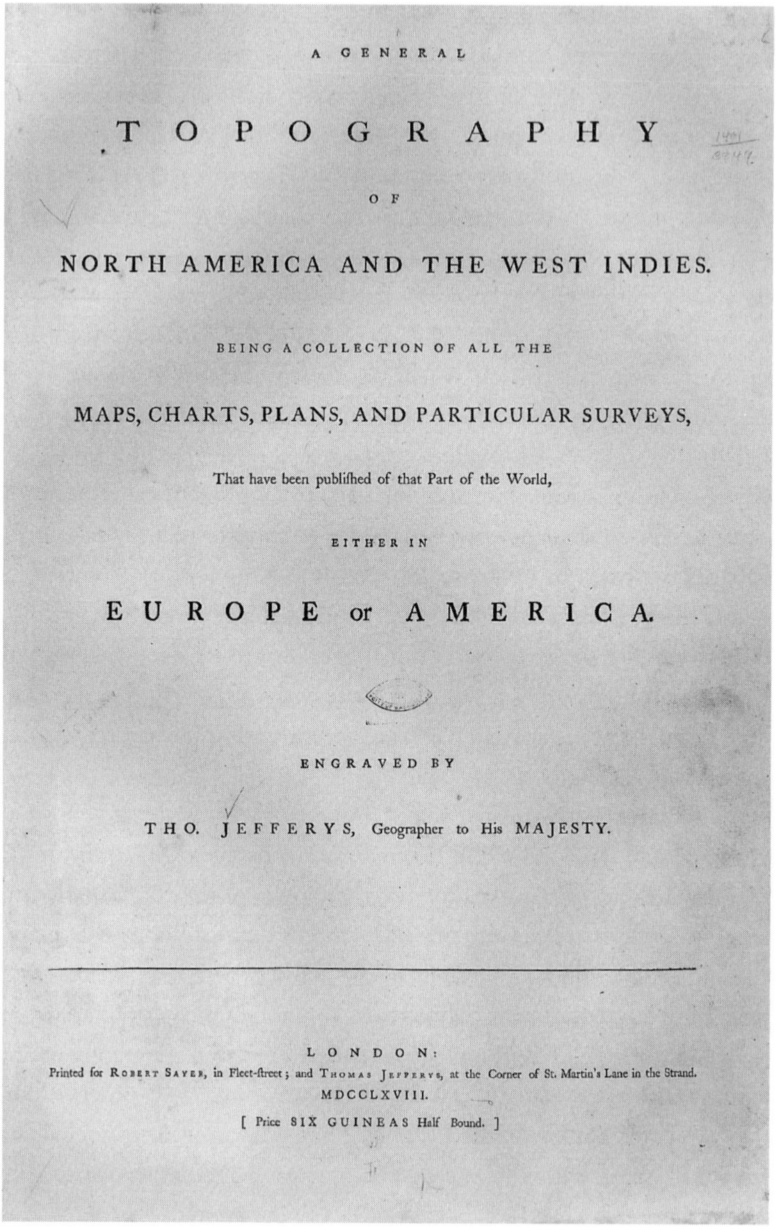

A GENERAL

TOPOGRAPHY

OF

NORTH AMERICA AND THE WEST INDIES.

BEING A COLLECTION OF ALL THE

MAPS, CHARTS, PLANS, AND PARTICULAR SURVEYS,

That have been publiſhed of that Part of the World,

EITHER IN

EUROPE or AMERICA.

ENGRAVED BY

THO. JEFFERYS, Geographer to His MAJESTY.

LONDON:
Printed for ROBERT SAYER, in Fleet-ſtreet; and THOMAS JEFFERYS, at the Corner of St. Martin's Lane in the Strand.
MDCCLXVIII.
[Price SIX GUINEAS Half Bound.]

Figure 16. The atlas epitomized: title page from *A General Topography of North America and the West Indies* (London: T. Jefferys, 1768). Library of Congress, Geography and Map Division.

about matters of class, status, and ethnicity, sharing the views of their patrons. Elsewhere, or in other periods in England, a cartography of protest can be discerned,[25] but few eighteenth-century atlas makers seem to have questioned the social and political order of their world or to have perceived their own craft as a social practice. On the contrary, the more they followed received cartographic practice, the more they were, if inadvertently, reinforcing and reciprocating the dominant social configuration of their age. Their atlases are at once cultural texts and visible models of the social relationships of eighteenth-century England. In this way, power is both implicit and explicit in the map makers' projection of an external geography onto the map page. The atlas maker approached his data with hard-headed expectations about the world he was mapping and a clear understanding of the rules of cartography by which the map image was to be produced—rules, such as those of social status, consistent with the rules of society at large. This is the process by which it revealed a terrain of internal power, as clearly delineated in implied social relationships as the engraved lines of rivers and mountain chains in the map image.

Patrons and Atlas Makers

In the context of the commercial mapping of eighteenth-century England, the atlas patrons were the agents by which external social power, exchanged through the map maker and a standardized technology, entered the atlases to become an interiorized form of power-knowledge. Such a study of the atlas *within* society—as opposed to one in which the atlas is removed from society for minute technical or bibliographical analysis—requires its own special approach. It becomes as important to reconstruct the social divisions and power relations within society as it is to understand the technical processes of map making. We have, therefore, to identify these patrons of eighteenth-century English atlas cartography and to show how they were brought into a close historical and geographical relationship with those who were engaged in the trade of making and selling maps.

Although the precise nature of the English social structure in the eighteenth century—its profile, changing character, and class tensions—has been the subject of much debate,[26] its basic anatomy is sufficient to show how power intersected the geographical knowledge reproduced in the atlases. English society in this period was arranged into a series of marked social divisions, each division having its own symbols of power, snobbery, and wealth. Despite a rigid hierarchy, one social historian has described eighteenth-century English society as a "one-class society," meaning that there was only one major class—comprising the strata of nobility, gentry, clergy, and the professional groups—who possessed a national consciousness of its own existence and influence.[27] Whatever the shortcomings of this diagnosis in historical sociology, it is a useful concept to explain some of the stereotyped images of the atlases, which do indeed appear to mirror the preoccupations of this dominant class in society.

Another major characteristic of English social structure in this period is the extent to which political power was derived from landed wealth. England's elite has been described as "a tight, privileged ring of landowners," while the nation resembled a "federal republic of country houses."[28] Nearly half the cultivated land in eighteenth-century England was owned by some five thousand families. At the apex of this domination, "four hundred families, in a population of some seven or eight million people, owned nearly a quarter of the cultivated land."[29] It is this relation between land and political power, and within which political power was used to protect property, which serves to frame the history of the atlas. Whether at the scale of the English county or of the overseas empire, maps were perceived as reinforcing the patterns of territorial ownership, and it is this potential which helps to explain both which geographical features were emphasized in the atlases and how these representations became a force in society.

Even a cursory inspection suggests that the patrons of English geographical atlases were likely to have been drawn from these upper ranks of society, the landowning class at large. Such groups represented perhaps no more than 5 percent of the total population yet they exerted a political and cultural hegemony disproportionate to their numbers. Just as was the case with the high art of the period, with its literature, and with its performed music and opera, so too the geographical atlases were regulated and made fashionable by the landed sector of English society. The fact that the sale price of a larger geographical atlas exceeded the average weekly wage of an artisan[30] likewise confirms a form of knowledge whose social distribution was heavily concentrated.

Several historical sources exist to link this social structure to the actual readership of the atlases, and from both sides of the map maker–patron divide.

As far as the map sellers were concerned, they regularly promoted the atlases to catch the eye of their patrons. In advertisements in the London newspapers, it was often the nobility and the gentry who were flattered into buying atlases, often by stressing features of particular interest to their class.[31] Similarly, in atlas dedications—both to the work in general and to the individual maps which comprised them—it is the nobility and gentry who are singled out, in addition to royalty, for attention. It is not by accident (as it will be shown) that coats of arms were so common a form of decoration on these maps.[32]

Even more central to our argument is the extent to which the atlases were actually purchased by those for whom they were intended. Here there is the evidence from the contents of individual libraries,[33] from book auction catalogs, and from subscription lists printed in the atlases themselves. The London auction lists are the subject of existing studies which confirm the regular purchase of geographical atlases by the nobility, gentry, and professional groups.[34] But it is the subscription lists, available for a dozen or so eighteenth-century English atlases, which provide the richest data for sociostructural analysis of map readership.[35] An analysis is given below of two of the surviving lists. It is a means of linking social structure to atlas production, and it also shows how cartography was caught up in an intricate network of wider power relations.

The first example is afforded by John Senex's *A New General Atlas,* published in London in 1721.[36] Naming himself in the Preface as Geographer to the Queen, he commended "the usefulness of a Book of this sort to Nobleman, Gentlemen, Commanders by Sea and Land, Divines, Lawyers, Physicians, and Merchants."[37] Eight categories of prospective reader were identified by Senex,[38] headed by "Sovereigns, with their Ministers" and ending with "Husbandmen, with Ordinary Mechanicks." For some reason, Senex made a special appeal to the last group. "This Science is necessary," he wrote, "for all Ranks of men, from the Prince to the Peasant" but we should not allow this egalitarian sentiment to distract us from the reality of his readership. Also in the preliminaries of the atlas, 1061 subscribers, identifying rank and title, are enumerated (see figure 17). Table 2 is a simple analysis of this list. While it cannot reflect the many fine gradations and nuances of contemporary English social structure, it nevertheless serves to underline how the subscribers to Senex's *Atlas* were drawn largely from groups in whose hands economic and political power was concentrated. Indeed, the alphabetical listings are a roll

Richard Newdigate Esq;
Bryan Nevill Esq;
John Nourse Esq;
John Napier Esq;
Rev. Mr. Newcomen, Rector of Braintree.
Rev. Mr. New come, Vicar of Abingdon.
Rev. Mr. Thomas Newman.
Rev. Mr. David Netto.
Fetherstone Nicholson of Liftock-Cas-tle in Cumberland Gent.
New-College Library in Oxon.
Mr. Thomas Nesbitt Merchant.
Mr. Nairne of Greenyards.
Mr. John Newman.
Mr. Peter Newhall.
Mr. John Nicholas.
Mr. Gilbert Neilson of Round-Court.
Mr. Robert Nicholson.

O.
Right Hon. the Earl of Orkney.
John Ogilvie of Balbegno Esq;
Sir Adolphus Oughton Bar.
John Olmius Esq;
Herman Olmius Esq;
Capt. Humphry Orme.
James Oglethorp Esq;
Cape Anthony Osburn.
Mr. Thomas Orbell.
Mr. H. Ogslton, Bookseller in Edinburgh.
Mr. Robert Owen, Bookseller in Dublin.

P.
Right Hon. Thomas Lord Parker, Lord High Chancellor of Great Britain.
Right Hon. John Earl Powlett.
Right Hon. the Lord Polwarth.
Hon. Thomas Pelham Esq;
Sir Robert Pollock Bar.
Sir James Pennyman Bar.
Hon. Maj. Gen. Thomas Pearce.
Popham Esq;
Thomas Paterson Esq;
John Pringle of Haning Esq;
Alexander Pitfield Esq;
Robert Pakenham Esq;
Charles Palmer of Ladebrook Esq;
John Phillips Esq;
John Peers Esq;
Will. Pitt Esq;
Tho. Palmer Esq;
John Parker Esq;
W. Mackworth Praed of Trevisham Esq;
Fitz-William Plumptre Esq;
William Petre Esq; 2 Books.
Dormer Parkhurst Esq;
James Pringle of Lees Esq;
Blackwell Parkyns of Leicester-Grange Esq;
Mark Pledwell of Colesel, Berks, Esq;
Nathaniel Payler Esq;
Rev. Charles Proby D. D. Rector of Tewing in Hertfordshire.
Rev. Mr. Robert Pickering, Rector of Cowlinge in Kent.
Rev. Mr. Peters.
Rev. Mr. Paschoud, of Little Chelsea.
Rev. Mr. Symon Pagett.
Rev. Mr. Thomas Perrot.
Major Richardson Pack.
Francis Patton Gent.
Christopher Pack M. D.
Mr. Robert Pattison of London Merch.
Mr. John Page.
Mr. Professior Pilgrim.
Mr. Henry Prude Apothecary.
Mr. Potter, Surgeon at Colchester.
Mr. William Pate.
Mr. Tho. Powel, Bookseller in Ludlow.
Mr. Baron Pretyman of Bacton.
Mr. Charles Pine.
Mr. Paton, Bookseller in Edinburgh.
Mr. Rich. Perkins of Coventgarden.
Mr. Jacob Portello, Merchant.
Mr. Thomas Prime.
Mr. Richard Parsons.
Mr. Joseph Penn, Bookseller in Bristol.

Q
His Grace the Duke of Queensberry and Dover.
The Marquis Du Quesne.
Queen's-College Library in Oxon.

R.
His Grace the Duke of Roxburghe.
Right Hon. Frederick Earl of Rochford.
Right. Hon. the Earl of Rothes.
Right Hon. the Earl of Roseberry.
Richard Rooth of Epsom Esq;
Benjamin Robinson Esq;
Edward Riggs Esq;
Ralph Radcliff Esq;
Moses Raper Esq;
Harry Radney Esq;
Col. Will. Rhett of South-Carolina.
Thomas Robe Esq;
Tho. Strangeways Robinson of York Esq
...ho nas Robinson of Rookby Esq;

John Ramsay Esq;
Dr. Raynes.
Rev. Balthasar Regis B. D. Rector of Adisham in Kent.
Rev. Mr. Richardson, Library-Keeper at St. Martins.
Rev. Mr. Richardson, Master of the Free School at Black-Heath.
Rev. John Rogers B. D.
Rev. Mr. Robert Rogers.
Rev. Mr. Simon Rowe.
Rev. Mr. Paul dela Roque.
Rev. Mr. Thomas Rodd, Rector of Rid-marley Dabilot in Worcestershire.
Captain Tancred Robinson.
Captain Francis Rodd.
Mr. Thomas Richardson.
Mr. Patrick Ramsay.
Mr. John Radhams.
Mr. William Rous.
Mr. Sam. Rogers, Bookseller in Rosst.
Mr. Richard Rider, Linendraper.
Mr. John Rede.
Mr. Samuel Ruffell.
Mr Joseph Rex of Waterford.
Mr. Tho. Ree of Waterford in Ireland.
Mr. George Resh Bookseller in Dublin.

S.
Right Hon. Thomas Earl of Stamford.
Right Hon. the Earl of Shaftesbury.
Right Hon. John Earl of Staire.
Right Hon. Thomas Earl of Strafford.
Right Hon. Talbot Earl of Sussex.
Right Hon. the Earl of Shrewsbury.
Right Hon. the Countess of Sandwich.
Right Hon. George Lord St. George.
Right Hon. the Ld Salton.
His Excellency Baron Schlenthall, Envoy from Denmark.
His Excellency Baron Spat, Envoy from Sweden.
Sir Robert Sutton, Minister from Great Britain to the Court of France.
Sir James Stewart of Goodtrees Bar.
Right Hon. Edward Southwell Esq;
Sir Philip Sydenham Bar.
Sir John Stanley Esq;
Sir Edw. Symmonds Bar.
Sir William Scot of Thirestan Bar.
Right Hon. John Smith Esq;
Brigadier-General Sutton.
Hon. Col. James Scott.
Sir Richard Steele.
Sir Sebastian Smith.
Sir William Scawen Kt.
Hon. D. Smith Esq; Governour of Nevis.
Chambers Slaughter Esq;
Thomas Scott Esq;
——Strangeways Esq;
John Shepard Esq;
Thomas Shallcrols Esq;
——Stevenson Esq;
Bennet Swayne Esq;
Walter Scott of Harden Esq;
John Spearman Esq;
Francis Smith Esq;
Jervase Scroop Esq;
Thomas Shairpe of Blanse Esq;
Jer. Sambroke of Cecil-Street Esq;
James Smith Esq; Surveyor General for Scotland.
John Scrimshire Esq;
James Strode Esq;
John Shugborg of Burton in Warwick-shire Esq;
John Smallwell Esq; Master-Joyner to his Majesty.
Henry Savile Esq; of Methly.
James Stuart Esq;
Alexander Strahan Esq;
Tho. Sherigley of the City of Dublin Esq;
George Sampson Gent.
Lieut. Col. John Shorey.
Rev. Dr. Shippen, Vice-Chanc. of Oxford.
Rev. Mr. James Sanxay, of Penzance.
Rev. Mr. Spratt, Archd. of Rochester.
Rev. Dr. Sydall, Prebend of Canterbury.
Rev. Dr. St. John Rector of Yeldean.
Rev. Mr. Steele, Sur-Master of St. Paul's School.
Rev. Mr. Shorthose, Rector of Stanton Barnard in Wiltshire.
Rev. Mr. Hugh Shorthose, Lecturer of Chelsey, and Chaplain to the Duke of Chandois.
Rev. Mr. Archdeacon Stubbs.
Rev. Dr. Joseph Smith.
Rev. Mr. Smith, Rector of Rougham.
Rev. Mr. Smith of Leicestershire.
Rev. Mr. George Storey, Rector of Isleworth.
William Swanton of Combebisset in Wilts Esq;
Arthur Shephard Gent. Blanse-Herald.
Samuel Symonds Gent.
Mr. William Smith Merchant.

Alexander Sandilands M. D.
Alexander Stewart M.D.
Mr. Sharpe, 7 Books.
Mr. Gilbert Stewart, Merchant in E-dinburgh.
Mr. John Salt of Coventgarden, Mercer.
Mr. Charles Stone Jun. of Bath.
Mr. Robert Scott Surgeon.
Mr. Edwin Sandys in Dublin.
Mr. William Sotheby.
Mr. John Smith, Merchant.
Mr. John Serle.
Mr Rob. Stockdale.
Mr. Edward Scarlet.
Mr. Richard Shirley.
Mr. Ward Smith.
Mr. John Smart.
Mr. Stone, Chymist.
Mrs. Stone.
Mr. Isaac Sierra.
Mr. Brand Henrick Schilden of Hannover.
Mrs. Squire of Yorkshire.
Mr. Stewart, Bookseller in Edinburgh.
Mr. Thomas Smith.
Mr. William Sagg, Bookseller in York.
Mr. Smithurst, Bookseller in Plimouth.
Mr. Robert Sparke.
Mr. John Smith of North Wiltshire.
Mr. Symmer, Bookseller in Edinburgh.
Mr. Sherigley of Dublin.
Mr. William Steare.
Mr. John Sherwill.
Mr. Richard Samborne.
Mr. Saunders of Highgate.
Mr. Richard Standfast Bookseller, 7 Books.
Mr. John Sherrer.
Mr. Spiker.
Mr. Peter Sahlgreen.

T.
Right Hon. the Earl of Tankerville.
Hon. Major-General Trelawney.
Right Hon. Richard Tighe Esq; one of the Privy Council of Ireland.
Samuel Thompson Esq;
Cholmley Turner Esq;
Philip Taylor Esq;
William Thompson Esq;
John Tolman Esq;
Clement Tudway Esq;
Moses Terry Esq;
Joas Tillard of the Inner-Temple Esq;
Ralph Thoresby of Leeds Esq;
Edward Turner Esq;
Marmaduke Tonstal Esq;
Nicholas Trott Esq; Chief-Justice of South-Carolina.
Thomas Tomkins Esq;
Tempeft Thornton Esq;
George-Lewis Teisier, M.D.
Rev. Mr. Thorold, Rector of St. Martin's Ludgate.
Rev Dr. Tippen, Rector of Camberwel.
Charles Thompson M. A.
Rev. Mr. Joseph Trapp.
Captain Edward Tyzack.
Mr. Tucker of Rye in Suffex.
Mr. Richard Taylor.
Mr. William Turing of Covent-garden.
Mr. John Tonkin.
Mr. Cornelius Taylor.
Mr. Ralph Thompson of Highgate.
Mr. Thomas Tooke, Jun. of St. Andrew's Helborn.
Mr. Nath. Thorne, Bookseller in Exon.
Mr. Thomas Thorhall.

U.
Right Hon. William Lord Vane.
Henry Vanderesch Esq;
William Vaughan of Newnton in Wiltshire Esq;
John Upton Esq; of Great Marlborough-Street.
Henry Verelst Esq;
Colonel Vans.
Alexander Urquhart of Newhall Esq;
Gerard Vanheytesen Esq;
Mr. William Vigor of the County of Somerset.
Mr. William Voyce.
Mr. Thomas Vergis Writing-Master.

W.
Right Hon. George Earl of Warrington.
Right Hon. the Countess Dowager of Winchelsea.
Right Hon. Willoughby de Brook, Dean of Windsor.
Right Rev. the Lord Bishop of Waterford.
Right Hon. James Lord Waldegrave.
His Excellency Lord Whitworth, Ambassador Extraordinary, and Plenipotentiary at the Congress to be held at Brunswick.
Right Hon. John Wallop Esq; one of the Lords of the Treasury.
Right Hon. Edward Webster Esq; Principal Secretary to the Ld Lieut. of Ireland.

Sir George Warrender of Lochend Bar.
Sir Thomas Webster Bar.
Hon. Thomas Willoughby Esq;
Major General Wade.
Major General Wightman.
Francis Whitworth Esq; Secretary to the Island of Barbadoes.
John Walkinshaw of Walkinshaw Esq;
John Ward Esq;
Christopher Wren Esq;
Richard Warburton of Timbertown in Ireland Esq;
Clement Wearg Esq;
William Wentworth of Wallis Esq;
George Waddell Esq;
John Willett Esq; one of his Majesty's Council in St. Christophers.
John Wills of Lincolns-Inn Esq;
William Walter of Chatham, Esq;
John Wafhler Esq;
John Williams of Dolecothy in Carmarthenshire, Esq;
Walter Waring Esq;
Edmond Warneford Esq;
Ezekiel Wallis Esq; of Lucknam in Wiltshire.
John Warburton Somerset Herald, 7 Books.
Humphry Weld Esq;
Thomas Wynn Esq; of Dyffryn-Aled, near Denbigh.
Anthony Welsden Esq;
Thomas White Gent.
John Wolfe Gent.
Thomas Wooly Gent.
Benj. Willoughby of Bristol Gent.
Rich. Washington of South-Cave in Yorkshire Gent.
Bryan Wheelock Gent.
Thomas Wilkinson Gent.
Robert Wood Gent.
Thomas Williamson Gent.
John Whithaw of Grays-Inn Gent.
Rev. Thomas Wise D. D. Chaplain to her Royal Highness the Princess of Wales.
Mr. T. Watts of the Accomptant's Office.
Isaac Warquin of New Romney in Kent, M. D.
Rev. Mr. Benjamin Wakefield, Rector of Woodhay.
Rev. Mr. James Wotton, Vicar of Ogburn St. George, Wilts.
Rev. Mr. Williams, Prebend of Chichester.
Rev. Mr. John Whitefide, Keeper of the Museum at Oxford.
Rev. Mr. John Willis of Lincoln.
Rev. Mr. Edward Wallyn.
Rev. Mr. Whiffler for Magdalen College Library.
Rev. Mr. Wood.
Rev. William Whifton M. A.
Rev. Mr. Samuel Wright.
Rev. Mr. John Willet.
Rev. William Webster M. A.
Mr. Joseph Walker, Attorney at Marlborough.
Mr. Arthur Wolley, Merchant.
Mr. Richard Woolfe Merchant.
Mr. Francis Woolley.
Mr. Thomas Weston of Greenwich
Mr. Thomas Watkins.
Mr. Thomas Wood.
Mr. J. Williamson, Attorney in Dublin.
Mr. John Wildman, Attorney.
Mr. William West Mercer.
Mr. John Weems, Surgeon.
Mr. James Wilde, Bookseller in Ludlow.
Mr. Ed. Wolley, Bookseller in Worcester.
Mr. Thomas Warner.
Mr. Watts.
Mr. John Watts.
Mr. Dabee Wells.
Mr. William Wogan.
Mr. Daniel White of Highgate.
Mr. Thomas Wilmott.
Mr. Roger Warne of Chippenham.
Mr. John Whormbey of Clapham.
Mr. James Winram, Sheriff Clerk of Berwick.

Y.
His Grace the Lord Archbishop of York.
John Yawle Esq;
Benj. Young of Plymouth Esq;
Rev. Mr. Arthur Young, of Thames-Ditton.
Arthur Young Gent.
Mr. Bartholomew Young of King's-College, Cambridge.
Mr. Samuel Young.
Mr. John Yarrow.
Mr. Philip Yeo, Bookseller in Exon.

Z.
Rev. Charles Zouch M. A. Vicar of Sandal Magna.

TABLE 2
Social Status of Subscribers to Senex's A New and General Atlas . . . *1721*

Recorded status in subscriber list*	Number of subscribers		Percent
1. Noblemen (includes Dukes, Earls, Marquess's, Viscounts, Barons) and Spiritual Lords (Archbishops and Bishops)	100	(Nobility)	10
2. Baronets and Knights	62		
3. Esquires	330	(Gentlemen)	41
4. Gentlemen	34		
5. Clergymen	105		10
6. "Professions"† (M.D.s, Lawyers, Merchants, Military Officers, etc.)	120		11
7. "Non-Gentry" (includes Yeomen, Husbandmen, Tradesmen, and Craftsmen)	296		28
Totals‡	1047		100

* These categories are adapted from the discussion in Peter Laslett, *The World We have Lost: Further Explored,* 3d ed. (London: Methuen, 1983), including Table 2, 38. Categories 1–6 provide approximately three-quarters of the subscribers (72%).
 † The term is Laslett's.
 ‡ Not all subscribers are identified by rank and occupation; the total number listed is 1061.

call of honorific titles. They enable us to locate the atlas patrons among the greater and minor nobility and, above all, from that class known as the gentry. While the designations do not always permit us to distinguish between those who were primarily landowners and those with other definite occupations— such as clergymen, court officials, diplomats, lawyers, merchants, military officers, schoolmasters and dons—there is no doubt that their common interest, and the class identity postulated by Laslett, lay in the possession of landed property. That such a class dominated atlas patronage is confirmed by the coats of arms engraved after the subscriber list (see figure 18). These were designed to single out those subscribers with the right to bear arms and it is significant that well over half (728) of the subscribers to Senex's *Atlas* came from the mainly landed families which possessed such a right.

The dominance of the landowners as atlas patrons must, however, be approached cautiously. During the eighteenth century their relative importance, numerically if not in terms of power, was slipping with the rise of an urban and industrial bourgeoisie. Even in Senex's *Atlas* of 1721—published at a time when Laslett's supposed one-class society was at its zenith—26 percent of the subscribers did not belong to the gentry or nobility. In London especially,

FACING PAGE

Figure 17. The patrons of atlas cartography: list of subscribers. John Senex, *A New General Atlas* (London: D. Browne, 1721). Library of Congress, Geography and Map Division.

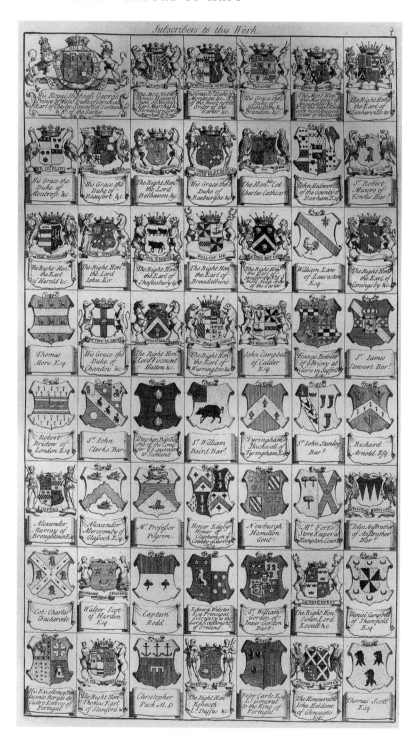

but also in the larger towns, a readership was growing for maps from the rising commercial and craft groups and among the artisan mathematical practitioners whose fortunes were enhanced by the expansion of agriculture, commerce, and industry.[39] Thus, even among Senex's subscribers, we find occupations such as those of apothecary, architect, bookseller, draper, goldsmith, limner (painter), mathematical-instrument maker, printer, watchmaker, and writing master.

By the late eighteenth century the numerical importance of these groups as patrons of cartography had further increased. More atlases were being published and some were cheaper in price. Maps in general were sharing the reality, by 1790, of "a well-developed print society," as compared with a century earlier.[40] Such was the background for our second example, Cary's *New and Correct English Atlas* (1787).[41] This includes a list containing approximately the same number of subscribers as Senex's *Atlas,* but Table 3 shows a striking difference in the social composition of the readership. The relative importance of the nobility had declined from 10 to 3 percent and that of the gentry had dropped, less markedly, from 41 to 36 percent. Clergymen remained a stable group of atlas buyers. Most outstanding was the rise of the "nongentry" subscribers to over 40 percent in Cary's atlas. Even if these two atlases are not representative of eighteenth-century atlases as a whole,[42]—or that Cary's was a smaller and cheaper work—the differences nevertheless alert us to the possibility of a changing relationship between social structure and cartography.

In attempting to understand how power becomes internal to cartographic practices, we also have to consider the context of map makers in their articulation of that power. The English geographical atlas of the eighteenth century can be seen as "the deposit of a social relationship."[43] On one side of the relationship were, as we have seen, the patrons of the atlas—a readership drawn predominantly from one class who purchased the atlases and recommended them to others in their circle. On the other side, there was the map maker who made the atlas or at least supervised its making. The balance of power in eighteenth-century England lay with the patron rather than with the craftsman who supplied his needs. Map makers and map sellers were located well

FACING PAGE

Figure 18. Subscribers' coats of arms: Senex, *A New General Atlas.* Library of Congress, Geography and Map Division.

TABLE 3
Social Status of Subscribers to Cary's New and Correct English Atlas *(1787)*

Recorded status in subscriber list*	Number of subscribers		Percent
1. Noblemen	39	(Nobility)	3
2. Baronets and Knights	27		
3. Esquires	396	(Gentry)	35.7
4. Gentlemen	—		
5. Clergymen	158		13
6. Miscellaneous † (M.D.s, Lawyers, Merchants, Military Officers, etc.)	44		4.5
7. "Non-Gentry"	520		43.8
Totals	1184		100.0

* For comparative purposes these groups are derived from Laslett (1983) as in Table 2, although the divisions, reflecting a configuration from the late seventeenth century, were increasingly inappropriate to English society by the end of the eighteenth century.

† The term is Laslett's.

down the hierarchy of social power. This meant that map making could never be an autonomous enterprise, especially for the atlas makers who were aiming a relatively expensive product at a quality market, and who could not hope to be entirely free and independent agents. Directly and indirectly, like most craft practitioners, the atlas maker's livelihood lay in the palms of the Great.[44]

By identifying the position of the atlas maker in eighteenth-century society we can begin to understand how their maps came to adopt and to reinforce the dominant social values of their patrons. Indeed, there would have been several reasons why the cartographic tradesmen may have been especially responsive to their patrons' social world and to their particular class's constructions of geographical knowledge. For one thing, atlas makers never formed a strong or cohesive craft group. At any one moment throughout the eighteenth century only a handful of named individuals—the Bowles family, the Bowens, Ovary, Dury, Dunn, Faden, Gibson, Jefferys, Kitchin, Moll, Sayer, and Senex—never more than a dozen or so, were dominant in this specialized form of geographical publishing. While their output may appear at first sight to be prolific, a closer look shows how they borrowed their cartography freely from a limited, and usually outdated, stock of original maps. Trading copperplates between publishers, they also engaged in serial publication and took shares in each other's atlases.[45] As their contemporaries realized, the trade was largely driven by the market rather than by any sustained notion of a "scientific" geography.[46] In such a publishing climate, we may suppose that the atlas makers had to be especially sensitive to the traditional values of their patrons as well as to changes of fashion in the print trade as a whole.

In fact, the term *atlas maker,* as we apply it to the eighteenth century, is the creation of modern cartobibliography. The production of maps in eighteenth-century England (as at other times) was a manifold process requiring the work of editor, draftsmen, engraver, printer, map colorer, publisher, and seller. In practice, these functions were sometimes combined into one workshop, but in other instances they were separated. More alien still to eighteenth-century eyes would have been our modern notion (which only emerged in nineteenth-century England) of the specialist atlas maker. Even the most specialized map makers diversified their businesses into a wide range of other publications. Bowen, Jeffreys, and Kitchin, for example, while styling themselves as "Geographers" and holding privileges to supply members of the royal household with maps, engaged in other branches of engraving, publishing, and print selling.[47] Thomas Kitchin published "hieroglyphicks" and other political prints;[48] Thomas Jefferys and Robert Sayer had a line in prints other than the strictly geographical;[49] and later in the century, Robert Sayer, while issuing specialist atlas catalogs was also a major publisher in other branches of the graphic arts.[50] For other "atlas makers," moreover, the geographical atlas was even more of an incidental line of business. Thomas and John Bowles, for example, may have been better known as publishers of prints of social satires than as map publishers.[51] Thus, in John Bowles's 1753 *Catalogue of Maps, Prints, Copy Books, &c.*, we read that "Merchants for Exportation, Gentlemen for Furniture, Shop-keepers to sell again, May be furnished with the greatest Variety of Maps and Prints, at the lowest Prices."[52] Bowles's phrase, "the greatest variety of maps and prints," reminds us to place the geographical atlas in the wider world of the graphic arts. Bowles and Son ran a wholesale and retail business selling sheet maps in various formats, but they also stocked a range of prints of different sizes and subjects. Historical, sporting, architectural, moral, religious, naval and military prints, perspective views, writing and drawing books, mezzotints—all passed through their hands. Only a small section of their 1753 Catalogue was devoted to "Books of Maps" (that is, atlases) and these were mixed in the stock with texts on architecture and on practical geometry and items such as "Gentleman's Guides" and "Pocket Companions."

The significance of such diversity is that there were many conduits from the wider world into the atlas maker's workshop. Far from being an esoteric craft, such cartography was borne along by the wider currents of social and political attitudes which flowed through English society. Atlas production in eighteenth-century England, linked both to the general expansion of the graphic arts and to the wider fields of geographical and historical publishing, was particularly well placed to articulate the social construction of geographical knowledge favored by its patrons.

The proximity of eighteenth-century atlas making to the seats of national power in London also reinforced this tendency. That production and distribution was overwhelmingly concentrated in the capital is well known, but its significance for the patronage of cartography needs to be stressed. While surveying skills were widely diffused in Great Britain and to a lesser extent in the overseas colonies, most of the map and atlas compilation, editing, engraving, printing, and publication—in common with the book and print trades— was concentrated in London.[53] For atlas production this domination may have been a nearly total one,[54] and it brought cartographers and patrons into potentially close proximity. London-based institutions such as the Court, Parliament, the departments of State, the law courts, the great chartered companies, as well as the social round, all drew the landed gentry away from the shires for at least part of the year. If the map maker only occasionally met his patron face-to-face, he would have been constantly reminded of his existence and of the need to manipulate knowledge to serve his interests. The eminences of social power were never far away from the map sellers' shops of St. Pauls and the Strand.

The map maker working in London also had easy access to a geographical knowledge already structured by power. The source materials of geographical atlases reveal their compilers as in tune not only with events in the domestic sphere impinging on their craft—the enactment of Parliamentary legislation relating to canals and turnpike roads, to take just one example—but also with military struggles in the European theater and, increasingly, with the national saga of the British overseas empires in North America, Asia, and the Pacific.[55] After the defeat of France in the Seven Years War (1756–1763), England's supremacy over the seas and imperial trade was greatly enhanced. Her hold on the non-European world was tightening and English geographical discovery, the events of which were often given prominence on new maps, was constantly serving colonial schemes. London became an *entrepôt* and clearinghouse for the geographical knowledge of a far-flung territorial system (see figure 19).

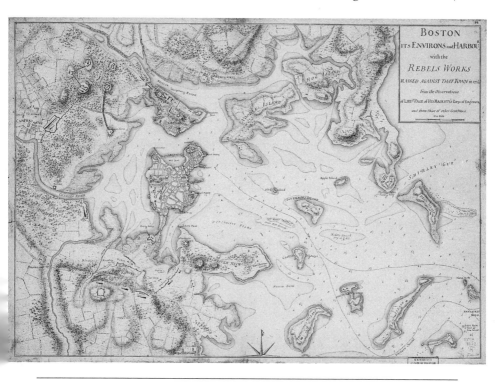

Figure 19. The raw materials of the atlas: manuscript maps. *Boston, Its Environs and Harbour with the Rebels Works . . . from the Observations of Lieut. Page of His Majesty's Corps of Engineers* (1775). Library of Congress, Geography and Map Division.

For the social history of the English atlas, its position at a crossroads of knowledge is a matter of considerable importance. The atlas maker had access—albeit sometimes indirectly or at several removes—to the geographical intelligence, including maps, which filtered into London through diplomatic, military, naval, and mercantile channels.[56] Located in an increasingly cosmopolitan city, the cartographer was being exposed to those ideas, political attitudes, ethnic stereotypes, cultural values and ideological convictions which permeated not just maps but a burgeoning knowledge industry in general.[57]

Representations of Power

We can now turn to see how power is represented in the maps of the atlases and try to gauge its influence. The argument focuses on the unarticulated aspects of power in the atlas, that is to say on the hidden agenda of social power which operates on the reader as an unconscious force and through the symbolic meaning of the image as much as through the literal facts of geography. In the discussion of historical influence, I am less concerned with the practical ways in which the atlases were used in the exercise of power—for administrative, diplomatic, military, propaganda, or surveillance purposes, all of which were well documented in the eighteenth century—than with the way the atlas maps worked to structure social attitudes and to support a preexisting geography of power relations. These tendencies—both of representation and of influence—will be illustrated in relation to the ideology in maps found in two groups of English geographical atlases: first, the county or regional atlases of England and Wales; and second, the general or universal atlases published before American independence. In the case of the latter, the discussion will be confined to examples of maps of North America.

County Atlases

Despite the continuing expansion of the English overseas world in the eighteenth century, the horizons of the majority of Englishmen were limited to the countrysides and towns of which they had direct experience. In practice, the county was the focus of the lives of the English nobility and gentry. It was through the county administrative and legal systems that regional patronage and power were exercised. It was within a county framework, too, that social power circulated, with the leading families arranged in their own county hierarchies and closely linked by ties of marriage and property.[58] The gentry may have held land in more than one county or have visited London and Bath in the season, but it was to their own counties that they returned and to which they felt the strongest loyalty. Much of the popularity of the county atlas—as of other works of county history and topography—rested on this county-gentry association. From the first publication of Saxton's atlas in 1579, the bonding of county atlas and county society was one of the active factors in the regionalization of English society. By the eighteenth century, the county atlas—in its many formats—had become entrenched as the dominant form of native English atlas publication.

But the county atlas–county society relationship was more than a matter of custom, format, and trade. Consensus and reciprocity between publisher and reader extended into the content and design of the maps. By 1700, the map makers had accumulated over a century's experience in pleasing their clients. Many features of seventeenth-century atlases—as well as some of the copper-plates themselves—passed into the new century with no more than cosmetic modification.[59] Throughout the eighteenth century, county atlases remained markedly conservative in the way they represented the class interests of their clients. Genuflections to rank and power are found in the decoration of each map, in its dedications, and in features such as lists of the "seats of nobility." The coats of arms of county nobility, towns, or institutions were a particularly common addition to county maps and atlases before 1750.[60] John Warburton made a point of advertising the provision of engraved coats of arms as the hallmark of his county maps. These would serve for "Persons of Distinction most of which are descended or enjoy Lands," he wrote snobbishly, "as an Index to shew the present Possessors of every individual Village, Castle, or Seat."[61] Even utility atlases, those designed for travelers, such as John Owen's roadbook *Britannia Depicta* (a combination of strip maps showing the roads and small county maps), were often dressed with features such as "The Arms of the Peers of this Realm who derive their Titles from places lying on, or near the Roads" and, to register the power of the established state religion, "The Arms of all ye Bishopricks & Denaries, their foundation, Extent, Yearly-Value, Number of Parishes &c."[62]

The general fashion for coats of arms was past by the middle of the century but confirmations of the structure of English society continued to be provided. In the atlases produced by Bowen and Kitchin these included dedications to the Lords Lieutenant of each county; marginal lists of "Seats of the Nobility and Gentry"; dates, going back to the Norman conquest, for those holding the rank of Earl; lists of Bishops ("Since the Reformation"); and dates of ancient borough charters (see figure 20).[63] This sort of historical information, whether added to the map itself or given in an accompanying text,[64] reflects in part the atlas makers' perception of the rise of antiquarian interests among the nobility and gentry in eighteenth-century England.[65] But it is also open to ideological interpretation. Coats of arms or engravings of cathedrals in the corners of maps may be read as emblems of power, transferring authority into the space of the map.[66] Likewise, an affirmation of antiquity can be seen as an act of unconscious legitimation, a symbol of social cohesion, and a displaying of the roots of institutions and hierarchical domination as a justification of their survival to the present time.[67]

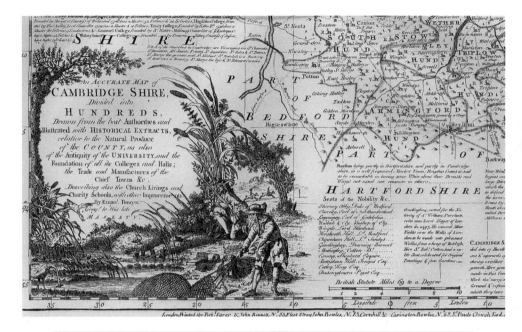

Figure 20. The atlas as social proclamation: detail showing seats of nobility, etc., in Cambridgeshire. Emmanuel Bowen, *The Royal English Atlas* (London: C. Bowles, 1778). Library of Congress, Geography and Map Division.

So much for the atlas in its general format and decoration. Turning now to the maps themselves, it is not difficult to see how they also had been made to suit the rights and priorities of the patron class. From 1750 onward, the county atlas maps were derived from more detailed original surveys,[68] but even so they continued to portray a decidedly partial view of the landscape of England and Wales. Social eminences such as country houses were surveyed as much as natural landmarks. The compilation of each map had clearly involved not only judgments about how things were in the landscape but also about the way the dominant group in society believed they ought to be. The beliefs and values of the nobility and gentry had thus structured a way of seeing, a way of surveying, and a way of interpreting the world so that the map became an image of their domination.

For instance, the boundaries of administrative units of jurisdiction and taxation—the county and the hundred—were always stressed. So too were the boroughs, from the courts of which justice was dispensed or which sent members to the Parliament at Westminster to represent the interests of this one national class and to enact its legislation. Similarly, the action and living space of the gentry and clergy was underlined on the maps, which served to confirm their social authority. The "seats," or houses, of gentlemen together with their parklands are especially prominent (see figure 21). Rectories, vicarages, and curacies were included as emblems of the social power of the established church, not just as records of the livelihood of a large group of subscribers. The content of the atlas maps did not, of course, remain unchanged throughout the century. In line with the growing percentage of subscribers to Cary's 1787 atlas who were associated with trade and manufactures, the image of some of Cary's atlas maps also began to reflect the care taken to locate the investment opportunities of this class in commercial and industrial enterprises. Coal mines, canals, turnpike roads, commons and heaths in process of enclosure, expanding towns and suburbs were all entered into maps as symbols of the new wealth. But it is the rise of new masters rather than a decline of power that these late-eighteenth-century maps portray. Instead of the old landscape of a predominantly landowning society, we detect in the new maps signs of a strengthening agrarian and industrial capitalism, that of the so-called agricultural and industrial revolutions.

As witnesses of the social order of Georgian England, the cartographic silences in the county atlas maps are as eloquent as the features that are mapped. Atlas maps, just like the English landscape paintings of the same period, idealized the countryside. They sought, if unwittingly, to hide the reality of rural poverty.[69] The only hint that another social class perhaps existed in England is the newly introduced sign for "charity schools."[70] Although individual parklands on late-eighteenth-century maps are crowded with the designs of landscape gardeners such as Capability Brown, beyond the wall of the park, where men and women toiled in the fields, the map landscape is often quite empty. No awkward manifestations of backwardness are shown. There are no map signs for poverty or squalor, and the bland washes of the map colorer denote a green and pleasant land. Even where there are vignettes of industrial activity on a map, it is sometimes only the tools of trade that are displayed while the workers themselves are either hidden from view or are presented in idealized compositions, smartly dressed and in situations of repose rather than of sweaty and grimy labor.[71] The inescapable conclusion is that we are viewing the paper world of an elite social class. Moreover, it was a world to be proud of. The county atlases, which in one sense also served as

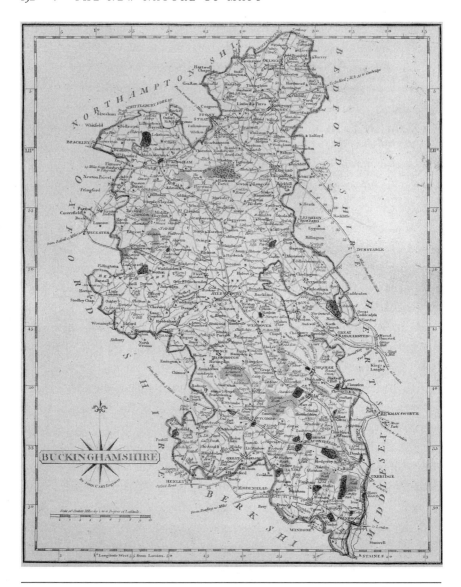

Figure 21. The Atlas as gentrified landscape: parklands in Buckinghamshire. John Cary, *New and Correct English Atlas* (London: J. Cary, 1787). Library of Congress, Geography and Map Division.

national atlases, are often prefaced by patriotic sentiments. Their county maps are full of regional pride, replete with the confidence of a ruling class, and evincing a strong belief in progress and improvement.

Some historians of maps have regarded these images of England as charming, innocent, and untainted by ideology. Because of the way social power had appropriated cartographic practices, however, the contrary view is more probable. We can now see how power worked in English eighteenth-century society through the county atlases. Two sets of connections were involved. The first was a necessary condition. What made the map-making process part of the diffusion of power was the social consensus about the proper hierarchy of landscape features selected for representation on a map. Perhaps this is obvious, but much less easily recognized is the second condition, the way the map-making workshops themselves cooperated in standardizing and reiterating that particular construction of the map on version after version of a particular landscape. Their activities constitute a contingent relationship, made up of the association of surveyors, editors, map draftsmen, engravers, and publishers who were all contributing toward the same end—the conformist-map image. The resultant mapped landscape would have been at once familiar and yet more robust to the eighteenth-century patrons of the atlas. But in other respects its very conservatism as a form of knowledge—even where new features were shown—made it unresponsive to change and oblivious to the everyday landscapes of ordinary people.

It has been said that it is "precisely through the process of making a power situation appear a fact in the nature of the world that traditional authority works."[72] So too the atlases made the power structures of eighteenth-century society appear normal and "in the nature of the world." They remind us how the internal power of cartography, though orchestrated by social values apparently external to its practice, exercised control and authority over the geographical features selected for mapping and the manner in which they were presented on the page or the style of the map sign used. And in the context of eighteenth-century England, the recurrent dominance of a relatively few landscape features in the county atlases helped endow those select topographies (castles, cathedrals, country houses and their parks, rectories) with an almost cosmological significance for the privileged society which received them. They represented a partly mythic England produced and read as a graphic ritual.[73] The comparison between ritual and cartography may be worth pursuing. Both activities are distinguished and stabilized above all by their repetitive and standardized nature.[74] Furthermore, the ritual itself becomes a powerful way of legitimizing what it stands for: "One of the reasons why ritual is such a potent means of legitimation is that it offers a way to unite a particular image of the universe with a strong emotional attachment to that image. Rituals are built out of symbols that embody certain views of how the world is constructed . . . rituals make these symbols salient and promote attachment to them."[75] There is little room to doubt that such an emotional attachment was felt by the gentry in eighteenth-century England for land and place and that the increasingly standardized maps in the county atlases they subscribed to served to link images of a set of local universes to that historically based attachment. County atlas maps thus became established as one of the culture symbols by which social power was retained by the gentry-nobility throughout the eighteenth century in England.

"General" or "Universal" Atlases: Some Representations from North America

The second group of atlases considered in this essay were international in scope. Symbolizing a sharp discontinuity between the perception of domestic and foreign space, they also contributed to the stereotyping and ritualization of social and geographical attitudes that must have been common in eighteenth-century English society. These are the atlases of the world as a whole, and the driving force in this case behind the cartographic power relations was that of a century of aggressive imperialism. Something of prevailing national attitudes is caught by Samuel Johnson. In 1766 (in a Dedication to George III) he could write of England's growing world hegemony:

> Your power is acknowledged by nations . . . whose names we know not yet how to write, and whose boundaries we cannot yet describe. But YOUR MAJESTY's lenity and benevolence give us reason to expect the time, when . . . multitudes, who now range the woods for prey, and live at the mercy of the winds and seasons, shall, by the paternal care of YOUR MAJESTY, enjoy the plenty of cultivated lands, the pleasures of society, the security of law, and the light of Revelation.[76]

Sentiments of chauvinism, patriotism, and prejudice such as these were frequently echoed in the geographical knowledge of the elite in eighteenth-century England.[77] Geography was a means by which to assert the superiority of the English nation against all other nations. Thus Moll could end the introduction to the *Atlas Minor* (1729) with a flourish: "the *British* Nation has no Superior upon the Globe, and the King of *Great Britain* no Equal."[78] In the concluding part of this essay, it will be shown how such attitudes were manifest in representations of North America in these world atlases.[79] As in the case of the county atlases, we shall focus on how cartography exerts power by legitimation rather than on how maps were a vital instrument in the practical management of colonial and imperial enterprises.[80] All that has to be borne in mind is that, given the colonial context, a different set of power relations was at work in the case of the American maps. An English social structure was transplanted into some of the North American colonies but, as the atlases reveal, power struggles between different European nations for overseas territory and, more unequally, the power relations between European and non-European peoples also play their role in producing the map image.

Until the War of Independence, the thirteen North American colonies were the jewel in the English imperial crown. While in all general European atlases the nations of Europe tended to be allocated space disproportionate to their size in the world,[81] in the atlases of the London cartographers, North America and the West Indies assumed increasing prominence throughout the eighteenth century. Even in the earlier atlases of Moll,[82] Senex, and Bowen, published before the French and Indian War (1756–1763), these colonies began to be highlighted for a domestic readership. After 1755, drawing on French sources and on a series of detailed maps of the individual English colonies,[83] the London atlas makers, notably Thomas Jefferys and his successors, began to produce detailed regional atlases for the North American and West Indian theaters of colonial activity. Some of these works, such as Jefferys's *A General Topography of North America and the West Indies* (1768) (see fig. 16), appeared before the beginning of the War of Independence but, in other instances, such as *The American Atlas, The North American Atlas,* and *The West India Atlas,* published between 1775 and 1777,[84] they were clearly rushed out by the owners of the copperplates as a deliberate attempt to cash in on the topicality of the mounting military and political crisis in the continent. Yet, whatever the changing historical or bibliographical context, it is the ideological repetitiveness of the images on the maps of North America which allows generalization about the way the world atlases manufactured and disseminated power.

In the eighteenth century, atlas making was already under the influence of a Science of Geography whose productions were unabashed handmaidens of imperialism.[85] On the American maps, this ideology is found in the wording of title pages, in dedications, and in the motifs for cartouches and other marginal emblems. Titles increasingly contain allusions to "British Dominions and Settlements throughout the World." Even if these imperial territories were not yet painted red, the British Empire had already appeared on the map, carrying with it implications of inevitability and right. "A Map of the British Empire, in North America," included in Thomas Jefferys's *The American Atlas* (1776) displays a note which states "The British Empire in North America contains": then it lists "The Hudsons Bay Company's Territories," "Canada or the Province of Quebec," followed by the individual colonies and then by "The Reserved Lands." The inventory-like arrangement of this table is striking.[86] It is in fact an inventory of the overseas property of the English crown. The function of the atlas maker was to inscribe its boundaries as legitimate and permanent. To strengthen the authority of representation, supporting allusions to international treaties appear on some maps. For instance, following the Treaty of Paris (1763), which gave England practically all North America east of the Mississippi as well as Canada, the relevant articles of the "Definitive Treaty" were engraved on maps, as if to confirm these extended bounds of the English empire (See figure 22).[87]

Yet it would be wrong to imply that North America was no more than a fief of the English crown. The same notions of status and proprietorship as those in the English county atlases can be found in the maps of America but they are applied to American society. Thus we find that the map of Pennsylvania in Jefferys's *American Atlas* is dedicated to "Thomas Penn and Richard Penn Esquires" (note the inclusion of their mark of social rank) as the "True and Absolute Proprietaries & Governors of the Province of Pennsylvania."[88] Even if this is a special case, these are key words: *True, Absolute, Proprietaries,* and *Governors* belong to the language of authority in eighteenth-century English. They epitomized the relevance of the concepts of right and of land ownership, held in an English county by a nobility with legal privileges, to the colonial world.

Many of the decorative features in the cartouches of English maps of North America reinforce these statements of power relations. The cartouche is the *pictura loquens* of cartography. Like the emblematic title page or frontispiece,

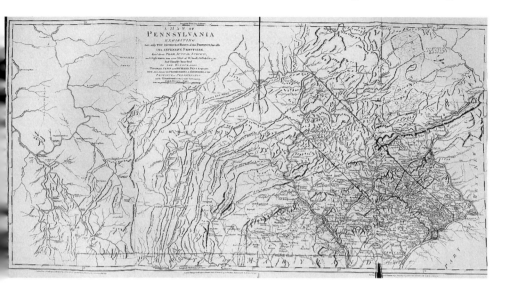

Figure 22. The atlas as colonial territory: W. Scull's map of Pennsylvania, 1775. *The American Atlas* (London: T. Jefferys, 1782). Library of Congress, Geography and Map Division.

it serves to abstract and epitomize some of the meaning of the work as a whole. A cartouche may thus be decorative, illustrative, programmatical, propagandist, doctrinal, or controversial.[89] All these elements recur in the English atlases of the eighteenth century but I am concerned here with how certain motifs are an integral part of the political rhetoric of the map as a whole. The King's coat of arms appeared on maps of America in the general atlases just as it had been nailed to trees on the ground as a mark of colonial sovereignty.[90] Other motifs such as the English crown, the national flag, or the coat of arms of English noblemen who were also colonial officials, are reminiscent of the emblemata of the county atlases. Equally recognizable to many patrons would have been the expression of royal power in George Willdey's map of North America. This was dedicated "To his Sacred & Most Excellent Majesty George by the Grace of God King of Great Britain."[91] The cartouche contains the standard emblems for North America. Above this is a portrait of the King, with crown and laurels. It is held over the landscape beneath by allegorical figures of Mercury and an angel. Thus, in Willdey's cartouche, English sovereignty, the cult of the crown, Anglican theology (in which traditional doctrines of the divine right of Kings persisted), and imperial commerce were firmly tied to the soil of America.

On other maps, the cartouches are used to develop a visual vocabulary of colonial exploitation by making them specific to America. A recurrent message is the cornucopia that the continent had become: various maps are decorated with the beaver, with hogshead of tobacco, with sugar cane, and with codfish. Ships with their sails furled stand in calm estuaries ready to convey this wealth back to the mother country. Such engravings tell us that the land of America belongs to the Euro-Americans and that sovereignty led to an appropriation of the wealth of the land. Even seemingly innocent cartouches may have reinforced these assumptions. The scene below Niagara Falls in the inset to Moll's "Beaver Map" is often reproduced (see figure 23).[92] At first glance, it might merely suggest an interest in natural history, or that the fur trade was a source of wealth to some of the atlas patrons. Yet a closer look shows an absence of people and especially of the native Americans upon whom the fur trade depended. In the final analysis, unless the beavers are intended as a symbol for the hard-working Europeans, it is just as likely that it was this negative aspect, the absence of people, which entered the reader's consciousness as any of the images of natural history or the fur trade. Such images, associated with the representation of the territory on the map, and becoming part of the process of persuasion and mythmaking, rendered legitimate the holding of English colonies in America.

It is true that many of these map emblems were added with little conscious thought by the atlas maker. But the fact remains that they served to further strengthen the perception of power relations between Europeans and non-Europeans. By the eighteenth century, the English colonies in North America had already been engaged in a long and bitter encounter both with native Americans and with the Africans in the New World. Popular images of this encounter, repeated in map cartouches and linked to the cartographic representation and symbolism of territory, helped to stereotype and to universalize the institutions they record. The cartouches confirm that the principal English encounter with African slaves was in the West Indies,[93] but that slave owning also extended throughout the thirteen colonies is brought home by Fry and Jefferson's map of Virginia of 1754.[94] The cartouche on this map shows a wharf scene. It is a silent parable of class relations in mid-eighteenth-century Virginia (see figure 24). The first tier of power lies in the dedication to the Earl of Halifax, the chief colonial official in England. His imprimatur served to enhance the authority of the map. At the next tier, the plantation

The Cataract of NIAGARA, some make this Water-Fall to be half a League while others reckon it no more than a hundred Fathom.

View of y̆ Industry of y̆ Beavers of Canada in making Dams to stop y̆ Course of y̆ R ivulet . in order to form a great Lake, about w ᶜʰ ey build their Habitations . To Effect this : they fell large Trees with their Teeth, in such a manner as to make them come Cross y̆ Rivu t. to lay y̆ foundation of y̆ Dam: they make Mortar. work up, and finish y̆ whole with great order and wonderfull Dexterity.

Figure 23. The beaver inset. Herman Moll, *A New and Exact Map of the Dominions of the King of Great Britain on ye Continent of North America* (London, 1715). Library of Congress, Geography and Map Division.

owner is shown seated. Below him are ranged men loading tobacco. Finally, beneath them all, are the black laborers and the black boy who is serving a glass of wine to the plantation owner.

Whites and Indians were frequently depicted in cartouches in clearly indicated relations of superiority and inferiority. Many of the eighteenth-century motifs were inherited from earlier centuries of colonial rule. The lifestyle of the Indian was represented as that of a "savage," often naked, emphasizing

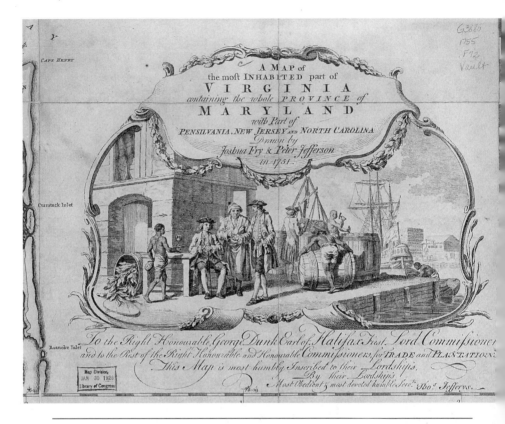

Figure 24. Cartouche in Joshua Fry and Peter Jefferson, *A Map of the Most Inhabited Part of Virginia Containing the Whole Province of Maryland* (London: T. Jefferys, 1755). Library of Congress, Geography and Map Division.

that in the European view, "the adoption of clothing symbolized the development of law, authority and power . . . whereas the naked Amerindian represented the state of nature."[95] The judgment that Indians could not be given the same rights as those who had attained the maturity of civility thus provided a justification for taking their land. To denigrate the indigenous population still further, on some eighteenth-century maps, Indians were represented as cannibals or monkeys with human heads.[96] While such images may not have been deliberately intended to inspire racial propaganda in our modern sense, they certainly would have consolidated European attitudes toward the Indian, dividing the North American population into the "other" and "they" as opposed to "us" and "we."[97] Even at best they were always shown subject to the settlers: the Indian stood by while the European was the principal actor.

On one map a suitably-tamed Indian is shown stroking a representation of the British lion.[98] Or in the iconography of the Revolutionary period, a Tory fights an American patriot while the Indian—always the loser—is depicted showing fear and apprehensiveness in case the protection of his colonial masters was withdrawn. Such were the prophecies of power which would run wherever colonies extended on the map.

The symbolism in Benjamin West's 1771 painting of "Penn's Treaty with the Indians"—a map is held by one of the group of colonists—is apt.[99] Yet such colonial maps were more than legal instruments enforcing Indian land treaties, more than strategic documents in colonial wars with the French, and more than a tool in the settled areas to divide the farmland or plat the city. They exercised power in other ways too. The maps in the general atlases—like those in the county atlases—entered power relations the way they standardized North American geography, erected social hierarchies in its landscape, and selectively omitted or emphasized features on the maps. For America as for England, the cartographic process was also the processing of power. Workshop techniques enabled the mass production of maps (in relative eighteenth-century terms) and, as private tradesmen, the English atlas makers used commerce to return these politically constructed geographies to those that held power.

This sort of cartographical circuit in power relations enabled a power-knowledge to be disseminated in such a way that it could be used to reinforce or to challenge earlier configurations of power. The most visible example of such a circuit in the preindependence period is the way English atlas makers championed national claims at a continental scale. In the run-up to the French and Indian War, both the French and English used maps as weapons of international propaganda or to sway domestic public opinion to support military action. It was the English map makers, however, who may have gone furthest—with or without direct patronage—in arbitrarily extending the boundaries of the thirteen colonies on their maps west toward the Mississippi. Yet, the increasingly ritualized depiction of these claims also shows the need to distinguish between external and internal power in cartographic representation. The ostensible mark of external power is that territorial claims were made on behalf of the nation, accompanied by partisan endorsements. The initial formulation of these claims, and their communication to the map makers, were probably deliberate acts of policy by a few leading colonial strategists who were using the atlases to promote their cause, but whose power was still located outside the workshop. At some point, however, these representations of power were internalized in cartographic practice. Diffused between a number of London map makers, external power became internal power. The English atlas maker could not take independent initiatives in choosing how particular configurations of colonial power were standardized, made more persuasive, or popularized in smaller-scale atlases.

During the eighteenth century these transfers of power were enacted on many occasions as the political realities changed or as new information became available. Ownership was constantly redefined or extended. Already, in the early eighteenth century, Moll's maps were annotated with anti-French propaganda. Maps by Morden and Senex claimed for England large parts of New France such as the Niagara peninsula of what is now Ontario, Canada. French maps were variously criticized for depicting their "political system of encroachment upon the territories of other nations," or as "an arbitrary Fiction, false and unjust,"[100] as the English atlas makers redrafted geography with bold sweeps of the burin to proclaim a manifest destiny of colonial expansion in North America (see figure 25). The zeal of some cartographers for the national cause went beyond the demands of patronage. They added their own polemics to the power they derived. Thomas Jefferys, in particular, was an active agent rather than a pawn in the power relations of colonialism. In one sense he could be described as the mouthpiece for Pitt's imperial strategies but in another he had also set himself up as the leading cartographic champion of his country's claims. In 1755, for example, on his *Map of North America from the French of Mr. D'Anville* he had included the argument that "the French are intruders into Canada, part of Cabot's discovery and have no Right but by Treaties."[101] By overstating the authority for the claim as well as by expanding its boundaries, the map had been manipulated to enhance its rhetoric. Jefferys had deliberately used the power of the atlas—as well as the armory of his workshop practices—to support the cause of imperial expansion.

Power did not have to be deliberately exerted, however, either by the cartographer or through the patron, for it to be effective. The depiction of the ordinary geography of North America in the atlases—the patterns of place-names, settlements, roads, and local administrative boundaries—illustrates this content forcibly. Like the landscapes of the English county atlases the geography of North America on the maps of the general atlases is a geography

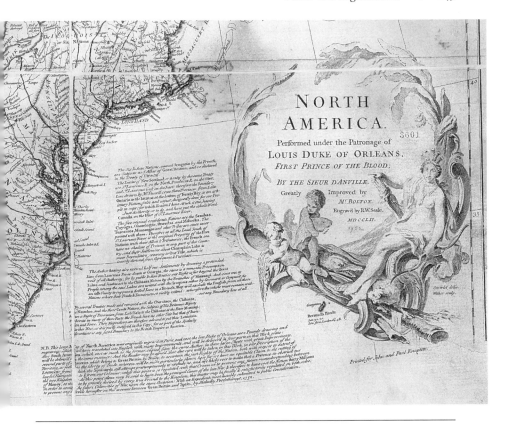

Figure 25. The atlas as political propaganda: Solomon Bolton's *North America* (London: printed for John and Paul Knapston, 1752). Library of Congress, Geography and Map Division.

with a hidden agenda. The maps of the thirteen colonies in the larger atlases are preeminently a record of colonial self-interest. They are an unconscious portrait of how successfully a European colonial society had reproduced itself in the New World. As maps of a new environment, they granted reassurance to settlers by reproducing the symbolic authority and place-names of the Old World. Some local administrative boundaries had been settled by the "King in Council." On the map of the "Island of St. John" in Jefferys's *American Atlas,* Kings County, Queens County, and Princes County are found adjacent to each other. Such loyalty to English social structure appears in innumerable instances.

Looking at the maps of the eastern seaboard, we find it is as if the Europeans had always lived there (see figure 19). In representing place, time had also been inserted into the landscape. If we forget geography for a moment, then it is possible to imagine oneself reading not maps of the New World but from an atlas of *English* counties. True, these American maps are emptier, but in settled areas it is the framework of a European geography that has taken shape. Wherever British influence was strong, as in New England, the names on the land constantly remind us of this coincidence.[102] Or again, on Jefferys's map of New England, place-names are derived from English or Scottish toponymy, from the personal names of British settlers, or from allusions to English nobility or the heroes of some English cause (see figure 26). Everywhere the maps served to emphasize the structures and consequences of colonialism on the land, reminding readers that the courthouses dispensed an English system of justice in its colonies, that the roads and trackways linked the New World settlements to the outposts of Empire trade, that the forts were there to defend the colonies, and even that the routes of navigation on charts served to facilitate His Majesty's ships. Not least, the atlas maker was helping construct a colonial history. Where historical events were recorded on the maps, they related to English discoveries, to English victories, to the surrender of native American peoples, to some atrocity committed by Indians, or to the defeat of England's colonial rivals such as the Dutch or the French.[103] It became an act of colonial promotion to encourage the portrayal of a landscape that was familiar and not hostile to English eyes. The map was inviting settlers. There were few obstacles in the paper landscape that would have seemed insurmountable.

The historical force of these carefully standardized maps may have been greater in a new society than in the old society portrayed in the English county atlases. Their power was as much psychological as practical. Their images were a metaphor for control. They made the new land believable. The wilderness was tamed on paper before the wilderness itself had been encountered. Space shrank. In the minds of administrators and settlers, the distant land was made domestic and the unknowable conquerable. Maps often ran ahead of the settled frontier, preceding the axe and the plough. Eastern North America was recolonized on paper by Europeans before it was recolonized on the ground.

The same maps were also the subliminal charters of colonial legitimation. As in the case of maps of the English landscape, English maps of the New World exercised power through the categories of their omissions. These

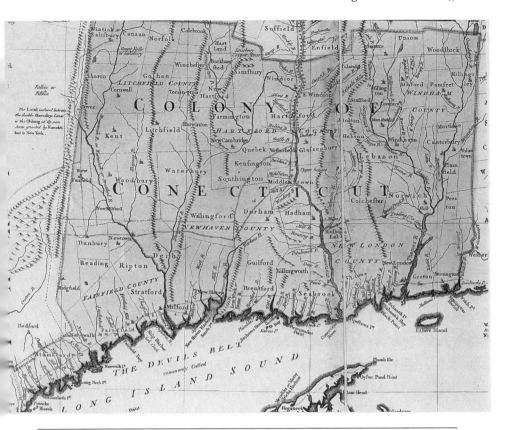

Figure 26. The atlas as England recreated: the colony of Connecticut from *A Map of the Most Inhabited Part of New England* (London: T. Jefferys, 1755). Library of Congress, Geography and Map Division.

silences applied especially to Indian civilization. We ask ourselves, where are the traces of Indian occupation on the land? At best they are only randomly preserved on the maps but, more often than not, as the frontier moved west, the traces of an Indian past were dropped altogether from the image. Although some maps mark "Indian houses and Plantations" and "English Plantations" separately,[104] more often than not, where Indian villages are identified or their nations named, it is usually on the margins of the European settlement, where they served as a guide to the fur trade, to military deployment, or ultimately to colonial appropriation. With the exception of the survival of the Indian names for natural features, such as rivers, lakes, and mountains, the maps seldom represented an Indian geography mapped in its own right and they were never a means of preserving ethnic integrity. Many eighteenth-century map makers preferred blank spaces to a relict Indian geography. This was defended on the grounds that it was good scientific practice to avoid mapping what could not be verified. Yet the ideological implications of the silence about Indian geography cannot be overlooked. It lent unwitting support to the legal doctrines of *terra nullus* and *vacuum domicilium,* which, since the earliest days of the colonies, had featured among the grounds for acquiring land title and assuming political jurisdiction. The English in particular believed that Indian land awaited their immediate settlement because it was vacant.[105] There is a moral neutrality about a blank space which is easily divided and ruled. In the end, we find it hard to believe that the Indians had ever lived on the land. The act of mapping had transformed what was being described and had given it new meanings and potentialities.

Conclusion

In this essay I have sought to deconstruct some map images in eighteenth-century English atlases. By this I mean that they have been interpreted in terms of their effects as a representation of power rather than as representations of the topographical reality of the English or American landscapes in the eighteenth century. The social power in question had become internal to cartography and was manufactured in its own workshop practices. It was in these workshops that the link with one reality was transformed and a new reality created. These processes are comparable to those of scientific procedures in the laboratory. The atlas maker disciplined and ordered geographical information, the grids and graticules of the map providing a framework of systematic domination. Through selection, classification, standardization, and the creation of mappable hierarchies, the atlas maker made mapped geography a more robust form of knowledge. By different means—regular mapping, decorative iconography, and textual glosses on maps—social power was represented. As a text of power rather than as a map of physical topography, it mattered less whether the image was a technically accurate representation of a landscape or an original rather than a plagiarized image. More important, it should be believable. It mattered that it represented power in ways which coincided with the values of contemporary society. Power relations such as the rights of the crown, the deferential ranking of power within

English society, and the inherent superiority of the English over other nations and especially non-Europeans, were all as important to cartographic practice as they were to other forms of knowledge in eighteenth-century England.

Once impregnated with power, cartographic knowledge worked through society in a number of ways. It worked both consciously and subliminally. It never operated alone but always in conjunction with other forms of knowledge and representation. Nevertheless, by its focus on the power relations both inherent and manifest in landscape and territory, it played a distinctive role in the social configuration of the age. Maps worked principally through legitimation. By representing territorial power relations as a normal part of the world, they enabled the status quo to be more easily accepted. The repetition of similar images through a succession of atlases strengthened this acceptance. In a society where many, even among the upper classes, lacked firsthand experience of other places, the map could become the only reality. Though divorced from the world on the ground, it acquired a mythic authority. As knowledge by force of tradition, its representations were more difficult to subvert, and indeed, many maps in the atlases had extraordinarily long lives which were independent of change in the world itself. The making and reading of maps, by constantly recycling a normalcy in power relations, is akin to a ritual, a ritual performed with knowledge and linked to attitudes and emotions widely held and expressed in English society. These included an attachment by the patrons to their own class and nation, a love of ownership and property, a bellicose chauvinism, and a tendency to despise the savages. Representing these emotions through maps tended not only to reinforce them but to associate them with ever wider geographical areas.

The answer to the initial question as to how were the atlases a force for change in society always depends on the context of power relations. In England itself, the county atlases tended toward conservatism and reaction and they helped to maintain the long-standing hegemony of a broad ruling class. In the North American colonies, however, the maps operated decisively in favor of the new society of Euro-Americans and at the expense of the Indians. Yet for both areas the atlas makers had produced a discourse of power. Even where the true nature of its dialectic was hidden from contemporaries, we can be sure that its reality was always socially constructed.

Deconstructing the Map

This chapter originally appeared in *Cartographica* 26, no. 2 (1989): 1–20.

A map says to you, "Read me carefully, follow me closely, doubt me not." It says, "I am the earth in the palm of your hand. Without me, you are alone and lost."

And indeed you are. Were all the maps in this world destroyed and vanished under the direction of some malevolent hand, each man would be blind again, each city be made a stranger to the next, each landmark become a meaningless signpost pointing to nothing.

Yet, looking at it, feeling it, running a finger along its lines, it is a cold thing, a map, humourless and dull, born of calipers and a draughtsman's board. That coastline there, that ragged scrawl of scarlet ink, shows neither sand nor sea nor rock; it speaks of no mariner, blundering full sail in wakeless seas, to bequeath, on sheepskin or a slab of wood, a priceless scribble to posterity. This brown blot that marks a mountain has, for the casual eye, no other significance, though twenty men, or ten, or only one, may have squandered life to climb it. Here is a valley, there a swamp, and there a desert; and here is a river that some curious and courageous soul, like a pencil in the hand of God, first traced with bleeding feet.

—BERYL MARKHAM,
West with the Night, 1983

The pace of conceptual exploration in the history of cartography—searching for alternative ways of understanding maps—is slow. Some would say that its achievements are largely cosmetic. Applying conceptions of literary history to the history of cartography, it would appear that we are still working largely in either a "premodern," or a "modern" rather than in a "postmodern" climate of thought.[1] A list of individual explorations would, it is true, contain some that sound impressive. Our students can now be directed to writings that draw on the ideas of information theory, linguistics, semiotics, structuralism, phenomenology, developmental theory, hermeneutics, iconology, marxism, and ideology. We can point to the names in our footnotes of (among others) Cassirer, Gombrich, Piaget, Panofsky, Kuhn, Barthes, and Eco. Yet despite these symptoms of change, we are still, willingly or unwillingly, the prisoners of our own past.

My basic argument in this essay is that we should encourage an epistemological shift in the way we interpret the nature of cartography. For historians of cartography, I believe a major roadblock to understanding is that we still accept uncritically the broad consensus, with relatively few dissenting voices, of what *cartographers* tell us maps are supposed to be. In particular, we often tend to work from the premise that mappers engaged in an unquestionably "scientific" or "objective" form of knowledge creation. Of course, cartographers believe they have to say this to remain credible but historians do not have that obligation. It is better for us to begin from the premise that cartography is seldom what cartographers say it is.

As they embrace computer-assisted methods and Geographical Information Systems, the scientific rhetoric of map makers is becoming more strident. The "culture of technics" is everywhere rampant. We are told that the journal now named the *American Cartographer* will become *Cartography and Geographical Information Systems.* Or, in a strangely ambivalent gesture towards the nature of maps, the British Cartographic Society proposes that there should be two definitions of cartography, "one for professional cartographers and the other for the public at large." A definition "for use in communication with the general public" would be "Cartography is the art, science and technology of making maps": that for "practicing cartographers" would be "Cartography is the science and technology of analyzing and interpreting geographic relationships, and communicating the results by means of maps."[2] Many may find it surprising that "art" no longer exists in "professional" cartography. In the present context, however, these signs of ontological schizophrenia can also be read as reflecting an urgent need to rethink the nature of maps from different perspectives. The question arises as to whether the notion of a progressive science is a myth partly created by cartographers in the course of their own professional development. I suggest that it has been accepted too uncritically by a wider public and by other scholars who work with maps.[3] For those concerned with the history of maps it is especially timely that we challenge the cartographer's assumptions. Indeed, if the history of cartography is to grow as an interdisciplinary subject among the humanities and social sciences, new ideas are essential.

The question becomes how do we as historians of cartography escape from the normative models of cartography? How do we allow new ideas to come in? How do we begin to write a cartographic history as genuinely revisionist as Louis Marin's "The King and His Geometer" (in the context of a seventeenth-century map of Paris) or William Boelhower's "The Culture of the Map" (in the context of sixteenth-century world maps showing America for the first time?[4] These are two studies informed by postmodernism. In this essay I also adopt a strategy aimed at the deconstruction of the map.

The notion of deconstruction[5] is also a password for the postmodern enterprise. Deconstructionist strategies can now be found not only in philosophy but also in localized disciplines, especially in literature, and in other subjects such as architecture, planning, and, more recently, geography.[6] I shall specifically use a deconstructionist tactic to break the assumed link between reality and representation which has dominated cartographic thinking, has led it in the pathway of "normal science" since the Enlightenment, and has also provided a ready-made and "taken for granted" epistemology for the history of cartography. The objective is to suggest that an alternative epistemology, rooted in social theory rather than in scientific positivism, is more appropriate to the history of cartography. It will be shown that even "scientific" maps are a product not only of "the rules of the order of geometry and reason" but also of the "norms and values of the order of social . . . tradition."[7] Our task is to search for the social forces that have structured cartography and to locate the presence of power—and its effects—in all map knowledge.

The ideas in this particular essay owe most to writings by Foucault and Derrida. My approach is deliberately eclectic because in some respects the theoretical positions of these two authors are incompatible. Foucault anchors texts in sociopolitical realities and constructs systems for organizing knowledge of the kind that Derrida loves to dismantle.[8] But even so, by combining different ideas on a new terrain, it may be possible to devise a scheme of social theory with which we can begin to interrogate the hidden agendas of cartography. Such a scheme offers no "solution" to a historical interpretation of the cartographic record, nor a precise method or set of techniques, but as a broad strategy it may help to locate some of the fundamental forces that have driven map making in both European and non-European societies. From Foucault's writings, the key revelation has been the omnipresence of power in all knowledge, even though that power is invisible or implied, including the particular knowledge encoded in maps and atlases. Derrida's notion of the rhetoricity of all texts has been no less a challenge.[9] It demands a search for metaphor and rhetoric in maps where previously scholars had found only measurement and topography. Its central question is reminiscent of Korzybski's much older dictum "The map is not the territory,"[10] but deconstruction goes further to bring the issue of how the map represents place into much sharper focus.

Deconstruction urges us to read between the lines of the map—"in the margins of the text"—and through its tropes to discover the silences and contradictions that challenge the apparent honesty of the image. We begin to learn that cartographic facts are only facts within a specific cultural perspective. We start to understand how maps, like art, far from being "a transparent opening to the world," are but "a particular human way . . . of looking at the world."[11]

In pursuing this strategy I shall develop three threads of argument. First, I shall examine the discourse of cartography in the light of some of Foucault's ideas about the play of rules within discursive formations. Second, drawing on one of Derrida's central positions I will examine the textuality of maps and, in particular, their rhetorical dimension. Third, returning to Foucault, I will consider how maps work in society as a form of power-knowledge.

The Rules of Cartography

One of Foucault's primary units of analysis is the discourse. A discourse has been defined as "a system of possibility for knowledge."[12] Foucault's method was to ask, it has been said,

> what rules permit certain statements to be made; what rules order these state-
> ments; what rules permit us to identify some statements as true and others
> as false; what rules allow the construction of a map, model or classificatory
> system . . . what rules are revealed when an object of discourse is modified or
> transformed . . . Whenever sets of rules of these kinds can be identified, we are
> dealing with a discursive formation or discourse.[13]

The key question for us then becomes, "What type of rules have governed the development of cartography?" Cartography I define as a body of theoretical and practical knowledge that map makers employ to construct maps as a distinct mode of visual representation. The question is, of course, historically specific: the rules of cartography vary in different societies. Here I refer particularly to two distinctive sets of rules that underlie and dominate the history of Western cartography since the seventeenth century.[14] One set may be defined as governing the technical production of maps and is made explicit in the cartographic treatises and writings of the period.[15] The other set relates to the cultural production of maps. These must be understood in a broader historical context than either scientific procedure or technique. They are, moreover, rules that are usually ignored by cartographers so that they form a hidden aspect of their discourse.

The first set of cartographic rules can thus be defined in terms of a scientific epistemology. From at least the seventeenth century onward, European map makers and map users have increasingly promoted a standard scientific model of knowledge and cognition. The object of mapping is to produce a "correct" relational model of the terrain. Its assumptions are that the objects in the world to be mapped are real and objective, and that they enjoy an existence independent of the cartographer; that their reality can be expressed in mathematical terms; that systematic observation and measurement offer the only route to cartographic truth; and that this truth can be independently verified.[16] The procedures of both surveying and map construction came to share strategies similar to those in science in general; cartography also documents a history of more precise instrumentation and measurement; increasingly complex classifications of its knowledge and a proliferation of signs for its representation; and, especially from the nineteenth century onward, the growth of institutions and a "professional" literature designed to monitor the application and propagation of the rules.[17] Moreover, although cartographers have continued to pay lip service to the "art and science" of map making,[18] art, as we have seen, is being edged off the map. It has often been accorded a cosmetic rather than a central role in cartographic communication.[19] Even philosophers of visual communication—such as Arnheim, Eco, Gombrich, and Goodman[20]—have tended to categorize maps as a type of congruent diagram—as analogs, models, or "equivalents" creating a similitude of reality—and, in essence, different from art or painting. A "scientific" cartography (so it was believed) would be untainted by social factors. Even today many cartographers are puzzled by the suggestion that political and sociological theory could throw light on their practices. They will probably shudder at the mention of deconstruction.

The acceptance of the map as "a mirror of nature" (to employ Richard Rorty's phrase)[21] also results in a number of other characteristics of cartographic discourse even where these are not made explicit. Most striking is the belief in progress: that, by the application of science ever more precise representations of reality can be produced. The methods of cartography have delivered a "true, probable, progressive, or highly confirmed knowledge."[22] This mimetic bondage has led to a tendency not only to look down on the maps of the past (with a dismissive scientific chauvinism) but also to regard the maps of other non-Western or early cultures (where the rules of map making were different) as inferior to European maps.[23] Similarly, the primary effect of the scientific rules was to create a "standard"—a successful version of "normal science"[24]—that enabled cartographers to build a wall around their citadel of the "true" map. Its central bastions were measurement and standardization and beyond there was a "not cartography" land where lurked an army of inaccurate, heretical, subjective, valuative, and ideologically distorted images. Cartographers developed a "sense of the other" in relation to nonconforming maps. Even maps such as those produced by journalists, where different rules and modes of expressiveness might be appropriate, are evaluated by many cartographers according to standards of "objectivity," "accuracy," and "truthfulness." In this respect, the underlying attitude of many cartographers is revealed in a recent book of essays on *Cartographie dans les Médias.*[25] One of its reviewers has noted how many authors attempt to exorcise from "the realm of cartography any graphic representation that is not a simple planimetric image, and to then classify all other maps as 'decorative graphics masquerading as maps' where the 'bending of cartographic rules' has taken place . . . most journalistic maps are flawed because they are inaccurate, misleading or biased."[26] Or in Britain, we are told, there was set up a "Media Map Watch" in 1984. "Several hundred interested members [of cartographic and geographic societies] submitted several thousand maps and diagrams for analysis that revealed [according to the rules] numerous common deficiencies, errors, and inaccuracies along with misleading standards."[27] In this example of cartographic vigilantism the "ethic of accuracy" is being defended with some ideological fervor. The language of exclusion is that of a string of "natural" opposites: "true and false"; "objective and subjective"; "literal and symbolic" and so on. The best maps are those with an "authoritative image of self-evident factuality."[28]

In cases where the scientific rules are invisible in the map we can still trace their play in attempting to normalize the discourse. The cartographer's "black box" has to be defended and its social origins suppressed. The hysteria among leading cartographers at the popularity of the Peters projection,[29] or the recent expressions of piety among Western European and North American map makers following the Russian admission that they had falsified their topographic maps to confuse the enemy give us a glimpse of how the game is played according to these rules. What are we to make of the 1988 newspaper headlines such as "Russians Caught Mapping" (*Ottawa Citizen*), "Soviets Admit Map Paranoia" (*Wisconsin Journal*) or (in the *New York Times*) "In West, Map Makers Hail 'Truth'" and "The rascals finally realized the truth and were able to tell it, a geographer at the Defense Department said"?[30] The implication is that Western maps are value free. According to the spokesman, our maps are not ideological documents, and the condemnation of Russian falsification is as much an echo of Cold War rhetoric as it is a credible cartographic criticism.

This timely example also serves to introduce my second contention that the scientific rules of mapping are, in any case, influenced by a quite different set of rules, those governing the cultural production of the map. To discover these rules, we have to read between the lines of technical procedures or of the map's topographic content. They are related to values, such as those of ethnicity, politics, religion, or social class, and they are also embedded in the map-producing society at large. Cartographic discourse operates a double silence toward this aspect of the possibilities for map knowledge. In the map itself, social structures are often disguised beneath an abstract, instrumental space, or incarcerated in the coordinates of computer mapping. And in the technical literature of cartography they are also ignored, notwithstanding the fact that they may be as important as surveying, compilation, or design in producing the statements that cartography makes about the world and its landscapes. Such an interplay of social and technical rules is a universal feature of cartographic knowledge. In maps it produces the "order" of its features and the "hierarchies of its practices."[31] In Foucault's sense the rules may enable us to define an *episteme* and to trace an archaeology of that knowledge through time.[32]

Two examples of how such rules are manifest in maps will be given to illustrate their force in structuring cartographic representation. The first is the well-known adherence to the "rule of ethnocentricity" in the construction of world maps. This has led many historical societies to place their own territories at the center of their cosmographies or world maps. While it may be dangerous to assume universality, and there are exceptions, such a rule is as evident in cosmic diagrams of pre-Columbian North American Indians as it is in the maps of ancient Babylonia, Greece, or China, or in the medieval maps of the Islamic world or Christian Europe.[33] Yet what is also significant in applying Foucault's critique of knowledge to cartography is that the history of the ethnocentric rule does not march in step with the "scientific" history of map making. Thus, the scientific Renaissance in Europe gave modern cartography coordinate systems, Euclid, scale maps, and accurate measurement, but it also helped to confirm a new myth of Europe's ideological centrality through projections such as those of Mercator.[34] Or again, in our own century, a tradition of the exclusivity of America was enhanced before World War II by placing it in its own hemisphere ("our hemisphere") on the world map.[35] Throughout the history of cartography ideological "Holy Lands" are frequently centered on maps. Such centricity, a kind of "subliminal geometry,"[36] adds geopolitical force and meaning to representation. It is also arguable that such world maps have in turn helped to codify, to legitimate, and to promote the world-views which are prevalent in different periods and places.[37]

A second example is how the "rules of the social order" appear to insert themselves into the smaller codes and spaces of cartographic transcription. The history of European cartography since the seventeenth century provides many examples of this tendency. Pick a printed or manuscript map from the drawer almost at random and what stands out is the unfailing way its text is as much a commentary on the social structure of a particular nation or place as it is on its topography. The map maker is often as busy recording the contours of feudalism, the shape of a religious hierarchy, or the steps in the tiers of social class[38] as the topography of the physical and human landscape.

Why maps can be so convincing in this respect is that the rules of society and the rules of measurement are mutually reinforcing in the same image. Writing of the map of Paris, surveyed in 1652 by Jacques Gomboust, the King's engineer, Louis Marin points to "this sly strategy of simulation-dissimulation":

> The knowledge and science of representation, to demonstrate the truth that its subject declares plainly, flow nonetheless in a social and political hierarchy. The proofs of its "theoretical" truth had to be given, they are the recognisable signs; but the economy of these signs in their disposition on the cartographic plane no longer obeys the rules of the order of geometry and reason but, rather, the norms and values of the order of social and religious tradition. Only the churches and important mansions benefit from natural signs and from the

visible rapport they maintain with what they represent. Townhouses and private homes, precisely because they are private and not public, will have the right only to the general and common representation of an arbitrary and institutional sign, the poorest, the most elementary (but maybe, by virtue of this, principal) of geometric elements; the point identically reproduced in bulk.[39]

Once again, much like "the rule of ethnocentrism," this hierarchicalization of space is not a conscious act of cartographic representation. Rather it is taken for granted in a society that the place of the king is more important than the place of a lesser baron, that a castle is more important than a peasant's house, that the town of an archbishop is more important than that of a minor prelate, or that the estate of a landed gentleman is more worthy of emphasis than that of a plain farmer. Cartography deploys its vocabulary accordingly so that it embodies a systematic social inequality. The distinctions of class and power are engineered, reified, and legitimated in the map by means of cartographic signs. The rule seems to be "the more powerful, the more prominent." To those who have strength in the world shall be added strength in the map. Using all the tricks of the cartographic trade—size of symbol, thickness of line, height of lettering, hatching and shading, the addition of color—we can trace this reinforcing tendency in innumerable European maps. We can begin to see how maps, like art, become a mechanism "for defining social relationships, sustaining social rules, and strengthening social values."[40]

In the case of both these examples of rules, the point I am making is that the rules operate both within and beyond the orderly structures of classification and measurement. They go beyond the stated purposes of cartography. Much of the power of the map, as a representation of social geography, is that it operates behind a mask of a seemingly neutral science. It hides and denies its social dimensions at the same time as it legitimates. Yet whichever way we look at it the rules of society will surface. They have ensured that maps are at least as much an image of the social order as they are a measurement of the phenomenal world of objects.

Deconstruction and the Cartographic Text

To move inwards from the question of cartographic rules—the social context within which map knowledge is fashioned—we have to turn to the cartographic text itself. The word *text* is deliberately chosen. It is now generally accepted that the model of text can have a much wider application than to literary texts alone. To nonbook texts such as musical compositions and architectural structures we can confidently add the graphic texts we call maps.[41] It has been said that "what constitutes a text is not the presence of linguistic elements but the act of construction" so that maps, as "constructions employing a conventional sign system,"[42] become texts. With Barthes we could say they "presuppose a signifying consciousness" that it is our business to uncover.[43] *Text* is certainly a better metaphor for maps than the mirror of nature. Maps are a cultural text. By accepting their textuality we are able to embrace a number of different interpretative possibilities. Instead of just the transparency of clarity we can discover the pregnancy of the opaque. To fact we can add myth, and instead of innocence we may expect duplicity. Rather than working with a formal science of communication, or even a sequence of loosely related technical processes, our concern is redirected to a history and anthropology of the image, and we learn to recognize the narrative qualities of cartographic representation[44] as well as its claim to provide a synchronous picture of the world. All this, moreover, is likely to lead to a rejection of the neutrality of maps, as we come to define their intentions rather than the literal face of representation, and as we begin to accept the social consequences of cartographic practices. I am not suggesting that the direction of textual enquiry offers a simple set of techniques for reading either contemporary or historical maps. In some cases we will have to conclude that there are many aspects of their meaning that are undecidable.[45]

Deconstruction, as discourse analysis in general, demands a closer and deeper reading of the cartographic text than has been the general practice in either cartography or the history of cartography. It may be regarded as a search for alternative meanings. "To deconstruct," it is argued, "is to reinscribe and resituate meanings, events and objects within broader movements and structures; it is, so to speak, to reverse the imposing tapestry in order to expose in all its unglamorously dishevelled tangle the threads constituting the well-heeled image it presents to the world."[46] The published map also has a "well-heeled image" and our reading has to go beyond the assessment of geometric accuracy, beyond the fixing of location, and beyond the recognition of topographical patterns and geographies. Such interpretation begins from the premise that the map text may contain "unperceived contradictions or duplicitous tensions"[47] that undermine the surface layer of standard objectivity. Maps are slippery customers. In the words of W. J. T. Mitchell, writing of languages and images in general, we may need to regard them more as "enigmas, problems to be explained, prison-houses which lock the understanding away from the world." We should regard them "as the sort of sign that presents a deceptive appearance of naturalness and transparence concealing an opaque, distorting, arbitrary mechanism of representation."[48] Throughout the history of modern cartography in the West, for example, there have been numerous instances of where maps have been falsified, of where they have been censored or kept secret, or of where they have surreptitiously contradicted the rules of their proclaimed scientific status.[49]

As in the case of these practices, map deconstruction would focus on aspects of maps that many interpreters have glossed over. Writing of "Derrida's most typical deconstructive moves," Christopher Norris notes that

> deconstruction is the vigilant seeking-out of those "aporias," blindspots or moments of self-contradiction where a text involuntarily betrays the tension between rhetoric and logic, between what it manifestly *means to say* and what it is nonetheless *constrained to mean*. To "deconstruct" a piece of writing is therefore to operate a kind of strategic reversal, seizing on precisely those unregarded details (casual metaphors, footnotes, incidental turns of argument) which are always, and necessarily, passed over by interpreters of a more orthodox persuasion. For it is here, in the margins of the text—the "margins," that is, as defined by a powerful normative consensus—that deconstruction discovers those same unsettling forces at work.[50]

A good example of how we could deconstruct an early map—by beginning with what have hitherto been regarded as its "casual metaphors" and "footnotes"—is provided by recent studies reinterpreting the status of decorative art on the European maps of the seventeenth and eighteenth centuries. Rather than being inconsequential marginalia, the emblems in cartouches and decorative title pages can be regarded as *basic* to the way they convey their cultural meaning,[51] and they help to demolish the claim of cartography to produce an impartial graphic science. But the possibility of such a revision is not limited to historic "decorative" maps. A recent essay by Wood and Fels on the Official State Highway Map of North Carolina[52] indicates a much wider applicability for a deconstructive strategy by beginning in the "margins" of the contemporary map. They also treat the map as a text and, drawing on the ideas of Roland Barthes of myth as a semiological system,[53] develop a forceful social critique of cartography which though structuralist in its approach is de-constructionist in its outcome. They begin, deliberately, with the margins of the map, or rather with the subject matter that is printed on its verso:

> One side is taken up by an inventory of North Carolina points of interest—illustrated with photos of, among other things, a scimitar horned oryx (resident in the state zoo), a Cherokee woman making beaded jewelry, a ski lift, a sand dune (but no cities)—a ferry schedule, a message of welcome from the then governor, and a motorist's prayer ("Our heavenly Father, we ask this day a particular blessing as we take the wheel of our car . . ."). On the other side, North Carolina, hemmed in by the margins of pale yellow South Carolinas and Virginias, Georgias and Tennessees, and washed by a pale blue Atlantic, is represented as a meshwork of red, black, green and yellow lines on a white background, thickened at the intersections by roundels of black or blotches of pink. . . . To the left of . . . [the] title is a sketch of the fluttering state flag. To the right is a sketch of a cardinal (state bird) on a branch of flowering dogwood (state flower) surmounting a buzzing honey bee arrested in midflight (state insect).[54]

What is the meaning of these emblems? Are they merely a pleasant ornament for the traveler or can they inform us about the social production of such state highway maps? A deconstructionist might claim that such meanings are un-decidable, but it is also clear that the State Highway Map of North Carolina is making other dialogical assertions behind its mask of innocence and trans-parence. I am not suggesting that these elements hinder the traveler getting from point A to B, but that there is a second text within the map. No map is devoid of an intertextual dimension and, in this case too, the discovery of intertextuality enables us to scan the image as more than a neutral picture of a road network.[55] Its "users" are not only the ordinary motorists but also the State of North Carolina that has appropriated its publication (distributed in millions of copies) as a promotional device. The map has become an instru-ment of State policy and an instrument of sovereignty.[56] At the same time, it is more than an affirmation of North Carolina's dominion over its territory. It also constructs a mythic geography, a landscape full of "points of interest," with incantations of loyalty to state emblems and to the values of a Christian piety. The hierarchy of towns and the visually dominating highways that connect them have become the legitimate natural order of the world. The map finally insists "that roads really *are* what North Carolina's all about."[57] The map idolizes our love affair with the automobile. The myth is believable.

A cartographer's stock response to this deconstructionist argument might well be to cry "foul." The argument would run like this: "Well after all it's a state highway map. It's designed to be at once popular and useful. We expect it to exaggerate the road network and to show points of interest to motorists. It is a derived rather than a basic map."[58] It is not a scientific map. The appeal to the ultimate scientific map is always the cartographers' last line of defense when seeking to deny the social relations that permeate their technology.

It is at this point that Derrida's strategy can help us to extend such an interpretation to all maps, scientific or nonscientific, basic or derived. Just as in the deconstruction of philosophy Derrida was able to show "how the supposedly literal level is intensively metaphorical,"[59] so too we can show how cartographic "fact" is also symbol. In "plain" scientific maps, science itself becomes the metaphor. Such maps contain a dimension of "symbolic realism" which is no less a statement of political authority and control than a coat of arms or a portrait of a queen placed at the head of an earlier decorative map. The metaphor has changed. The map has attempted to purge itself of ambiguity and alternative possibility.[60] Accuracy and austerity of design are now the new talismans of authority culminating in our own age with computer mapping. We can trace this process very clearly in the history of Enlightenment mapping in Europe. The topography as shown in maps, increasingly detailed and planimetrically accurate, has become a metaphor for a utilitarian philosophy and its will to power. Cartography inscribes this cultural model upon the paper and we can examine it in many scales and types of maps. Precision of instrument and technique merely serves to reinforce the image, with its encrustation of myth, as a selective perspective on the world. Thus maps of local estates in the European *ancien régime,* though derived from instrumental survey, were a metaphor for a social structure based on landed property. County and regional maps, though founded on scientific triangulation, were an articulation of local values and rights. Maps of the European states, though constructed along arcs of the meridian, served still as a symbolic shorthand for a complex of nationalist ideas. And world maps, though increasingly drawn on mathematically defined projections, nevertheless gave a spiralling twist to the manifest destiny of European overseas conquest and colonization.[61] In each of these examples we can trace the contours of metaphor in a scientific map. This in turn enhances our understanding of how the text works as an instrument operating on social reality.

In deconstructionist theory the play of rhetoric is closely linked to that of metaphor. In concluding this section of the essay I will argue that notwithstanding "scientific" cartography's efforts to convert culture into nature, and to "naturalize" social reality,[62] it has remained an inherently rhetorical discourse. Another of the lessons of Derrida's criticism of philosophy is "that modes of rhetorical analysis, hitherto applied mainly to literary texts, are in fact indispensable for reading *any* kind of discourse."[63] There is nothing revolutionary in the idea that cartography is an art of persuasive communication. It is now commonplace to write about the rhetoric of the human sciences in the classical sense of the word rhetoric.[64] Even cartographers—as well as their critics—are beginning to allude to the notion of a rhetorical cartography but what is still lacking is a rhetorical close reading of maps.[65]

The issue in contention is not whether some maps are rhetorical, or whether other maps are partly rhetorical, but the extent to which rhetoric is a universal aspect of all cartographic texts. Thus for some cartographers the notion of "rhetoric" would remain a pejorative term. It would be an "empty rhetoric" which was unsubstantiated in the scientific content of a map. "Rhetoric" would be used to refer to the "excesses" of propaganda mapping or advertising cartography or an attempt would be made to confine it to an "artistic" or aesthetic element in maps as opposed to their scientific core. My position is to accept that rhetoric is part of the way all texts work and that all maps are rhetorical texts. Again we ought to dismantle the arbitrary dualism between "propaganda" and "true," and between modes of "artistic" and "scientific" representation as they are found in maps. All maps strive to frame their message in the context of an audience. All maps state an argument about the world and they are propositional in nature. All maps employ the common devices of rhetoric such as invocations of authority (*especially* in "scientific" maps)[66] and appeals to a potential readership through the use of colors, decoration, typography, dedications, or written justifications of their method.[67] Rhetoric may be concealed but it is always present, for there is no description without performance.

The steps in making a map—selection, omission, simplification, classification, the creation of hierarchies, and "symbolization"—are all inherently rhetorical. In their intentions as much as in their applications they signify subjective human purposes rather than reciprocating the workings of some "fundamental law of cartographic generalisation."[68] Indeed, the freedom of rhetorical maneuver in cartographer is considerable: the map maker merely omits those features of the world that lie outside the purpose of the immediate discourse. There have been no limits to the varieties of maps that have been developed historically in response to different purposes of argument, aiming at different rhetorical goals, and embodying different assumptions about what is sound cartographic practice. The style of maps is neither fixed in the past nor is it today. It has been said that "The rhetorical code appropriates to its map the style most advantageous to the myth it intends to propagate."[69] Instead of thinking in terms of rhetorical versus nonrhetorical maps it may be more helpful to think in terms of a theory of cartographic rhetoric which accommodated this fundamental aspect of representation in all types of cartographic text. Thus, I am not concerned to privilege rhetoric over science, but to dissolve the illusory distinction between the two in reading the social purposes as well as the content of maps.

Maps and the Exercise of Power

For the final stage in the argument I return to Foucault. In doing so I am mindful of Foucault's criticism of Derrida that he attempted "to restrict interpretation to a purely syntactic and textual level,"[70] a world where political realities no longer exist. Foucault, on the other hand, sought to uncover "the social practices that the text itself both reflects and employs" and to "reconstruct the technical and material framework in which it arose."[71] Though deconstruction is useful in helping to change the epistemological climate, and in encouraging a rhetorical reading of cartography, my final concern is with its social and political dimensions, and with understanding how the map works in society as a form of power-knowledge. This closes the circle to a context-dependent form of cartographic history.

We have already seen how it is possible to view cartography as a discourse—a system which provides a set of rules for the representation of knowledge embodied in the images we define as maps and atlases. It is not difficult to find for maps—especially those produced and manipulated by the state—a niche in the "power/knowledge matrix of the modern order."[72] Especially where maps are ordered by government (or are derived from such maps) it can be seen how they extend and reinforce the legal statutes, territorial imperatives, and values stemming from the exercise of political power. Yet to understand how power works through cartographic discourse and the effects of that power in society further dissection is needed. A simple model of domination and subversion is inadequate and I propose to draw a distinction between *external* and *internal* power in cartography. This ultimately derives from Foucault's ideas about power-knowledge, but this particular formulation is owed to Joseph Rouse's recent book on *Knowledge and Power,*[73] where a theory of the internal power of science is in turn based on his reading of Foucault.

The most familiar sense of power in cartography is that of power *external* to maps and mapping. This serves to link maps to the centers of political power. Power is exerted *on* cartography. Behind most cartographers there is a patron; in innumerable instances the makers of cartographic texts were responding to external needs. Power is also exercised *with* cartography. Monarchs, ministers, state institutions, the Church, have all initiated programs of mapping for their own ends. In modern Western society maps quickly became crucial to the maintenance of state power—to its boundaries, to its commerce, to its internal administration, to control of populations, and to its military strength. Mapping soon became the business of the state: cartography was early nationalized. The state guards its knowledge carefully: maps have been universally censored, kept secret, and falsified. In all these cases maps are linked to what Foucault called the exercise of "juridical power."[74] The map becomes a "juridical territory": it facilitates surveillance and control. Maps are still used to control our lives in innumerable ways. A mapless society, though we may take the map for granted, would now be politically unimaginable. All this is power *with* the help of maps. It is an external power, often centralized and exercised bureaucratically, imposed from above, and manifest in particular acts or phases of deliberate policy.

I come now to the important distinction. What is also central to the effects of maps in society is what may be defined as the power *internal* to cartography. The focus of inquiry therefore shifts from the place of cartography in a juridical system of power to the political effects of what cartographers do when they make maps. Cartographers manufacture power: they create a spatial panopticon. It is a power embedded in the map text. We can talk about the power of the map just as we already talk about the power of the word or about the book as a force for change. In this sense maps have politics.[75] It is a power that intersects and is embedded in knowledge. It is universal. Foucault writes of "the omnipresence of power: not because it has the privilege of consolidating everything under its invincible unity, but because it is produced from one moment to the next, at every point, or rather in every relation from one point to another. Power is everywhere; not because it embraces every-thing, but because it comes from everywhere."[76] Power comes from the map and it traverses the way maps are made. The key to this internal power is thus cartographic process. By this I mean the way maps are compiled and the categories of information selected; the way they are generalized, a set of rules for the abstraction of the landscape; the way the elements in the landscape are formed into hierarchies; and the way various rhetorical styles that also re-produce power are employed to represent the landscape. To catalog the world is to appropriate it,[77] so that all these technical processes represent acts of control over its image which extend beyond the professed uses of cartography. The world is disciplined. The world is normalized. We are prisoners in its spa-tial matrix. For cartography as much as other forms of knowledge, "All social action flows through boundaries determined by classification schemes."[78] An analogy is to what happens to data in the cartographer's workshop and what happens to people in the disciplinary institutions—prisons, schools, armies, factories—described by Foucault:[79] in both cases a process of normalization occurs. Or similarly, just as in factories we standardize our manufactured goods so in our cartographic workshops we standardize our images of the world. Just as in the laboratory we create formulaic understandings of the processes of the physical world so too, in the map, nature is reduced to a graphic formula.[80] The power of the map maker was not generally exercised over individuals but over the knowledge of the world made available to people in general. Yet this is not consciously done and it transcends the simple categories of "intended" and "unintended" altogether. I am not suggesting that power is deliberately or centrally exercised. It is a local knowledge which at the same time is universal. It usually passes unnoticed. The map is a silent arbiter of power.

What have been the effects of this "logic of the map" upon human con-sciousness, if I may adapt Marshall McLuhan's phrase ("logic of print")?[81] Like him I believe we have to consider for maps the effects of abstraction, uniformity, repeatability, and visuality in shaping mental structures and in imparting a sense of the places of the world. It is the disjunction between those senses of place and many alternative visions of what the world is, or what it might be, that has raised questions about the effect of cartography in society. Thus, Theodore Roszak writes, "The cartographers are talking about their maps and not landscapes. That is why what they say frequently becomes so paradoxical when translated into ordinary language. When they forget the difference between map and landscape—and when they permit or persuade us to forget that difference—all sorts of liabilities ensue."[82] One of these "liabilities" is that maps, by articulating the world in mass-produced and stereotyped images, express an embedded social vision. Consider, for example, the fact that the ordinary road atlas is among the best selling paperback books in the United States[83] and then try to gauge how this may have affected ordinary Americans' perception of their country. What sort of an image of America do these atlases promote? On the one hand, there is a patina of gross simplicity. Once off the interstate highways the landscape dissolves into a generic world of bare essentials that invites no exploration. Context is stripped away and place is no longer important. On the other hand, the maps reveal the ambivalence of all stereotypes. Their silences are also inscribed on the page: where, on the page, is the variety of nature, where is the history of the landscape, and where is the space-time of human experience in such anonymized maps?[84]

The question has now become: do such empty images have their consequences in the way we think about the world? Because all the world is designed to look the same, is it easier to act upon it without realizing the social effects? It is in the posing of such questions that the strategies of Derrida and Foucault appear to clash. For Derrida, if meaning is undecidable so must be, *pari passu,* the measurement of the force of the map as a discourse of symbolic action. In ending, I prefer to align myself with Foucault in seeing all knowledge[85]—and hence cartography—as thoroughly enmeshed with the larger battles which constitute our world. Maps are not external to these struggles to alter power relations. The history of map use suggests that this may be so and that maps embody specific forms of power and authority. Since the Renaissance they have changed the way in which power was exercised. In colonial North America, for example, it was easy for Europeans to draw lines across the territories of Indian nations without sensing the reality of their political identity.[86] The map allowed them to say, "This is mine; these are the boundaries."[87] Similarly, in innumerable wars since the sixteenth century it has been equally easy for the generals to fight battles with colored pins and dividers rather than sensing the slaughter of the battlefield.[88] Or again, in our own society, it is still easy for bureaucrats, developers, and "planners" to operate on the bodies of unique places without measuring the social dislocations of "progress." While the map is never the reality, in such ways it helps to create a different reality. Once embedded in the published text the lines on the map acquire an authority that may be hard to dislodge. Maps are authoritarian images. Without our being aware of it maps can reinforce and legitimate the status quo. Sometimes agents of change, they can equally become conservative documents. But in either case the map is never neutral. Where it seems to be neutral it is the sly "rhetoric of neutrality"[89] that is trying to persuade us.

Conclusion

The interpretive act of deconstructing the map can serve three functions in a broad enquiry into the history of cartography. First, it allows us to challenge the epistemological myth (created by cartographers) of the cumulative progress of an objective science always producing better delineations of reality. Second, deconstructionist argument allows us to redefine the historical importance of maps. Rather than invalidating their study, it is enhanced by adding different nuances to our understanding of the power of cartographic representation as a way of building order into our world. If we can accept intertextuality then we can start to read our maps for alternative and sometimes competing discourses. Third, a deconstructive turn of mind may allow map history to take a fuller place in the interdisciplinary study of text and knowledge. Intellectual strategies such as those of discourse in the Foucauldian sense, the Derridian notion of metaphor and rhetoric as inherent to scientific discourse, and the pervading concept of power-knowledge are shared by many subjects. As ways of looking at maps they are equally enriching. They are neither inimical to hermeneutic enquiry nor antihistorical in their thrust. By dismantling we build. The possibilities of discovering meaning in maps and of tracing the social mechanisms of cartographic change are enlarged. Postmodernism offers a challenge to read maps in ways that could reciprocally enrich the reading of other texts.

CHAPTER SIX

New England Cartography and the Native Americans

This chapter originally appeared in Emerson W. Baker, Edwin A. Churchill, Richard S. D'Abate, Kristine L. Jones, Victor A. Konrad and Harald E. L. Prins, eds., *American Beginnings: Exploration, Culture, and Cartography in the Land of Norumbega* (Lincoln: University of Nebraska Press, 1994), 287–313.

ictims of a Map is the title of a book of poems by the Palestine poet Mahmud Darwish and others.[1] Like the modern tragedy of the dispossessed Palestinian people, the much older tragedy in American history saw the map as an instrument through which power was exercised to destroy an indigenous society. The maps of seventeenth-century New England provide a text for studying the territorial processes by which the Indians were progressively edged off the land. This was not achieved without resistance on the part of the Indians, nor was it a simple process. I do not suggest that maps were the prime movers in the events of territorial appropriation and ethnic alienation. However, as a classic form of power-knowledge, maps occupy a crucial place—in both a psychological and a practical sense—among the colonial discourses that had such tragic consequences for the native Americans. By trying to view the place of maps in the encounter and their role as they impinged on Indian affairs, one can add a different dimension to cartographic history.

Hidden Geographies

One of the ironies of the exclusion of the Indians from the map is that the Indians undoubtedly played a significant part in the construction of the first maps by the English of their North American colonies. In a recent essay, James Axtell posed the question, "What would colonial America have been like without the Indians?"[2] What, in particular, would have been the direction of discovery and exploration without Indian guides to the New World? Extending these questions, we can speculate on how the seventeenth-century English maps of America might have looked had the navigators and explorers arrived in an empty land. Beyond the narrow strip of coastal settlement, the details on the maps would undoubtedly have been much sparser. Without Indian contributions to the cartography of the interior, a map of continental scale would have unrolled far more slowly in front of European eyes.

The recognition that early maps are an epitome of the encounter—a set of reciprocal relationships between Native American and European peoples—rather than a chapter in "discovery" history is relatively new. As recently as

1981, the mapping of the New England region was seen as characterized by "an almost complete lack of a cartographic or abstract literacy in Algonquian culture."[3] Today such an opinion may be compared with the following perspective:

> Early colonizers . . . found native North Americans to be proficient cartographers whose geographical knowledge greatly expedited the first European explorations of the region. For a century and a half, information imparted by means of ephemeral maps scratched in the sand or in the cold ashes of an abandoned campfire, sketched with charcoal on bark, or painted on deerskin was incorporated directly into French and English maps, usually enhancing their accuracy.[4]

The cultivation of such an ethnocartographic history involves two initial steps. The first is to accept the existence of an indigenous cartography in many American cultures from the time of Columbus onward. The second is to try to reconstruct the Indian contribution to the "European" maps of the New World. From these steps, we learn that the Indian contribution was a major one.

The fullest evidence of an indigenous cartography as a significant form of local knowledge is found in Middle America. Screen folds and other artifacts, usually manuscripts painted on animal skins, contain major cartographic elements.[5] Elsewhere, in eastern North America, for instance, though there are far fewer artifacts, the notion of a "complete lack of a cartographic . . . literacy" is hardly born out by the record. Gregory Waselkov points out that in the early seventeenth century, the Powhatan Algonquians "spontaneously produced maps on at least three occasions." These ranged "in scope from a simple one showing the course of the James River to an ambitious map depicting their place at the center of a flat world, with England represented by a pile of sticks near the edge" (see figure 27).[6] Clearly, some if not all the American Indians could draw maps at the time of their first contact with the English.

There is much evidence that geographical knowledge flowed from Indian guides and informants to Europeans and subsequently was incorporated into surviving manuscript or printed maps. Indeed, it may be said that most European maps showing the Americas, from that of Juan de la Cosa (ca. 1500) onward, disguise a hidden stratum of Indian geographical knowledge. During much of the English and French exploration of the coast of North America, the presence of Indian guides—who sometimes made maps—was a matter of

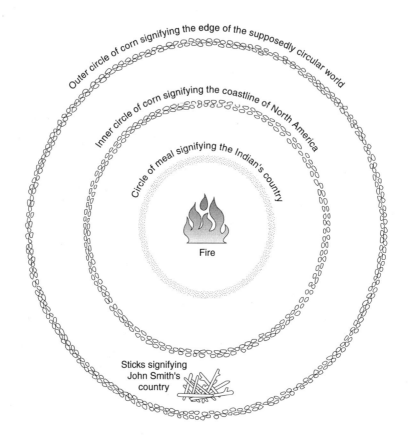

Figure 27. A reconstruction of a model of the world made on the ground by Powhatan Indians in 1607. Drawn by Sandra Mather.

routine. In 1607, for example, John Smith noted that when he was some eighteen miles upstream from Jamestown, Virginia, he had met an Indian who offered to draw the James River "with his foote" and who eventually drew with pen and paper "the whole River from Chesseian [Chesapeake] bay to the end of it so far as passadg was for boates."[7] There can be no doubt that Smith's *Map of Virginia* (1612) was fleshed out by several such encounters. The readers of this map were specifically instructed to observe "that as far as you see the little Crosses on rivers, mountaines, or other places, have been discovered; the rest was had by information of the *Savages,* and are set downe according to

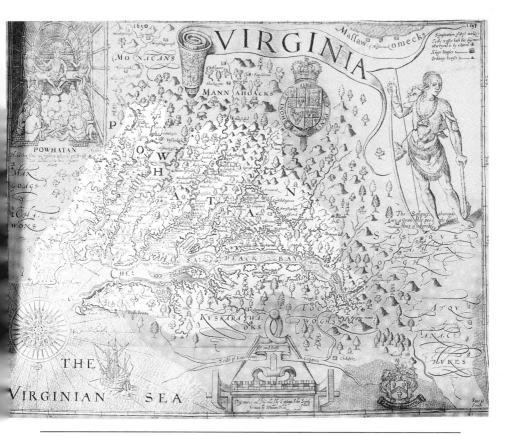

Figure 28. John Smith, *Map of Virginia,* 1612, with the area derived from Native American sources shaded. Courtesy of Osher Cartographic Collection, University of Southern Maine.

their instructions."[8] In the key of the map a small Maltese cross appears with the note, "To the crosses have bin discovered what beyond is by relation." If one shades these areas, the extent of the Indian contribution to this particular map becomes clear (figure 28). Indian geographical knowledge was also filtered into Smith's *Map of Virginia* through other, intermediate documents. On March 12, 1611, Spain's ambassador to England, Don Alonso de Velasco, sent a large manuscript map of northeastern North America to Spain. By comparing the details of the Chesapeake area on this map with Smith's Virginia map, we see that the two maps must have been drawn from a common prototype.[9] Moreover, a gloss on the Velasco map is explicit about its reliance on Indian sources. Of the details shown in the interior, we are told that "al the blue is done by the relations of the Indians,"[10] an admission similar to that of Smith.

Not all printed European maps are as well documented as these, but turning to Smith's map of New England of 1616 (figure 29), one can hardly doubt that it was similarly underpinned by Indian knowledge. Smith acknowledged that in ranging along the coast, in addition to his crew, "The main assistance next God, I had . . . was my acquaintance among the Salvages, especially with Dohannida, one of their greatest Lords, who had lived long in England."[11] One may assume, for example, that Indian names to identify places along the coast were supplied by these Indian guides, and the text of Smith's *Description of New England* points to this substratum of knowledge in the map that accompanied the book.[12] Nor was Smith a lone figure in making use of the Indians in this way. Along the New England coast, Bartholomew Gosnold is said to have benefited from a chalk drawing that the local Indians had prepared for him.[13] As he traveled along the coast of Maine and New Hampshire, Samuel de Champlain had Indians with him specifically to serve as guides, and he used their knowledge to compile a map of the coast. He wrote:

> After I had drawn for them with a charcoal the bay and the Island Cape, where we then were, they pictured for me with the same charcoal another bay which they represented as very large. Here they placed six pebbles at equal intervals, giving me thereby to understand that each one of these marks represented that number of chiefs and tribes. Next they represented within the said bay a river which we had passed, which is very long and has shoals.[14]

Champlain's vessel was off Cape Ann at that moment, and the Indians sketched Massachusetts Bay and the Merrimack River and positioned the villages of local Indians on their map by means of pebbles.[15] In yet other cases, Indians were kidnapped and sent back to England to be debriefed in depth about their geographical knowledge.[16] Such events all confirm the vital role of Indian sources of information in the early European mapping of the New England coast.

As the permanent settlements of the English expanded, Indian guides continued to convey geographical information—some of it in map form—from inland journeys.[17] Relating this contribution to individual European maps is a more difficult task, though traces of Indian geography have been identified in some seventeenth-century New England maps. For instance, Malcolm Lewis has suggested that such an influence—even an Indian map—

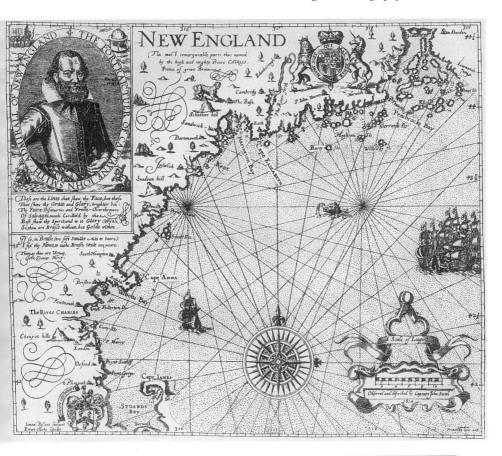

Figure 29. John Smith, *New England Observed,* 1616. Courtesy of Osher Cartographic Collection, University of Southern Maine.

can be detected beyond the limit of English settlement in John Foster's *A Map of New-England* (1677). Winnipesaukee Lake lends the giveaway clues of such a native source: the shape is artificially rounded; the islands are randomly scattered on its surface; and the lake is far too large in size in relation to everything else on the map (figure 30). Lewis concluded that the English compiler of the map or its prototype may have misunderstood information received from Indian sources.[18] Through such researches, the "intertextual" character of the "English" maps of New England in the seventeenth century— derived from both Indians and settlers—becomes abundantly clear.

Once we accept that Indians made significant contributions to these regional maps, we can also search for shadows of their knowledge in local maps.

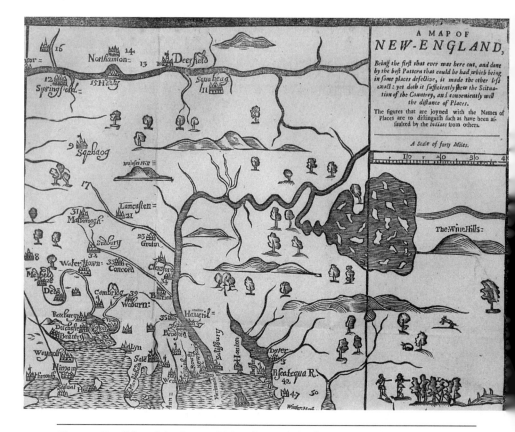

Figure 30. Detail from John Foster, *A Map of New-England*, 1677. Taken from an 1888 reprint. Courtesy of Osher Cartographic Collection, University of Southern Maine.

One such contribution was to maps of land claims and boundary disputes involving Indian territory. So it was with the map of "the Pequids, theire Country," drawn by an unknown draftsman in 1662 and showing part of Connecticut or Rhode Island.[19] As Peter Benes says, "While this is an English document, it shows a characteristic Indian reliance on place names rather than on measured points of reference."[20] Somewhat similar is the map (figure 31) by the Christianized Indian John Sassamon of Plymouth Colony, giving "the

FACING PAGE

Figure 31. Map and deed for land sold in 1666 by the Wampanoag sachem King Philip. The map was probably drawn by John Sassamon. In "Indian Deeds: Treasurer Accounts; Lists of Freemen." Courtesy of Plymouth County Commissioners. Photography courtesy of Plimoth Plantation, Plymouth, Massachusetts.

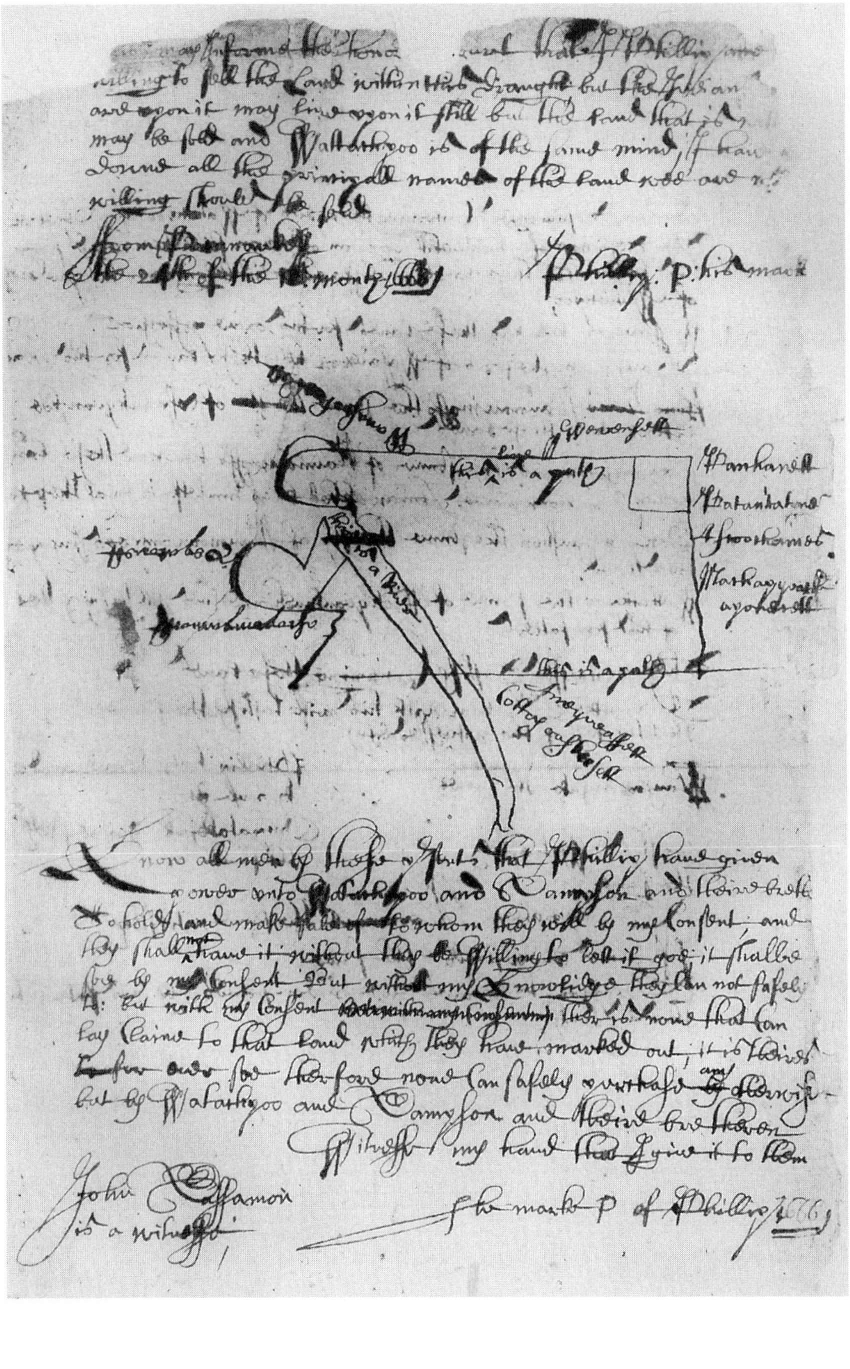

... may informe the hono[illegible] ... that Phillip are willing to sell the land within this draught but the Indians are upon it may live upon it still but the land that is may be sold and Watarhgoo is of the same mind. I have donne all the principall names of the land wee are not willing should be sold

from Pawmpmasset
the 24 of the 12 month 1665

Phillip P his mark

Know all men by these presents that Phillip have given unto Watarhgoo and Samson and their brethren to hold and make sale of to whom they will by my consent and they shall not have it without they be willing to let it goe, it shall be by my consent but without my knowledge they can not safely do it but with my consent [illegible] there is none that can lay claime to that land which they have marked out, it is theirs for ever so therefore none can safely purchase any of them but by Watarhgoo and Samson and their brethren

Witness my hand that I give it to them

John Sassamon is a witness

the mark P of Phillip 1666

prinsipall names of the land we are now willing should be sold" (1666). This maps also relied on the naming of ecological landmarks rather than on geometrical positions or the metes and bounds that had characterized English estate mapping from the beginning of colonization.[21]

It is appropriate to offer some preliminary generalizations about the cartographic encounter and its significance in the wider ideological and political struggle between Indians and whites for the territory of New England. Indian and European maps *were* different, just as their notions of space, territory, and function were often poles apart. As Gregory Waselkov explains, Indian maps often "contain considerable geographical detail," but "their main function was to portray social and political relationships." He continues:

> Such a shift in the mapmakers' perspective required a new set of conventions to represent their social world. . . . Social distance (based, for example, on the degree of kin relatedness between social groups) and political distance (the degree of cooperation between groups, or the extent of control over groups) could be effectively mapped, but only by replacing absolute measures of Euclidean distance with a flexible, topological view of space.[22]

It is thus not so much questions of "accuracy" from a European perspective but the historical consequences of such Indian maps that merit reflection. The fact that English settlers failed to appreciate the social geometry and the cosmological nuances of Indian cartography is suggested by their frequent "mistranslation" into European maps.[23] Equally significant, in a colonial society where English law and documentary formulas prevailed, the Indians' approach to mapping did not serve them well in resisting the colonial appropriation of their lands. In a European culture, where land was conveyed by precise measurement and with a fixing of position by latitude and longitude, the Indians' maps, as we shall see, put them at a technological disadvantage. Undoubtedly, some Indians grasped the different geometric principles of the English maps, but they lacked the resources in seventeenth-century New England to develop strategies of resistance by adapting European-type maps to their own ends.[24]

Eradicating Place-names

Place-names have always been implicated in the cultural identity of the people who occupy the land. Naming a place anew is a widely documented act of political possession in settlement history.[25] Equally, the taking away of a name is an act of dispossession. Meron Benvenisti, the historian and former deputy mayor of Jerusalem, has described the process of Hebraizing the names on the ordnance map of Eretz Israel. He wrote, "Like all immigrant societies, we attempted to erase all alien names." Benvenisti added, "The Hebrew map of Israel constitutes one stratum in my consciousness, underlaid by the stratum of the previous Arab map."[26] Or again, if we move back in time and north-westward across space, we reach the scene of Brian Friel's play *Translations,* set in nineteenth-century Ireland. The action is built around the British ordnance surveyors who are making their maps in the Gaelic West. We are told that the cartographer's task "is to take each of the Gaelic names—every hill, stream, rock, even every patch of ground which possessed its own distinctive Irish name—and Anglicize it, either by changing it into approximate English sound or by translating it into English words."[27] As we listen to local Irish people reacting to these changes—and despite the lack of historical realism in some aspects of the dialogue[28]—we can perhaps experience what it might feel like to be Irish, or Palestinian, or Algonquian and have to learn new names for places previously pronounced in a native tongue. It must be like being written out of history.

The disappearing stratum of ethnic consciousness embodied in the Indian names of Norumbega and those strata on the maps of Ireland and Israel have much in common. In a similar way, maps were important agents in the Anglicization of the toponymy of seventeenth-century New England.[29] They were a medium in a wider colonial discourse for redescribing topography in the language of the dominant society. Yet this was far from a simple process. Not all maps were equally influential, and the pace of adoption of new names varied with both the nature of English settlement and the linguistic geography of the associated Indian groups.[30] Anglicization got off to a slow start. The sixteenth-century voyages of exploration made on behalf of France and Spain, such as those of Giovanni da Verrazzano and Estevan Gomes, left relatively few traces in the regional toponymy of New England.[31] Only when we move from the age of imperial reconnaissance—when the search for a route to the Indies was paramount—to a phase of permanent colonial settlement does the process of renaming the land assume wider significance for the indigenous peoples of America.

In New England the founding document of European colonization, as well as of its modern cartographic and topynymic history, is John Smith's map of 1616. Like Smith's earlier map of Virginia, and Champlain's map of New France, its aim was to encourage permanent colonial settlement with a visible and highly symbolic image of the land to be occupied. In common with planting the flag or raising the cross, rituals of possession were enacted on innumerable occasions along the shores of America. Naming the land was one such baptismal rite for early European colonial societies in the New World. By choosing the name "New England" for the part of America that "hath formerly beene called Norumbega," Smith had in mind to promote English sovereignty in the face of Spanish, French, and Dutch claims in the same region. As he explained, "In this voyage I tooke the description of the coast as well by map as writing, and called it *New-England:* but malicious mindes amongst Sailers and others, drowned that name with the eccho of *Nusconcus, Canaday,* and *Penaquid;* till . . . our most gracious King *Charles,* then Prince of *Wales,* was pleased to confirme it by that title."[32]

New England was thus prominently placed on Smith's map, giving it additional authority and currency. Naming was possessing, at least in part possession. A few years later Sir William Alexander would name "New Scotlande" (Nova Scotia) on his *Mapp of New Englande* (1624).[33] Both men doubtless saw the promotional advantages of such toponymic rhetoric in seeking domestic backers for the new colonies, just as the names "New Netherlands," "New France," or "New Spain" made legible the colonial aspirations of those nations in the Americas.[34]

We know that Algonquian place-names had originally been collected by Smith during the exploration that resulted in his map. Such names were later published in his book,[35] but once back in England, the names on the draft map were subjected to an act of intellectual appropriation when the Indian names were struck from the map and replaced by English substitutes. In the older histories of New England this story is reduced to an antiquarian anecdote. It is also, however, an event of considerable ideological significance. Smith himself told how a fair drawing of the map was presented to "our most gracious King Charles, then Prince of Wales." Dismissing the Indians with contemptuous arrogance, Smith continued to address the king, "I heere present your Highness the description in a Map; my humble sute is, you would please to change their Barbarous names, for such English, as Posterity may say, Prince Charles was their Godfather."[36]

Transplanting England in the paper landscape was an easy game to play. The young prince named "Cape James" (Cape Cod) for his father; "Stuart's Bay" (Cape Cod Bay) after the reigning family; "Cape Elizabeth" for his sister; "Cape Anna" after his mother; and "The River Charles" for himself. Smith commemorated his own surname in the Isles of Shoals, which became "Smith Isles." Even the London printer James Reeve would later get into the act by naming a promontory on the Maine coastline "Point Reeves."[37]

Few of these royal inventions survived, but Smith's map became a paradigm for further Anglicization. The Massachusetts Bay Company set up a court that, among other things, decreed the name for each new township in the colony. By the date of the 1635 reissue of Smith's map (figure 32), a number of new English names—such as South Hampton on the New Hampshire coast and Salem, Charles towne, Water towne, Boston, Dorchester, and Medford— had been added to the copperplate.[38] As previously, this naming process was far more than merely an administrative or legal convenience. In New England as elsewhere, the maps were a means of ideological reproduction as well as practical tools in the history of English colonialism. A roll call of familiar place-names made the unbelievable seem more familiar, the unknown more knowable, and the wilderness less wild. For the English, the map becomes "a narrative of ethnogenesis,"[39] but for the Indians, the reverse was true. They became aliens in their own land. What we still have to tease out of the historical record is the nature of the Indian reaction to this obliteration of the language for their familiar topography. What were the social consequences of the destruction of names preserved through generations of an oral culture and of the redescription of an anciently settled landscape?

Once the process of New England settlement had begun, the record of toponymic colonialism became more complex. In the half century or so between Smith's map and the publication of John Foster's woodcut map in 1677, many more English names were created, and there also seems to have been a hardening of English attitudes, unconsciously or deliberately, toward recognizing an Indian geography in the landscape. Sometimes it was as if renaming was the final act of reprisal against Indian tribes who had tried to resist the English expansion in New England. Thus, after the Pequot massacre at Mystic Fort in May 1637, and after the final dispersal and destruction of the remaining members of the tribe, the very word *Pequot* was wiped from the map. The river of that name became the Thames, and the former Pequot

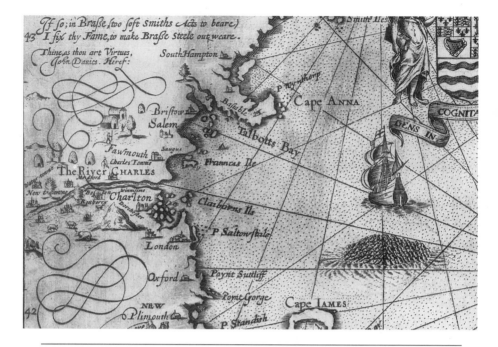

Figure 32. Detail from John Smith's map *New England Observed,* originally published in 1616, showing new English place-names. The version reproduced is from the 1635 edition of G. Mercator, *Historia Mundi,* courtesy of the National Archives of Canada (NMC 55020).

village became New London.[40] Even years after their successful persecution of the Pequot War, the United Colonies of New England passed a resolution disallowing the conquered Pequots to be a distinct people or "to retayne the name of Pequatts, or to settle in the Pequatt country."[41] A name could be a potentially dangerous symbol of survival as much as its elimination was public proof of conquest.

Within the main areas of English settlement, the practice of naming may appear more benign or "peaceful," but it was no less thorough in its removal of the traces of earlier Indian culture. Naming the micro features of the New England landscape was an uncoordinated process—part and parcel of the process of agricultural settlement—and it was probably taken for granted by the settlers. Characteristic are the names found on the detailed land surveys that were made of the area around Boston in the mid-seventeenth century. Sometimes simple English generic names were added to landscape features.[42] In other cases (just as with the Ordnance Survey and the Gaelic names of nineteenth-century Ireland), attempts were made to translate or transliterate Indian names. "Elsabeth River" is thus a corruption of the native "Assebet" to English spelling.[43] Yet in many cases, the Indian population was so sparse that the Algonquian roots of the names of settlements were effectively buried with their former inhabitants. A greater number of Indian names of physical features survive, but for purposes of settlement, their toponymy had been replaced by a distinctive regional category of New England place-names consisting of topographical terms such as *brook, hill, pond, river,* and *swamp.*[44]

Moreover, as William Cronon has noted, even the objectives of English and Indian naming of landscape features were different. Thus, the English "frequently created arbitrary place-names which either recalled localities in their homeland or gave a place the name of its owner," whereas the "Indians used ecological labels to describe how the land could be used."[45] Given such fundamental cultural differences, it is not surprising to discover that only one of all the names on Sassamon's map of Plymouth Colony can be identified on a modern map.[46] These may not have been deliberate acts of cultural genocide, but the fact remains that the land had been effectively redescribed in the vocabulary of the conquerors.

Place-name scholars tend to concentrate on linguistic aspects of the process of naming. Here, however, it is the ideological implications that are stressed. The use of English on the maps—names in an alien language—helped to create a further barrier between the Indians and the settlers. Even where attempts were made to record Indian place-names in maps, this was hardly an innocent expression of scholarly curiosity. As the anthropologist Johannes Fabian stated, "By putting regions on a map and native words on a list, explorers laid the first, and deepest, foundations for colonial power."[47] In French maps, in particular, the recording and mapping of tribal areas and settlements were calculated acts of commercial, political, and religious control.

In New England one reads another variation of this hidden agenda between the lines of William Wood's *New England's Prospect* (1634).[48] The book provides not only a short general glossary of "some of the Natives language" but also geographical lists of "the names of the *Indians* as they be divided into severall Countries," "the names of the noted Habitations," and "at what places be Rivers of note." Some of these names appear in the small map *The South part of New-England, as it is Planted this yeare, 1634* (figure 33), which was included as a frontispiece to the volume. In this map, partly based on Gover-

The South part of New-England, as it is Planted this yeare, 1639.

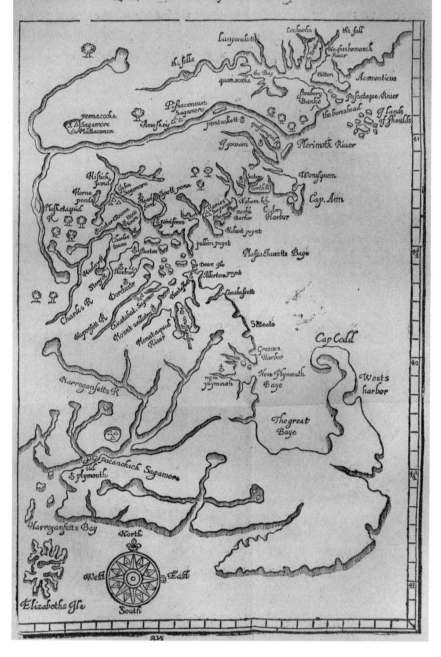

nor John Winthrop's manuscript map of the Bay Colony plantations of the previous year,[49] Indian and English villages are distinguished by different cartographic signs as well as by place-names. Indian settlements are depicted by small triangles for wigwams (sometimes palisaded) and the Puritans' places with a small circle surmounted by a cross. Thus paganism versus Christianity is inscribed in the coded language of the map, which empowers it with much more than simple locational or record value in the expansion of the frontier. The act of mapping can also be an act of apartheid. By making legible the idea of a separate existence, Wood's map, in its own way, helped, and still helps, perpetuate and legitimate the notion of inferiority and superiority. Once translated into John Eliot's fourteen "praying towns" of Massachusetts Bay, the notion became one of mutually exclusive patterns of occupation on the land.[50]

By 1677, the tendency to eradicate Indian geography had gone yet another stage further. This was the year of publication of William Hubbard's *The Present State of New-England, Being a Narrative of the Troubles with the Indians.*[51] The map that accompanied it—John Foster's woodcut *A Map of New-England*—reduces the Indian presence even further (figure 34). In the brief explanation associated with the title of the map, a new twist is given to the representation of place-names. We read that "the figures joyned with the Names of Places are to distinguish such as have been assaulted by the Indians" from others. Turning to the *Narrative* itself, we find "a Table shewing the Towns and Places which are inhabited by the English in New England: those that are marked with figures, as well as expressed by their names, are such as were assaulted by the Indians, during the late awful Revolutions of Providence."[52]

Linked to the map, and cross-referenced to the fuller account of events in the main text, the message is of "a litany of burned barns, slaughtered stock, and human massacre"[53] for which the Indians are solely responsible. It is not difficult to imagine the propaganda effects of this strident piece of cartographic rhetoric, much like a modern map of a war zone. Foster's map would have further hardened settlers' attitudes toward the Indians. The spotlight

FACING PAGE

Figure 33. William Wood, *The New South Part of New-England, as It Is Planted This Yeare, 1639,* in William Wood, *New England's Prospect,* 1639. This is a corrected state of this woodblock map, which was first issued in 1634. The 1634 edition was reproduced in the original version of this chapter. Courtesy of Osher Cartographic Collection, University of Southern Maine.

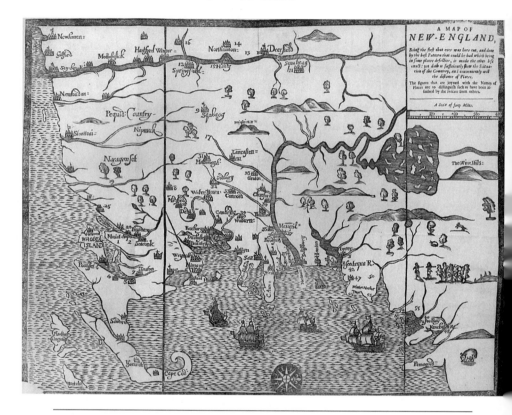

Figure 34. John Foster, *A Map of New-England*, 1677. Taken from an 1888 reprint. Courtesy of Osher Cartographic Collection, University of Southern Maine.

plays on the location of assaults. The map gives less emphasis to places that were not attacked, and the record is silent about the colonial violence of the Puritans. The selection of place-names is consciously partial. By declaration, it is a map of "Towns and Places which are inhabited by the English in New England." The scattered trees suggest an English parkland rather than a colonial semiwilderness. The Indian has been made even more marginal. In the heartland of Puritan civilization, the signs for towns and villages are exaggerated. Here there are no wigwams, only church spires, crosses, and the reassuring flag. It has been observed: "It is only across the Merrimack in Maine (from Pascataqua to Pemmaquid) and thus outside the colonial confederation of the Massachusetts Bay, Plymouth, and Connecticut . . . that the cartographer acknowledges the wilds. There the trees are larger, wild animals (rabbit, bear, wolf) evident, and Indians drawn in."[54]

The polemic of cartographic discourse should never surprise us. It is in the nature of all maps, including the "scientific" maps of our own day, to construct a world in the image of society rather than to hold a mirror to an "objective" reality. In Hubbard's map, one observes a religious iconography. The representation affirms the support of the Lord for the Puritan conquest of both the Indians and the wilderness they inhabit. New England can be identified with ancient Israel, and Hubbard's map is not dissimilar to the maps of the Holy Land in the Calvinist Bibles of the same period.[55] It is designed to illustrate, with a belief in literality essential to Puritan thought,[56] the events of a providential history. The maps' progress in plotting New England's geography is a pilgrim's progress,[57] for indeed to some it was the "New English Canaan" that was being represented.[58] The map is a *geographia sacra,* and the names are themselves the habitations of a chosen people. In an age when place-names are recognized as an aspect of cultural survival, and when more Indian names are beginning to be restored to the maps of North America,[59] it is worthwhile to explore some of the historical antecedents and consequences of their original disappearance.

Dividing the "Wilderness"

In Joseph Conrad's Victorian novel *The Heart of Darkness,* the character Marlowe says, "At that time there were many blank spaces on the earth, and when I saw one that looked particularly inviting on a map (but they all look that) I would put my finger on it and say, When I grow up I will go there."[60] The passage is often quoted as an example of how maps stir the geographical imagination. But it also demonstrates the map's double function in colonialism of both opening up and later closing a territory. Conrad's delight in the blank spaces on the map—like that of other writers[61]—is also a symptom of a deeply ingrained colonial mentality that was already entrenched in seventeenth-century New England. In this view the world is full of empty spaces that are ready for taking by Englishmen. America in particular was seen as the "vacant wilderness."[62] In early colonial New England, maps gave much unwitting psychological support to the idea of boundless available land awaiting occupation. The maps also fostered the image of a dehumanized geometrical space—a land without the encumbrance of the Indians—whose places could be controlled by coordinates of latitude and longitude. By the mid-seventeenth century, maps were becoming a necessary device for juridical control of territory. Now, America not only could be desired from afar but also—having been conquered—could be appropriated, bounded, and subdivided. It was as divorced a process as "remote sensing."

We can specifically trace a growing map consciousness among the leaders of the New England colonies. As early as 1641, the General Court of Massachusetts Bay Colony enacted a law requiring every new town within its jurisdiction to have its boundaries surveyed and recorded in a plan.[63] The authority of the map was thus added to the authority of legal treatises, written histories, and the sacred books in sanctioning the taking of the lands of the Indians. The map had become "an epiphenomenon of imperial control."[64]

Consider first the psychological impact of the blank spaces that fill so many of the early printed maps of New England. It could be said that cartographers helped to invent the American wilderness. Take an example chosen almost at random—A Map of New England, first published by Robert Morden and William Berry in 1676 (fig. 35).[65] Possibly published to cash in on the newsworthiness of the region just after King Philip's War ("King Philip's Countrey" is shown above the name "Plymouth Colony"), it contains two clearly different images of New England. One portrays a coastal area filled with the huddled villages and towns of the English settlement. The other, beyond and to the northwest, shows an empty map. The presence of America's native inhabitants is denied. The names of a few Indian groups are attached to the land, but "New England" is engraved in large letters forming a great arc over much of the territory. One can interpret this territorial void as a reflection of geographical ignorance or even of scientific probity on the part of the mapmaker, since he avoided including terrain details for which he had no information. But what about the *unintended* consequences of the representation of these vast uninhabited areas? What sort of message did the map send to colonial speculators? How were they received? How far was the map believed, and to what extent did it affect the individual or the group consciousness of the principal actors in England and America?

Answers to such questions must in part lie in the maps themselves. However, the maps have to be seen as part of a wider colonial discourse,[66] one that helped to render Indian peoples invisible in their own land. Cartographers contrived to promote a durable myth of an empty frontier.[67] Maps were yet another form of knowledge—a euphemism for the harshness of control—that

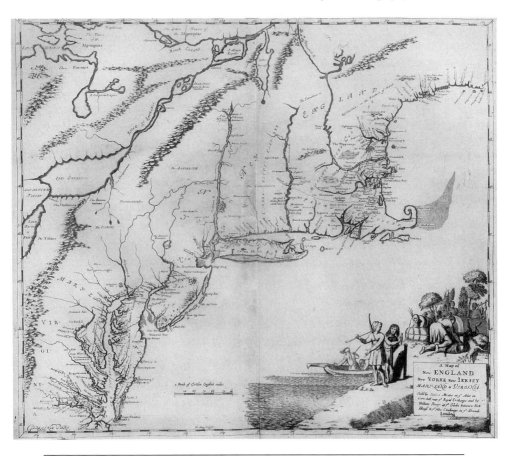

Figure 35. Robert Morden and William Berry, *A Map of New England,* 1676. Courtesy of the John Carter Brown Library at Brown University.

allowed the English conveniently to ignore the realities of the Indian societies that they encountered in the New World. They enabled Crown and colonists alike to brush aside evidence they may have had of a well-defined political organization among the northeastern Indians[68] and of a territorial integrity of the Indian nations, an integrity that the French were more willing than the English to accept in their maps.[69] Given the English maps of the period, it became more unlikely that the policymakers would accept, as Francis Jennings put it, that "Indians were as much tied to particular localities as were Europeans."[70] And even if some colonists understood—like Edward Winslow, who had noted in 1624 that every sachem in New England knew "how far the bounds and limits of his own countrey extendeth"[71]—this recognition was not translated into cartography. Maps were largely silent about the Indian territories. Had King Philip been able to see Foster's or Morden's maps of New England, his worst fears about the broken treaties and territorial encroachments of the English would have been confirmed.

Thus cartography and the legal code of New England went hand in hand in the process of exclusion. Both the law and the map were forms of colonial discourse that helped to push the Indian off the land or into the confinement of a reservation system that was already taking shape by the mid-seventeenth century.[72] Maps with their empty spaces can be, and were, read as graphic articulations of the widely held doctrine that colonial expansion was justified when it occurred in "empty" or "unoccupied" land. Sir Thomas More, in the incipient age of English colonialism in North America, had referred to the continent his Utopians colonized whenever their own island became overcrowded. "The natives there," he wrote, "have more land than they can use, so some of it lies fallow." He continued, "Utopians regard a war as just if it is waged to oust a people who refuse to allow vacant land to be used according to the very law of nature."[73] In a similar vein, in 1629, Governor Winthrop of Massachusetts had declared that most land in America "fell under the legal rubric of *vacuum domicilium* because the Indians had not 'subdued' it."[74] The maps would have lent him support, and they would have likewise confirmed the belief of John Cotton, who wrote, "In a vacant soyle, he that taketh possession of it, and bestoweth culture and husbandry upon it, his Right it is."[75] In the words of the title of Samuel Danforth's well-known sermon to the Massachusetts Bay Colony in 1670, the map becomes an icon of an "Errand into the Wilderness."[76] And although a scriptural metaphor was intended, the implications of John Flavel's "Proposition" for the Puritan settlement of lands held by the Indians is unmistakable. "*Husbandmen* divide and separate their lands from other mens, they have their Landmarks and Boundaries by which property is preserved. So are the People of God wonderfully separated, and distinguisht from the People of the earth. It is a special act of Grace, to be inclosed by God out of the Waste Howling Wilderness of the World."[77]

In this passage, the rights of the Puritan cultivator and encloser are given a divine authority greater than the Indian mode of occupation of the land. In the blank spaces of the map, European and Amerindian settlements are also "wonderfully separated."

But if maps were a reinforcing image of a virgin land, they were also the practical documents on which the subdivision and bounding of Indian territories would occur. Because the map was not the territory—and because it was an abstract geometrical space—this was usually an arbitrary process, with little reference to indigenous peoples.[78] In the nineteenth-century "scramble for Africa," native territories were carved up by European powers on maps. Likewise one can talk about an English "scramble" for early-seventeenth-century New England. The attitude of potential "proprietors" was cavalier in the extreme when it came to disposing of the land rights of Indian nations. "Sir Humphrey Gilbert carved (on paper) estates of millions of acres in the vicinity of Narragansett Bay which he had never seen and which, in all probability, had never been sighted by any Englishman."[79] An almost archetypal story of how colonial lands in New England were divided with the help of a map was related by John Smith. The Council for New England had decided in 1623 to procure "new Letters Patent from King James" so that territory could be allocated between a group of twenty prominent colonial speculators. The method adopted was to cut up Smith's map of New England into pieces so that lots could be drawn to divide a "tract of land from the North Sea to the South Sea."[80] Smith's testimony is independently confirmed in another document in which we are told that on 29 June 1623 there was presented to the king at Greenwich

> a plot of all the coasts and lands of New England, divided into twenty parts, each part containing two shares, and twenty lots containing the said double shares, made up in little bales of wax, and the names of twenty patentees by whom these lots were to be drawn. And for that the Lord Duke of Buckingham was then absent, his Majesty was graciously pleased to draw the first lot in his grace's behalf, which contained the eighth number or share. And the rest of the lots were drawn as follows.[81]

The king also drew for two other absent members. There were only eleven patentees present, who drew for themselves. Nine lots were drawn for absent members. In such a way, by means of a partly absentee lottery,[82] the Indian territories were redistributed to an elite in English society. A map of New England recording this process, and listing the names set down in the order they were drawn from the lottery, was published in 1624. It accompanied Sir William Alexander's *Encouragement to Colonies* (figure 36)[83] and shows the hypothetical territories running back from the coast like the long lots in a French township system.

What is revealing about this incident is the arbitrariness of the mode of division that was executed with the help of a map. As it happened, these arrangements were not implemented,[84] but in one form or another, such a process of bounding and dividing—fragmenting the Indian jurisdictions—was repeated at many different junctures and at scales ranging from the local to the regional in New England colonial history. The map was never far from the action. It is clear, for example, that the colonial patents and charters for the New England colonies were drafted with the help of maps. One could go further and say that they could not have been drafted in the form in which they survived had no maps been available. Maps do not accompany the charters, but these documents nevertheless define territory in a language of verbal cartography that is unmistakable and presupposes that maps were available to the Privy Council and law officers during the complicated legal process of obtaining a royal charter.[85] In the very first charter of Virginia (1606), for example, that from which the territory of New England would be carved, a demarcation in what was largely terra incognita had to be given in terms of latitude. This presumably was read from a map or globe: "that part of *America* commonly called Virginia . . . situate, lying, and being all along the Sea Coasts, between four and thirty Degrees of *Northerly* Latitude from the Equinoctial Line, and five and forty Degrees of the same Latitude, and in the main Land between the same four and thirty five and forty Degrees . . . or within one Hundred Miles of the Coast thereof."[86]

In this well-known passage, the map is being used to cast a sweeping net of control over a largely unknown land and its people. In the same charter, the Native Americans were already categorized as living "in Darkness and miserable Ignorance of the true Knowledge and Worship of God" and as "Infidels and Savages." This situation, as in Spanish America over a century earlier, became "just" cause, often sanctioned by ecclesiastical and international law, for the appropriation of Indian lands.[87] The Virginia charter went on to permit the establishment of two settlements within this abstract space. One would lie between thirty-four and forty-five degrees north and the other between thirty-eight and forty-five degrees north.[88] Each settlement—irrespective of Indian political organization or the nature of the land—had claims to resources fifty miles north and south and one hundred miles west.

As the maps became more detailed, the language of the characters became

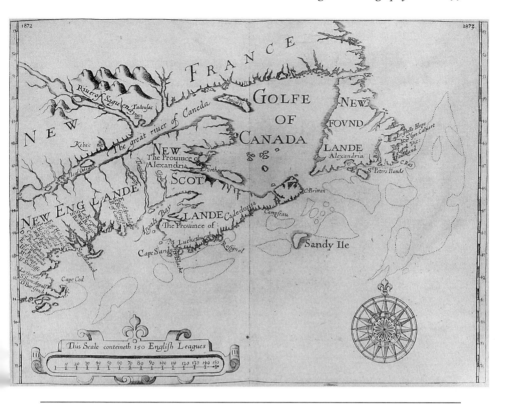

Figure 36. Sir William Alexander, *A Mapp of New Englande,* in Samuel Purchas, *Hacklytus Posthumus or Purchas His Pilgrimes,* 1625. Courtesy of Osher Cartographic Collection, University of Southern Maine.

geographically more explicit. The better the map, or the more exact the chain and the compass, the better the charters were as instruments of appropriation. Advances in cartography enabled the English settlers to begin to exclude the Indians more definitively from the land and from the resources of the colonial territories. The two Maine charters of 1622 and 1639 point to this process. In the grant to Sir Ferdinando Gorges and Captain John Mason of 1622, the patent was written in terms of latitudes.[89] However, in the grant of Maine by Charles I to Sir Ferdinando Gorges in 1639, it is as if the finger of a lawyer is verbalizing the boundaries of the colony as traced from the best map available to him. To quote only the opening of the passage, Gorges was to receive "all that part . . . of the mainland of New England . . . beginning at the entrance of Passcattaway Harbor and so to pass up the same into the river of Newichewanock, and through the same unto the farthest head thereof, and from there northwestwards till sixty miles be finished, and from Passcattaway Harbor aforesaid northeastwards along the sea coast to Sagadohock."[90]

This is the language of the map. It alone gives the charter its territorial structure. Such indirect evidence for the use of maps as the territorial authority for colonial expansion is reflected in many other New England sources.[91] As new patents were granted, as territories were annexed from the Netherlands and France, as disputes arose about the positioning of particular boundaries between individual colonies,[92] as the Office of Plantations in London sought to impose stronger central control over the American colonies—for example, the proposal to create a "Dominion of New England"[93]—and as land treaties became a way of acquiring Indian tribal lands, maps came to be increasingly used.

Nor was the scale of cartographic influence confined only to the creation of the large political territories of New England. The same symbiosis between cartography and colonialism permeated the creation of local territories in seventeenth-century New England. Many charters of the individual colonies were worded in abstract fashion as if the tabula rasa of the map rather than the land was being divided, and once again, the boundaries had the effect of excluding the Indians while incorporating the English settlers. The power of boundary making, conferring almost feudal power within a Euclidean cage, was comprehensive. Turning again to the grant for the province of Maine in 1639, Sir Ferdinando Gorges was given

> full power and authority to divide all or any part of the territories hereby granted . . . into provinces, counties, cities, towns, hundreds, and parishes, or such other parts of portions as he . . . shall think fit, and in them . . . to appoint and allot out such portions of land for public uses, ecclesiastical and temporal, of what kind soever and to distribute, grant, assign, and set over such particular portions of the said territories, counties, lands, and premises unto such our subjects or the subjects of any other state or prince then in amity with us.[94]

Reading the formulaic language of the charters, we can see that a role for maps is implicit in the mechanism for creating territorial hierarchies and settlements that would structure colonial society. The charters were as much a license for the map makers as they were for the landowners, the lawyers, and the politicians. In their Indian policies, all four groups were mapping the common ground of territorial expansion. By the end of the seventeenth century, when New England cartographic history was gathering momentum, maps were being made to describe all tiers of territory, from the individual estate to the colonies as a whole. Even at a local level, they often tended to stress boundaries rather than other features.[95] This is characteristic of a type of European colonial mapping that focused on private property but failed to make legible the usufructuary rights of conquered peoples. Such maps are more than an image of the landscapes of English colonization in New England. They are a discourse of the acquisition and dispossession that lie at the heart of colonialism.

Conclusion

Maps were surely a two-edged weapon in the colonial history of New England. Historiography has tended to look at cartography only from the point of view of the English Crown or settlers, or as an image of the roots of the Anglo-American experience. Indeed, for the colonists, the filling-in of the map was a potent emblem for their own presence on the land. They may have started to appreciate how maps assisted their endeavors in both practical and psychological ways. They would have recognized that maps had become tools of boundary making, of charter framing, of settlement planning, and of strategic value in the war of attrition against the Indians. Not least, and more subtlely, a few would have come to see how maps were the best testimony for the exclusion of the Indians from the territories of New England and how maps were a mirror to God's providence. Documents that enabled the settlers to think territorially were bound to become an integral part of the whole colonial agenda.

But is it also possible to look at New England cartographic history from the Indian point of view? Here the historiography is full of holes. There is no sustained ethnohistorical perspective on maps; one has to read for a geography of absences. It is not known how many Indians saw and understood the English maps of the seventeenth century or how those who saw reacted to the obliteration of their own geography. But at least one can begin to imagine what it was like to be on the wrong side of the map, to see the English place-names advancing across the map, or to feel the sharpness of the boundary as it cut through the ancient territory of an Indian nation. It remains to be seen whether scholars can write a cartographic history that will accommodate both a European and an Indian perspective on the American past.

CHAPTER SEVEN

Can There Be a Cartographic Ethics?

This chapter originally appeared in *Cartographic Perspectives* 10 (summer 1991): 9–16.

In time you may discover all there is to discover—but your progress will only be progress away from mankind. The gulf between you and the people will become so great that one day you will cry out in jubilation over a new achievement—and be greeted by a cry of universal horror. —BERTHOLT BRECHT, *The Life of Galileo*, 1980

*I*n an event little reported in the media during the recent Iraq war, a demonstration was held outside the U.S. Defense Mapping Agency in St. Louis. It concerned the crucial role of maps in our ability to wage modern warfare: official estimates stated that by 2 January 1991 some 35 million maps had been shipped to some 300,000 U.S. troops stationed in the Persian Gulf area.[1] Whatever our views about the morality of war, the incident serves to remind us that the making of maps can raise profound ethical issues. In my case, it led me to reflect on the apparent lack of ethical discussion in the professional literature of cartography. Search long among the key words of periodical articles or books and "ethics" is usually missing. This means that in its failure to engage in a full and frank debate about ethics, cartography is out-of-step with other academic disciplines and professions. On the contrary, the discipline could be accused of complacency. Cartography seems to be uncritical of its own practices, and both their intentional and unintentional consequences. It certainly lacks a substantial literature in applied ethics comparable to that generated by many of its peer professions in science and technology. There is no group in cartography comparable to, for example, "Computer Professionals for Social Responsibility," founded in 1984. And there are no or few features such as the "Legal and Ethical" case notes, now published in the ACSM [American Congress on Surveying and Mapping] *Bulletin,* in cartographic journals. In short, for many map makers ethics remains a gray area, lost somewhere in the abyss that separates logic from the swamp of subjective opinion.

All this surely has to change in the new few years. I am writing this essay in response to a pioneering "roundtable commentary" on "Ethical Problems in Cartography"—the first of its kind—published in the fall 1990 issue of *Car-*

tographic Perspectives.[2] Ethics was defined there as the "principles of conduct guiding the practices of an individual or professional group." Among the varied issues raised at the roundtable were some which may not immediately have struck all readers as obviously ethical problems. For instance, while the so-called "ethic" of being "precise, accurate, and exact" was plain enough, the moral aspects of the perennial copyright problem or the impact of new technology on the ability to maintain traditional standards and values raise finer points of definition. What, for a start, *are* the "traditional standards and values" and have they ever existed except as a social construction of cartographers? Or why should commercial cartographers feel threatened by copyright violations other than for reasons of profit which may or may not be an ethical question? Other issues considered are the claim that some aspects of cartographic practice—such as the design and choice of symbols—are ethically neutral, and that "the false impression" that is sometimes given "that cartography is a science, based on objective principles and criteria," is also ultimately a matter of ethics.

I did not find myself in agreement with all of the contributors and here I take issue with certain stated viewpoints. For example, the emphasis on the copyright question as a major ethical issue seems to be misplaced. The old English rhyme tells us

> The law locks up both man and woman
> Who steals the goose from off the common
> But lets the greater felon loose
> Who steals the common from the goose[3]

I suggest that the individual who "steals" the information on a copyrighted map may be stealing the goose, but the greater moral dilemma is that the map, when it fails to be anything less than a socially responsible representation of the world, is being stolen from everyone. This is to put the issue rather starkly but I feel *strongly* that some different questions should be squarely posed. Can there be an ethically informed cartography and what should be its agenda? How can we go about formulating principles and rules that would allow us to arbitrate moral judgments in particular cartographic circumstances? Can we debate cartographic ethics in the narrow arena of internal practice, looking for a pragmatic code of professional conduct, or should we be concerned with transcendental values that go to the heart of social justice in the world at large? Rather than engage in generalities at this stage, I confine myself here to addressing these three questions, taking the last first.

THE DEBATE opened in *Cartographic Perspectives* is based, in my view, on a fundamental fallacy. This is the "cartographers know best" fallacy, the notion that over the years cartographic practice and experience has resulted in normative rules and principles that are, because a consensus exists about their value, in themselves ethical. If they are widely accepted, and so long as they are followed, the profession is "clean," and there will be no need to ask questions in an ethical context such as "What kind of map is good?" or "What sort of cartography is just?" Michael Dobson produces an argument that enshrines this fallacy. He writes "in my opinion . . . most of the substandard cartographic products [substandard here is equated with unethical] are the result of individuals who have not been properly trained and not the work of individuals who are consciously trying to mislead their audience."[4] However, such a premise, far from addressing fundamental ethical questions, bypasses them entirely. Questions about the rightness of technical practice are being confused with questions about the rightness of the social consequences of map making. While there may be moral aspects to both cases, I would argue that it is the ethics of the latter that should be addressed rather than value judgments concerning the permissibility or impermissibility of this or that technical practice. For instance, in every map made by a professional cartographer, some sort of judgment has to be made as to how to represent the world. Yet cartographers, though they are fully aware how maps *must* distort reality, often engage in double-speak when defending their subject. We are told about the "paradox" in which "an accurate map," to "present a useful and truthful picture," must "tell white lies."[5] Even leaving aside the element of special pleading in this statement (the map can be "truthful" and "accurate" even when it is lying), there is the corollary that cartographers instinctively attribute the worst forms of "ignorance," "blunders," and "distortions," and so on to noncartographers. For instance, when they come to talk about propaganda maps or the cartographic distortions presented by the popular media, a quite different order of moral debate is entered into. The *cause célèbre* of the Peters projection led to an outburst of polemical righteousness in defense of "professional standards." But ethics demand honesty. The real issue in the Peters case is power: there is no doubt that Peters's agenda was the empowerment of those nations of the world he felt had suffered a historic cartographic discrimination. But equally, for the cartographers, it was their power and "truth claims" that were at stake. We can see them, in a phenomenon well known to sociologists of science, scrambling to close ranks to defend their established ways of representing the world. They are still closing ranks. I was invited to publish a version of this paper in the ACSM *Bulletin.* After submission, I was informed by the editor that my remarks about the Peters projection were at variance with an official ACSM pronouncement on the subject and that it had been decided not to publish my essay! Cartography will be unable to engage in an ethical debate while it continues to appeal only to its own internal standards yet is morally blind to issues in the world outside.

A similarly introspective technophilia is enshrined in the view that some aspects of cartography lie beyond the need for ethical consideration. In the roundtable discussion it is suggested in the context of cartographic education that

> The majority of information we impart to students . . . had little to do with ethics. Recommendations on what line widths or what lettering sizes are harmonious or discriminate from one another are perceptual and aesthetic issues, not ethical ones. Suggestions on title placement is a design issue, not an ethical one. Conventions on coloring a forested area green, or a water body blue are iconicity issues, not ethical ones.[6]

But is this really the case? It is well known—not the least in advertising—that every map represents a world-view in miniature and its design is fraught with potential ethical consequences. Aesthetics is not a value-free science and it is as much a prisoner of ideology as the empirical content of the map.[7] The way a word is written, the choice of name size, the selection of a color to represent an area, or the type of point symbol employed, are all part of the persuasive rhetoric of map making. They may wield considerable power over the way we understand the world. For example, the symbols designed to represent towns or villages on a map may privilege some settlements while discriminating against others. In a recent study of small-scale South African mapping we are told how policies of apartheid have "created dormitory Black townships adjacent to practically every White town in the country" and also a cartography that naturalizes this discrimination: "With the prevalent design approach used by cartographers, many of these Black settlements have been made invisible. This process of subjective generalization has been achieved subtly in recent years by mapping a selection of Black settlements for which the style of symbolization used to mark them is downgraded."[8] Here is a clear instance of where design and a moral judgment are inseparable. Though it is claimed that such maps were "more an act of negligence than a deliberate attempt to deceive,"[9] from an ideological standpoint the map supports the powerful against the disenfranchised and makes notions of white supremacy seem more legitimate.

It is the apparent ethical innocence of map design that can be so misleading. Mark Monmonier has reminded us about the "seductiveness of color" but he cannot blame it all on "misuse by cartographically illiterate commercial artists."[10] Thus, despite his assertion that "the blueness of the water might exist largely in the minds of wishful environmentalists, self-serving tourist operators, and gullible map readers,"[11] it is also a perception traditionally perpetuated by cartographers more than anyone else. So too is the decidedly Eurocentric convention that brown is the best color for terrain, contours, and land representation. It is a dubious logic that brown is assumed to be "the fundamental color of soil . . . evident in fresh tilled soil in spring," a statement that might apply to middle latitude humid forest and steppe-land soils but is untrue for much of the rest of the world.[12] Once it is accepted that certain conventions are "natural" or "normal," the danger is that they acquire a coercive and manipulative authority. The simplistic belief that "graphical excellence" and "graphical integrity" can be achieved by the application of hard-and-fast design rules[13] similarly lessens cartographers' maneuverability to portray the world ethically, that is to say, in ways that are sensitive to social needs. I am not advocating a form of design anarchy here, but merely suggesting that cartography runs the risk of being reduced to a series of graphic formulas detached from the consequences of representation.

With the development of new institutionalized technologies such as Geographical Information Systems and automated cartography the likelihood increases that this will occur. The drive for standardization becomes ever more crucial to allow interchange between systems and to reduce confusion over technology. With this in mind, the U.S. Geological Survey is developing a national cartographic data standard.[14] Yet is this entirely a step forward? It could result in a further narrowing of the ways in which the diversity of local landscape is mapped and it is saying, in effect, that there is only one way of showing a particular geographic feature despite any potential insensitivity to social and environmental issues in that form of representation.

"Method" has thus become a main criterion for truth; moreover, it becomes in itself a specific category of truth, that of "cartographic truth." Invented by cartographers, map "truth" runs the danger of becoming a knowledge available *only* to the technical specialists and this (as Einstein once put it) "is almost as bad for art as for the artists, or religion for the priests."[15] It is thus clear that the debate must be moved beyond a narrow internalist formulation of what is ethical in cartography. If we are truly concerned with the social consequences of what happens when we make a map, then we might also decide that cartography is too important to be left entirely to cartographers.

I FIND two fundamental issues in the second question: how can we go about formulating principles and rules that would support moral judgments in particular cartographic circumstances? The first concerns the philosophy of cartography; the second the content of maps. The basic philosophy of many cartographers, as Sona Andrews points out in the roundtable discussion, would probably be that they are "doing a science" that is correct, accurate, and objective.[16] I agree that this is a key ethical issue and, indeed, it is this positivism, fueled by recent technological developments, that is beckoning cartographers away from the very ethical issues now espoused by other professions. Even as the twin themes of innovation and technological revolution are loudly proclaimed (the latter with almost Maoist fervor),[17] so the social implications of the cartographic Prometheus unbound—such as increased surveillance of the individual—are largely overlooked. The tendency is to shrug off alternative views of the nature of maps, especially those that open up humanistic perspectives. The result is the sort of tunnel vision that must have led Duane Marble to remark of map projections, which he sees merely as a mathematical transformation, that "It escapes me how politics, etc, can enter into it."[18] With views like this, there will be no truly open debate until cartographers shed at least some of their notions of scientific essentialism. My argument is that this traditional philosophical foundation should be critically examined. Alternative views about the nature of maps need to be seriously evaluated. Could it be that what cartographers do, albeit unwittingly, is to transform by mapping the subject they seek to mirror so as to create not an image of reality, but a simulacrum that *redescribes* the world?[19] This alternative view of what a map is would allow us to embrace a much more open, self-critical, socially sensitive, politically street-wise approach to the practice of map making and the objectives of cartographic activity.

Thus even the apparently arcane ontological and epistemological questions must be part of the debate. They too raise issues of practical ethical concern. Our philosophy—our understanding of the nature of maps—is not merely a part of some abstract intellectual analysis but ultimately a major strand in the web of social relations by which cartographers project their values into the world.

Second, there is the content of maps. Not only how cartographers believe they represent the world, but even more what they emphasize and what they silence, and how features are classified and given hierarchy, adds up, in effect, to a moral statement. Each map is a manifesto for a set of beliefs about the world. In many unremarked instances a map may be an act of empowerment or of disenfranchisement in the construction of social relationships. Thus, the content of maps will increasingly become a moral dilemma for cartographers if they accept their responsibilities for reconstructing the world that the surveyor has deconstructed. Whether through choice or through the "advance" in technology we are increasingly witnessing the death of the map author, a situation in which the cartographer, in most cases, has ceased to be the initiator of the map.[20] This is largely related to what Patrick McHaffie defines as the organization of the cartographic labor process.[21] But it is also ironic that this loss of cartographic autonomy has been promoted by the cartographers' own narrowing of their field of operations, designed to enhance their image as an independent profession, but effectively confining their role to the design and generalization of *other* people's data. Apart from the fact that this undermines cartography's claim to be a science even in any normal understanding of that word, it embodies an ethical dimension. Maps, rather than resulting from primary observations of the world, are increasingly derived from secondary packages of predetermined information. Thus, when the data arrives in the cartographer's hands the map is already "pre-censored"; it is often too late to challenge its content from an ethical standpoint.

Such restrictions placed on what a map can show is a key ethical issue. If the moral contours of the shape of the world have already been drawn by others—usually those in positions of power—then the danger is that the cartographer is relegated to becoming a robotic arm of an institutional or commercial patron. Map makers have to ask themselves how, if they so desire, they can recapture control over the morality of the map, so that the cartographic author is able to exercise ethical judgment. Otherwise we may create a design masterpiece but it will merely be a projection of an unethical landscape in whose making we have no part and for whose social consequences we have abrogated responsibility.

FINALLY, an answer to the first question, "Can there be an ethically informed cartography, and, if so, what should be its agenda?" is more difficult to arrive at. As I hope I have made clear, from issues that are already surfacing, the answer to the first part is "yes." Where to go next is less clear. What cartographers most earnestly seek is probably not so much a theoretical as a practical ethics, a set of principles that can be used to clarify moral disagreements or conflicts with the goal of resolving them. It would certainly help, as a first step, to have more *documented* facts about ethical issues in cartography.[22] What are the motives and personal engagements of cartographers with the maps they make? What are the relationships between production and consumption in cartography and GIS? How do practices such as the limitation of access to official information (through the policies of secrecy or pricing it beyond the means of ordinary citizens),[23] the omission of toxic waste sites from USGS maps, the inclusion of pejorative ethnic names on maps,[24] or the Eurocentrism of many maps and atlases,[25] actually influence the way people think about and *act* upon social issues in a democracy? What are the moral benefits or deficits of particular ways of mapping the world? This should be the bottom line of the balance sheet of cartography, and the time may be overdue when such questions about the human consequences of making particular kinds of maps are researched in our graduate schools.

A second step would be to try to resolve underlying conceptual disagreements about the claims to truth of cartography. This would involve a reexamination of the nature of maps along the lines I have suggested. But, thirdly, there should be an effort to link cartographic ethics to wider social questions. What are the principles of social justice that ought to be endorsed by cartographers? Should maps merely be an inert mirror of majority values or can they play a wider role in the struggle for social improvement? Can there be a normative ethics or do we slide into a cozy relativism in which cartographic values vary with different societies, generations, social groups, or individuals?

Can any of us have a privileged claim to ethical truth or must we accept the idea that what might be a good map for one society, culture, or group might be harmful for another? Where such conflicts occur is there a principled way of judging between them if there are no transcendental or absolute moral values?

Cartographers have yet to grapple with these difficult questions. Many are likely to be resolved only at the level of social policy. Indeed, the final ethical question may be one of just how far cartographers of all shades of opinion are prepared to be politically active in altering the conditions under which they make maps. How much do they care about the world they portray? Institutional rules, regulations, and laws (such as those that govern federal or corporate cartographers) all have an ethical dimension that may clash with the individual conscience. Those who believe that the map is impartial and value-neutral may argue that cartographers—as befits a "scientific" profession—must remain neutral at every cost. Yet this reminds me of a remark made by the video-cult personality Max Headroom, who says "I only invent the bomb, I don't drop it."[26] We could paraphrase this for those cartographers who say "I only draw the map, I'm not responsible for how it's used or what it does."

For others, however, there is a different moral position. It involves accepting the linkage between knowledge and power. Only then will we agree with those who have already pointed out that cartography *is* politicized and it always has been:

> We will only be able to *think* clearly about our situation once this is recognized. We will not be able to make intelligent choices until, having accepted our political instrumentality, we fully debate our situation with this in mind. There will materialize Cartographers for Peace and Cartographers for a Strong Defense, but at least we will be through pretending that we are not completely involved.[27]

Being involved on matters of conscience is an important aspect not only of social responsibility but also of true professionalism. At a moment when global technology is weaving an ever more impenetrable curtain between the makers and users of maps this has become urgent:

> . . . we have to learn new standards of responsible conduct in our use of information technology; we need to reformulate what's right and what's wrong, especially in a world in which human and social relations, increasingly, are

endlessly reprogrammable, after the fashion of human/machine interfaces. Ethics is very much back on the agenda for intellectuals in a technology where efficiency and rationality are seen as presiding, without passion, over a regime of instrumental problem-solving.[28]

Can there be a cartographic ethics? It is doubtful if either more internal design "solutions," or the unfettered working of a free market in commercial cartography,[29] will result in the truly ethical map. Ethics cannot be divorced from questions of social justice. To do nothing would be to sanction a world closer to Bertholt Brecht's vision of the future than one in which morally responsible cartographers would choose to live.

Preface

1. Obituaries include the following: Paul Laxton, *Independent* (London), 27 December 1991, with an additional comment by Lionel M. Munby, 29 February 1992; Paul D. A. Harvey, *Guardian* (London), 28 December 1991; [William Ravenhill], *Times* (London), 30 December 1991; Alan R. H. Baker, *Daily Telegraph* (London), 7 January 1992; Richard Lawton, *Journal of Historical Geography* 18 (1992): 210–12; R. R. O[liver], "Brian Harley, 1932–1991: Historian of the Ordnance Survey—and Much Else," *Sheetlines* 33 (1992): 5; David Woodward, "John Brian Harley, 1932–1991," *Imago Mundi* 44 (1992): 120–25; William Ravenhill, "John Brian Harley, 1932–1991," *Transactions of the Institute of British Geographers*, n.s., 17 (1992): 363–69; Eila M. J. Campbell, *Geographical Journal* 158 (1992): 252–53; Ferjan Ormeling, "Brian Harley's Influence on Modern Cartography," *Cartographica* 29 (1992): 62–65; Matthew H. Edney, "J. B. Harley (1932–1991): Questioning Maps, Questioning Cartography, Questioning Cartographers," *Cartography and Geographic Information Systems* 19 (1992): 175–78; David Woodward with Paul Laxton, Tony Campbell, Helen Wallis, Roger Kain, and Ed Dahl, *Map Collector* 58 (1992): 40–41. There was also a brief notice in the *New York Times,* 27 December 1991, under the headline "Prof. John Brian Harley, Expert on History of Maps, Is Dead at 59." A symposium on "J. B. Harley and Cartographic Theory: Review and Commentary" was held at the 89th annual meeting of the Association of American Geographers in Atlanta, Georgia, in April 1993. Three speakers assessed aspects of Harley's scholarship: his theoretical writings (Matthew Edney), his "abiding interest in historical geography and in reading the landscape" (Anne Godlewska), and his interest in Ordnance Survey maps, which undermines the belief that he was a "technophobe" (David Woodward). Two other speakers applied Harley's ideas to mentalities in cartography: the debate over the Peters Projection (Jeremy Crampton) and a theoretical argument that maps cannot represent a reality (Denis Wood). I am grateful to Matthew Edney for supplying me with copies of the abstracts published in the conference program.

2. Harley formally submitted the proposal in late November 1991, three weeks before he died. Two chapters in the present volume were published posthumously.

3. A bibliography submitted by William Ravenhill to the *Transactions of the Institute of British Geographers* was abbreviated in publication (see note 1). Matthew Edney's bibliography corrects errors and omissions and contains all Harley's posthumous publications.

4. [W. R. Ravenhill and others], "A Celebration of the Life and Work of J. B. Harley 1932–1991" (privately circulated, 1992) contains brief appreciations from eleven colleagues at a meeting chaired by Professor Bill Ravenhill. A lunch was held to launch the J. B. Harley Fellowships in the History of Cartography, which continue to offer scholars assistance while they work in the London map collections. Harley's papers are in the Map Room of the British Library but still have to be processed before they can be made available to scholars.

5. This impression is confirmed by letters I sometimes receive, as his literary executor, from students preparing dissertations, asking for personal or other information about Brian Harley. Together with other personal correspondence and conversations, these requests suggest that his acquired status as a map guru is significant to young scholars. The publication of *Le pouvoir des cartes: Brian Harley et la cartographie* (Paris: Anthropos, 1995), edited by Peter Gould and Antoine Bailly, suggests a similar interest among French students.

6. A particularly unfortunate piece of hagiography appears in a "personality box" in a recent textbook for undergraduates, offering the authors' speculations about Harley's struggle for recognition against a hostile establishment: Daniel Dorling and David Fairbairn, *Mapping: Ways of Representing the World* (Harlow, Essex: Addison Wesley Longman, 1997), 74–75.

7. A book manuscript, "The Interpretation of Early Maps," was proposed (and indeed advertised by a publisher) in 1976, with Paul Laxton as the third author, but it did not materialize. John Andrews is the author of *A Paper Landscape: the Ordnance Survey in Nineteenth-Century Ireland* (Oxford: Oxford University Press, 1975).

8. J. H. Andrews, "Meaning, Knowledge, and Power in the Map Philosophy of J. B. Harley," *Trinity Papers in Geography* 6 (Dublin: Trinity College, 1994).

9. The misgivings were expressed in Andrews's review of J. B. Harley and Michael J. Blakemore's "Concepts in the History of Cartography," *Imago Mundi* 34 (1982): 99. They were stated more directly in private correspondence.

10. Harley was probably well aware of the risks he took in flirting with conspiracy theories. For an example of his posthumous adoption as patron saint, exposing cartographers as accomplices in repressive authoritarianism, see Peter J. Taylor, "Politics in Maps, Maps in Politics—a Tribute to Brian Harley," *Political Geography* 11 (1992): 127–29.

11. Although three of these seven papers have been posthumously republished (full details can be found in the bibliography), only one was republished in a modified

form: "Deconstructing the Map" in Trevor J. Barnes and James S. Duncan, eds., *Writing Worlds: Discourse, Text, and Metaphor in the Representation of Landscape* (London: Routledge, 1992), 231–47. In the modified version the epigraph and opening three paragraphs were rewritten and two minor changes were made later in the text; other editorial modifications did not alter the text. However, the substantial material in the notes was removed, and it is chiefly for that reason that the original version is republished in this volume.

In chapter 1 notes have been provided (none existed in the original version) and references to other essays in *From Sea Charts to Satellite Images* have been either removed or noted, as appropriate. In chapters 5 and 7, footnotes have ben renumbered because in each case note 1, accompanying the epigraph, is now redundant. In chapter 3 new numbers have been assigned to the last two notes to allow for the removal of a note marker erroneously inserted into the text.

12. After 1971, in works on English county maps and the history of the Ordnance Survey, Harley collaborated with twelve scholars, five of whom had been his students.

13. In addition, his substantial work as an editor across the field of historical geography ran in parallel with his research. Unhappily, no complete list of his published book reviews exists; they also reveal his ideas and priorities.

14. These comments owe a great deal to long conversations with Catherine Delano Smith, to whom I am very grateful. I am also grateful to Jeremy Crampton of George Mason University for the opportunity to argue with him about Harley's map philosophy. Like the rest of this preface, these comments represent a personal view. Matthew Edney, in a highly perceptive evaluation of Harley's period as a map philosopher and his multidisciplinary approach, sometimes gives the impression that his agenda was long-term and formalized. He *may* be right, but I doubt it. Matthew H. Edney, "J. B. Harley (1932–1991)."

15. I owe these comments on "The Map as Ideology" to drafts in the possession of Catherine Delano Smith and to her recollections of helping Brian Harley prepare them. The quotation marks around the word language reflect Harley's insistence that the term *language of cartography* is far more problematical than its common usage would suggest. Michael J. Blakemore and J. B. Harley, "Concepts in the History of Cartography: A Review and Perspective," *Cartographica* 17, no. 4 (1980) *Monograph* 26: 87–106. John Andrews (see note 5 of his introduction) suggests that while the word *ideology* survived in the title of his proposed "The Map as Ideology" (on the evidence of an early draft of "Maps, Knowledge, and Power"), Harley's enthusiasm for it waned in the late 1980s. An equally plausible explanation, however, is that editorial policy required "Maps, Knowledge, and Power" to be cut; much of the theoretical discussion was removed, and the paper was none the worse for it.

16. Harley's presentation, undertaken with initial reluctance, was to the Visual Documentation Group of the History Workshop Centre for Social History, founded by Raphael Samuel at Ruskin College in 1967. The outline of "The Map as Ideology"

was sent to Routledge and Kegan Paul in 1984, and most of the work was drafted in that year, the year in which he presented his published work to the University of Birmingham for the degree of D. Litt and the only year after 1960 in which he did not publish articles or books. A further draft with revised section titles was prepared by 1985, but I do not know how much more was written or revised after Harley's move to the University of Wisconsin-Milwaukee in 1986. By that time he was busy with many other projects, not least the *History of Cartography.*

17. This is from his comment written on the new outline and sent to Catherine Delano Smith in 1986.

18. Barbara Belyea, "Images of Power: Derrida/Foucault/Harley," *Cartographica* 29 (1992): 1–9. This piece was written before Harley's death but published after it.

19. The *Science Citation Index, Social Science Citation Index,* and *Arts and Humanities Citation Index* carry between them eighty-seven citations of his works from 1991 to mid-1998, excluding reviews of his books (see note 13 above) and Matthew Edney's tribute. Fifty-five of the citations refer to the works reproduced in this volume. "Maps, Knowledge, and Power," with seventy-two recorded journal citations since its publication, is by far Harley's most cited paper; it continues to be so.

20. Jeremy Black, *Maps and History. Constructing Images of the Past* (New Haven: Yale University Press, 1997).

21. To Andrews's comment one should, of course, add in parentheses, "at the time that he wrote it." The words "key texts Harley himself selected" may be a little misleading; after "Concepts in the History of Cartography" (1980) they were the only texts he could have offered without revising the unfinished typescript of "The Map as Ideology."

22. David Woodward, "A Devon Walk: The History of Cartography" in Ravenhill et al., *A Celebration,* 13.

Introduction

I am indebted to Edward Dahl, Richard Haworth, Paul Laxton, William Ravenhill, Eileen Russell, Catherine Delano Smith, and David Woodward for help in tracing Harley's writings; and to Gordon Herries Davies, Arnold Horner, Paul Laxton, William Ravenhill, Anngret Simms, Catherine Delano Smith, and Matthew Stout for valuable comments on earlier drafts of this essay.

1. Obituaries and assessments of Harley are listed in note 1 of the Preface to this volume. The papers that formed the symposium on "J. B. Harley and Cartographic Theory: Review and Commentary," held at the annual meeting of the Association of American Geographers in 1993, have not been used in the present work. Several of the obituaries include reminiscences of a personal nature, and perhaps another such

statement will be permitted here. Like many students of map history, I am indebted to Brian Harley for inspiration, friendly encouragement, and helpful discussion, including numerous exchanges of uninhibited comment on work in progress. Most of this correspondence took place during what might be called Harley's positivist period, but some of it related to his earlier philosophical typescripts. My remarks on the latter were on occasion strongly critical, in one instance eliciting the reply that Harley's "first reaction was to abandon the whole thing" (Harley to J. H. Andrews, 20 April 1982), but it was only after a disagreement over his definition of the word *map* (in a draft preface to what later appeared as J. B. Harley and David Woodward, eds., *The History of Cartography,* vol. 1 (Chicago: University of Chicago Press, 1987) that Harley seems to have decided that my views on such matters were now too unsympathetic for future comments to be helpful. However, it was not conflicts over questions of principle but the treatment of particular historical issues that caused me to start work on the present essay shortly before his death.

2. In 1979 Harley wrote privately about what he called "a little flush of enthusiasm" for philosophical matters, adding: "I imagine it will be very short-lived" (Harley to Andrews, 6 November 1979). A curriculum vitae of September 1980 anticipated this shift of interest in a statement that gave little hint of his later radicalism: "Most recently the main thrust of my work has been in trying to measure and isolate the influence of maps in fashioning attitudes and decisions in past societies." Among historical geographers the desire to find a deeper and broader theoretical context for scholarly research had been influential throughout the 1970s, and, in his quest for a further understanding of the place of maps in history, Harley acknowledged as his first inspiration the writings of Alan R. H. Baker (J. B. Harley, "The Map and the Development of the History of Cartography," in Harley and Woodward, eds., *History of Cartography,* 1:1). The works by Baker cited in Harley's previous publications are "Historical Geography: Understanding and Experiencing the Past," *Progress in Human Geography* 2 (1978): 495–504, and "Historical Geography: A New Beginning," *Progress in Human Geography* 3 (1979): 560–70.

3. This impression is confirmed by colleagues who remained in close touch with Harley until the end of his life. A hint to the same effect from private correspondence is: "You continue to chide me about Darwinian paradigms but that was a long time ago" (Harley to Andrews, 1 November 1988). The Darwinian or evolutionary view of map history had been criticized in M. J. Blakemore and J. B. Harley, "Concepts in the History of Cartography: A Review and a Perspective," *Cartographica,* 17, no. 4 (1980), Monograph 26: 17–23, and my brief defense of it in the context of Irish county history appeared, without chiding Harley or even mentioning him, seven years later (J. H. Andrews, "Landmarks in early Wexford Cartography," in Kevin Whelan, ed., *Wexford: History and Society* [Dublin: Geography Publications, 1987], 448). In fact, Harley's opposition to evolutionism seems hardly to have diminished (J. B. Harley,

"L'histoire de la cartographie comme discours," in "Dossier: La cartographie et ses methodes," edited by Christian Jacob and Hervé Théry, *Préfaces. Les Idées et les Sciences dans la Bibliographie de la France,* [1987–88], 5:74).

4. For Harley's alleged failure fully to assimilate the works of Foucault and Derrida, see Barbara Belyea, "Images of Power: Derrida/Foucault/Harley," *Cartographica* 29 (1992): 1–9.

5. See, however, J. B. Harley, "Maps, Knowledge, and Power," in Denis Cosgrove and Stephen Daniels, eds., *The Iconography of Landscape: Essays on the Symbolic Representation, Design, and Use of Past Environments,* Cambridge Studies in Historical Geography 9 (Cambridge: Cambridge University Press, 1988), 285–86. At some point in his career, Harley lost some of his enthusiasm for the term *ideology.* In a preliminary draft of "Maps, Knowledge, and Power" (kindly made available by Dr. Catherine Delano Smith) entitled "Early Maps as Ideology," this word and its derivatives appear at least eighty times. In the published version, more than seventy of these occurrences have been removed, without in any way altering the essay's general thrust. Similarly, Harley's essay on "Power and Legitimation in the English Geographical Atlases of the Eighteenth Century" (in John A. Wolter and Ronald E. Grim, eds., *Images of the World: The Atlas through History* [New York: McGraw-Hill, 1997], 161–204) was originally entitled "Society, Ideology, and the English Geographical Atlas in the Eighteenth Century" (Harley, "Maps, Knowledge, and Power," 309, n. 78). On the other hand, the title of Harley's proposed book, "The Map as Ideology," appears to have been left unchanged until the end.

6. The question of objectivity among pre-Harleian map historians is raised in "L'histoire de la cartographie," *passim.*

7. Harley, "The Map and the Development of the History of Cartography," 30–31.

8. J. B. Harley, "Deconstructing the Map," *Cartographica* 26, no. 2 (1989): 2. Republished with modifications in T. J. Barnes and J. S. Duncan, eds., *Writing Worlds: Discourse, Text, and Metaphor* (London: Routledge, 1992), 231–47. Most of the changes in the 1992 version were designed to remove Harley's argument from the context of map history to that of human geography. Unless otherwise stated, page references below are to the earlier version.

9. Richard Helgerson, "Dismantling to Build," in Edward H. Dahl, ed., "Responses to J. B. Harley's article 'Deconstructing the Map,' . . . ," *Cartographica* 26 (1989): 99–100.

10. Robert Baldwin, in Dahl, ed., "Responses," 90.

11. J. B. Harley, "Historical Geography and the Cartographic Illusion," *Journal of Historical Geography* 15 (1989): 84, 85, 86; Harley, "Deconstructing," 4; J. B. Harley, "Introduction: Texts and Contexts in the Interpretation of Early Maps," in David Buisseret, ed., *From Sea Charts to Satellite Images: Interpreting North American History through Maps* (Chicago: University of Chicago Press, 1990), 4. I have collected more

than 320 definitions of the word *map,* ranging in date from the mid-seventeenth century to the present day. None of them describes a map as objective, neutral, detached, or transparent, and the only occurrence of the term *mirror* is in a definition attributed by Harley to fellow cartographic specialists whom he does not name ("Introduction: Texts and Contexts," 3).

12. Harley, "Deconstructing," 1–2; J. B. Harley, "Cartography, Ethics, and Social Theory," *Cartographica* 27, no. 2 (1990): 7–10; J. B. Harley, "Can There Be a Cartographic Ethics?" *Cartographic Perspectives* 10 (1991): 9–16, *passim.* There are many references to ethical questions among the writings under review, but in a philosophical study of Harley's opinions this is not a subject that calls for extended comment. We can agree that in the course of map making it is possible for cartographers to act either rightly or wrongly, even though their profession (unlike, say, medicine, politics, or the law) can hardly be expected to receive much attention in a treatise on ethics. As for the notion of goodness, we can share Harley's approval of the question "What kind of map is good?" ("Can There Be an Ethics," 10) while noting that in "Concepts in the History of Cartography" (99) he had been reluctant to write of maps as "better" or "best" without putting these words in quotation marks (see note 96 below). His opinion that maps are not "value-free" is irrelevant to this issue: it refers to the expression of moral judgements, not to the possession of moral qualities.

13. Harley, "Historical Geography and the Cartographic Illusion," 83. See also Harley's statement that "there are a number of geographers who make their living by asserting that cartography and GIS deliver a positive knowledge that is value-neutral and culture-independent" ("The Culture of the Map in Western History," *Cartographica* 30, no. 1 [1993]: 107, abstract of a paper that has not been published and was perhaps never completed). Some references to particular map experts are given in "Deconstructing" (4–5), but they do not seem to justify the strength of Harley's language. His criticisms are largely concerned with the hostile response of professional cartographers to a now-famous map projection promoted by Arno Peters, but the so-called Peters phenomenon is untypical of cartographic literature in general and much of the hostility in question came from geographers rather than cartographers. For discussion and references, see Russell King, *Visions of the World and the Language of Maps,* Trinity Papers in Geography 1 (Dublin: Trinity College, 1990), 8–10.

14. Harley, "Maps, Knowledge, and Power," 278. Even in a purely graphic context, the term *Euclidean* is not particularly helpful. Lines on maps differ from Euclid's in possessing breadth as well as length, while the truths conveyed by maps are synthetic and not analytic like those of geometry.

15. Harley, "Introduction: Texts and Contexts," 4; also J. B. Harley, "What Happens When We've Made a Map," lecture, Penn State University, 1991, privately circulated, 2.

16. Harley, "Deconstructing," 1, 2: here and elsewhere, unless otherwise stated, emphasis is mine. The same strong view is expressed by G. N. G. Clarke: "Maps are

not so much objective and scaled equivalents of the land, as . . . visual texts which map the culture's image of the land" ("Taking Possession: The Cartouche as Cultural Text in Eighteenth-Century American Maps," *Word and Image* 4, no. 2 [1988]: 455).

17. "The history of cartography—and cartography—requires the syncretism of both positivist and deconstructionist strategies if it is to flourish" (Harley, "Cartography, Ethics, and Social Theory," 11). The word *supplement* is applied to this relationship in J. B. Harley, "Meaning and Ambiguity in Tudor Cartography," in Sarah Tyacke, ed., *English Map-Making 1500–1650, Historical Essays* (London: The British Library, 1983), 22, and in an unpublished statement the same paper is said to "supplement but not supersede in any way our more literal understanding of cartography" (Harley to Andrews, 25 March 1982). The stronger view appears in the conclusion that "we thus *move* the reading of maps *away* from the canons of traditional cartographical criticism" ("Maps, Knowledge, and Power," 278), and also in Harley's claim that a number of his papers "*subvert* the positivist model of cartography *replacing* it with one that is grounded in an iconological and semiotic theory of the nature of maps" (Harley to a private correspondent, 25 November 1991).

18. Harley, "Meaning and Ambiguity," 40; J. B. Harley, "The Iconology of Early Maps," in Carla C. Marzoli, ed., *Imago et Mensura Mundi: Atti del IX Congresso Internationazionale di Storia della Cartographia* (Rome: Instituto della Enciclopedia Italiana, 1985), 1:37; Harley, "Maps, Knowledge, and Power," 289; Harley, "Cartography, Ethics, and Social Theory," 1, 12.

19. Harley, "Maps, Knowledge, and Power," 278; Harley, "Deconstructing," 1; Harley, "What Happens," 2.

20. A. Kolacny, "Cartographic Information—a Fundamental Concept and Term in Modern Cartography," *Cartographic Journal* 6 (1969): 47–49. For a review of subsequent literature on the same subject, see C. Board, "The Development of Concepts of Cartographic Communication with Special Reference to the Role of Professor Ratajski," *International Yearbook of Cartography* 23 (1983), 19–29.

21. Blakemore and Harley, "Concepts in the History of Cartography," 36–37; Harley, "Cartography, Ethics, and Social Theory," 9.

22. Harley, "Introduction: Texts and Contexts," 4. Taken as a whole, this definition is rendered circular by incorporating the phrase "through the medium of cartography."

23. Crusoe's fleeting appearance in Blakemore and Harley's "Concepts in the History of Cartography" (102) is a response to my comments on an early draft of this paper (J. H. Andrews to J. B. Harley, 28 October 1980). The issue on that occasion, however, was whether maps could be conceived as acts of communication (including a cartographer's communication with himself), not whether map making necessarily implies the existence of one or more social groups.

24. Harley, "Cartography, Ethics, and Social Theory," 6.

25. Harley, "What Happens," 16. Perhaps Crusoe could also have invented the

clock (described by Harley in "Maps, Knowledge, and Power," 285, as "a graphic symbol of centralised political authority") and the calendar.

26. James A. Williamson, *The Voyages of the Cabots and the English Discovery of North America under Henry VII and Henry VIII* (London: Argonaut Press, 1929), 279. Another classic statement is R. A. Skelton's: "for every detail in an early map, its author must be assumed to have had some reason, which it is the business of the student to uncover" (*Looking at an Early Map* [Lawrence, Kansas: University of Kansas Libraries, 1965], 28). For a much earlier statement of the same principle, see William Martin, "The Interpretation of Maps of the Sixteenth and Seventeenth Centuries," *South Eastern Naturalist* (1910): 38–51.

27. J. B. Harley, "Uncultivated Fields in the History of British Cartography," *Cartographic Journal* 4 (1967): 9; J. B. Harley, "The Evaluation of Early Maps: Towards a Methodology," *Imago Mundi* 22 (1968): 68–70; J. B. Harley, *Maps for the Local Historian: A Guide to the British Sources* (London: National Council of Social Service for the Standing Conference for Local History, 1972), 5; J. B. Harley, "Ancient Maps Waiting to Be Read," *Geographical Magazine* 53, no. 5 (1981): 314. For similar statements by other authors from the same period, see Ferjan Ormeling, "Brian Harley's Influence on Modern Cartography," *Cartographica* 29 (1992): 62. The same theme reappears under a postpositivist umbrella in Harley's "Maps, Knowledge, and Power," 281.

28. Blakemore and Harley, "Concepts in the History of Cartography," 87–106; Harley, "Meaning and Ambiguity," 24–31; Harley, "Iconology of Early Maps," 30–34; Harley, "Introduction: Texts and Contexts," 11–13. The works cited by Harley are Erwin Panofsky, *Studies in Iconology: Humanistic Themes in the Art of the Renaissance* (Oxford: Oxford University Press, 1939) and Erwin Panofsky, *Meaning in the Visual Arts* (New York: Doubleday, 1955).

29. Harley, "Meaning and Ambiguity," 25.

30. J. H. Andrews, "Map and Language: A Metaphor Extended," *Cartographica* 27 (1990): 3–5. Other linguistic analogies in the present text are explained in the same paper.

31. J. B. Harley, "Secrecy and Silences: The Hidden Agenda of State Cartography in Early Modern Europe," *Imago Mundi* 40 (1988): 65; Harley, "Deconstructing," 13–14. Another version of this thesis is that European-designed symbols (e.g., for hills and trees) suppress the individuality of the American landscape, which could be better represented by putting the tree symbols closer together (J. B. Harley, "New England Cartography and the Native Americans," in Emerson W. Baker et al., eds., *American Beginnings: Exploration, Culture and Cartography in the Land of Norumbega* [Lincoln, Nebraska: University of Nebraska Press, 1994], 303; J. B. Harley, "Rereading the Maps of the Columbian Encounter," *Annals of the Association of American Geographers* 82 [1992]: 531). A contrary train of thought appeared in Harley's "Meaning and Ambigu-

ity," 25, where the standardizing function of primary symbols seems to be accepted as an advantage.

32. A peculiarity of statistical thematic maps is that the cartographer can sometimes exploit his freedom to choose class intervals by favoring patterns similar to those associated with possible explanatory variables, thus highlighting evidence for whatever causal theory he wishes to promote. This is no doubt why thematic maps have been described as essentially persuasive—a function noted briefly and without explanation in Denis Wood's review of Arthur H. Robinson's *Early Thematic Mapping in the History of Cartography* (Chicago: University of Chicago Press, 1982), *Cartographica* 20, no. 3 (1983): 111–12, and by Harley in "Historical Geography and the Cartographic Illusion," 86; J. B. Harley, "The Myth of the Great Divide," unpublished paper given to the 13th International Conference on the History of Cartography, Amsterdam, 1989, typescript, 21 (where thematic maps are said to "beg and cajole"); Harley, "Introduction: Texts and Contexts," 5; and Harley, "What Happens," 16. Not all thematic maps should count as persuasive in this sense, however. It can be confidently stated from personal experience that some are produced by authors who have not yet decided, and may never decide, which hypothesis they would like to prove. The belief attributed by Harley to certain cartographers that thematic maps are more objective than nonthematic maps ("Historical Geography and the Cartographic Illusion," 85, 86; "Cartography, Ethics, and Social Theory," 17) seems unconnected with the issue of persuasiveness: it probably rests on the fact that thematic maps usually record the whole of a distribution pattern as known to the compiler, whereas a nonthematic map may be deliberately—and subjectively—incomplete (Andrews, "Map and Language," 15–16).

33. Harley, "Cartography, Ethics, and Social Theory," 17. Not everyone will share Harley's opinion that thematic maps are harder to read than topographical maps.

34. This, it must be admitted, is no more than an impression: hints appear in "Secrecy and Silences," 65; "Deconstructing," 13–14; and "Can There Be an Ethics," 5.

35. Blakemore and Harley, "Concepts in the History of Cartography," 78. Harley makes the same point when writing without a coauthor in "Meaning and Ambiguity," 26, and "Introduction: Texts and Contexts," 12.

36. Harley, "Historical Geography and the Cartographic Illusion," 86; Harley, "Deconstructing," 10–11; Harley, "Introduction: Texts and Contexts," 5.

37. Harley, "Historical Geography and the Cartographic Illusion," 86; Harley, "Deconstructing," 11.

38. Harley, "Meaning and Ambiguity," 31.

39. *Monarchy* here replaces Harley's phrase "the royal image," which refers not to a meaning but to the carrier of meaning and which is therefore out of place in his list. His phrase "emblems for cosmographies and religious systems" is similarly incongruous.

40. Harley, "Meaning and Ambiguity," 31.

41. Harley, "Deconstructing," 8.

42. See, for example, J. B. Harley and Yolande O'Donoghue, *The Old Series Ordnance Survey Maps of England and Wales* (Lympne Castle, Kent: Harry Margary, 1975), 1:xviii.

43. In Harley's words, "meaning can be iconographically identified from a wider repertoire of images within a culture," ("Maps, Knowledge, and Power," 295).

44. Blakemore and Harley, "Concepts in the History of Cartography," 86.

45. Harley, "Meaning and Ambiguity," 29–30.

46. Harley, "Iconology," 37.

47. Harley, "Meaning and Ambiguity," 36. See also Blakemore and Harley, "Concepts in the History of Cartography," 81–85; Harley, "Maps, Knowledge, and Power," 297; Harley, "Deconstructing," 9. For another interpretation of decorative matter, namely as a boundary between metalanguage and object language, see Andrews, "Map and Language," 14.

48. Harley, "Cartography, Ethics, and Social Theory," 11.

49. This can be established by comparing the manuscript and printed versions of a map (see for example Coolie Verner, *Captain Collins' Coasting Pilot,* Map Collectors' Series 58 [1969], 8) and by noting the occurrence of different draftsmen's or engravers' signatures on different parts of the same sheet, a form of specialization well exemplified in Mary Sponberg Pedley, "The Map Trade in Paris, 1650–1825," *Imago Mundi* 33 (1981): 40.

50. Yet this is the map that Harley chooses to illustrate the idea of a total image ("Meaning and Ambiguity," 36).

51. For an example, see J. H. Andrews, "Henry Pratt, Surveyor of Kerry Estates," *Journal of the Kerry Archaeological and Historical Society* 13 (1980): 14–16.

52. J. H. Andrews, "The Earliest Map of Dublin," *Proceedings of the Royal Irish Academy* 83 C (1983): 223–37.

53. Examples are his discussions of the North Carolina state highway map ("Deconstructing," 9–10) and of a historical atlas of Canada ("Historical Geography and the Cartographic Illusion," 88).

54. Harley, "Deconstructing," 6. Harley apparently finds political significance not just in a cartographer's choice of projection but in "the use of cartographic grids to organise space" ("Maps, Knowledge, and Power," 308, n. 68). Unfortunately he does not develop this latter theme: the implication may be that people who put grids on their maps are likely to impose a similar pattern on a landscape already occupied by less geometrically minded inhabitants, as in the Roman practice of centuriation or the rectangular land system of the United States (Harley, "Power and Legitimation," 191).

55. Harley, "Deconstructing," 7. Elsewhere Harley argues that the omission of Irish cabins from "otherwise 'accurate' maps" reflected "the religious tensions and class relations in the Irish countryside" ("Maps, Knowledge, and Power," 290–92). If

accurate here means *complete*, as the word *otherwise* seems to suggest, then, in my experience, there were no such maps. An Irish map that showed all other landscape features would also have shown cabins. However, in lease maps, which were the commonest form of early Irish estate cartography, many landscape features (including cabins) were omitted because the rent of the survey area was fixed by competitive bidding per acre on the part of would-be tenants and not by quality. Where monetary value was relevant to the purpose of a survey, cabins were often omitted simply because they were too small and insubstantial to affect a surveyor's valuation. No doubt if cartographers had chosen to depict the smallest size of Irish dwelling, Harley would have interpreted their house-symbols ideologically—as the record of an exploitable labor force, for instance.

56. Harley writes as if Mercator's projection necessarily puts Europe in its center, but on this projection (as on all cylindrical and conical projections) any line of longitude can serve as the central meridian and any country can occupy a central position (Harley, "Maps, Knowledge, and Power," 290). See also Harley, "Deconstructing," but there the reference to Mercator (6) was omitted in the second version (236).

57. Harley, "Maps, Knowledge, and Power," 283, 287, 294–95; Harley, "Deconstructing," 11; Harley, "Can There Be an Ethics," 11–12. For Orwell's comment, see *Tribune*, 11 February 1944, reprinted in Sonia Orwell and Ian Angus, eds., *The Collected Essays, Journalism and Letters of George Orwell* (London: Penguin, 1970), 3:114. Orwell notes other tendentious uses of cartography and, unlike many map historians, even makes reference to projections. The use of red for British possessions was first recorded in 1831 and became common in the later nineteenth century (Geoff Armitage, *Daily Mail* (London), 7 July 1994). Orwell's statement about other countries appears to have met no direct response from cartographic historians, though there are some interesting general comments in King, *Visions of the World,* 13.

58. Harley, "Cartography, Ethics, and Social Theory," 2–4. This subject is complicated by the following passage in Harley's "Rereading" (530): "What . . . about those cases [in America] where the Indian names were retained by the conquerors and entered on a map? Surely these denote a cultural exchange and provide an index of Indian contribution to mapping? This might be true at one level. . . . Equally, however, it can be argued that the very adoption of native toponyms by the colonists was initially an act of appropriation and control." This seems a good example of Harley's heads-I-win-tails-you-lose style of argumentation.

59. Harley, "Maps, Knowledge, and Power," 299–300.

60. Harley, "Deconstructing," 10. No formal definition of the words *science* and *scientific* has been noticed in Harley's works.

61. G. N. G. Clarke also considers that undecorated maps symbolize something, though without making clear what this is: "Thus a 'plain' map, as it were, can be deceptive as to what it offers the eye. The iconography has, in one sense been

hidden—inscribed into the lines *of* the map—so absorbed that one is hardly aware of it. . . . The line here is the iconography; the word is the image. . . . The values which look on the land have wholly inscribed themselves into the look of the map. In these examples the cartouche *is* the map" (Clarke, "Taking Possession," 473–74; italics in original).

62. Harley, "Secrecy and Silences," 58. On this subject Harley acknowledges particularly Bernard P. Dauenhauer, *Silence: the Phenomenon and Its Ontological Significance* (Bloomington, Ind.: Indiana University Press, 1980) and Max Picard, *The World of Silence*, trans. Stanley Godman (Chicago: H. Regnery, 1952). The relation of silence to censorship needs clarifying. Censorship may mean (1) restricting the accessibility of a map, or (2) withholding or removing information from a map. It seems preferable to reserve the word *silence* for the second of these processes.

63. Harley, "Cartography, Ethics, and Social Theory," 14. This example makes it inconsistent for Harley to complain of apartheid when crosses are used for Christian but not pagan settlements (Harley, "New England Cartography," 301; Harley, "Power and Legitimation," 51–52; see also Harley, "Can There Be an Ethics," 1). In discussing archaeological monuments he does not mention Ormeling's suggestion that these might be omitted to protect them from "carto-literate" vandals (Ormeling, "Brian Harley's Influence," 2).

64. Harley, "Cartography, Ethics, and Social Theory," 5–6.

65. Harley, "Power and Legitimation," 34. On this point Harley seems to be at fault in a purely factual sense. "Activities of the county" were an accepted feature of marginal compositions (E. M. Rodger, *The Large Scale County Maps of England, 1596–1850*, 2d ed., [Oxford: Bodleian Library, 1972], ix), and even without access to a large map collection it is not hard to find twenty-odd human figures at work in the cartouches of eighteenth-century county maps.

66. "Saxton deserves a place beside Shakespeare as an interpreter of the national consciousness, unity and pride which were the greatest achievements of Elizabethan England" (Edward Lynam, *British Maps and Map-Makers* (London: William Collins, 1944), 20, quoted in Harley, "Meaning and Ambiguity," 36). See also Lynam's *The Mapmaker's Art: Essays on the History of Maps* (London: Batchworth Press, 1953), 91.

67. Harley, "Maps, Knowledge, and Power," 290. For the term *egocentric* in this context, see N. J. W. Thrower, *Maps and Man: an Examination of Cartography in Relation to Culture and Civilization* (Englewood Cliffs: Prentice-Hall, 1972), 15.

68. Harley, "Deconstructing," 10.

69. Harley, "Maps, Knowledge, and Power," 298–99.

70. Ibid., 299. This example is not quite conclusive: no territorial claim would necessarily be implied if Africans were shown with photographic realism engaged in suitably unrhetorical activities.

71. Ibid., 283–84.

72. Harley, "Power and Legitimation," 51–53.

73. Harley, "Maps, Knowledge, and Power," 292–94.

74. For an early example, see Thomas Hearne's comment of 1711 on a settlement ignored in Robert Morden's map of Bedfordshire: "This omission is unpardonable, because 'tis a high spire, and the church stands upon a hill" (*Remarks and Collections of Thomas Hearne*, 11 vols. [Oxford: Oxford Historical Society, 1888–1921], 3:145).

75. Harley, "Maps, Knowledge, and Power," 292.

76. For contemporary allegations of minuteness beyond any requirement of utility in early Ordnance Survey maps, see J. H. Andrews, *A Paper Landscape: The Ordnance Survey in Nineteenth-Century Ireland* (Oxford: Oxford University Press, 1975), 142.

77. Harley, "Secrecy and Silences," 70; Harley, "New England Cartography," 304–8; Harley, "Power and Legitimation," 51–52.

78. Harley, "Deconstructing," 14. Harley recognizes the existence of nonpolitical silences due to geographical ignorance, lack of data, error, limitations of scale, and "deliberate design," though in his own terms these might better have been described as blank spaces ("Secrecy and Silences," 57). We can accept the implication (at first sight self-contradictory) that in certain circumstances a design feature may be non-deliberate, but it is hard to understand the corollary that deliberation and politicality are in some way incompatible.

79. A widely circulated instance of this Harley-inspired propensity occurs in the BBC television series *Tales from the Map Room* (6 May 1993):

> All maps are the creation of their makers, each of them with their own truth to uncover, their axe to grind, their propaganda to peddle, and their fiction to realise. Maps bear all the appearance of truth, when in fact in a myriad of ways they're a tissue of lies. People nowadays tend to feel that maps are accurate, therefore they're true, but in fact this can't actually be so. However accurately you measure the earth's surface you can't put all that measurement on to the map.

Like the series itself, this comment is not credited to any particular author. For other statements of the same kind, see Mark Monmonier, *How to Lie with Maps* (Chicago: University of Chicago Press, 1991), 1, and J. Crampton, *Harley's Critical Cartography: In Search of a Language of Rhetoric* (Department of Geography, University of Portsmouth, Working Papers xxvi, 1993), 5.

80. For an example from Harley's work, see J. H. Andrews, "The Cartography of Celtic Placenames," *Ulster Local Studies* 14 (1992): 17–21, and "Notes for a Future Edition of Brian Friel's *Translations*," *Irish Review* 13 (1992–93): 93–106. The latter article is cited as "The Playwright as Historian" in Harley's "New England Cartography," 365, n. 28.

81. J. E. Cirlot, *A Dictionary of Symbols*, 2d ed., trans. Jack Sage (London: Routledge and Kegan Paul, 1971).

82. Harley, "Iconology," 37–38.

83. Harley, "Historical Geography and the Cartographic Illusion," 84. Later *truth* was described by Harley as "a harder word than I would choose to apply to any form of representation" ("Cartography, Ethics, and Social Theory," 11).

84. Harley, "Historical Geography and the Cartographic Illusion," 84, 86; Harley, "Deconstructing," 11. Elsewhere Harley grants propositional status to third-level messages by describing them as abstract truths ("Iconology," 29; J. B. Harley, "The Map as Ideology: Knowledge and Power in the History of Cartography," typescript, n.d., 9).

85. Harley, "Maps, Knowledge, and Power," 282, 294, 302–3; Harley, "Secrecy and Silences," 66; Harley, "Deconstructing," 7, 14; Harley, "Power and Legitimation," 28.

86. Harley, "Deconstructing," 9–10; Harley, "Introduction: Texts and Contexts," 13. Harley's analysis is based on that of Denis Wood and John Fels in "Designs on Signs: Myth and Meaning in Maps," *Cartographica* 23, no. 3 (1986): 54–103, but the phrase quoted seems to be his own.

87. Arthur H. Robinson, *Early Thematic Mapping in the History of Cartography* (Chicago: University of Chicago Press, 1982), 155–88. Good examples of anti–status-quo cartography are the distribution maps of public houses produced by Victorian temperance interests (Ralph Hyde, "Cartographers versus the Demon Drink," *Map Collector* 3 [1978]: 22–27). But here the counterinterpretation can itself be countered: a large unpublished map of Dublin's public houses, formerly in the National Library of Ireland, was generally accepted as an aid to serious drinking rather than as any kind of deterrent. This theme is addressed again below as "the cartography of protest."

88. Harley, "Secrecy and Silences," 70; Harley, "Deconstructing," 14; Harley, "New England Cartography," 307–8; J. B. Harley, *Maps and the Columbian Encounter: An Interpretive Guide to the Travelling Exhibition*, assisted by Ellen Hanlon and Mark Warhus (Milwaukee: The Golda Meir Library, University of Wisconsin-Milwaukee, 1990), 56, 89, 136; Harley, "Rereading," 531.

89. Harley, "Secrecy and Silences," 68; Harley, "Power and Legitimation," 50; Harley, "Rereading," 531.

90. A cartographic example of disharmony between style and third-level meaning is the unusually decorative script used by the left-wing English cartographer J. F. Horrabin to depict a world which he surely had no desire to "celebrate" (Angela Bithell, "The Maps and Diagrams of J. F. Horrabin," *Bulletin of the Society of University Cartographers* 18 [1984]: 85–91).

91. T. R. Nicholson, *Wheels on the Road: Maps of Britain for the Cyclist and Motorist 1870–1940* (Norwich: Geo Books, 1983), plates 7 and 9. G. N. G. Clarke adds "thickness of lines" as an ideological-cultural-political indicator, but this generally suggests importance rather than moral worth (Clarke, "Taking Possession," 455–56).

92. We know that Harley preferred topographic to thematic maps (Harley, "Cartography, Ethics, and Social Theory," 17–19), and we even know which topographic map-sheet he liked best (J. B. Harley, "My Favourite Map. The Map as Biography:

Thoughts on Ordnance Survey Map, Six-Inch Sheet Devonshire CIX, SE, Newton Abbot," *The Map Collector* 41 [1987]: 18–20).

93. Harley, "Power and Legitimation," 177.

94. Harley, "Maps, Knowledge, and Power," 277; Harley, "Secrecy and Silences," 58.

95. No doubt by modern methods terrain can be automatically surveyed and the results plotted, drawn, and printed without any human eye inspecting either the ground or the map and without any human mind entertaining any beliefs—without the term *knowledge* becoming applicable, in other words. Even with live cartographers and live readers, some features of a map may remain unknown: the exact number of building-blocks on a nineteenth-century one-inch Ordnance Survey map of Britain is not knowledge until someone has counted them.

96. For examples of this habit, see Harley, "Meaning and Ambiguity," 26; Harley, "Iconology," 32; J. B. Harley, "Innovation, Social Context and the History of Cartography: Review Article," *Cartographica* 24, no. 4 (1987): 60; "Maps, Knowledge, and Power," 301, n. 2; "Secrecy and Silences," 66; "Historical Geography and the Cartographic Illusion," 82, 83, 84; "Myth of the Great Divide," 17; "Deconstructing," 4, 5; "Cartography, Ethics, and Social Theory," 11, 12; "Can There Be an Ethics," 12; and "Map as Ideology," 8. Other straws in the same philosophical wind are the statement that without first-hand geographical experience "the map could become the only reality" ("Power and Legitimation," 192) and the phrase "cartography of reality," used in a context that seems to equate reality with feelings, percepts, and beliefs ("Concepts in the History of Cartography," 105; "Historical Geography and the Cartographic Illusion," 87).

97. Harley, "Deconstructing," 2. This sentence forms a jumping-off point for much of Crampton's cogent and persuasive analysis (*Harley's Critical Cartography*).

98. Harley, "Deconstructing," 13. Another example is the capacity of maps to help "fashion" geographical features (Harley, "Maps, Knowledge, and Power," 277). The whole tendency is well summarized in the title of one of Harley's last papers, "The Map Is the Territory: Cartography and the Frontier in Eighteenth-Century North America," Conference on "Re-examining America's Frontier Heritage," Shenandoah University, Winchester, Va., October 1991, typescript. The equation of map and territory also appears in Harley, "What Happens," 19, 20. It apparently derives from David Turnbull's *Maps Are Territories, Science Is an Atlas* (Chicago: University of Chicago Press, 1989). Turnbull reverses a proposition stated as a truism by Alfred Korzybski in *Science and Sanity: An Introduction to Non-Aristotelian Systems and General Semantics* (Lancaster, Pa.: International Non-Aristotelian Library Co., 1941).

99. Harley, "Deconstructing," 16, n. 10. Several critics point out that in the end Harley abjures the antirealism that they believe to be entailed by deconstruction (e.g., Belyea, "Images of Power," 4).

100. Harley, "Deconstructing," 13. (*Panopticon* was the term coined by Jeremy Bentham for a prison in which all the inmates are constantly visible to the staff from a central point.) See also Harley, "Maps, Knowledge, and Power," 279–80; Harley, "Cartography, Ethics, and Social Theory," 12; Harley, "Power and Legitimation," 162.

101. Harley, "Deconstructing," 12–13; Harley, "Power and Legitimation," especially 162–67. Harley derives this distinction from Joseph Rouse, *Knowledge and Power: Toward a Political Philosophy of Science* (Ithaca: Cornell University Press, 1987).

102. Harley, "Power and Legitimation," 165. The period in question is the eighteenth century.

103. Harley, "Can There Be an Ethics," 14. In pondering this "executive" concept of the map, we may remember Harley's earlier statement that "Maps, like other documents or material remains of the past, are passive objects" ("Evaluation of Early Maps," 74).

104. Harley, *Maps and the Columbian Encounter*, 99.

105. Harley, "Maps, Knowledge, and Power," 282.

106. Outside the present context, this danger is admittedly ignored in the terminology of certain measurable physical quantities like candlepower and horsepower, but nothing analogous to these measurements has yet been identified in cartography.

107. Harley, "What Happens," 12–15.

108. Harley quotes a verbal boundary delimitation from seventeenth-century North America. His gloss, "This is the language of the map," probably means no more than that the writer appears to have consulted a map ("New England Cartography," 311). This may well have been true of the case quoted, but quite complex verbal boundary definitions can be formulated without cartographic assistance (J. H. Andrews, *Plantation Acres: An Historical Study of the Irish Land Surveyor and His Maps* [Belfast: Ulster Historical Foundation, 1985], 8), unless of course it is argued that to perambulate a boundary itself constitutes making a map at a scale of one to one.

109. Roger J. P. Kain and Elizabeth Baigent, *The Cadastral Map in the Service of the State: A History of Property Mapping* (Chicago: University of Chicago Press, 1992), 340.

110. This problem is implicitly stated, though not discussed at length, in P. D. A. Harvey, *The History of Topographical Maps: Symbols, Pictures and Surveys* (London: Thames and Hudson, 1980), 36, 48, 86.

111. Arthur H. Robinson, Randall D. Sale, Joel L. Morrison, and Phillip C. Muehrcke, *Elements of Cartography*, 5th ed. (New York: John Wiley, 1985), 5. My arguments for the psychological authority of maps—their inability either to produce nonsense or to contradict themselves—fall into the same category (Andrews, "Map and Language," 10–11).

112. Harley, "Maps, Knowledge, and Power," 284; Harley, "Secrecy and Silences," 66; Harley, "Deconstructing," 14.

113. Harley, "Maps, Knowledge, and Power," 289, 294; Harley, "Secrecy and Si-

lences," 58, 66; Harley, "Deconstructing," 6, 7, 10, 14; Harley, "Cartography, Ethics, and Social Theory," 4; Harley, "New England Cartography," 301; Harley, "Power and Legitimation," 183, 192; Harley, "Rereading," 530.

114. The distinction between cartographers' and noncartographers' boundaries is not always clear in Harley's work. He writes of territory being "sliced through by the pen of the mapmaker as in the scramble for Africa" ("What Happens," 17), but here the culprits were surely politicians rather than map makers. Much the same applies to cartographers' and noncartographers' place-names ("What happens," 4–11). This is an increasingly common "category-mistake" among map historians. Another example is the reference to maps "erecting" (rather than simply recording) social hierarchies in the American landscape ("Power and Legitimation," 187). For more on this subject, see Andrews, "The Cartography of Celtic Placenames," 7.

115. Harley, "What Happens," 5–12 (quotation from 9); though see Harley, "New England Cartography," 297, for a less radical view.

116. Harley, "New England Cartography," 296; Harley, *Maps and the Columbian Encounter,* 135–36.

117. Jean Jacques Rousseau, *Emile,* trans. Barbara Foxley (1780; London: Everyman's Library, J. M. Dent and Sons, 1938), 7.

118. Harley, "Power and Legitimation," 195, n. 25. Also see Harley, *Maps and the Columbian Encounter,* 121, and Harley, "Rereading," 527–28. "Cartography of Protest" is a section heading in an early draft of the table of contents for Harley's proposed book "The Map as Ideology."

119. Harley, "Maps, Knowledge, and Power," 300–301. Harley finds no fundamental difference in format and style between maps made in preconquest America to assert the territorial control of a native aristocracy and those used by the same class to dispute the legitimacy of colonial occupation (Harley, "Rereading," 527–28).

120. Ernie O'Malley, *On Another Man's Wound* (Dublin: Sign of the Three Candles, 1936), 75, 146, 210, 222. The extent to which Irishmen in the previous century had "resisted" the Ordnance Survey because of the power-wielding capacity of its maps is doubtful. Harley's evidence ("What Happens," 18) on this point is probably the fact that surveyors' poles were sometimes removed by local residents in the 1820s and 1830s (Andrews, *Paper Landscape,* 43), but thieves may have simply had their own uses for the poles. On the whole the Ordnance Survey's map-making activities encountered remarkably little popular opposition in Ireland throughout its history and there was almost no politically motivated criticism of the survey until Irish placenames became an issue for language enthusiasts after 1890.

121. "Iconology," 34, 38; "Maps, Knowledge, and Power," 278, 281, 287, 292, 300; "Secrecy and Silences," 65, 70, 71; "Historical Geography and the Cartographic Illusion," 86; "Myth of the Great Divide," 16, 19, 21; "Deconstructing," 2, 3, 6, 9, 10, 11; "Cartography, Ethics, and Social Theory," 8, 12; "New England Cartography," 304;

"Introduction: Texts and Contexts," 5, 6, 10; "What Happens," 16; "Can There Be an Ethics," 11, 13.

122. Harley, "Maps, Knowledge, and Power," 287; Harley, "Deconstructing," 11; Harley, "Introduction: Texts and Contexts," 5.

123. For Harley's willingness to admit exceptions, see "Meaning and Ambiguity," 30; "Iconology," 32; "Maps, Knowledge, and Power," 300.

124. Harley, "Iconology," 8.

125. Harley, "Cartography, Ethics, and Social Theory," 11.

126. Harley, "Maps, Knowledge, and Power," 300.

127. Harley, "Iconology," 36.

128. Harley, "Meaning and Ambiguity," 40. Examples include "embedding," "inscribing" and "enmeshing." For anyone incurably antipathetic to Harley's ideas, these metaphors, wherever encountered, can almost serve as a signal to stop reading.

129. Harley, "Cartography, Ethics, and Social Theory," 9.

130. Harley, "Myth of the Great Divide," 23; Harley, "Introduction: Texts and Contexts," 10.

131. Harley, "Maps, Knowledge, and Power," 280–81.

132. Harley, "Deconstructing," 14.

133. This is in spite of Harley's own maxim that "it is the analysis of content that serves as the point of departure" ("Iconology," 31).

134. Harley's training as a "social scientist" (Catherine Delano Smith, in Ravenhill et al., *A Celebration,* 20) is described in more detail by his obituarists (see preface, note 1).

135. Harley and Woodward, *History,* 1:23–39.

136. The most important exception is Denis Wood, at least nine of whose publications, ranging from 1977 to 1989, are cited in Harley's writings.

137. J. B. Harley, Review of Arthur H. Robinson and Barbara Bartz Petchenik, *The Nature of Maps: Essays toward Understanding Maps and Mapping* (Chicago: University of Chicago Press, 1976), *Imago Mundi* 30 (1978): 111.

138. R. A. Skelton, *Maps: A Historical Survey of Their Study and Collecting* (Chicago: University of Chicago Press, 1972), 103–8; David Woodward, "The Study of the History of Cartography: A Suggested Framework," *American Cartographer* 1 (1974): 101–15.

139. Brief statements of Harleian principles appear isolated among many pages of wholly positivist history in A. S. Bendall, *Maps, Land and Society: A History with a Carto-bibliography of Cambridgeshire Estate Maps, c. 1600–1836* (Cambridge: Cambridge University Press, 1992), ch. 2; Kain and Baigent, *Cadastral Map,* 344; P. D. A. Harvey, *Maps in Tudor England* (London: Public Record Office and the British Library, 1993), 24; and Matthew Edney, "Mathematical Cosmography and the Social Ideology of British Cartography, 1780–1820," *Imago Mundi* 46 (1994): 101, 112. Edney's paper on the social status of cartographers and surveyors requires a further

comment. It begins and ends with a Harleian characterization of "cartographic mimesis" as an illusion and otherwise gives a historiographically orthodox account of an admittedly unusual subject. The interest and validity of its arguments are unaffected by whether or not Edney is right about cartographic mimesis being an illusion.

140. In the first two volumes (1987, 1992) of Harley and Woodward's *History*, the most striking result of Harley's radicalism is an emphasis on celestial cartography and cosmological iconography consequent on a widened definition of the word *map*. There is little trace of the "social epistemology" discussed in the present essay. On the contrary, the authors express many opinions and attitudes that Harley had already come to dislike. Examples from volume one are the distinction between decorative and nondecorative maps (230), the "privileging" of maps regarded as scientific (245) and of "the basic cartographic concept of a map drawn to scale" (478), the implicit contrast between "true" and less-than-true cartographers (178), the branding of an early map for its "obvious failings" (209) or for being "behind its time" (173), and the associated idea that by a process of "cartographic advancement" (482) maps get closer to geographical reality (152). One of Harley's favorite generalizations is brusquely denied in the statement that "it would of course be absurd to read meanings of this kind [i.e., symbolic, metaphorical meanings] into sketch maps that were demonstrably drawn for practical and ephemeral purposes" (493).

These examples may seem captious, but when writing under his own name Harley was equally quick to pounce on the same attitudes in the work of other scholars (see for example "Concepts in the History of Cartography," 17–18; "Meaning and Ambiguity," 36; "Myth of the Great Divide," 9–10; "Deconstructing," 6). However, in considering these early volumes of the *History* we must recognize that, to judge from Harley's choice of examples elsewhere, ancient and medieval cartography have for one reason or another proved generally unresponsive to his approach. For the seventeenth and eighteenth centuries he intended the *History* to "take a more ideological line" (Anne Godlewska, assistant director, *History of Cartography*, to J. H. Andrews, 30 November 1984). Among the other nonphilosophical publications of Harley's last decade, it would be unfair to judge *Old Series Ordnance Survey Maps of England and Wales* by ideological criteria: two volumes of this series had appeared in the 1970s and it was clearly desirable for the remainder to adopt a matching traditionalist posture. On the other hand, much of *Maps and the Columbian Encounter* can stand as a successful politicization of regional map history.

141. David Woodward, "John Brian Harley, 1932–1991," *Imago Mundi* 44 (1992): 121.

ONE ◆ *Texts and Contexts in the Interpretation of Early Maps*

1. Robert I. Rotberg and Theodore K. Rabb, *Art and History: Images and Their Meaning* (Cambridge: Cambridge University Press, 1988).

2. Helen M. Wallis and Arthur H. Robinson, *Cartographical Innovations: An International Handbook of Mapping Terms to 1900* (Tring, Hertfordshire: Map Collector Publications, 1987).

3. D. F. McKenzie, *Bibliography and the Sociology of Texts*, the Panizzi Lectures (London: the British Library, 1985).

4. Arthur H. Robinson et al., *Elements of Cartography*, 5th ed. (New York: John Wiley and Sons, 1984).

5. Robert Karrow and Ronald E. Grim, "Two Examples of Thematic Maps: Civil War and Fire Insurance Maps," in David Buisseret, ed., *From Sea Charts to Satellite Images* (Chicago: University of Chicago Press, 1990), 213–37.

6. Denis Wood and John Fels, "Designs on Signs: Myth and Meaning in Maps," *Cartographica* 23, no. 3 (1986): 54–103.

7. Dominick La Capra, *Rethinking Intellectual History: Texts, Contexts, Language* (Ithaca: Cornell University Press, 1983).

8. J. A. Williamson, *The Voyages of John and Sebastian Cabot* (London: Argonaut Press, 1929).

9. R. A. Skelton, *Looking at an Early Ma*p (Lawrence, Kans.: University of Kansas Libraries, 1965).

10. Wallis and Robinson, *Cartographical Innovations*.

11. Charles Singer et al., eds., *A History of Technology*, vols. 1–4 (Oxford: Clarendon Press, 1954–78).

12. David Woodward, "The Study of the History of Cartography: A Suggested Framework," *American Cartographer* 1, no. 2 (1974): 101–15.

13. R. A. Skelton, *Maps: A Historical Survey of Their Study and Collecting* (Chicago: University of Chicago Press, 1972); J. B. Harley, "The Map and the Development of the History of Cartography," in *Cartography in Prehistoric, Ancient, and Medieval Europe and the Mediterranean*, vol. 1 of *The History of Cartography*, ed. J. B. Harley and David Woodward (Chicago: University of Chicago Press, 1987), 1:1–42.

14. Morris M. Thompson, *Maps for America: Cartographic Producers of the U.S. Geological Survey and Others*, 2d ed. (Reston, Va.: U.S. Department of the Interior, 1981).

15. Michael Baxandall, *Painting and Experience in Fifteenth Century Italy: A Primer in the Social History of Pictorial Style* (Oxford: Clarendon Press, 1972).

16. Matthew H. Edney, "Politics, Science, and Government Mapping Policy in the United States, 1800–1925," *American Cartographer* 13, no. 4 (1986): 295–306.

17. J. K. Wright, "Map Makers Are Human: Comments on the Subjective in Mapping," *Geographical Review* 32 (1942): 527–44.

18. Ronald E. Grim, "Maps of the Township and Range System," in Buisseret, ed., *From Sea Charts to Satellite Images*, 91.

19. Walter Ristow, *American Maps and Mapmakers: Commercial Cartography in the Nineteenth Century* (Detroit: Wayne State University Press, 1985).

20. Tony Campbell, "Knowledge and Market Mechanism as Impulses for Map Publishing," in *Abstracts, 13th International Conference on the History of Cartography* (Amsterdam, 1989), 55–56.

21. J. B. Harley, "The Evaluation of Early Maps: Towards a Methodology," *Imago Mundi* 22 (1968): 62–74.

22. La Capra, *Rethinking Intellectual History.*

23. A. E. Nordenskiöld, *Facsimile-Atlas to the Early History of Cartography with Reproductions of the Most Important Maps Printed in the XV and XVI Centuries* (Stockholm; New York: Dover Publications, 1973).

24. J. L. Morrison, "Recommendations for the Classification of the Extent Maps of the Great Lakes," Unpublished report to the Hermon Dunlap Smith Center for the History of Cartography, Newberry Library, Chicago.

25. David Buisseret, "Spanish and French Mapping of the Gulf of Mexico in the Sixteenth and Seventeenth Centuries," in *The Mapping of the American Southwest*, ed. Denis Reinhartz and Charles C. Colley (College Station, Tex.: A & M University Press, 1987), 3–17.

26. Ibid., 4.

27. Skelton, *Looking at an Early Map.*

28. Jonathan Lanman, *On the Origin of Portolan Charts* (Chicago, The Hermon Dunlap Smith Center, the Newberry Library, 1987); Skelton, *Looking at an Early Map.*

29. W. F. Ganong, *Crucial Maps in the Early Cartography and Place-Nomenclature of the Atlantic Coast of Canada*, with an introduction, commentary, and map notes by Theodore E. Layng (Toronto: University of Toronto Press, 1964).

30. W. A. R. Richardson, "Jave-la-Grande: A Place Name Chart of Its East Coast," *Great Circle* 6, no. 1 (1984): 1–23; W. A. R. Richardson, "Jave-la-Grande: A Case Study of Place-Name Corruption," *Globe* 22 (1984): 9–32.

31. Helen Wallis, ed., *The Maps and Texts of the Boke of Idrography Presented by Jean Rotz to Henry VIII* (Oxford: Roxburghe Club, 1981).

32. Richardson, "Jave-la-Grande: A Place Name Chart."

33. Skelton, *Looking at an Early Map.*

34. R. W. Karrow, "Carto-bibliography," *AB Bookman's Yearbook*, part 1 (Clifton, N.J.: AB Bookman, 1976) 43–52; C. Verner, "The Identification and Designation of Variants in the Study of Early Printed Maps," *Imago Mundi* 19 (1965): 100–105; C. Verner, "Carto-bibliographical Description: The Analysis of Variants in Maps Printed from Copperplates," *American Cartographer* 1 (1974): 77–87.

35. Justin Winsor, *Narrative and Critical History of America*, 8 vols. (Boston: Houghton, Mifflin, and Co., 1884–89); C. I. Wheat, *Mapping the Transmississippi West, 1540–1861*, 5 vols. (San Francisco: Institute of Historical Cartography, 1957–63); William P. Cumming, *The Southeast in Early Maps*, rev. ed. (Princeton: Princeton University Press, 1962).

36. David Woodward, ed., *Five Centuries of Map Printing* (Chicago: University of Chicago Press, 1975).

37. Skelton, *Looking at an Early Map*, 28–29.

38. Michel Foucault, *The Archaeology of Knowledge and the Discourse on Language*, trans. A. M. Sheridan Smith (New York: Pantheon Books, 1972).

39. Raymond Williams, *The Sociology of Culture*, American ed. (New York: Schocken Books, 1982).

40. G. N. G. Clarke, "Taking Possession: The Cartouche as Cultural Text in Eighteenth-Century American Maps," *Word and Image* 4, no. 2 April–June 1988): 455–74.

41. Gerald Danzer, "Bird's-Eye Views of Towns and Cities," in Buisseret, ed., *From Sea Charts to Satellite Images*, 144.

42. J. B. Harley, "Silences and Secrecy: the Hidden Agenda of Cartography in Early Modern Europe," *Imago Mundi* 40 (1988): 57–76.

43. J. B. Harley, "Deconstructing the Map," *Cartographica* 26, no. 2 (1989): 1–20.

44. J. B. Harley, "Power and Legitimation in the English Geographical Atlases of the Eighteenth Century," in *Images of the World: The Atlas through History*, edited by John A. Wolter and Ronald E. Grim (New York: McGraw-Hill, 1997), 161–204.

45. Clarke, "Taking Possession."

46. Harley, "Power and Legitimation."

47. E. Panofsky, *Meaning in the Visual Arts* (New York: Doubleday, 1955).

48. J. B. Harley, "Meaning and Ambiguity in Tudor Cartography," in *English Map-Making 1500–1650: Historical Essays*, ed. Sarah Tyacke (London: British Museum Publications, 1983), 22–45.

49. M. J. Blakemore and J. B. Harley, *Concepts in the History of Cartography: A Review and Perspective*, Monograph, *Cartographica* 17, no. 4 (1980).

50. J. Schulz, "Jacopo de' Barbari's View of Venice: Map Making, City Views, and Moralized Geography before the Year 1500," *Art Bulletin* 60 (1978): 425–74.

51. John R. Stilgoe, "Mapping Indiana: Nineteenth-Century School Book Views," in John R. Stilgoe, Roderick Nash, and Alfred Runte, *Perceptions of the Landscape and Its Preservations*, Indiana Historical Society Lectures, 1983.

52. John R. Stilgoe, *Common Landscape of America, 1580–1845* (New Haven: Yale University Press, 1982).

53. William Belhower, "Inventing America: A Model of Cartographic Semiosis," *Word and Image* 4, no. 2 (April–June 1988): 475–97; Harley, "Deconstructing."

54. Marshall McLuhan, *The Gutenberg Galaxy: The Making of Typographic Man* (Toronto: University of Toronto Press, 1962); E. L. Eisenstein, *The Printing Press as an Agent of Change: Communications and Cultural Transformations in Early-Modern Europe* (Cambridge: Cambridge University Press, 1979).

T W O ◆ *Maps, Knowledge, and Power*

This paper was given in a preliminary form at a meeting of the Visual Documentation Group of the History Workshop Centre for Social History, held at Ruskin College, Oxford, in February 1984. It has subsequently been presented in seminars at the Department of Art History and Theory in the University of Essex and at the Department of Geography at the University of Wisconsin at Madison. I am grateful for the constructive suggestions received on those occasions and, for helpful comments, to John Andrews, Peter Barber, Mark Blacksell, Mark Cleary, Catherine Delano Smith, Anne Godlewska, Derek Gregory, Nicola Gregson, Roger Kain, Richard Oliver, Raphael Samuel, and David Woodward.

1. Geographical maps are but one aspect of the wider discourse of maps, which extends to embrace other genres such as cosmological and celestial representations and maps of fictional areas.

2. Historians are also primarily concerned with the extent to which the evidence of maps can be evaluated as a "true" record of the facts of discovery, colonization, exploration, or other events in space.

3. On this view, see Margarita Bowen, *Empiricism and Geographical Thought from Francis Bacon to Alexander von Humboldt* (Cambridge: Cambridge University Press, 1981); and D. R. Stoddard, ed., *Geography, Ideology and Social Concern* (Oxford: Blackwell, 1981), esp. 11, 58–60.

4. Carl O. Sauer, "The Education of a Geographer," *Annals of the Association of American Geographers* 46 (1956): 287–99, esp. 289.

5. W. J. T. Mitchell, *Iconology: Image, Text, Ideology* (Chicago: University of Chicago Press, 1986), 9–14.

6. Cf. the analysis of art in "Art as Ideology," in Janet Wolff, *The Social Production of Art* (New York: St. Martin's Press, 1981), 49.

7. How widely this is accepted across disciplines is demonstrated in W. J. T. Mitchell, ed., *The Language of Images* (Chicago: Phoenix Books, 1980).

8. Arthur H. Robinson and Barbara Bartz Petchenik, *The Nature of Maps: Essays toward Understanding Maps and Mapping* (Chicago: University of Chicago Press, 1976), discuss the analogy at length. It is rejected by J. S. Keates, *Understanding Maps* (London: Longman, 1982), 86, although he continues to employ it as a metaphor for the ways maps "can be studied as ordered structures." Another recent discussion is C. Grant Head, "The Map as Natural Language: A Paradigm for Understanding," in Christopher Board, ed., *New Insights in Cartographic Communication,* Monograph 31, *Cartographica* 21, no. 1 (1984): 1–32, and Hansgeorg Schlichtmann's "Discussion" of the Head article, ibid., 33–36.

9. Jacques Bertin, *Semiology of Graphics: Diagrams, Networks, Maps,* trans. William J. Berg (Madison: University of Wisconsin Press, 1983); see also Hansgeorg

Schlichtmann, "Codes in Map Communication," *Canadian Cartographer* 16 (1979): 81–97; also Hansgeorg Schlichtmann, "Characteristic Traits of the Semiotic System 'Map Symbolism,'" *Cartographic Journal* 22 (1985): 23–30. A humanistic application of semiology to maps is found in Denis Wood and John Fels, "Designs on Signs: Myth and Meaning in Maps," *Cartographica* 23, no. 3 (1986): 54–103.

10. Robert Scholes, *Semiotics and Interpretation* (New Haven: Yale University Press, 1982), 144.

11. In accepting that maps can be regarded as an agent of change in history we can draw on the ideas of Lucien Febvre and Henri-Jean Martin, *The Coming of the Book: The Impact of Printing 1450–1800,* trans. David Gerard (London: NLB, 1976); see also Kenneth E. Carpenter, ed., *Books and Society in History: Papers of the Association of College and Research Libraries Rare Books and Manuscripts Preconference 24–28 June 1980, Boston, Massachusetts* (New York: R. R. Bowker, 1983).

12. Erwin Panofsky, *Studies in Iconology: Humanistic Themes in the Art of the Renaissance* (Oxford: Oxford University Press, 1939).

13. A preliminary discussion is in M. J. Blakemore and J. B. Harley, "Concepts in the History of Cartography: A Review and Perspective," Monograph 26, *Cartographica* 17, no. 4 (1980): 76–86, and in J. B. Harley, "The Iconology of Early Maps," *Imago et Mensura Mundi: Atti del IX Congresso Internazionale di Storia della Cartographia,* ed. Carla Marzoli, 2 vols. (Rome: Instituto della Enciclopedia Italiana, 1985), 1: 29–38. A narrower context is found in J. B. Harley, "Meaning and Ambiguity in Tudor Cartography," in Sarah Tyacke, ed., *English Map-Making 1500–1650: Historical Essays* (London: The British Library, 1983), 22–45. For another application see Patricia Gilmartin, "The Austral Continent on Sixteenth-Century Maps: An Iconological Interpretation," *Cartographica* 21, no. 4 (1984): 85–90. See also Brian S. Robinson, "Elizabethan Society and Its Named Places," *Geographical Review* 63 (1973): 322–33.

14. W. H. Stahl, "Representation of the Earth's Surface as an Artistic Motif," in *Encyclopedia of World Art* (New York: McGraw-Hill, 1960), 851–54.

15. Mitchell, *Iconology,* 38.

16. See "Questions on Geography," in Colin Gordon, ed., *Power/Knowledge: Selected Interviews and Other Writings 1972–1977 of Michel Foucault,* trans. Colin Gordon, Leo Marshall, John Mepham, Kate Soper (New York: Pantheon Books, 1980), 63–77, esp. 74–75.

17. Mark Poster, "Foucault and History," *Social Research* 49 (1982): 116–42, esp. 118–19.

18. Ibid.

19. M. Foucault, *Discipline and Punish: The Birth of the Prison,* trans. Alan Sheridan (London: Allen Lane, 1977), esp. 195–228.

20. Anthony Giddens, *The Contemporary Critique of Historical Materialism: Power, Property and the State* (London: Macmillan, 1981), 94 (emphasis added).

21. Ibid., 5.

22. See, for example, Nelson Goodman, *Languages of Art: An Approach to a Theory of Symbols* (Indianapolis: Bobbs-Merrill, 1968), 170–73.

23. These arguments will be more fully developed in J. B. Harley, *The Map as Ideology: Knowledge and Power in the History of Cartography* (London, forthcoming). [This work, which was never published, is described in the preface to this volume].

24. Oswald Ducrot and Tzvetan Todorov, *Encyclopedic Dictionary of the Sciences of Language,* trans. Catherine Porter (Oxford: Blackwell, 1981), 333–38.

25. J. B. Harley and David Woodward, "Concluding remarks," in J. B. Harley and David Woodward, eds., *Cartography in Prehistoric, Ancient, and Medieval Europe and the Mediterranean* vol. 1 of *The History of Cartography* (Chicago: University of Chicago Press, 1987), 506.

26. Ibid.

27. Islamic cartography is most authoritatively described in E. van Donzel, B. Lewis, and Ch. Pellat, eds., *Encyclopaedia of Islam* (Leiden: Brill, 1978), 4: 1077–83.

28. Joseph Needham, *Science and Civilisation in China* (Cambridge: Cambridge University Press, 1959), vol. 3, sec. 22.

29. B. Castiglione, *The Courtier,* trans. George Bull (1528; Harmondsworth: Penguin, 1967), 97; Thomas Elyot, *The Boke Named the Gouernour,* edited from the first edition of 1531 by H. H. S. Croft, 2 vols. (London, 1880), 1: 45, 77–78; Niccolo Machiavelli, *Arte della Guerra e Scritti Politici Minori,* ed. S. Bertelli (1521; Milan: Feltrinelli, 1961), 457–78.

30. For the classical empires see O. A. W. Dilke, *Greek and Roman Maps* (London: Thames and Hudson, 1985), 41–53 (on Agrippa's map) and 169–70 (on the world map of Theodosius II). Maps of the British Empire became popular during the Victorian era: see Margaret Drabble, *For Queen and Country: Britain in the Victorian Age* (London: Deutsch, 1978), where the map by Maclure and Co., London, 1886, is reproduced. The geopolitical message of such maps and globes is unequivocally conveyed by G. K. Chesterton, "Songs of Education: II Geography," quoted on 294–95 above.

31. Samuel Y. Edgerton, Jr., "From Mental Matrix to *Mappamundi* to Christian Empire: The Heritage of Ptolemaic Cartography in the Renaissance," in David Woodward, ed., *Art and Cartography* (Chicago: University of Chicago Press, 1987), 22.

32. Hildegard Binder Johnson, *Order upon the Land: The U.S. Rectangular Land Survey and the Upper Mississippi Country* (New York: Oxford University Press, 1976).

33. Claude Raffestin, *Pour une Géographie du Pouvoir* (Paris: Libraries Techniques, 1980), 131.

34. Alexander's bull regarding the demarcation line is given in Anne Fremantle, ed., *The Papal Encyclicals in Their Historical Context* (New York: Putnam, 1956), 77–81.

35. D. W. Meinig, *The Shaping of America: A Geographical Perspective on 500 Years of History,* vol. 1, *Atlantic America, 1492–1800* (New Haven: Yale University Press,

1986), 232. A similar point is made by Robert David Sack, *Human Territoriality: Its Theory and History* (Cambridge: Cambridge University Press, 1986), 11.

36. See P. A. Penfold, ed., *Maps and Plans in the Public Record Office,* vol. 3: *Africa* (London: HMSO, 1982), passim; J. Stengers, "King Leopold's Imperialism," in Roger Owen and Bob Sutcliffe, eds., *Studies in the Theory of Imperialism* (London: Longman, 1972), 248–76.

37. For a vivid reconstruction of Radcliffe's partition of India employing relatively small-scale maps see Larry Collins and Dominique Lapierre, *Freedom at Midnight* (London: William Collins, 1982), 245–8.

38. Chandra Mukerji, *From Graven Images: Patterns of Modern Materialism* (New York: Columbia University Press, 1983), 83. See also Giuseppe Dematteis, *Le Metafore della Terra: La Geografia Umana tra Mito e Scienzia* (Milan: Feltrinelli, 1985), 54–59.

39. On early map collections see R. A. Skelton, *Maps: A Historical Survey of Their Study and Collecting* (Chicago: University of Chicago Press, 1972), 26–61; Harley, "The Map and the Development of the History of Cartography," in Harley and Woodward, eds., *History of Cartography,* 6–12.

40. For early examples of state involvement in topographical mapping see Lloyd A. Brown, *The Story of Maps* (Boston: Little, Brown, and Co., 1949), esp. 241–71.

41. Daniel J. Boorstin, *The Discoverers* (New York: Random House, 1983), 267–69; on the Dutch East India Company's policy see Gunter Schilder, "Organization and Evolution of the Dutch East India Company's Hydrographic Office in the Seventeenth Century," *Imago Mundi* 28 (1976): 61–78; for an English example, Helen Wallis, "The Cartography of Drake's Voyage," in Norman J. W. Thrower, ed., *Sir Francis Drake and the Famous Voyage, 1577–1580* (Berkeley: University of California Press, 1985), 133–37.

42. Mukerji, *From Graven Images,* 91; see also Chandra Mukerji, "Visual Language in Science and the Exercise of Power: The Case of Cartography in Early Modern Europe," *Studies in Visual Communications* 10, no. 3 (1984): 30–45.

43. Official map-making agencies, usually under the cloak of "national security," have been traditionally reticent about publishing details about what rules govern the information they exclude, especially where this involves military installations or other politically sensitive sites.

44. Christopher Duffy, *Siege Warfare: The Fortress in the Early Modern World 1494–1660* (London: Routledge and Kegan Paul, 1979), esp. 81; and Duffy, *Siege Warfare: The Fortress in the Age of Vauban and Frederick the Great 1660–1789* (London: Routledge and Kegan Paul, 1985), esp. 29, 72, 142. On the effect of cartography on more mobile warfare see R. A. Skelton, "The Military Surveyor's Contribution to British Cartography in the Sixteenth Century," *Imago Mundi* 24 (1970): 77–83.

45. Phillip C. Muehrcke, *Map Use: Reading, Analysis, and Interpretation* (Madison: J. P. Publications, 1978), 299–301.

46. Probably the majority of published battle plans and campaign maps issued "after the event" in Europe down to the end of the eighteenth century fall either into this category or illustrated histories justifying the conduct of warfare.

47. A comparison can be made here with written documents; see, for example, M. T. Clanchy, *From Memory to Written Record: England 1066–1307* (London: Edward Arnold, 1979), esp. 149–265.

48. O. A. W. Dilke, *The Roman Land Surveyors: An Introduction to the Agrimensores* (Newton Abbot: David and Charles, 1971).

49. P. Anderson, *Passages from Antiquity to Feudalism* (London: New Left Books, 1974), esp. 147–53, 185, 188–89, 207–8.

50. P. D. A. Harvey, *The History of Topographical Maps: Symbols, Pictures and Surveys* (London: Thames and Hudson, 1980), passim.

51. Mukerji, *From Graven Images,* 84; Immanuel Wallerstein, *The Modern World-System,* vol. 2, *Mercantilism and the Consolidation of the European World Economy, 1600–1750* (New York: Academic Press, 1980), offers many clues to this process. Appropriately enough, the frontispiece to the volume is a world map by Jan Blaeu (1638).

52. J. R. Hale, *Renaissance Europe 1480–1520* (London: Fontana, 1971), 52–53.

53. F. M. L. Thompson, *Chartered Surveyors: The Growth of a Profession* (London: Routledge and Kegan Paul, 1968).

54. David S. Landes, *Clocks and the Making of the Modern World* (Cambridge: Harvard University Press, 1983), xix, 2, 25, 228–30, 285–86; and Stephen Kern, *The Culture of Time and Space* (London: Weidenfeld and Nicolson, 1983), 10–35.

55. There is an extensive literature on maps in the prewar German school of geopolitics. See, for example, Hans Speir, "Magic Geography," *Social Research* 8 (1941): 310–30; Louis O. Quam, "The Use of Maps in Propaganda," *Journal of Geography* 42 (1943): 21–32; Louis B. Thomas, "Maps as Instruments of Propaganda," *Surveying and Mapping* 9 (1949): 75–81; and John Ager, "Maps and Propaganda," Society of University Cartographers, *Bulletin* 11 (1977): 1–14.

56. Muehrcke, *Map Use,* 295.

57. Geoffrey Parker, *The Thirty Years' War* (London: Routledge and Kegan Paul, 1984), plates 10, 13.

58. T. J. Jackson Lears, "The Concept of Cultural Hegemony: Problems and Possibilities," *American Historical Review* 90 (1985): 567–93.

59. J. B. Harley and Yolande O'Donoghue, *The Old Series Ordnance Survey Maps of England and Wales, Scale: 1 Inch to 1 Mile* (Lympne Castle: Harry Margary, 1981), 3:xxxiv.

60. Speir, "Magic Geography," 320; F. J. Ormeling, Jr., "Cartographic Consequences of a Planned Economy—Fifty Years of Soviet Cartography," *American Cartographer* 1, no. 1 (1974): 48–49; "Soviet Cartographic Falsifications," *Military Engineer* 62, no. 410 (1970): 389–91.

61. For "security" reasons not even the existence of these practices is reported,

although in Britain, for example, in recent years they have been unearthed by investigative journalism: see *New Statesman,* 27 May 1983, 6, which reported that "Moles within the Ordnance Survey have sent us a most interesting secret manual which lists and defines the places in Britain which do not officially exist, and therefore cannot appear on maps."

62. For example, in West Germany, the publishers of atlases have been obliged to obey a set of detailed ministerial regulations relating to political boundaries for maps that are to be used in schools. These did not receive approval for publication unless they showed the 1937 boundaries of Germany as well as those of today: K. A. Sinnhuber, "The Representation of Disputed Political Boundaries in General Atlases," *Cartographic Journal* 1, no. 2 (1964): 20–28.

63. Numerous examples occur in the eighteenth-century British and French maps of North America: Percy G. Adams, *Travelers and Travel Liars 1660–1800* (New York: Dover Publications, 1980), 64–79, who, however, misses the ideological significance of the cartographic falsification he describes. See also J. B. Harley, "The Bankruptcy of Thomas Jefferys: An Episode in the Economic History of Eighteenth-Century Map-Making," *Imago Mundi* 20 (1966); 28–48, esp. 33–40. For a nineteenth-century example see Charles E. Nowell, *The Rose-Colored Map: Portugal's Attempt to Build an African Empire from the Atlantic to the Indian Ocean* (Lisbon: Junta de Investigaóes Científicas do Ultramar, 1982).

64. For political aspects of carto-philately see Bruce Davis, "Maps on Postage Stamps as Propaganda," *Cartographic Journal* 22, no. 2 (1985); 125–30.

65. H. R. Wilkinson, *Maps and Politics: A Review of the Ethnographic Cartography of Macedonia* (Liverpool University of Liverpool Press, 1951).

66. F. J. Ormeling, *Minority Toponyms on Maps: The Rendering of Linguistic Minority Toponyms on Topographic Maps of Western Europe* (Utrecht: Drukkerij Elinkwijk Bu, 1983).

67. The idea of the hidden rules of cartography comes from Michel Foucault, *The Order of Things, an Archaeology of the Human Sciences,* trans. Alan Sheridan-Smith (London, 1966; repr. New York: Vintage Books, 1973).

68. These geometrical elements also include the manipulation of scale and orientation and the use of cartographic grids to organize space. On the wider social significance of these geometries see Robert Sack, *Conceptions of Space in Social Thought: A Geographic Perspective* (London: Macmillan, 1980), passim.

69. The phrase is that of Edgerton, "From Mental Matrix to *Mappamundi,*" 26.

70. On European examples see Harley and Woodward, *The History of Cartography,* vol. 1; on Chinese maps, Needham, *Science and Civilisation in China,* vol. 3; and on Islamic maps, *Encyclopaedia of Islam,* vol. 4.

71. The concept is E. H. Gombrich's *The Sense of Order: A Study in the Psychology of Decorative Art* (Ithaca: Cornell University Press, 1979), 155–56.

72. Edgerton, "From Mental Matrix to *Mappamundi,*" 27. For potential insights

into how maps could have contributed to the social cosmologies, see Michael Harbsmeier, "On Travel Accounts and Cosmological Strategies: Some Models in Comparative Xenology," *Ethnos* 50, nos. 3–4 (1985); 273–312.

73. Denis E. Cosgrove, *Social Formation and Symbolic Landscape* (London: Croom Helm, 1984), 8.

74. Arno Peters, *The New Cartography*, trans. Ward Kaiser, D. G. Smith, and Heim Wohlers (New York: Friendship Press, 1983), 63; see also Terry Cook, "A Reconstruction of the World: George R. Parkin's British Empire Map of 1893," *Cartographica* 21, no. 4 (1984): 53–65, for the deliberate use of Mercator's projection in a map promoting the "New Imperialism" of the pan-Britannic world of the late nineteenth century. The recent reaction of cartographers towards the "unscientific" nature of the alternative "Peters' projection," which adjusts some of these distortions in favor of the Third World, provides a contemporary gloss on the entrenched scientism among map makers which still gives credibility to the mathematically constructed map while ignoring the possibility of the social and political effects on its imagery. For example, see the comments by John Loxton, "The Peters' Phenomenon," *Cartographic Journal* 22, no. 2 (1985): 106–8, which attempt to discredit Peters as a "Marxist" and "socialist." "The so-called Peters' projection," in ibid., 108–10, which is presented as the considered view of the German Cartographical Society is in some respects more polemical than Loxton in its "defence of truthfulness and pure scientific discussion." See also A. H. Robinson, "Arno Peters and His New Cartography," *American Cartographer* 12 (1985): 103–11, and Phil Porter and Phil Voxland, "Distortion in Maps: The Peters' Projection and Other Devilments," *Focus* 36 (1986): 22–30.

75. J. H. Andrews, *Plantation Acres: An Historical Study of the Irish Land Surveyor and His Maps* (Belfast: Ulster Historical Foundation, 1985), 157–58.

76. J. B. Harley, "The Re-Mapping of England 1750–1800," *Imago Mundi* 19 (1965): 56–67; Paul Laxton, "The Geodetic and Topographical Evaluation of English County Maps, 1740–1840," *Cartographic Journal* 13, no. 1 (1976): 37–54.

77. Cf. Juergen Schulz, "Jacopo de' Barbari's View of Venice: Map Making, City Views and Moralized Geography before the Year 1500," *Art Bulletin* 60 (1978): 425–74; Harley, "Meaning and Ambiguity in Tudor Cartography," 28–32.

78. For the development of this argument see J. B. Harley, "Power and Legitimation in the English Geographical Atlas of the Eighteenth Century," in John A. Wolter, and Ronald E. Grim, eds., *Images of the World: The Atlas through History* (New York: McGraw-Hill, 1997), 161–204.

79. James R. Akerman, "National Geographical Consciousness and the Structure of Early World Atlases," Paper presented at the Eleventh International Conference on the History of Cartography, Ottawa, Canada, July 1985.

80. I am indebted to Catherine Delano Smith for discussion and the sight of a draft manuscript on "Cartographic Signs in the Renaissance," to be published in J. B. Harley and David Woodward, eds., *The History of Cartography*, vol. 3, *Cartogra-*

phy in the Age of Renaissance and Discovery (Chicago: University of Chicago Press, forthcoming).

81. Catherine Delano Smith, "Cartographic Signs on European Maps and Their Explanation before 1700," *Imago Mundi* 37 (1985): 9–29, where Mercator's *Advice for the Use of Maps: Atlas sive Cosmographicae. Meditationes de Fabrica Mundi et Fabricati Figura* (1595) is quoted, 25–26.

82. See Christian Sgrothen's maps of the Netherlands (1573) where towns such as Bruges, Brussels, and Ghent are depicted in high oblique in such a way—and with so large a sign—as to ensure ample scope for the detailed display of the attributes of their commercial success and civic pride.

83. Edward Lynam, "Boazio's Map of Ireland," *British Museum Quarterly* 11 (1937): 92–95.

84. François de Dainville, *Le Langage des Géographes: Termes, Signes, Couleurs des Cartes Anciennes, 1500–1800* (Paris: A. et J. Picard, 1964), 236–44.

85. François de Dainville, "Le Signe de 'justice' dans les Cartes Anciennes," *Revue Historique de Droit Français et Etranger,* 4th ser., 34 (1956): 111–14. For a broader context see Yi-Fu Tuan, *Landscapes of Fear* (Oxford: Blackwell, 1980).

86. Buchotte, *Les Règles du Dessin et du Lavis* (Paris, 1721), plate facing 124.

87. Helen Wallis, "Globes in England up to 1660," *Geographical Magazine* 35 (1962–63): 267–79.

88. David Woodward, "Medieval *Mappaemundi,*" in Harley and Woodward, eds., *The History of Cartography,* vol. 1, 334–42.

89. Victor Morgan, "The Literary Image of Globes and Maps in Early Modern England," in Tyacke, ed., *English Map-Making 1500–1650,* 46–56.

90. For other meanings of the globe see James Hall, *Dictionary of Subjects and Symbols in Art* (London: John Murray, 1974), 139; and J. E. Cirlot, *A Dictionary of Symbols,* 2d ed., trans. Jack Sage (London: Routledge and Kegan Paul, 1971), 118–19.

91. Juergen Schulz, "The Map Mural Cycles of the Renaissance," in Woodward, ed., *Art and Cartography,* 97–120.

92. Reproduced in *Arte e Scienza per il Disegno del Mondo* (Milan: Electa, 1983), 57; see also the plate on 56.

93. Roberto Almagià, *Monumenta Cartographica Vaticana,* 4 vols. (Vatican City: Biblioteca Apostolica Vaticana, 1952), vol. 3: *Le Pitture Murali della Galleria delle Carte Geografiche,* 7, 12.

94. *Cartes et Figures de la Terre* (Paris: Centre Georges Pompidou, 1980), 354; *A la Decouverte de la Terre. Dix Siècles de Cartographie* (Paris: Bibliothèque Nationale, 1979), facing 57.

95. Abel Gance, *Napoleon* (France, 1927); Charles Chaplin, *The Great Dictator* (U.S., 1940). On the Gance film see Peter Pappas, "The Superimposition of Vision: *Napoleon* and the Meaning of Fascist Art," *Cineaste: A Magazine on the Art and Politics of the Cinema* (1983), 5–13.

96. A. G. Hodgkiss, *Understanding Maps: A Systematic History of Their Use and Development* (Folkestone: Dawson, 1981), 184–98; MacDonald Gill, "Decorative Maps," *Studio* 128 (1944): 161–69.

97.   So Geographers in *Afric*-Maps
      With Savage-Pictures fill their Gaps;
      And o'er unhabitable Downs
      Place Elephants for want of Towns.

          —Jonathan Swift, *On Poetry: A Rhapsody*

"Savage-Pictures," "Elephants," and a "want of Towns" (towns being one of the hallmarks of European civilization), suggest that a stereotype of African geography, promoted by maps, was already in existence. On present-day attitudes towards decoration, see R. A. Skelton, *Decorative Printed Maps of the Fifteenth to Eighteenth Centuries* (London: Spring Books, 1952), 1.

98. These have been treated as decorative ephemera for collectors: R. V. Tooley, *Title Pages from Sixteenth to Nineteenth Century,* Map Collectors' Series 107 (London: Map Collectors' Circle, 1975). Historians of cartography still have to attempt the depth of iconographic analysis revealed in M. Corbett and R. Lightbown, *The Comely Frontispiece: The Emblematic Title-Page in England 1550–1660* (London: Routledge and Kegan Paul, 1979), or, F. A. Yates, *Astraea: The Imperial Theme in the Sixteenth Century* (London: Routledge and Kegan Paul, 1975), 63.

99. Harley, "Meaning and Ambiguity in Tudor Cartography," 37–38; Hilda Marchant, "A 'Memento Mori' or 'Vanitas' Emblem on an Estate Map of 1612," *Mapline* 44 (1986): 1–4.

100. In different contexts compasses have other meanings: see Hall, *Dictionary of Subjects and Symbols,* 73.

101. Helen Wallis, ed., *The Maps and Texts of The Boke of Idrography Presented by Jean Rotz to Henry VIII, Now in the British Library* (Oxford: Roxburgh Club, 1981), esp. 67–72; Bernadette Bucher, *Icon and Conquest: A Structural Analysis of the Illustrations of de Bry's Great Voyages* (Chicago: University of Chicago Press, 1981).

102. On the female personifications for America, see Hugh Honour, *The New Golden Land: European Images of America from the Discoveries to the Present Time* (New York: Pantheon Books, 1975), 85–117, and Clare Le Corbeiller, "Miss America and Her Sisters: Personifications of the Four Parts of the World," Metropolitan Museum of Art, *Bulletin* 19, new ser. (1961): 209–23. I owe these two references to Howard Deller.

103. Oscar I. Norwich, *Maps of Africa: An Illustrated and Annotated Carto-Bibliography* (Johannesburg: Ad. Donker, 1983). For comparison see Leonard Bell, "Artists and Empire: Victorian Representations of Subject People," *Art History* 5, no. 1 (1982): 73–86.

104. R. Rees, "Historical Links between Cartography and Art," *Geographical Re-*

view 70 (1980): 60–78; David Woodward, "Introduction," in Woodward, ed., *Art and cartography,* vol. 2.

105. The continued symbolic significance of the map is indicated by Louis XIV's dismay in the thought that his kingdom had shrunk as a result of more accurate survey. Brown, *Story of Maps,* facing 246. On biblical maps see the prefatory "epistle" to the 1559 Geneva Bible of Nicolas Barbier and Thomas Courteau where the usefulness of the maps in interpreting the scriptures is explained: I owe this reference to Catherine Delano Smith.

106. Göran Therborn's argument in *The Ideology of Power and the Power of Ideology* (London: New Leaf Books, 1980), 81–84, about "affirmative symbolism or *ritual*" is relevant to maps; see also Eric Hobsbawm and Terence Ranger, eds., *The Invention of Tradition* (Cambridge: Cambridge University Press, 1983), esp. 1–100, 211–62.

107. Deborah J. Warner, *The Sky Explored: Celestial Cartography 1500–1800* (New York: A. R. Liss, 1979), xi–xii, discusses the iconographies of constellations produced by astronomers supporting the Reformation and the Counter Reformation respectively.

108. There is a parallel here to some of the tendencies identified by Robert David Sack, "Human Territoriality: A Theory," *Annals of the Association of American Geographers* 73, no. 1 (1983): 55–74; the ideas are more fully developed in Sack, *Human Territoriality: Its Theory and History* (Cambridge: Cambridge University Press, 1986).

THREE ◆ *Silences and Secrecy*

This paper was given in a preliminary form at a seminar in the Department of Geography, York University, Canada, in March, 1987; it was subsequently presented at the Twelfth International Conference on the History of Cartography in Paris in September 1987 and at the "Geography and the Environment Workshop," in the University of Chicago, in November 1987; I am grateful for the encouragement and suggestions received on those occasions. I am also indebted to Howard Deller of the American Geographical Society Collection for crucial bibliographical assistance, to Kevin Kaufman for supplying me with references on the early history of cartographic secrecy in Portugal; to David Quinn for a number of other examples of sixteenth and seventeenth century policies of cartographic secrecy; and to Michael Conzen, Catherine Delano Smith, Richard Eversole, Michael Mikos, Denis Wood, and David Woodward for commenting on a draft of the essay.

1. J. B. Harley, *The Map as Ideology,* forthcoming. [This work, which was never published, is described in the preface to this volume.]

2. An interesting variant of modern censorship is provided by remote sensing from satellites. The resolution of the instruments used for military intelligence is now

so extraordinarily fine that satellites for civilian use (LANDSAT 1, launched in 1972, and LANDSAT 5, in 1984) have their imagery deliberately degraded; see: Peter Gould, *The Geographer at Work* (London: Routledge and Kegan Paul, 1985), 162–63, 211–13. For a shift of policy see: William J. Broad, "U.S. Ends Curb on Photographs from Satellites," *New York Times,* 21 January 1988.

3. For an indication of the importance of this theme see James R. Akerman and David Buisseret, *Monarchs, Ministers, and Maps: A Cartographic Exhibit at the Newberry Library* (Chicago: Newberry Library, 1985).

4. Joseph Anthony Mazzeo, *Renaissance and Seventeenth-Century Studies* (New York: Columbia University Press, 1964), 148.

5. The word *discourse* has so many interpretations in linguistic and literary studies that it is necessary to define it here. I take the sense nearest to my own from Peter Hulme, *Colonial Encounters: Europe and the Native Caribbean, 1492–1797* (London: Methuen, 1986), 2, where he writes of "colonial discourse, meaning by that term an ensemble of linguistically-based practices unified by their common deployment in the management of colonial relationships." I am also concerned with how "linguistically-based practices," broadly defined as both verbal and nonverbal language and systems of graphic representation including maps, have been used as political instruments. The sense is, therefore, also that of Michel Foucault, *The Archaeology of Knowledge and the Discourse on Language,* trans. A. M. Sheridan-Smith (New York: Pantheon Books, 1972), who is concerned with discourse as a social practice with a set of meanings and effects that can be determined within particular historical societies.

6. Silences can be detected, for example, in most of the technical stages of map production modeled by David Woodward, "The Study of the History of Cartography: A Suggested Framework," *American Cartographer* 1 (1974): 101–15.

7. While he did not specify silences, an excellent discussion of the difficulty of assigning the nuances of cartographic representation to particular cultural or technical causes is given by H. R. Wilkinson, *Maps and Politics: A Review of the Ethnographic Cartography of Macedonia* (Liverpool: University of Liverpool Press, 1951), 314–23.

8. I have found Bernard P. Dauenhauer's *Silence: The Phenomenon and Its Ontological Significance* (Bloomington: Indiana University Press, 1980) to be particularly helpful; see also Max Picard, *The World of Silence,* trans. Stanley Godman (Chicago: H. Regnery, 1952). I owe these references to Dr. Walter Mignolo of the University of Michigan, Ann Arbor.

9. Dauenhauer, *Silence,* 23.

10. Ibid., 4.

11. See Don Ihde, *Experimental Phenomenology* (New York: Putnam, 1977), 68, 129.

12. The "reader-response" to maps in historical contexts has been neglected: for its place in literary studies see: Wolfgang Iser, "The Reading Process: A Phenomenological Approach," in Jane P. Tompkins, ed., *Reader-Response Criticism. From Formalism to*

Post-Structuralism (Baltimore, 1980), 50–51. The extent to which silences in maps may have stimulated their readers' participation is worth pursuing. While early map makers—unlike Laurence Sterne in *Tristram Shandy,* where the reader is invited to add to the story on a provided blank page (see Laurence Sterne, *The Life and Opinions of Tristram Shandy, Gentleman,* ed. James Aiken Work (New York: Odyssey Press, 1940), 470—may not have generally envisaged such participation, it is possible to investigate its historical effects in the social construction of *terrae incognitae.* I owe the references in this note to Dr. Richard Eversole.

13. The negative—even derisory—attitude towards blank spaces on maps was already well established by the eighteenth century most famously in Jonathan Swift, *On Poetry: A Rhapsody* (London, 1733), 12 in his well-known lines beginning "So geographers in *Afric*-maps" For a modern continuation see Lewis Carroll, "Bellman's map," *The Hunting of the Snark,* quoted by R. A. Skelton in *Looking at an Early Map* (Lawrence, Kansas: University of Kansas Libraries, 1965), 3.

14. Dauenhauer, *Silence,* 4.

15. Recent anthropological research, revealing different cultural and contextual interpretations given to silence in speech patterns, can serve as a preliminary warning about the danger of overgeneralizing about the silences in maps. See, for example, K. H. Basso, " 'To give up on words': Silence in Western Apache Culture," in Pier Paolo Giglioli, ed., *Language and Social Context: Selected Readings* (Harmondsworth: Penguin, 1972), 67–86. For a sociolinguistic example see Jennifer Coates, *Women, Men and Language: A Sociolinguistic Account of Sex Differences in Language* (London: Longman, 1986), 33–34. I owe these references to Dr. Michael Mikos.

16. For an earlier step see J. B. Harley, "Maps, Knowledge, and Power," in D. Cosgrove and S. J. Daniels, eds., *The Iconography of Landscape* (Cambridge: Cambridge University Press, 1988), 277–312.

17. Among Foucault's commentators and critics I have found to be particularly helpful for this paper J. G. Merquior, *Foucault* (Berkeley: University of California Press, 1987) and Mark Poster, *Foucault, Marxism and History: Mode of Production versus Mode of Information* (Cambridge: Polity Press, 1984).

18. Foucault, Michel, *Discipline and Punish: The Birth of the Prison,* trans. Alan Sheridan (London: Allen Lane, 1977), 27.

19. Foucault, Michel, *Power/Knowledge: Selected Interviews and Other Writings 1972–1977,* ed. Colin Gordon, trans. Colin Gordon, Leo Marshall, John Mepham, Kate Sopher (New York: Pantheon Books, 1980), 74–75, during the interview "Questions on Geography."

20. Foucault, *Archaeology,* 216.

21. *Discourse* here being a word for thought and knowledge as a social practice: Merquior, *Foucault,* 18.

22. Foucault, Michel, *The Order of Things: An Archaeology of the Human Sciences,* trans. Alan Sheridan-Smith (New York: Vintage Books, 1930), Preface.

23. Ibid., xxii, Foucault also argues that the *episteme* "defines the mode of being of the objects that appear in that field, provides man's everyday perception with theoretical powers, and defines the conditions in which he can sustain a discourse about things that is recognized to be true."

24. Ibid., xxii.

25. For literary parallels to cartographic censorship, which help us to view its practice as taken for granted rather than exceptional in early modern Europe, see Annabel Patterson, *Censorship and Interpretation: The Conditions of Writing and Reading in Early Modern England* (Madison: University of Wisconsin Press, 1984).

26. See, for example, Joseph Needham and Wang Ling, *Science and Civilization in China,* vol. 3, *Mathematics and the Sciences of the Heavens and the Earth* (Cambridge: Cambridge University Press, 1959), 193; J. B. Harley, and David Woodward, eds., *The History of Cartography,* vol. 1, *Cartography in Prehistoric, Ancient, and Medieval Europe and the Mediterranean* (Chicago: University of Chicago Press, 1987), 254; and William Davenport, "Marshall Islands Navigational Charts," *Imago Mundi* 15 (1967): 19–26.

27. In terms of Foucault, *Discipline and Punish* (23 n), 18, it was also a "technology of power" closely enmeshed with the will to dominate in both domestic and overseas spheres. See also Akerman and Buisseret, *Monarchs, Ministers, and Maps,* passim for examples of an increasing use of maps by the emergent states as tools of government.

28. Chandra Mukerji, "Visual Language in Science and the Exercise of Power: The Case of Cartography in Early Modern Europe," *Studies in Visual Communication* 10, no. 3 (1984): 30–45; Robert David Sack, *Human Territoriality: Its Theory and History* (Cambridge: Cambridge University Press, 1986).

29. See Michael Mann, *The Sources of Social Power,* vol. 1, *A History of Power from the Beginning to A.D. 1760* (Cambridge: Cambridge University Press, 1986), 8, where he distinguishes between "authoritative power," which "comprises definite commands and conscious obedience" and "diffused power" which "spreads in a more spontaneous, unconscious, decentered way . . . not explicitly commanded." My *intentional* and *unintentional* silences in maps can be allocated to this broad distinction.

30. Jonathan D. Spence, *The Memory Palace of Matteo Ricci* (New York: Viking, 1984), 97.

31. For example, in England, the crown had fully grasped the strategic importance of maps by the mid-sixteenth century. In 1551, for example, a chance visit to Portsmouth by a French ambassador en route for Scotland, in the company of an engineer/map maker, was sufficient to alarm the English authorities into ordering the refortification of its castle: W. K. Jordan, ed., *The Chronicle and Political Papers of King Edward VI* (London: Allen and Unwin, 1966), 97 (26 December 1551). I owe this reference to Peter Barber. In France, the models in the *Musée des Plans-Reliefs,* first constructed after 1668 for Louis XIV, were kept locked away in the Great Gallery of the Louvre and "few visitors were allowed to see them because examination by a potential enemy could have threatened military security": George A. Rothrock,

"Maps and Models in the Reign of Louis XIV," *Proceedings of the Annual Meeting of the Western Society for French History* 14 (1987): 50; also Josef W. Konvitz, *Cartography in France, 1660–1848: Science, Engineering, and Statecraft* (Chicago: University of Chicago Press, 1987), 93. The same was true of other maps prepared for military purposes. Geoffrey Parker cites the case of the Duke of Alva who had a map of the Franche-Comté made for his pioneer march of 1567, but this was so accurate that he delayed its publication for a decade. See Geoffrey Parker, *The Army of Flanders and the Spanish Road 1567–1659: The Logistics of Spanish Victory and Defeat in the Low Countries' Wars* (Cambridge: Cambridge University Press, 1972), 83.

32. Johannes Keuning, "Isaac Massa, 1586–1643," *Imago Mundi* 10 (1953): 66–67; Leo Bagrow, *A History of Russian Cartography up to 1800*, ed. Henry W. Castner (Wolfe Island, Ontario: Walker Press, 1975), 51.

33. Bagrow, *A History of Russian Cartography,* 4–7.

34. Eckhard Jager, *Prussia-Karten 1542–1810. Geschichte der Kartographischen Darstellung Ostpreussens vom 16. bis zum 19, Jahrhundert. Entstehung der Karten-Kosten-Vertrieb. Bibliographischer Katalog* (Weissenhorn: A. H. Konrad, 1982), 168–71.

35. Vladimiro Valerio, "The Neapolitan Saxton and His Survey of the Kingdom of Naples," *Map Collector* 18 (1982): 14–17. The survey, intended to be produced as an atlas, remained unpublished because it was perceived as a threat to both the interests of Spain and the security of the Kingdom.

36. Akerman and Buisseret, *Monarchs, Ministers, and Maps,* 9, although this is debated.

37. Eduard Imhof, *Cartographic Relief Presentation,* ed. H. J. Steward (New York: De Gruyter, 1982), 7.

38. R. A. Skelton, *Saxton's Survey of England and Wales. With a Facsimile of Saxton's Wall-Map of 1583* (Amsterdam: N. Israel, 1974), 15–18.

39. William Lambarde, the sixteenth-century English historian, for example, had encountered opposition to the publication of a map of beacons in Kent, see: William Lambarde, *A Perambulation of Kent* (London, 1596), 69, where he wrote "And now, if any man shall thinke that this laying open of the Beacons, is a point not meete to bee made publike: I pray him to give me leave to dissent in that opinion from him. For, as the profit to the Realme and subiect is manifest, in that it speedeth the service, where speed is the most profitable: so there is no secret hereby disclosed, whereof the enimie may take advantage."

40. R. Helgerson, "The Land Speaks: Cartography, Chorography, and Subversion in Renaissance England," *Representations* 16 (1986): 51–85.

41. Victor Morgan, "Lasting Image of the Elizabethan Era," *Geographical Magazine* 52 (1980): 401–8.

42. Helgerson, "The Land Speaks," 81.

43. Immanuel Wallerstein, *The Modern World-System,* vol. 1, *Capitalist Agriculture and the Origins of the European World-Economy in the Sixteenth Century,* and vol. 2,

Mercantilism and the Consolidation of the European World-Economy, 1600–1750 (New York: Academic Press, 1974, 1980).

44. Jaime Cortesão, "The Pre-Columbian Discovery of America," *Geographical Journal* 89 (1937): 29–42.

45. Chandra Mukerji, *From Graven Images: Patterns of Modern Materialism* (New York: Columbia University Press, 1983), 91.

46. See, for example, Richard Eden's statement in the mid-sixteenth century: "As touching these trades and voyages, as in manner of all the sciences, there are certain secrets not to be published and made common to all men." Quoted by E. G. R. Taylor in "John Dee and the Map of North-East Asia," *Imago Mundi* 12 (1955): 103; also George Best, *A True Discourse of the Late Voyage of Discoverie, for Finding a Passage to Cathaya, under M. Frobisher, General* (London, 1578); and Richard Hakluyt, who refers to a forthcoming "very large and most exact terrestriall Globe, collected and reformed according to the newest, secretest, and latest discoveries, both Spanish, Portugall, and English" in *The Principal Navigations Voiages and Discoveries of the English Nation. A Photo-Lithographic Facsimile with an Introduction by David Beers Quinn and Raleigh Ashlin Skelton and with a New Index by Alison Quinn* (London, 1589; Cambridge: Cambridge University Press for the Hakluyt Society and Peabody Museum, Salem, 1965), xlviii–xlix.

47. Helen Wallis, "The Cartography of Drake's Voyage," in Norman J. W. Thrower, ed., *Sir Francis Drake and the Famous Voyage, 1577–1580. Essays Commemorating the Quadricentennial of Drake's Circumnavigation of the Earth* (Berkeley: University of California Press, 1984), 121–63.

48. Bailey W. Diffie, "Foreigners in Portugal and the 'Policy of Silence,'" *Terrae Incongnitae* 1 (1969): 23–34; see also Armando Cortesão, *History of Portuguese Cartography*, 2 vols. (Coimbra: Junta de Investigaóes Científicas do Ultramar, 1969–71), 2:76, 116–18.

49. Helen Wallis, ed., *The Maps and Text of the Boke of Idography Presented by Jean Rotz to Henry VIII Now in the British Library* (Oxford: Roxburghe Club, 1981), 40.

50. Cortesão, "The Pre-Columbian Discovery of America," 31, n. 44; see also George H. Kimble, "Portuguese Policy and Its Influence on Fifteenth Century Cartography," *Geographical Review* 23 (1933): 653–59.

51. A. Teixeira da Mota, "Some notes on the Organization of Hydrographical Services in Portugal before the Beginning of the Nineteenth Century," *Imago Mundi* 28 (1976): 51–60.

52. Ibid., 53–54.

53. Edward L. Stevenson, "The Geographical Activities of the Casa de la Contratación," *Annals of the Association of American Geographers* 17 (1927): 39–59.

54. J. H. Parry, *The Spanish Seaborne Empire* (London: Hutchinson, 1966), 54–58.

55. Stevenson, "The Geographical Activities," 41.

56. Ibid., 42.

57. Marcel Destombes, *Cartes Hollandaises: La Cartographie de le Compagnie des Indes Orientales, 1593–1743* (Saigon, 1941), 5.

58. Gunter Schilder, "Organization and Evolution of the Dutch East India Company's Hydrographic Office in the Seventeenth Century," *Imago Mundi* 28 (1976): 61–78.

59. I owe this point to Professor David B. Quinn: on the so-called "Secret Atlas of the East India Company," F. C. Wieder, *Monumenta Cartographica,* vol. 5, (The Hague: M. Nijhoff, 1933), 145–95. See also Tony Campbell, "A Descriptive Census of Willem Blaeu's Sixty-Eight Centimetre Globes," *Imago Mundi* 28 (1976): 21–50, esp. 27.

60. G. R. Crone, and R. A. Skelton, "Collections of Voyages and Travels, 1625–1846," in E. Lynam, ed., *Richard Hakluyt and His Successors* (London: Hakluyt Society, 1946), 65–140, esp. 67.

61. D. W. Moodie, "Science and Reality: Arthur Dobbs and the Eighteenth-Century Geography of Rupert's Land," *Journal of Historical Geography* 2 (1976): 293–309; Glyndwr Williams, "The Hudson's Bay Company and Its Critics in the Eighteenth Century," *Transactions of the Royal Historical Society,* 5th series, 20 (1970): 150–51.

62. R. I. Ruggles, "Governor Samuel Wegg: Intelligent Layman of the Royal Society," *Notes and Records of the Royal Society of London* 32 (1978): 181–99.

63. Williams, "The Hudson's Bay Company."

64. I owe this point to Professor David B. Quinn.

65. See, for example, Armando Cortesão, in *Cartografia e Cartógrafos Portugueses dos Séculos XV et XVI* (Lisbon: Edição da "Seara Nova, 1935), 1: 142–44, describes the acquisition of the Cantino map by the Duke of Ferrara. Alberto Cantino was sent to Lisbon under cover to obtain information on the progress of the Portuguese discoveries. In 1502, a letter from Cantino to the Duke states that he had bribed a Portuguese map maker, probably one connected to the *Casa da India,* with twelve gold *ducados* to copy a map, probably the official *padrão.* Cantino left Lisbon with the planisphere at the end of October 1502, and through the intermediary of Francesco Cataneo, the duke had the map in his library by December. I owe this reference to Kevin Kaufman.

66. R. A. Skelton, "Raleigh as a Geographer," *Virginia Magazine of History and Biography* 71 (1963): 131–49.

67. Lamb, Ursula, "Science by Litigation: A Cosmographic Feud," *Terrae incognitae* 1 (1969): 40–57.

68. Following the distinction of Michael Mann, *Sources of Social Power,* 8.

69. Foucault, Michel, "Résponse au cercle d'épistémologie," *Cahiers pour l'analyse* 9 (summer 1968), quoted by Merquior, *Foucault,* 81.

70. Foucault, *Archaeology,* 153–54, for a fuller discussion of the concept of the *episteme* as it relates to social constraints on the creation of knowledge.

71. Merquior, *Foucault,* 46, these two characteristics comprise what Foucault termed the "classical *episteme.*"

72. The appearance of the characteristic sheet on maps offers a diagnostic criterion for the formalization of this taxonomic tendency: see E. M. J. Campbell, "The Development of the Characteristic Sheet, 1533–1822," *Proceedings of the 7th General Assembly—17th Congress—of the International Geographical Union* (Washington: International Geographical Union, 1952), 426–30. For other aspects of the early history of adoption of this device see Catherine Delano Smith, "Cartographic Signs on European Maps and Their Explanation before 1700," *Imago Mundi* 37 (1985): 9–29.

73. These are, in effect, the assumptions of "normal science" and they represent an important epistemological thread in the development of cartography.

74. For an earlier statement of this view see Gerald R. Crone, *Maps and Their Makers: An Introduction to the History of Cartography* (London, 1953), xi. Crone writes that "the history of cartography is largely that of the increase in the accuracy with which . . . elements of distance and direction are determined and . . . the comprehensiveness of the map content." That the interpretation persists is demonstrated, for example, by the Foreword by Emmanuel Le Roy Ladurie to Konvitz, *Cartography in France,* xi–xiv, where he writes in terms of concepts such as "enormous progress," "realistic understanding of space," "perfection of terrestrial concepts" and concludes that "the progress of French cartography at the time of the Enlightenment was linked to collaborations between state and science" yet without, in the main, pursuing the ideological implications of the state interest in mapping.

75. See Campbell, "Development of the Characteristic Sheet," fig. 2.

76. For the effects of print culture on social thought with relevance to the argument in this paper see: Walter J. Ong, *Orality and Literacy: The Technologizing of the Word* (London: Methuen, 1982), esp. 117–23.

77. Foucault sees this as inherent in the process of graphic representation: see Merquior, *Foucault,* 46–47; Sack, *Human Territoriality,* 131, makes the same point in his discussion of "abstract metrical territorial definition of social relationships," imposed through maps.

78. In relation to the concept of a "normal science" *episteme,* a weakness of Foucault's formulation is that he insists that "in any given culture and at any given moment, there is always only one *episteme* that defines the conditions of possibility of all knowledge": Foucault, *The Order of Things,* 168.

79. For an understanding of patronage in the history of cartography in early modern Europe there is much to be derived from Michael Baxandall, *Painting and Experience in Fifteenth-Century Italy: A Primer in the Social History of Pictorial Style* (Oxford: Clarendon Press, 1972). He writes (1): "A fifteenth-century painting is the deposit of a social relationship. On one side there was a painter who made the picture, or at least supervised its making. On the other side there was somebody else who asked him to make it, provided funds for him to make it and, after he had made it,

reckoned on using it in some way or other. Both parties worked within institutions and conventions—commercial, religious, perceptual, in the widest sense social—that were different from ours and influenced the forms of what they together made."

80. By the nineteenth century the place-names associated with linguistic minorities in many European states were being deliberately suppressed but the origins of such policies as an agent of statecraft still have to be described in the history of cartography: see F. J. Ormeling, *Minority Toponyms on Maps: The Rendering of Linguistic Minority Toponyms on Topographic Maps of Western Europe* (Utrecht: Drukkerij Elinkijk Bu, 1983).

81. Tzvetan Todorov, *The Conquest of America: The Question of the Other,* trans. Richard Howard (New York: Harper, 1984) is a revisionist essay with important ideological pointers to the way we view the silences of the New World cartography of the "Discoveries" period.

82. Four styles of cross are used to identify ecclesiastical rank. The smallest category of civil settlement is identified by a plain dot while other settlements are shown by pictorial signs. These are not clearly distinguished but range from small to large.

83. For a discussion of the impact of Reformist issues upon the content of maps of the Holy Land, see Catherine Delano Smith, "Maps in Bibles in the Sixteenth Century," *Map Collector* 39 (1987): 2–14: for other examples see Kenneth Nebenzahl, *Maps of the Holy Land: Images of Terra Sancta through Two Millennia* (New York: A. R. Liss, 1986), esp. 70–133.

84. For an analysis of the religious content in *mappaemundi* see David Woodward, "Medieval *Mappaemundi,*" in J. B. Harley and David Woodward, eds., *The History of Cartography,* vol. 1 (Chicago: University of Chicago Press, 1987), 286–370.

85. For example, N. Claudianus' map of Bohemia (1518) may have been prepared for the purpose of showing the distribution and status of Papal and Hussite adherents, since so little topographical information is included; P. de la Beke's map of Flanders (1538), stronghold of Protestanism, concentrates on categories of religious institutions; C. Radziwiłł's map of Lithuania (1613) for its part distinguishes Orthodox from Roman bishops.

86. Suggestions of such a silence of religious conviction come from John Norden, the late-sixteenth- and early-seventeenth-century English map maker. Norden was anti-Catholic and on only one of his county maps, *Middlesex* (1593), does he show "Bishops sees" and then with a curious starlike sign rather than a cross (a papal symbol abhorred by some protestants). On the other hand, his unusual inclusion of chapels of ease on most of his other maps can be attributed to his deep interest in ecclesiastical matters. I owe this example to Catherine Delano Smith.

87. Again further contextual research is needed to establish whether we can regard these silences as an action prophesying the ultimate triumph of Christendom or merely a failure to update old images and texts. On the persistence of an old topography of the Holy Land and its meaning, see Yael Katzir, "The Conquests of Jerusalem,

1099 and 1178: Historical Memory and Religious Topology," in Vladimir P. Goss and Christine Verzar Bornstein, eds., *The Meeting of Two Worlds: Cultural Exchange between East and West during the Period of the Crusades* (Kalamazoo, Mich.: Medieval Institute Publications, Western Michigan University, 1986), 103–31; for the continuing consequences of the mental set of the crusaders in Holy Land cartography, see Nebenzahl, *Maps of the Holy Land,* passim.

88. This may have been an indirect expression of the sumptuary laws which regulated how the members of some European social groups should dress. In the case of England and her colonies it has been suggested that the purpose of these laws was "that no one would be able to slip over into a status to which he did not belong": see Karen Ordahl Kupperman, *Settling with the Indians: The Meeting of English and Indian Cultures in America, 1580–1640* (Totowa, N.J.: Rowmand and Littlefield, 1980), 3. For a wider discussion of the social significance of dress codes in early modern Europe see Fernand Braudel, *Civilization and Capitalism 15th–18th Century,* vol. 1, *The Structures of Everyday Life: The Limits of the Possible,* trans. Sian Reynolds (London: William Collins, 1981), 311–33.

89. Kupperman, *Settling,* 2.

90. Key in northeast corner of John Smith's "Virginia," 1612. For a detailed description of this influential map and its various printed states see Collie Verner, "The First Maps of Virginia, 1590–1673," *Virginia Magazine of History and Biography* 58 (1950): 3–15.

91. For a somewhat later example of the deliberate use of maps in this way see Louis De Vorsey, Jr., "Maps in Colonial Promotion: James Edward Oglethorpe's Use of Maps in 'Selling' the Georgia Scheme," *Imago Mundi* 38 (1986): 35–45.

92. For reproductions see Seymour I. Schwartz and Ralph E. Ehrenberg, *The Mapping of America* (New York: Harry N. Abrams, 1980), chapter 4, "Permanent Colonization Reflected on Maps: 1600–1650," 84–109.

93. Kupperman, *Settling,* 33.

94. Ibid., 1.

95. This silence, like others, cannot be regarded as a historical constant. By the nineteenth century it has been pointed out that even popular maps were showing the location of Indian tribes in the American West and Southwest. This "probably confirmed in the reader's mind an image of the . . . [region] as a place heavily peopled by hostile Indians": Dennis Reinhartz and Charles C. Colley, eds., *The Mapping of the American Southwest* (College Station, Tex.: Texas A&M University Press, 1987), 67.

96. For a discussion relevant to the depictions of scenes of cannibalism on early manuscript and printed maps of the New World see Gina Kolata, "Are the Horrors of Cannibalism Fact—or Fiction," *Smithsonian* 17, no. 12 (1978): 150–70; for wider implications see also William Arens, *The Man-Eating Myth* (New York: Oxford University Press, 1979).

97. Helgerson, "The Land Speaks," 81.

98. M. S. Monmonier, "Cartography, Geographic Information, and Public Policy," *Journal of Geography in Higher Education* 6, no. 2 (1982): 99–107.

99. The notion of the "unthought" (*impensé*) is that of Foucault.

100. In the cartographic literature see, notably, the two recent essays by Wood: Denis Wood and John Fels, "Designs on Signs: Myth and Meaning in Maps," *Cartographica* 23, no. 3 (1986): 54–103; and Denis Wood, "Pleasure in the Idea: The Atlas as Narrative Form," in R. J. B. Carswell, A. J. A. de Leeuw, and N. M. Waters, eds., *Atlases for Schools: Design Principles and Curriculum Perspectives, Cartographica* 24, no. 1 (1987, Monograph 36), 24–45.

101. Helgerson, "The Land Speaks," is an example of how "The new historicism" in literary studies has brought maps within its purview as an aspect of representation; it is taken for granted that the map would be read as any other text: I owe this point to Dr. Richard Eversole of the University of Kansas at Lawrence.

102. Phillip C. Muehrcke, *Map Use: Reading, Analysis, and Interpretation* (Madison, 1978); 103. Foucault, *Archaeology*, chapter 6, "Science and Knowledge," 178–195, refuses to make a distinction between "science" and "ideology." This places him apart from traditional marxism in which "science" and "ideology" have always been regarded as separate categories of knowledge. It is this latter position, derived from positivist science, which has established itself within cartography (and the history of cartography), and is reflected, for example, in the assumed major cleavage between "propaganda maps" and "truth maps." For similar conclusions about the artificiality of this divide, taking examples from present-day maps, see Bjørn Axelsen and Michael Jones, "Are All Maps Mental Maps?" *Geo Journal* 14, no. 4 (1987): 447–64, and (much earlier) Denis Wood, *I Don't Want to, But I Will. The Genesis of Geographic Knowledge: A Real-Time Developmental Study of Adolescent Images of Novel Environments* (Worcester, Mass.: Clark University Cartographic Library, 1973), passim.

103. Michael Mann, *Sources of Social Power,* 1:524–25. While he does not mention cartography specifically it is clearly part of "the infrastructure available to power holders" and is among "the social inventions that have crucially increased power capacities."

104. The notion of "truth effects" is that of Foucault.

FOUR ◆ *Power and Legitimation in the English Geographical Atlases of the Eighteenth Century*

In the four years since this paper was originally presented in a preliminary form in Washington, D.C., I have accumulated more debts than I can hope to properly acknowledge. In preparing this new version for publication, however, I am especially indebted to Howard Deller, Ellen Hanlon, and Sarah Wilmot for bibliographical assistance and to Dalia Varanka, who has supplied me with some new examples of cartouches on North American maps. For making valuable comments on a draft of the essay I am also particularly grateful to James R. Akerman, Catherine Delano Smith, Matthew Edney, and Barbara McCorkle, and to John Wolter and his staff in the Geography and Map Division of the Library of Congress for help with selecting illustrations and in other editorial matters.

1. Lucien Febvre and Henri-Jean Martin, *L'Apparition du Livre* (Paris: Edition Albin, 1958); English edition, *The Coming of the Book: The Impact of Printing, 1450–1800,* new ed., ed. Geoffrey Nowell-Smith and David Wootton, trans. David Gerard (London: NLB, 1976).

2. Ibid., 248.

3. Elizabeth L. Eisenstein, *The Printing Press as an Agent of Change: Communications and Cultural Transformations in Early Modern Europe,* 2 vols. (Cambridge: Cambridge University Press, 1979).

4. D. F. McKenzie, *Bibliography and the Sociology of Texts. The Panizzi Lectures* (London: The British Library, 1986), esp. 34–39. I share his view that Arthur H. Robinson and Barbara Bartz Petchenik, *The Nature of Maps: Essays toward Understanding Maps and Mapping* (Chicago: University of Chicago Press, 1976), 43, were fundamentally wrong when they wrote "the two systems, map and language, are essentially incompatible." Unfortunately, even in the history of cartography, it has led (in the words of McKenzie, 37) to a view of maps as solely "silent, visual, spatial, and a-temporal."

5. For a general discussion see J. B. Harley, "Maps, Knowledge, and Power," in Denis Cosgrove and Stephen Daniels, eds., *The Iconography of Landscape* (Cambridge: Cambridge University Press, 1988), 277–312.

6. Joseph Rouse, *Knowledge and Power: Toward a Political Philosophy of Science* (Ithaca: Cornell University Press, 1987).

7. Recently, see James R. Akerman and David Buisseret, *Monarchs, Ministers, and Maps: A Cartographic Exhibit at the Newberry Library* (Chicago: Newberry Library, 1985).

8. Michel Foucault, *Power/Knowledge: Selected Interviews and Other Writings, 1972–1977,* ed. Colin Gordon, trans. Colin Gordon, Leo Marshall, John Mepham, Kate Soper (New York: Pantheon Books, 1980), 88; see also Rouse, *Knowledge and Power,* 209–10.

9. J. B. Harley, "Silences and Secrecy: The Hidden Agenda of Cartography in Early Modern Europe," *Imago Mundi* 40 (1988): 111–30.

10. Rouse, *Knowledge and Power,* 17–24.

11. Ibid., 213–26.

12. An analogy may be drawn here between the "construction of microworlds" in the scientific laboratory and the construction of geographical knowledge in the cartographer's workshop. In both cases the key is standardization: Rouse, *Knowledge and Power,* 95–125. On the effect of standard tools, techniques, and procedures on the

creation of scientific knowledge, see also Jerome R. Ravetz, *Scientific Knowledge and Its Social Problems* (Oxford: Clarendon Press, 1971), 194–202.

13. Marshall McLuhan, *The Gutenberg Galaxy* (Toronto: University of Toronto Press, 1962), passim. Quoted in Alvin Kernan, *Printing Technology, Letters, and Samuel Johnson* (Princeton: Princeton University Press, 1987), 50; I find Kernan's whole discussion of "Print Logic," 48–55, particularly helpful to my understanding of atlas cartography.

14. Kernan, *Printing Technology,* 51.

15. The trade practices of the eighteenth-century cartographic workshop still have to be fully constructed but on engraving and printing maps see Coolie Verner, "Copperplate Printing," in David Woodward, ed., *Five Centuries of Map Printing* (Chicago: University of Chicago Press, 1975), 51–75.

16. Josef W. Konvitz, *Cartography in France, 1660–1848. Science, Engineering, and Statecraft* (Chicago: University of Chicago Press, 1987), 3–4, compares the development of geographical mapping in England and France in this respect.

17. William Gerard De Brahm, *Report of the General Survey in the Southern District of North America,* ed. and with an introduction by Louis De Vorsey, Jr. (Columbia: University of South Carolina Press, 1971), 3–6.

18. J. B. Harley, "The Origins of the Ordnance Survey," in W. A. Seymour, ed., *A History of the Ordnance Survey* (Folkestone: Dawson, 1980), 1–20; J. B. Harley and Y. O'Donoghue, "The Ordnance Survey Becomes a Map Publisher, 1801–1820," in ibid., 67–78.

19. For details see H. G. Fordham, *John Cary: Engraver, Map, Chart and Print-Seller and Globe-Maker; 1754 to 1835* (Cambridge: Cambridge University Press, 1925; rpt., Folkestone: Dawson, 1976).

20. R. A. Skelton, *James Cook Surveyor of Newfoundland. Being a Collection of Charts of the Coasts of Newfoundland and Labradore, &c. Drawn from Original Surveys Taken by James Cook and Michael Lane. London, Thomas Jefferys, 1769–1770,* with an introductory essay by R. A. Skelton (San Francisco: David Magee, 1965), 7.

21. J. B. Harley, "The Bankruptcy of Thomas Jefferys: An Episode in the Economic History of Eighteenth Century Map-Making," *Imago Mundi* 20 (1966): 35–37.

22. Donald Hodson, *County Atlases of the British Isles Published after 1703* (Terwin, Hertfordshire: Terwin Press, 1984) 1:xi.

23. For example, the earliest of these, *A General Topography of North America and the West Indies* (1768), published by Sayer and Jefferys and consisting of 100 maps on 109 sheets was described as "a collection of all the maps, charts, plans, and particular surveys that have been published of that part of the world, either in Europe or America"; it was issued with both a French and English title page and contents. In general, however, the composite atlas was declining in the English map trade after 1700 and was to disappear around the middle of the nineteenth century.

24. For a fuller discussion see Harley, "Silences and Secrecy," 119–20.

25. A cartography of protest against established power relations is an accepted part of present-day cartography. A recent prototype, originally published in one-sheet form by the Society for Human Exploration, is *The Nuclear War Atlas* (Victorianville, Quebec: The Society, 1982); it was republished as William Bunge, *The New World Atlas* (New York: Blackwell, 1988). Other recent examples of cartography as protest include Michael Kidron and Ronald Segal, *The New State of the World Atlas* (New York: Simon and Schuster, 1984); Joni Seager and Ann Olson, *Woman in the World: An International Atlas* (New York: Simon and Schuster, 1986) and Barbara Gimla Shortridge, *Atlas of American Women* (New York: Macmillan, 1987).

26. See, for example, the diversity of interpretation expressed by Peter Laslett, *The World We Have Lost: Further Explored,* 3d ed. (London: Methuen, 1965, 1983); Harold Perkin, *The Origins of Modern English Society 1780–1880* (London: Routledge and Kegan Paul; Toronto: University of Toronto Press, 1969); R. S. Neale, *Class in English History, 1680–1850* (Oxford: Blackwell, 1981), esp. chapter 3; Roy Porter, *English Society in the Eighteenth Century* (London: Penguin, 1982); L. Stone and J. C. F. Stone, *An Open Elite? England, 1540–1880* (Oxford: Clarendon Press; New York: Oxford University Press, 1984); J. C. D. Clark, *English Society, 1688–1932. Social Structure and Political Practice During the Ancien Régime* (Cambridge: Cambridge University Press, 1985).

27. Laslett, *The World We Have Lost,* 1983, 22–52.

28. Porter, *English Society,* 69, 78.

29. Raymond Williams, *The Country and the City* (London: Chatto and Windus, 1973), 60.

30. This type of analysis still has to be undertaken for English cartography, but the raw material exists in price data on atlases in trade catalogs and in standard series of wage data. On the former see the interim list by Antony Griffiths, "A Checklist of Catalogues of British Print Publishers, c. 1650–1830," *Print Quarterly* 1 (1984): 4–22; on the latter see W. J. T. Mitchell and Phyllis Deane, *Abstract of British Historical Statistics* (Cambridge: Cambridge University Press, 1962) and J. E. Thorold Rogers, *Six Centuries of Work and Wages: The History of English Labour,* new ed., with a new preface by G. D. H. Cole (London: Allen and Unwin, 1949).

31. For examples of these advertisements, which appear throughout the eighteenth century, see Sarah Tyacke, *London Map-sellers, 1660–1720* (Tring, Hertfordshire: Map Collector Publications, 1978) and Hodson, *County Atlases,* vol. 1.

32. The general European practice of displaying coats of arms in atlas maps was already common by the mid-seventeenth century; in the English atlases the fashion was at its height in the early eighteenth century.

33. See, for example, John Harrison, *The Library of Isaac Newton* (Cambridge: Cambridge University Press, 1978), who records that Newton, as well as some seventy-six books relating to voyages, travel, and geography, owned a copy of Senex's *The English Atlas* (1714) and Moll's *A New Description of England and Wales . . .* (1724); his library as a whole comprised 2,100 volumes at the time of his death. Also R. A.

Harvey, "The Private Library of Henry Cavendish (1731–1810)," *Library,* Sixth Series, 2 (1980): 281–92; as well as many books of travel and voyages, Cavendish had collected maps, plans, and surveys, comprising 656 sheets bound together in six giant volumes, each measuring 22 × 16½ inches.

34. J. B. Harley and Gwyn Walters, "William Roy's Maps, Mathematical Instruments, and Library: The Christie's Sale of 1790," *Imago Mundi* 29 (1977): 9–22; J. B. Harley and Gwyn Walters, "English Map Collecting, 1790–1840: A Pilot Survey of the Evidence in Sotheby Sale Catalogues," *Imago Mundi* 30 (1978): 31–53. References to atlases can also be found among *Sale Catalogues of Libraries of Eminent Persons,* 12 vols., gen. ed. A. N. L. Munby (London: Mansell with Sotheby Parke-Bernet Publications, 1971–1974). Volume 2, *Scientists,* ed. and introduced by H. A. Fiesenberger (London, 1975), has references to atlases. The whole topic of eighteenth-century English map ownership requires a systematic study.

35. They are listed in F. J. G. Robinson and P. J. Wallis, *Book Subscription Lists: A Revised Guide* (Newcastle upon Tyne: Harold Hill and Son for the Book Subscription List Project, 1975); occasional typewritten supplements have been issued. Advance subscription was a standard way of financing book publication in the eighteenth century but though it was widely employed in financing the English county surveys of the period it was not generally used for atlas publication. On the county surveys see, for example, William Yates, *A Map of the County of Lancashire, 1786* (Liverpool: Historic Society of Lancashire and Cheshire, 1968), 48. See Paul Laxton, *250 Years of Mapmaking in the County of Hampshire,* introduction to a collection of facsimiles (Lympne Castle, Kent: Harry Margary, 1976), on Isaac Taylor's map of that county.

36. John Senex, *A New General Atlas, . . . Containing a Geographical and Historical Account of all the Empires, Kingdoms, and Other Dominions of the World* (London, 1721).

37. Ibid., preface.

38. The following categories given in Senex's introduction provide an eighteenth-century perspective on the value of maps, not least where questions of power relations are involved: "Sovereigns, with their Ministers . . . find it necessary for Civil Government; and particularly for understanding the Interests, Extent, Situation, Wealth and Strength of their own Dominions, and those of their neighbors"; "Generals, and other Commanders of Armies, find this Study absolutely needful for directing their Marches, Encampments, Fortifications, &c"; "Divines find it no less necessary, for understanding several Religions of the World"; "Tis no less useful to the Gentlemen of the Long Robe, for knowing the Laws and Customs of all Nations"; "It is equally necessary to Physicians, for knowing the several Conditions and Diseases of People; and what Provision the bountiful Hand of Providence has made for the Preservation & Cure of Mankind"; "Historians, Poets and Philosophers cannot be ignorant of it for no part of history, or even so much as a Gazette, can be understood without it"; "Above all, it is useful to Merchants and Sailors, for Directing them in their Com-

merce or Navigation"; "nor can Travellers by Sea or Land be without it . . ."; and "Nay, the very Husbandmen, with ordinary Mechanicks, and their Families, must be convinc'd of its Usefulness to inform them of the Quality and Product of the Soil which Mankind lives upon."

39. On the increasing number of mathematical practitioners in the eighteenth century, which drew interested persons from all layers of society, see E. G. R. Taylor, *The Mathematical Practitioners of Hanoverian England, 1714–1840* (Cambridge: Cambridge University Press, 1966).

40. For this wider context to atlas history see Terry Belanger, "Publishers and Writers in Eighteenth-Century England," in Isabel Rivers, ed., *Books and Their Readers in Eighteenth-Century England* (London: St. Martin's Press, 1982), 5–25.

41. John Cary, *Cary's New and Correct English Atlas, Being a New Set of County Maps from Actual Surveys, etc.* (London, 1787).

42. For example, the smaller atlases like the geography texts in octavo were aimed at a more general market than the larger folio atlases for which the readership was more restricted. One of the problems in generalizing about English atlas cartography is that there is no cartobibliography of the world atlases or of atlases in general. Driven by the collector interest, emphasis has been placed on bibliographies of county atlases or of the maps of individual counties. Work on the world atlases is a desideratum for future research.

43. Michael Baxendall, *Painting and Experience in Fifteenth-Century Italy: A Primer in the Social History of Pictorial Style* (Oxford: Clarendon Press, 1972), 1.

44. Porter, *English Society*, 86.

45. The most scholarly analysis of the practices of the eighteenth-century London atlas trade is that of Hodson, *County Atlases*, vol. 1. For a discussion of a particular atlas, see *The Royal English Atlas: Eighteenth-Century County Maps of England and Wales by Emanuel Bowen and Thomas Kitchen*, with an introduction by J. B. Harley and Donald Hodson (Newton Abbot: David and Charles Ltd., 1971).

46. See, for example, the comment of Richard Gough, *British Topology*, 2 vols. (London, 1780), 1:xvi that "as to the several sets of county maps professing to be drawn from the *latest* observations, they are almost invariably copies of those that preceded them." A high level of plagiarism was also characteristic of the English geographies in the same period.

47. For the complexity of the eighteenth-century London print trades with which atlas making was intermeshed, see H. M. Atherton, *Political Prints in the Age of Hogarth* (Oxford: Clarendon Press, 1974), esp. chapter 1, "Printshops of London and Westminister," and chapter 2, "Of Prints and Their Makers."

48. Ibid., 8; the term *hieroglyphicks* refers to the use of hieroglyphic emblems in the design of the prints.

49. Mary Pedley, "Gentlemen Abroad: Jefferys and Sayer in Paris," *Map Collector*

37 (1986): 20–23; for Sayer's print stock in this period, see also Robert Sayer and John Bennett, *Catalogue of Prints for 1775* (rpt., London: Holland Press, 1970).

50. Robert Sayer, *Atlases, Both Ancient and Modern, Books of Maps, Surveys, and Catalogue of Single Maps, of all the Empires, Kingdoms, States, &c. in the Universe* (London, 1788); *Catalogue of Pilots, Neptunes, and Charts, Both General and Particular; for the Navigation of All the Seas and Coasts of the Universe* (London, 1787); *Catalogue of New and Interesting Prints Consisting of Engravings and Metzotintos of Every Size and Price, Likewise Paintings on Glass, Books of Architecture & Ornaments, Penmanship, &c. &c. &c.* (London, 1786).

51. Atherton, *Political Prints,* 5.

52. For locations of Bowles's and other eighteenth-century trade catalogs, see Griffiths, "A Checklist of Catalogues of British Print Publishers, c. 1650–1830."

53. John Feather, *The Provincial Book Trade in Eighteenth-Century England* (Cambridge: Cambridge University Press, 1985), chapter 1, "London and the Country," 1–11.

54. Unlike the eighteenth-century geographies, for example, which were also published in Edinburgh, Glasgow, Montrose, Dublin, Eton, Oxford, and Manchester.

55. See, for example, the discussion of one atlas maker's geographical sources in J. B. Harley, "The Bankruptcy of Thomas Jefferys: An Episode in the Economic History of Eighteenth-Century Mapmaking," *Imago Mundi* 20 (1966): 27–48.

56. For examples, see ibid., 33–41; the manuscript "Catalogue of Drawings & Engraved Maps, Charts and Plans; the Property of Mr. Thomas Jefferys, Geographer to the King, 1775," Manuscript list in the Collections of the Royal Geographical Society, London, contains almost 200 items for North America and the West Indies alone.

57. On the increasing cosmopolitanism of eighteenth-century London, with many implications for the growth of geographical knowledge, see Thomas M. Curley, *Samuel Johnson and the Age of Travel* (Athens: University of Georgia Press, 1976), esp. chapter 1, "Johnson's Lifetime, 1709–1784: The Age of Travel," 7–46; on the growing English knowledge of the world, see also P. J. Marshall and Glyndwr Williams, *The Great Map of Mankind: British Perceptions of the World in the Age of Enlightenment* (London: Dent, 1982). The same point is borne out by E. A. Reitan, "Expanding Horizons: Maps in the *Gentlemen's Magazine,* 1731–1754," *Imago Mundi* 37 (1985): 54–62.

58. Porter, *English Society,* 70–71; see also J. V. Beckett, *The Aristocracy in England, 1160–1914* (Oxford: Blackwell, 1986), esp. chapters 3 and 10 for fuller details of the ties of marriage and property in English county societies.

59. This is most fully documented in Hodson, *County Atlases.* Until the publication of later volumes of Hodson's work, we have to rely on older bibliographies such as Thomas Chubb, *The Printed Maps in the Atlases of Great Britain and Ireland. A*

Bibliography, 1579–1870 (London: E. J. Burrow, 1927) or on the cartobibliographies of individual counties for which Donald Hodson, *The Printed Maps of Hertfordshire, 1577–1900* (London: Dawsons, 1974) also provides a model.

60. In England, heraldic art may be said to have reached its maturity by the fourteenth century: see Anne Payne, "Medieval Heraldry," 55–59, in Jonathan Alexander and Paul Binski, eds., *Age of Chivalry: Art in Plantagenet England, 1200–1400* (London: Royal Academy of Arts in association with Weidenfeld and Nicolson, 1987). During the Middle Ages an important task of the heralds at tournaments had been the receipt, the certification, and the display (nailing up) of a participant's coat of arms, and this custom survived at tournaments until Elizabethan times: see Alan Young, *Tudor and Jacobean Tournaments* (New York: Sheridan House, 1987), 46.

61. Quoted in Hodson, *County Atlases*, 171.

62. Ibid., 78–95. The atlas was reissued in many editions down to the 1760s. A facsimile was published as *Britannia Depicta or Ogilgby Improved* by Emanuel Bowen (Newcastle upon Tyne: Frank Graham, 1970) with an Introduction by J. B. Harley.

63. This type of marginal note was systematically added to Emanuel Bowen and Thomas Kitchen, *The Royal English Atlas: Being a New and Accurate Set of Maps of all the Counties of South Britain, Drawn from Surveys, and the Best Authorities . . . by Emanuel Bowen, Geographer to His Late Majesty, Thomas Kitchen, Geographer, and Others. The Whole Comprised in Forty-four Sheet Maps* (London, 1763).

64. See, for example, *England Displayed. Being a New, Complete, and Accurate Survey and Description of the Kingdom of England, and Principality of Wales . . . by a Society of Gentlemen . . . Revised, Corrected, and Improved, by P. Russell, Esq; and . . . Mr. Owen Price* (London, 1769). In this case, the small county maps—derived from John Rocque's *The Small British Atlas*—served as illustrations to a topographical and historical text rather than providing an atlas in the usual sense.

65. See *The Old Series Ordnance Survey Maps of England and Wales. Scale: 1 Inch to 1 Mile. A Reproduction of the 110 Sheets of the Survey in Early State in 10 Volumes, Vol. 3, South-Central England,* Introduction by J. B. Harley and Yolande O'Donoghue (Lympne Castle, Kent: Harry Margary, 1975), xxii–xxx, "The Birth of Archaeological Cartography."

66. For other examples of this process, see Harley, "Maps, Knowledge, and Power," 296–98.

67. For insights into the use of the past in this way, see Eric Hobsbawm, "Introduction: Inventing Traditions," in Eric Hobsbawm and Terence Ranger, eds., *The Invention of Tradition* (Cambridge: Cambridge University Press, 1983), 1–14.

68. J. B. Harley, "The Remapping of England, 1750–1800," *Imago Mundi* 19 (1965): 56–67.

69. See John Barrell, *The Dark Side of Landscape: The Rural Poor in English Painting, 1730–1840* (Cambridge: Cambridge University Press, 1980).

70. Charity Schools were supported by endowments or subscriptions given by the

philanthropically inclined. They were intended to teach the "Three Rs" to children of the "lower classes" who would not need Latin and other subjects taught in the grammar schools: see Mary G. Jones, *The Charity School Movement: A Study of Eighteenth-Century Puritanism in Action* (Cambridge: Cambridge University Press, 1938).

71. In the vignette for Northumberland in the *Royal English Atlas,* for example, three coal workers are seated on piles of coal, one smoking a pipe. For examples of such tendencies in the art of the period, see Hugh Prince, "Art and Agrarian Change, 1710–1815," in Denis Cosgrove and Stephen Daniels, eds., *The Iconography of Landscape* (Cambridge: Cambridge University Press, 1988), 98–118.

72. Maurice Bloch, "Symbols, Song, Dance and Features of Articulation: Is Religion an Extreme Form of Traditional Authority?" *European Journal of Sociology* 15 (1974): 79; quoted in David I. Kertzer, *Ritual, Politics, and Power* (New Haven: Yale University Press, 1988), 40.

73. Émile Durkheim, *The Elementary Forms of the Religious Life* (1915), trans. Joseph Swain (Glencoe: Free Press, 1974) argued that through ritual people project the secular sociopolitical order in which they live onto a cosmological plane. It is through ritual that people symbolize the "system of socially approved 'proper' relations between individuals and groups." See the discussion in Kertzer, *Ritual, Politics, and Power,* 37.

74. Kertzer, *Ritual, Politics, and Power,* 40, notes that standardization "along with its repetitive nature, gives ritual its stability." See also Hobsbawm, "Introduction: Inventing Traditions," 1, where " 'Invented tradition' is taken to mean a set of practices, normally governed by overtly or tacitly accepted rules and of a ritual or symbolic nature, which seek to inculcate certain values and norms of behavior by repetition, which automatically implies continuity with the past."

75. Kertzer, *Ritual, Politics, and Power,* 40.

76. Samuel Johnson, Dedication for George Adams's *Treatise on the Globes* (London, 1766); quoted in Curley, *Samuel Johnson,* 12.

77. Examples abound, but see, for example, Charles Theodore Middleton, *A New and Complete System of Geography* (London, 1778), which presents a view of Europe not only advanced in culture, but dominant over the world. The frontispiece shows allegories of the four continents presided over by an angelic Europe with a verse beneath which develops the theme:

> Europe *by Commerce, Arts, and Arms obtains*
> *The Gold of Afric, and her Sons enchains,*
> *She rules luxurious* Asia's *fertile Shores,*
> *Wears her bright Gems, and gains her richest Stores.*
> *While from America thro' Seas she brings*
> *The Wealth of Mines, and various useful things.*

Reproduced in Margarita Bowen, *Empiricism and Geographical Thought from Francis Bacon to Alexander von Humboldt* (Cambridge: Cambridge University Press, 1981),

170. Apart from the picturing of Great Britain as the delight, envy, and mistress of the world, the English geographies were particularly racist in their descriptions of Africa. For example, in the Preface to William Guthrie's *A New System of Modern Geography* (London: printed for C. Dilly and G. G. and J. Robinson, 1795), it is concluded that "In Africa the human mind seems degraded below its natural state. To dwell long on the manners of this country . . . would be disgusting to every lover of mankind."

78. H. Moll, *Atlas Minor* (London, 1729).

79. Much of the argument could be applied to other continents. For the role of geographical knowledge in the European construction of colonial power relations, see Edward W. Said, *Orientalism* (London: Penguin Books, 1985), esp. 215–19, but referring to the nineteenth-century use of geography.

80. For an early example of practical uses involving the creation of an atlas for English colonial administration in North America at the beginning of our period, see Jeanette D. Black, *The Blathwayt Atlas,* vol. 2, *Commentary* (Providence, R.I.: Brown University Press, 1975). The extent to which the colonial government for North America used maps is also indicated by the maps in the records of the "Lords of Trade and Plantations," a book which was abolished in 1782: Ralph B. Pugh, *The Records of the Colonial and Dominions Offices* (London, PRO Handbook no. 3, HMSO, 1964), 5–6. These maps are listed in Peter A. Penfold, ed., *Maps and Plans in the Public Record Office,* 2, *America and West Indies* (London: HMSO, 1974), passim.

81. James R. Akerman, "National Geographical Consciousness and the Structure of Early World Atlases," paper presented at the Eleventh International Conference on the History of Cartography, Ottawa, Canada, July 1985.

82. On Moll, see Dennis Reinhartz, "Herman Moll, Geographer: An Early Eighteenth-century European View of the American Southwest," in Dennis Reinhartz and Charles C. Colley, eds., *The Mapping of the American Southwest* (College Station, Tex.: Texas A&M University Press, 1987), 18–36; an Appendix to the volume, 79–83, is a "Selected Cartobibliography of the Works of Herman Moll Depicting the American Southwest" and, in effect, provides a list of the geographical atlases by Moll relevant to this chapter. The popularity of Moll's atlases—along with voyages, travels, and other geographical works—is suggested by Frederick Bracher, "The Maps in Gulliver's Travels," *Huntingdon Library Quarterly* 8 (1944): 60–64.

83. For a description of these maps, see William P. Cumming, *British Maps of Colonial America* (Chicago: University of Chicago Press, 1974), esp. chapters 1 and 2; see also Seymour I. Schwartz and Ralph E. Ehrenberg, *The Mapping of America* (New York: Harry N. Abrams, 1980), esp. chapters 6 and 7.

84. For lists of the maps in these regional atlases and in some of the other eighteenth-century English atlases depicting North America, see P. L. Phillips, *A List of Geographical Atlases in the Library of Congress,* vols. 1–4 (Washington, D.C.: Government Printing Office, 1909–14; rpt., Amsterdam: Theatrum Orbis Terrarum, 1967).

85. Bowen, *Empiricism and Geographical Thought,* 169.

86. "A Map of the British Empire in North America," by Samuel Dunn, Mathematician, improved from the Surveys of Capt. Carver; sheet 8 in Thomas Jefferys, *The American Atlas or, a Geographical Description of the Whole Continent of America* (London: Sayer and Bennett, 1776).

87. For example, "A Map of the Whole Continent of America . . . with a Copious Table Fully Showing the Several Possessions of Each European Province & State, as Settled by the Definitive Treaty Concluded at Paris, Feby. 10th, 1763" in Thomas Kitchin, *A General Atlas* (London, editions 1773–1793). The boundary is also marked and the treaty referred to in the map of North America in the same atlas: "An Accurate Map of North America Describing and Distinguishing the British and Spanish Dominions on this Great Continent, According to the Definitive Treaty."

88. "A Map of Pennsylvania Exhibiting Not Only the Improved Parts of that Province, but also its Extensive Frontiers: Laid Down from Actual Surveys, and Chiefly from the Late Map of W. Scull Published in 1770," sheet 20 in Jefferys, *The American Atlas.*

89. This reading is adapted from Karl Josef Holtgen, *Aspects of the Emblem. Studies in the English Emblem Tradition and the European Context* (Kassel: Reichenberger, 1986), 92.

90. Cornelius J. Jaenen, "Characteristics of French-Amerindian Contact in New France," in Stanley H. Palmer and Dennis Reinhartz, eds., *Essays on the History of North American Discovery and Exploration* (College Station, Tex.: Texas A&M Press, 1988), 90; other symbolic acts of sovereignty by European powers in North America included planting crosses and burying inscribed lead plates to establish a claim in the face of European rivals.

91. The cartouche is reproduced in Schwartz and Ehrenberg, *The Mapping of America,* 163.

92. Herman Moll, "A New and Exact Map of the Dominions of the King of Great Britain on ye Continent of North America," 1715, published in Moll's *The World Described* (London, 1708–20).

93. By 1710, there were already 50,000 black slaves in the American colonies. See James Egert Allen, *Black History Past and Present* (New York: Exposition Press, 1971). See also Larissa Brown, *Africans in the New World, 1493–1834: An Exhibition at the John Carter Brown Library* (Providence, R.I., 1988) for examples of literature and attitudes towards blacks in the eighteenth century. The Chesapeake region already contained 40,000 black slaves by 1720: A. Roger Ekirch, *Bound for America: The Transportation of British Convicts to the Colonies, 1718–1775* (Oxford: Oxford University Press, 1988).

94. Joshua Fry and Peter Jefferson, "A Map of the Most Inhabited Part of Virginia, Containing the Whole Province of Maryland with Part of Pennsylvania, New Jersey and North Carolina," 1751. Bibliographical details of the inclusion of this map in

various atlases appear in Coolie Verner, "The Fry and Jefferson Map," *Imago Mundi* 21 (1967): 70–94. For the context behind the social structure in the cartouche, see Allan Kulikoff, *Tobacco and Slaves* (Chapel Hill: University of North Carolina Press, 1986).

95. Olive Patricia Dickason, "Old World Law, New World Peoples, and Concepts of Sovereignty," in Palmer and Reinhartz, eds., *Essays on the History of North American Discovery and Exploration*, 60.

96. For a discussion of the origins of this image in art, see H. W. Janson, *Apes and Ape Lore in the Middle Ages and the Renaissance* (London: The Warburg Institute and the University of London, 1952).

97. On the question of the Other with implications for cartographic discourse, see Henry Louis Gates, Jr., ed., *"Race," Writing, and Difference* (Chicago: University of Chicago Press, 1986); Francis Barker et al., eds., *Europe and Its Others*, 2 vols. (Colchester: University of Essex, 1985).

98. A very limp-looking lion or lion hide in the cartouche for D'Anville and Robert, "A New and Correct Map of North America with the West India Islands," 1779: in *A General Atlas Describing the Whole Universe* (London, 1782).

99. Reproduced in Schwartz and Ehrenberg, *The Mapping of America*, 118.

100. "North America. Performed under the Patronage of Louis Duke of Orleans, First Prince of the Blood; by the Sieur D'Anville Greatly Improved by Mr. Bolton . . . 1752," in J. Savary de Bruslans, *The Universal Dictionary of Trade* (London, 1757), 1: plates 1–4. Quoted in Conrad E. Heidenreich, "Mapping the Great Lakes: The Period of Imperial Rivalries, 1700–1760," *Cartographica* 18, no. 3 (1981): 74–109.

101. Thomas Jefferys, *North America from the French of Mr. D'Anville* (1755) in *The Natural and Civil History of the French Dominions* (London, 1760), 134. Quoted in Heidenreich, "Mapping the Great Lakes."

102. On New England names, see Arthur J. Krim, "Acculturation of the New England Landscape: Native and English Toponymy of Eastern Massachusetts," in *New England Prospect: Maps, Place Names, and the Historical Landscape* (Boston: Boston University, The Dublin Seminar for New England Folklife: Annual Proceedings, 1980), 69–88.

103. This emphasis is paralleled in the text of the eighteenth-century English geographies. It is the colonial presence which is usually stressed—what crops settlers raise, what schools they have founded, their churches, towns, and villages. I owe this point to Barbara McCorkle.

104. Emanuel Bowen, *A Complete Atlas or Distinct View of the Known World, Exhibited in 68 Maps* (London, 17—), map 38, "A New and Accurate Map of Virginia and Maryland."

105. See the discussion in Robert F. Berkhofer, Jr., *The White Man's Indian: Images of the American Indian from Columbus to the Present* (New York: Vintage Books, 1979), 115–26. Francis Jennings, *The Invasion of America: Indians, Colonialism, and the Cant of Conquest* (New York: Norton, 1976), also stresses how the English colonists had

rigged rationales as well as legal procedures to favor themselves in land dealings; we can add atlas cartography to the rationale.

FIVE ◆ *Deconstructing the Map*

These arguments were presented in earlier versions at "The Power of Places" Conference, Northwestern University, Chicago, in January 1989, and as a 'Brown Bag' lecture in the Department of Geography, University of Wisconsin at Milwaukee, in March 1989. I am grateful for the suggestions received on those occasions and for other helpful comments received from Sona Andrews, Catherine Delano Smith, and Cordell Yee. I am also indebted to Howard Deller of the American Geographical Society Collection for a number of references and to Ellen Hanlon for editorial help in preparing the paper for press.

1. For these distinctions see Terry Eagleton, *Literary Theory: An Introduction* (Minneapolis: University of Minnesota Press, 1983); for an account situated closer to the direct concerns of cartography see Maurizio Ferraris, "Postmodernism and the Deconstruction of Modernism," *Design Issues* 4, nos. 1 and 2, Special Issue (1988): 12–24.

2. Reported in *Cartographic Perspectives: Bulletin of the North American Cartographic Information Society* 1, no. 1 (1989): 4.

3. Others have made the same point: see, especially, the trenchantly deconstructive turn of the essay by Denis Wood and John Fels, "Designs on Signs/Myth and Meaning in Maps," *Cartographica* 23, no. 3 (1986): 54–103.

4. Louis Marin, *Portrait of the King,* trans. Martha M. Houle, *Theory and History of Literature* 57 (Minneapolis: University of Minnesota Press, 1988), 169–79; William Boelhower, *Through a Glass Darkly: Ethnic Semiosis in American Literature* (Venezia: Edizioni Helvetia, 1984), esp. 41–53. See also Boelhower's "Inventing America: A Model of Cartographic Semiosis," *Word and Image* 4, no. 2 (1988): 475–97.

5. Deriving from the writings of Jacques Derrida: for exposition see the translator's preface to Jacques Derrida, *Of Grammatology,* trans. Gayatri Chakratvorty Spivak (Baltimore: The Johns Hopkins University Press, 1976), ix–lxxxvii; Christopher Norris, *Deconstruction: Theory and Practice* (London: Methuen, 1982); and Christopher Norris, *Derrida* (Cambridge: Harvard University Press, 1987).

6. On architecture and planning see, for example, Paul L. Knox, ed., *The Design Professions and the Built Environment* (London: Croom Helm, 1988); Derek Gregory, "Postmodernism and the Politics of Social Theory," *Environment and Planning D: Society and Space* 5 (1987): 245–48; on geography see Michael Dear, "The Postmodern Challenge: Reconstructing Human Geography," *Transactions, Institute of British Geographers,* New Series, 13 (1988): 262–74.

7. Marin, *Portrait of the King,* 173, the full quotation appears later in this article.

8. As an introduction I have found to be particularly useful Edward W. Said, "The

Problem of Textuality: Two Exemplary Positions," *Critical Inquiry* 4, no. 4 (summer 1978): 673–714; also the chapters "Jacques Derrida" by David Hoy and "Michel Foucault" by Mark Philp in Quentin Skinner, ed., *The Return of Grand Theory in the Human Sciences* (Cambridge: Cambridge University Press, 1985), 41–64, 65–82.

9. On the other hand, I do not adopt some of the more extreme positions attributed to Derrida. For example, it would be unacceptable for a social history of cartography to adopt the view that nothing lies outside the text.

10. Alfred Korzybski, *Science and Sanity: An Introduction to Non-Aristotelian Systems and General Semantics,* 3d ed. with new pref. (Lakeville, Conn.: The International Non-Aristotelian Library Pub. Co., 1948), 58, 247, 498, 750–51.

11. H. G. Blocker, *Philosophy and Art* (New York: Charles Scribner's Sons, 1979), 43.

12. Mark Philp, "Michel Foucault," 69.

13. Ibid.

14. "Western cartography" is defined as the types of survey mapping first fully visible in the European Enlightenment and which then spread to other areas of the world as part of European overseas expansion.

15. The history of these technical rules has been extensively written about in the history of cartography, though not in terms of their social implications nor in Foucault's sense of discourse: see, for example, the later chapters of G. R. Crone, *Maps and Their Makers: An Introduction to the History of Cartography* (1953; 5th ed. Folkestone, Kent: Dawson; Hamden, Conn.: Archon Books, 1978).

16. For a discussion of these characteristics in relation to science in general see P. N. Campbell, "Scientific Discourse," *Philosophy and Rhetoric* 6, no. 1 (1973); also Steve Woolgar, *Science: The Very Idea* (Chichester, Sussex: Ellis Horwood, 1988), esp. chapter 1, and R. Hooykaas, "The Rise of Modern Science: When and Why?" *British Journal for the History of Science* 20, no. 4 (1987); 453–73, for a more specifically historical context.

17. For evidence see John A. Wolter, "The Emerging Discipline of Cartography," Ph.D. diss., University of Minnesota, 1975; also, "Cartography—an Emerging Discipline," *Canadian Cartographer,* 12, no. 2 (1975): 210–16.

18. See, for example, the definition of cartography in International Cartographic Association, *Multilingual Dictionary of Technical Terms in Cartography,* ed. E. Meynen (Wiesbaden: Franz Steiner Verlag, 1973), 1, 3: or, more recently, Helen M. Wallis and Arthur H. Robinson, eds., *Cartographical Innovations: An International Handbook of Mapping Terms to 1900* (Tring, Herts: Map Collector Publications and International Cartographic Association, 1987), xi, where cartography "includes the study of maps as scientific documents and works of art."

19. See the discussion in J. Morris, "The Magic of Maps: The Art of Cartography," M.A. diss., University of Hawaii, 1982.

20. Rudolf Arnheim, "The Perception of Maps," in Rudolf Arnheim, *New Essays*

on the Psychology of Art (Berkeley: University of California Press, 1986), 194–202; Umberto Eco, *A Theory of Semiotics* (Bloomington: Indiana University Press, 1976), 245–57; E. Gombrich, "Mirror and Map: Theories of Pictorial Representation," *Philosophical Transactions of the Royal Society of London,* Series B, vol. 270, Biological Sciences (1975): 119–49; and Nelson Goodman, *Languages of Art: An Approach to a Theory of Symbols* (Indianapolis and New York: Bobbs-Merrill, 1968), 170–71, 228–30.

21. Richard Rorty, *Philosophy and the Mirror of Nature* (Princeton: Princeton University Press, 1979).

22. Larry Laudan, *Progress and Its Problems: Toward a Theory of Scientific Growth* (Berkeley: University of California Press, 1977), 2.

23. For a discussion of these tendencies in the historiography of early maps see J. B. Harley. "L'Histoire de la cartographie comme discours," *Préfaces* 5 (December 1987–January 1988): 70–75.

24. In the much-debated sense of Thomas S. Kuhn, *The Structure of Scientific Revolutions* (Chicago: University of Chicago Press, 1962). For challenges and discussions, see Imre Lakatos and Alan Musgrave, eds., *Criticism and the Growth of Knowledge* (Cambridge: Cambridge University Press, 1970).

25. M. Gauthier, ed., *Cartographie dans les Médias* (Québec: Presses de l'Université du Québec, 1988).

26. Sona Karentz Andrews, review of *Cartography in the Media* in *American Cartographer* 16 (1989).

27. W. G. V. Balchin, "The Media Map Watch in the United Kingdom," in Gauthier, ed., *Cartographie dans les Médias,* 33–48.

28. The phrase is that of Ellen Lupton, "Reading Isotype," *Design Issues* 3, no. 2 (1986): 47–58 (quote on 53).

29. Arno Peters, *The New Cartography* (New York: Friendship Press, 1983). The responses included John Loxton, "The Peters Phenomenon," *Cartographic Journal* 22, no. 2 (1985): 106–8; "The So-called Peters Projection," in ibid., 108–10; A. H. Robinson, "Arno Peters and His New Cartography," *American Cartographer* 12 (1985): 103–11; Phil Porter and Phil Voxland, "Distortion in Maps: The Peters' Projection and Other Devilments," *Focus* 36 (1986): 22–30; and, for a more balanced view, John P. Snyder, "Social Consciousness and World Maps," *Christian Century,* 24 February 1988, 190–92.

30. "Soviet Aide Admits Maps Were Faked for 50 Years" and "In West, Map Makers Hail 'Truth,'" *New York Times,* 3 September 1988; "Soviets Admit Map Paranoia," *Wisconsin State Journal,* 3 September 1988; "Soviets Caught Mapping!" *Ottawa Citizen,* 3 September 1988; "Faked Russian Maps Gave the Germans Fits," *New York Times,* 11 September 1988; and "National Geo-glasnost?" *Christian Science Monitor,* 12 September 1988.

31. Michel Foucault, *The Order of Things: An Archaeology of the Human Sciences,* a translation of *Les Mots et les Choses* (New York: Vintage Books, 1973), xx.

32. Ibid., xxii.

33. Many commentators have noted this tendency. See, for example, Yi-Fu Tuan, *Topophilia: A Study of Environmental Perception, Attitudes, and Values* (Englewood Cliffs, N.J.: Prentice-Hall, 1974), chapter 4, "Ethnocentrism, Symmetry, and Space," 30–44. On ancient and medieval European maps in this respect, see J. B. Harley and David Woodward, eds., *The History of Cartography*, vol. 1, *Cartography in Prehistoric, Ancient, and Medieval Europe and the Mediterranean* (Chicago: University of Chicago Press, 1987). On the maps of Islam and China see ibid., vol. 2, *Cartography in the Traditional Islamic and Asian Societies.*

34. Peters, *The New Cartography*, passim.

35. For the wider history of this "rule" see Arthur P. Whitaker, *The Western Hemisphere Idea: Its Rise and Decline.* Ithaca, New York: Cornell University Press, 1954; also S. Whittemore Boggs, "This Hemisphere," *Department of State Bulletin* 12, no. 306 (6 May 1945): 845–50; Alan K. Henrikson, "The Map as an 'Idea': The Role of Cartographic Imagery During the Second World War," *American Cartographer* 2, no. 1 (1975): 19–53.

36. J. B. Harley, "Maps, Knowledge, and Power," in Denis Cosgrove and Stephen Daniels, eds., *The Iconography of Landscape* (Cambridge: Cambridge University Press, 1988), 289–90.

37. The link between actual mapping, as the principal source of our world vision, and *mentalité* still has to be thoroughly explored. For some contemporary links see Alan K. Henrikson "Frameworks for the World," Preface in Ralph E. Ehrenberg, *Scholars' Guide to Washington, D.C., for Cartography and Remote Sensing Imagery* (Washington, D.C.: Smithsonian Institution Press, 1987), viii–xiii. For a report on research that attempts to measure this influence in the cognitive maps of individuals in different areas of the world see Thomas F. Saarinen, *Centering of Mental Maps of the World* (Tucson: Department of Geography and Regional Development, Tucson, Arizona, 1987).

38. For a general discussion see Harley, "Maps, Knowledge, and Power," 292–94; in my essay on "Power and Legitimation in the English Geographical Atlases of the Eighteenth Century," in John A. Wolter and Ronald E. Grim, eds., *Images of the World: The Atlas through History* these "rules of the social order" are discussed in the maps of one historical society.

39. Marin, *Portrait of the King*, 173.

40. Gifford Geertz, "Art as a Cultural System" in *Local Knowledge: Further Essays in Interpretive Anthropology* (New York: Basic Books, 1983), 99.

41. This is cogently argued by D. F. McKenzie, *Bibliography and the Sociology of Texts* (London: British Library, 1986), esp. 34–39, where he discusses the textuality of maps. Arthur H. Robinson and Barbara Bartz Petchenik, *The Nature of Maps: Essays toward Understanding Maps and Mapping* (Chicago: University of Chicago Press, 1976), 43, reject the metaphor of map as language: they state that "the two systems,

map and language are essentially incompatible," basing their belief on the familiar grounds of literality that language is verbal, that images do not have a vocabulary, that there is no grammar, and the temporal sequence of a syntax is lacking. Rather than isolating the differences, however, it now seems more constructive to stress the *similarities* between map and text.

42. McKenzie, *Bibliography,* 35.

43. Roland Barthes, *Mythologies: Selected and Translated from the French by Annette Lavers* (London: Paladin, 1973), 110.

44. The narrative qualities of cartography are introduced by Denis Wood in "Pleasure in the Idea: The Atlas as Narrative Form," in *Atlases for Schools: Design Principles and Curriculum Perspectives,* ed. R. J. B. Carswell, G. J. A. de Leeuw and N. W. Waters, *Cartographica* 24, no. 1 (1987): 24–45 (Monograph 36).

45. The undecidability of textual meaning is a central position in Derrida's criticism of philosophy: see the discussion by Hoy, "Jacques Derrida."

46. Terry Eagleton, *Against the Grain* (London: Verso, 1986), 80, quoted in Edward W. Soja, *Postmodern Geographies* (London: Verso, 1989), 12.

47. Hoy, "Jacques Derrida," 540.

48. W. J. T. Mitchell, *Iconology: Image, Text, Ideology* (Chicago: University of Chicago Press, 1986), 8.

49. J. B. Harley, "Silences and Secrecy: The Hidden Agenda of Cartography in Early Modern Europe," *Imago Mundi* 40 (1988): 57–76.

50. Christopher Norris, *Derrida* (Cambridge: Harvard University Press, 1987), 19.

51. Most recently, C. N. G. Clarke, "Taking Possession: The Cartouche as Cultural Text in Eighteenth-Century American Maps," *Word and Image* 4, no. 2 (1988): 455–74; also Harley, "Maps, Knowledge, and Power," esp. 296–99 and J. B. Harley, "Meaning and Ambiguity in Tudor Cartography," in Sarah Tyacke, ed., *English Map-Making, 1500–1650: Historical Essays* (London: British Library Reference Division Publications, 1984), 22–45; and Harley, "Power and Legitimation in the English Geographical Atlases."

52. Wood and Fels, "Designs on Signs."

53. Roland Barthes, "Myth Today," in Barthes, *Mythologies,* 109–59.

54. Wood and Fels, "Designs on Signs," 54.

55. On the intertextuality of all discourses—with pointers for the analysis of cartography—see Tzvetan Todorov, *Mikhail Bakhtin: The Dialogical Principle,* trans. Wlad Godzich (Minneapolis: University of Minnesota Press, 1984), 60–74; also M. M. Bakhtin, *The Dialogic Imagination: Four Essays,* ed. Michael Holquist, trans. Caryl Emerson and Michael Holquist (Austin: University of Texas Press, 1981). I owe these references to Dr. Cordell Yee, History of Cartography Project, University of Wisconsin at Madison.

56. Wood and Fels, "Designs on Signs," 63.

57. Ibid., 60.

58. The "basic" and "derived" division, like that of "general purpose" and "thematic," is one of the axiomatic distinctions often drawn by cartographers. Deconstruction, however, by making explicit the play of forces such as intention, myth, silence, and power in maps, will tend to dissolve such an opposition for interpretive purposes except in the very practical sense that one map is often copied or derived from another.

59. Hoy, "Jacques Derrida," 44.

60. I derive this thought from Eagleton, *Literary Theory*, 135, writing of the ideas of Roland Barthes.

61. These examples are from Harley, "Maps, Knowledge, and Power," 300.

62. Eagleton, *Literary Theory*, 135–36.

63. Norris, *Deconstruction*, 19.

64. See, for example, Donald N. McCloskey, *The Rhetoric of Economics* (Madison: University of Wisconsin Press, 1985); and John S. Nelson, Allan Megill, and Donald N. McCloskey, eds., *The Rhetoric of the Human Sciences: Language and Argument in Scholarship and Public Affairs* (Madison: The University of Wisconsin Press, 1987).

65. For a notable exception see Wood and Fels, "Designs on Signs." An interesting example of cartographic rhetoric in historical atlases is described in Walter Goffart, "The Map of the Barbarian Invasions: A Preliminary Report" *Nottingham Medieval Studies* 32 (1988): 49–64.

66. In Wood and Fels, "Designs and Signs," 99, the examples are given for topographical maps of reliability diagrams, multiple referencing grids, and magnetic error diagrams; on thematic maps "the trappings of F-scaled symbols and psychometrically divided greys" are a similar form of rhetorical assertion.

67. The "letter" incorporated into Gomboust's map of Paris, as discussed by Marin, *Portrait of the King*, 169–74, provides an apposite example.

68. This is still given credence in some textbooks: see, for example, Arthur H. Robinson, Randall D. Sale, Joel L. Morrison, and Phillip C. Muehrcke, *Elements of Cartography*, 5th ed. (New York: John Wiley & Sons, 1984), 127.

69. Wood and Fels, "Designs on Signs," 71.

70. Hoy, "Jacques Derrida," 60; for further discussion see Norris, *Derrida*, 213–20.

71. Hoy, "Jacques Derrida," 60.

72. Philp, "Michel Foucault," 76.

73. Joseph Rouse, *Knowledge and Power: Toward a Political Philosophy of Science* (Ithaca: Cornell University Press, 1987).

74. Michel Foucault, *Power/Knowledge: Selected Interviews and Other Writings, 1972–1977*, ed. Colin Gordon, trans. Colin Gordon, Leo Marshall, John Mepham, Kate Sopher (New York, Pantheon Books, 1980), 88; see also Rouse, *Knowledge and Power*, 209–10.

75. I adapt this idea from Langdon Winner, "Do Artifacts Have Politics?", *Daedalus* 109, no. 1 (1980): 121–36.

76. Michel Foucault, *The History of Sexuality,* vol. 1, *An Introduction,* trans. Robert Hurley (New York: Random House, 1978), 93.

77. Adapting Roland Barthes, "The Plates of the *Encyclopedia,*" in *New Critical Essays* (New York: Hill and Wang, 1980), 27, who writes much like Foucault, "To catalogue is not merely to ascertain, as it appears at first glance, but also to appropriate." Quoted in Wood and Fels, "Designs on Signs," 72.

78. Robert Darnton, *The Great Cat Massacre and Other Episodes in French Cultural History* (New York: Basic Books, 1984), 192–93.

79. Rouse, *Knowledge and Power:* 213–26.

80. Indeed, cartographers like to promote this metaphor of what they do: read, for example, Mark Monmonier and George A. Schnell, *Map Appreciation* (Englewood Cliffs, N.J.: Prentice Hall, 1988), 15. "Geography thrives on cartographic generalization. The map is to the geographer what the microscope is to the microbiologist, for the ability to shrink the earth and generalize about it . . . The microbiologist must choose a suitable objective lens, and the geographer must select a map scale appropriate to both the phenomenon in question and the 'regional laboratory' in which the geographer is studying it."

81. Marshall McLuhan, *The Gutenberg Galaxy: The Making of Typographic Man* (Toronto: University of Toronto Press, 1962), passim.

82. Theodore Roszak, *Where the Wasteland Ends: Politics and Transcendence in Postindustrial Society* (New York: Doubleday, 1972), 410; Roszak is using the map as a metaphor for scientific method in this argument, which again points to the widespread perception of how maps represent the world.

83. Andrew McNally, "You Can't Get There from Here, with Today's Approach to Geography," *Professional Geographer* 39 (November 1987): 389–92.

84. This criticism is reminiscent of Roland Barthes's essay on "The *Blue Guide,*" *Mythologies,* 74–77, where he writes of the *Guide* as "reducing geography to the description of an uninhabited world of monuments" (we substitute "roads"). More generally, this tendency is also the concern of Janos Szegö, *Human Cartography: Mapping the World of Man,* trans. Tom Miller (Stockholm: Swedish Council for Building Research, 1987). See also Roszak, *Where the Wasteland Ends,* where he writes (408) that "We forfeit the whole value of a map if we forget that it is *not* the landscape itself or anything remotely like an exhaustive depiction of it. If we do forget, we grow rigid as a robot obeying a computer program; we lose the intelligent plasticity and intuitive judgement that every wayfarer must preserve. We may then know the map in fine detail, but our knowledge will be purely academic, inexperienced, shallow."

85. See Paul Rabinow, ed., *The Foucault Reader* (New York: Pantheon Books, 1984), 6–7.

86. J. B. Harley, "Victims of a Map: New England Cartography and the Native Americans." Paper read at the Land of Norumbega Conference, Portland, Maine, December 1988.

87. Boelhower, *Through a Glass Darkly,* 47, quoting François Wahl, "Le Désir d'Espace," in *Cartes et Figures de la Terre* (Paris: Centre Georges Pompidou, 1980), 41.

88. For a modern example relating to Vietnam see Phillip C. Muehrcke, *Map Use: Reading, Analysis, and Interpretation,* 2d ed. (Madison, Wisc.: J.P. Publications, 1986), 394, where, however, such military examples are classified as "abuse" rather than a normal aspect of actions with maps. The author retains "maps mirror the world" as his central metaphor.

89. There is a suggestive analogy to maps in the example of the railway timetable given by Robin Kinross, "The Rhetoric of Neutrality," *Design Issues,* 2, no. 2 (1985): 18–30.

SIX ♦ *New England Cartography*

1. Mahmud Darwish, Samid al-Qasim, and Adonis, *Victims of a Map,* trans. Abdullah al-Udhari (London: Al Saqi Books, 1984).

2. James Axtell, "Colonial America without the Indians: A Counterfactual Scenario," in Frederick E. Hoxie, ed., *Indians in American History: An Introduction* (Arlington Heights, Ill.: Harlan Davidson, 1988), 47–65.

3. Peter Benes, *New England Prospect: A Loan Exhibition of Maps at the Currier Gallery of Art, Manchester, New Hampshire* (Boston: Boston University for the Dublin Seminar for New England Folklife, 1981), 76.

4. Gregory A. Waselkov, "Indian Maps of the Colonial Southeast," in Peter H. Wood, Gregory A. Waselkov, and M. Thomas Hatley, eds., *Powhatan's Mantle: Indians in the Colonial Southeast* (Lincoln: University of Nebraska Press, 1989), 292–343, quotation on page 292. This had also been noted earlier. See, for example, Louis De Vorsey, "Amerindian Contributions to the Mapping of North America: A Preliminary View," *Imago Mundi* 30 (1978): 71–78, in which De Vorsey wrote, "It is clear from the narratives and journals of scores of explorers, from Columbus onward, that Amerindian cartographers and guides in every region of the continent contributed significantly to the outlining and filling up of the North American map" (71).

5. Donald Robertson, *Mexican Manuscript Painting of the Early Colonial Period* (New Haven: Yale University Press, 1959); Donald Robertson, "The Pinturas (Maps) of the Relaciones Geográficas, with a Catalog," in *Handbook of Middle American Indians,* vol. 12, *Guide to Ethnohistorical Sources,* part 1, ed. H. F. Cline (Austin: University of Texas Press, 1972), 243–78; Mary Elizabeth Smith, *Picture Writing from Ancient Southern Mexico: Mixtec Place Signs and Maps* (Norman: University of Oklahoma Press, 1973). Some examples in the context of the Columbian encounter are given in J. B. Harley, *Maps and the Columbian Encounter: An Interpretive Guide to the Travelling Exhibition* (Milwaukee: Golda Meir Library, 1990).

6. Waselkov, "Indian Maps," 292. For the source of the cosmological map, see Philip L. Barbour, ed., *The Jamestown Voyages under the First Charter, 1606–1609,*

Hakluyt Society, 2d ser. 136–37 (Cambridge: Cambridge University Press for the Hakluyt Society, 1969), 82; for a graphic reconstruction, see G. Malcolm Lewis, "The Indigenous Maps and Mapping of North American Indians," *Map Collector* 9 (1979): 25–32.

7. Barbour, ed., *Jamestown Voyages,* 82.

8. See [John Smith], "A Map of Virginia, with a Description of the Country, by Captain Smith," in *The Complete Works of Captain John Smith,* ed. Philip L. Barbour, 3 vols. (Chapel Hill: University of North Carolina Press, 1986), 1:140–41, for a reproduction of the map.

9. Smith, *Complete Works of Captain John Smith,* 1:123.

10. Don Alonso de Velasco, Untitled map of the east coast of North America (1611), MS, Estado., Log. 2588, fol. 22, Archivo General de Simancas, Simancas, Spain. This is reproduced in part in G. Malcolm Lewis, "Indicators of Unacknowledged Assimilations from Amerindian *Maps* on Euro-American Maps of North America: Some General Principles Arising from a Study of La Vérendrye's Composite Map, 1728–29," *Imago Mundi* 38 (1986): 9–34, where the possible Indian content of the map is discussed.

11. [John Smith], "A Description of New England; or, Observations and Discoveries in North America, 1616," in Smith, *Complete Works* 1:351. I am grateful to Harald E. L. Prins for this reference.

12. Ibid., 1:291–370.

13. Gabriel Archer, "The Relation of Captaine Gosnols Voyage to the North Part of Virginia . . . 1602," in Samuel Purchas, *Hakluytus Posthumus or Purchas His Pilgrimes,* 20 vols. (1906; reprint, New York: AMS Press, 1965), 18:304.

14. Samuel de Champlain, *The Works of Samuel de Champlain,* ed. H. P. Biggar, 6 vols. (Toronto: Champlain Society, 1922–36), 1:335–36.

15. G. Malcolm Lewis, "Native North Americans' Cosmological Ideas and Geographical Awareness," in John L. Allen, ed., *North American Exploration* (Lincoln: University of Nebraska Press, 1997), 1:71–126.

16. George Weymouth was serving the interests of Ferdinando Gorges, later lord proprietor of Maine. Once in England, the Indians were imprisoned in Somerset Castle for a "full three years," and Weymouth was able to learn from them of their homeland with its "goodly Rivers, stately Islands, and safe harbours." Furthermore, he got them to set "downe what great Rivers ran up into the Land, what Men of note were seated on them, what power they were of, how allyed [and] what enemies they had." Ferdinando Gorges, *A Briefe Narration of the Original Undertakings of the Advancement of Plantations into the Parts of America* (London: Printed by E. Brudenell, 1658), 4. The Indians were later returned to New England to act as guides and interpreters. Quoted by Lewis, "Native North Americans' Cosmological Ideas."

17. The use of Indian geographical knowledge is implied in William Wood, *New England's Prospect* (1634; reprint, Boston: Publications of the Prince Society, 1865), 1–

2, where, in describing "the Situation, Bayes, Havens, and Inlets," Wood noted that New England is "surrounded on the North-side with the spacious River *Canada,* and on the South with *Hudsons River . . .* these two Rivers . . . having their rise from the great Lakes which are not farre off one another, as the *Indians* doe certainely informe us."

18. Lewis, "Indicators of Unacknowledged Assimilations," 28. Lewis also discussed distortions in European colonial maps as being related to their misunderstanding of information supplied by Indians. G. Malcolm Lewis, "Misinterpretation of Amerindian Information as a Source of Error on Euro-American Maps," *Annals of the Association of American Geographers* 77 (1987): 542–63.

19. Benes, *New England Prospect,* 27–28.

20. Ibid., 28.

21. Ibid., 75–76.

22. Waselkov, "Indian Maps," 300.

23. For examples, see Lewis, "Indicators of Unacknowledged Assimilations."

24. See Michel de Certeau, *The Practice of Everyday Life,* trans. Steven Rendall (Berkeley: University of California Press, 1984), xiii, who wrote of the Indians in New Spain: "Submissive, and even consenting to their subjection, the Indians nevertheless often *made* of the rituals, representations, and laws imposed on them something quite different from what their conquerors had in mind; they subverted them not by rejecting or altering them, but by using them with respect to ends and references foreign to the system they had no choice but to accept." An example in cartographic history of such a subversion would be the "Mapa Mundi" of Felipe Guamán Poma de Ayala in the *Nueva Corónica y Buen Gobierno,* 1613. See Rolena Adorno, *Guaman Poma: Writing and Resistance in Colonial Peru* (Austin: University of Texas Press, 1986), and Gordon Brotherston, *The Image of the New World: The American Continent Portrayed in Native Texts,* translations prepared in collaboration with Ed Dorn (London: Thames and Hudson, 1979).

25. F. J. Ormeling, *Minority Toponyms on Maps: The Rendering of Linguistic Minority Toponyms on Topographic Maps of Western Europe* (Utrecht: Drukkerij Elinkwijk Bu, 1983).

26. Meron Benvenisti, *Conflicts and Contradictions* (New York: Villard Books, 1986), epilogue, 191–202.

27. Brian Friel, *Translations* (London: Faber and Faber, 1981), 34.

28. For a critique of Friel's *Translations* as an authentic historical document, as opposed to creative fiction, see John Andrews, "The Playwright as Historian," in *Essays for Brian Friel* (forthcoming). [Not published: See under Andrews in the bibliography to this volume.]

29. Justin Winsor, "Early Maps of New England," in Justin Winsor, ed., *Narrative and Critical History of America,* 8 vols. (Boston: Houghton Mifflin, 1884), 3:381–84;

Clarice E. Tyler, "Topographical Terms in the Seventeenth-Century Records of Connecticut and Rhode Island," *New England Quarterly* 2 (1929): 382–401.

30. For some of its complexities, in a study making systematic use of manuscript and printed maps, see Arthur J. Krim, "Acculturation of the New England Landscape: Native and English Toponymy of Eastern Massachusetts," in Peter Benes, ed., *New England Prospect: Maps, Place Names, and the Historical Landscape* (Boston: Boston University, 1980), 69–88.

31. Justin Winsor, "The Earliest Maps of Massachusetts Bay and Boston Harbor," in Justin Winsor, ed., *Memorial History of Boston*, 4 vols. (Boston: James E. Osgood, 1888), 1:39–61. The most authoritative modern summary of the early mapping of New England is William P. Cumming, "The Colonial Charting of the Massachusetts Coast," in *Seafaring in Colonial Massachusetts: A Conference Held by the Colonial Society of Massachusetts, November 21 and 22, 1975* (Boston: Colonial Society of Massachusetts, 1980).

32. Smith, *Complete Works of Captain John Smith*, 3:278.

33. William Alexander, *The Map and Description of New England* (London, 1624).

34. Smith, *Complete Works of Captain John Smith*, 2:440, 442, tells us how he spent the summer of 1616 visiting the towns and gentry in Devon and Cornwall, "giving them Bookes and Maps." He also presented "one thousand with a great many maps, both of Virginia and New England . . . to thirty of the Chief Companies in London at their halls." For examples of the later use of maps in colonial promotion, see Jeannette D. Black, "Mapping the English Colonies in North America: The Beginnings," in Norman J. W. Thrower, ed., *The Compleat Plattmaker: Essays on Chart, Map, and Globe Making in England in the Seventeenth and Eighteenth Centuries* (Berkeley: University of California Press, 1978), 101–25, esp. 115–18.

35. The old and new names are tabulated by Smith in a leaf inserted in some copies of *A Description of New England* in *Complete Works of Captain John Smith*, 1:319.

36. Ibid., dedication "To the High Hopeful Charles, Prince of Great Britaine," 1:309. The story is garbled in some popular histories of American cartography. See Seymour I. Schwartz and Ralph E. Ehrenberg, *The Mapping of America* (New York: Harry N. Abrams, 1980), 96, where it is stated that the place-names were "demanded by the fifteen-year-old Prince Charles of Scotland."

37. Benes, *New England Prospect: A Loan Exhibition of Maps*, 5–6.

38. Winsor, "Earliest Maps of Massachusetts Bay," 1:52–56.

39. The phrase is that of William Boelhower, "Inventing America: The Culture of the Map," *Revue Française D'Etudes Américaines* 36 (1988): 211–24.

40. Ronald Sanders, *Lost Tribes and Promised Lands: The Origins of American Racism* (Boston: Little, Brown and Co., 1978), 339–40.

41. Benes, *New England Prospect: A Loan Exhibition of Maps*, 27.

42. Krim, "Acculturation of the New England Landscape," 75–78.

43. Ibid., 79.

44. Wilbur Zelinsky, "Some Problems in the Distribution of Generic Terms in the Place-Names of the Northeastern United States," *Annals of the Association of American Geographers* 45 (1955): 319–49.

45. William Cronon, *Changes in the Land: Indians, Colonists, and the Ecology of New England* (New York: Hill and Wang, 1983), 66.

46. Benes, *New England Prospect: A Loan Exhibition of Maps,* 76.

47. Johannes Fabian, *Language and Colonial Power: The Appropriation of Swahili in the Former Belgian Congo, 1880–1938* (Cambridge: Cambridge University Press, 1986), 27.

48. Wood, *New England's Prospect.* For a modern edition, see William Wood, *New England's Prospect,* ed. Alden T. Vaughan (Amherst: University of Massachusetts Press, 1977).

49. Or on a common prototype. On the map, see Justin Winsor, "The Winthrop Map," in *Narrative and Critical History,* vol. 3, after p. 380, and Judge Chamberlain, "Early Map of Eastern Massachusetts," *Massachusetts Historical Society Proceedings,* 2d ser., 1 (1884), 211–14.

50. William Hubbard, *The Present State of New-England, Being a Narrative of the Troubles with the Indians 1677* (New York: York Mail-Print, 1972). On the "praying towns," see Neal Salisbury, "Red Puritans: The 'Praying Indians' of Massachusetts Bay and John Eliot," *William and Mary Quarterly* 31 (1974): 27–54. On the policy of breaking up tribal units and confining them to artificially established plantations or reservations, see also Yasu Kawashima, "Jurisdiction of the Colonial Courts over the Indians in Massachusetts, 1689–1763," *New England Quarterly* 42 (1969): 532–50.

51. Hubbard, *The Present State.* The "Table" is printed on seven pages of the original text following p. 131.

52. Ibid., xv.

53. Ibid., xiii.

54. Cecelia Tichi, introduction to Hubbard, *The Present State,* xiii.

55. See Catherine Delano Smith, "Maps in Bibles in the Sixteenth Century," *Map Collector* 39 (1987): 2–14; also Catherine Delano Smith and Elizabeth M. Ingram, *Maps in Bibles, 1500–1600: An Illustrated Catalogue* (Geneva: Librarie Droz, 1991).

56. Hubbard, *The Present State,* vii, clearly regarded a realistic geographical framework as important to his narrative, believing that truth suffered when events occurred in amorphous space undefined by familiar landmarks. He wrote, "For our Souldiers in the pursuit of their Enemies being drawn into many desert places, inaccessible Woods, and unknown Paths, which no Geographers hand ever measured, scarce any Vultures eye had ever seen, there was a necessity to take up many things in reference thereunto upon no better credit sometimes than common Report."

57. I adopt this sentence from Boelhower, "Inventing America."

58. Thomas Morton, *The New England Canaan, or New Canaan: Containing an*

Abstract of New England Composed in Three Books (Boston: Prince Society, 1883). For the broader context of these attitudes toward the territory, see Mason I. Lowance, Jr., *The Language of Canaan: Metaphor and Symbol in New England from the Puritans to the Transcendentalists* (Cambridge: Harvard University Press, 1980).

59. See, for example, "What's in a Name? For Indians, Cultural Survival," *New York Times,* 4 August 1988 (the restoration of Apache names in an Arizona reservation), or "NWT Natives Seek to Put Own Stamp on Map of North," *Globe and Mail* (Toronto), 12 October 1987 (on the restoration of traditional Indian and Inuit names to the Northwest Territories, Canada), and "A Town with a History, but Whose?" *New York Times International,* 20 April 1991 (the debate about restoring the Indian name *Aquinnah* to the town of Gay Head on Martha's Vineyard, Massachusetts).

60. Joseph Conrad, *Heart of Darkness: An Authoritative Text, Backgrounds and Sources, Criticism,* ed. Robert Kimbarough (New York: W. W. Norton and Co., 1971), 8; for Conrad's other writing on geography and maps, see also 99–104.

61. See also Sir Richard Burton, *Personal Narrative of Pilgrimage to Al-Medinah and Meccah,* 2 vols. (New York: Dover, 1964), 1:1, where he wrote of "that opprobrium to modern adventure, the huge white blot which in our maps still notes the Eastern and the Central regions of Arabia," with the implication that it is the duty of the European explorer to fill it.

62. Even allowing for the fact that the local Indian populations had been greatly reduced by disease by the time the Puritan settlers arrived, the notion of "emptiness" is as exaggerated as it is deeply ingrained in American historiography. Perry Miller, *Errand into the Wilderness* (Cambridge: Harvard University Press, 1964), vii, wrote of "the massive narrative of the movement of European culture into the vacant wilderness of America." See the discussion in Jane Tompkins, " 'Indians': Textualism, Morality, and the Problem of History," *Critical Inquiry* 13 (1986): 101–19.

63. Benes, *New England Prospect: A Loan Exhibition of Maps,* 36.

64. Lewis Pyenson, "Cultural Imperialism and Exact Science: German Expansion Overseas, 1900–1930," *History of Science* 20 (1982): 1–43.

65. For a description, see Jeannette D. Black, *The Blathwayt Atlas,* vol. 2, *Commentary* (Providence: Brown University Press, 1970–75), map 11, 82–85.

66. For this wider discourse, which could have been written with seventeenth-century maps in mind, see especially "Bounding the Land," chapter 4 in Cronon, *Changes in the Land,* 54–81.

67. For its present-day survival, see James Axtell, "Europeans, Indians, and the Age of Discovery in the American History Textbooks," *American Historical Review* 92 (1987): 621–32.

68. For the evidence for this organization, see Anthony F. C. Wallace, "Political Organization and Land Tenure among the Northeastern Indians, 1600–1830," *Southwestern Journal of Anthropology* 13 (1957): 301–21. Early European accounts demonstrate that tribal territories were clearly delimited by natural features such as rivers,

lakes, and watershed lines. For example, see "The Description of the Country of Mawooshen," (an eastern Abenaki account recorded in 1605) in David B. Quinn and Alison M. Quinn, eds., *The English New England Voyages, 1602–1608,* 2d ser., no. 161 (London: Hakluyt Society, 1983), 469–76. The description was obtained from one of the Indians captured by Weymouth and taken back to England (see note 16 above).

69. On the background to French representation of Indian territories on maps, see Cornelius J. Jaenen, "Characteristics of French-Amerindian Contact in New France," in Stanley H. Palmer and Dennis Reinhartz, eds., *Essays on the History of North American Discovery and Exploration* (College Station: Texas A & M University Press, 1988), 79–101.

70. Francis Jennings, *The Invasion of America: Indians, Colonialism, and the Cant of Conquest* (New York: W. W. Norton and Co., 1976), 67.

71. Ibid., quoting Edward Winslow, "Good Newes from New England," in Alexander Young, ed., *Chronicles of the Pilgrim Fathers of the Colony of Plymouth from 1602 to 1625* (Boston: C. C. Little and J. Brown, 1841), 361.

72. On the origins of the reservation system in New England, see Yasu Kawashima, "Legal Origins of the Indian Reservation in Colonial Massachusetts," in Bruce A. Glasrud and Alan M. Smith, eds., *Race Relations in British North America, 1607–1783* (Chicago: Nelson-Hall, 1982), 65–83.

73. Thomas More, *The Essential Thomas More,* ed. and trans. James J. Greene and John P. Dolan (New York, 1967), 61, quoted in Sanders, *Lost Tribes and Promised Lands,* 327.

74. John Winthrop, Sr., "General Considerations for the Plantation in New England, with an Answer to Several Objections," *Winthrop Papers* 2:120, in Jennings, *Invasion of America,* 82.

75. Quoted in Cronon, *Changes in the Land,* 56–57.

76. Quoted in Lowance, *The Language of Canaan,* 57, from Samuel Danforth, *A Briefe Recognition of New England's Errand into the Wilderness* (Boston, 1671).

77. Ibid., 71, quoting John Flavel, *Husbandry Spiritualized* (Boston, 1709).

78. Robert David Sack, *Human Territoriality: Its Theory and History* (Cambridge: Cambridge University Press, 1986), 134; see also D. W. Meinig, *The Shaping of America: A Geographical Perspective on 500 Years of History,* vol. 1, *Atlantic America, 1492–1800* (New Haven: Yale University Press, 1986), 232–33.

79. W. P. Cumming, R. A. Skelton, and D. B. Quinn, *The Discovery of North America* (London: Paul Elek, 1971), 21.

80. John Smith, "The True Travels, Adventures, and Observations of Captaine John Smith," 892, and "Advertisements; or, The Path-way to Experience to Erect a Plantation," 946–47, in Smith, *Complete Works* 3:222, 286.

81. J. P. Baxter, ed., *Documentary History of the State of Maine,* 24 vols., 2d ser. (Portland: Various Publishers, 1869–1916), 7:73–75.

82. The method of dividing land by lottery was also used to allocate land at the township level in New England. See, for example, John Smith, "The Generall Historie of Virginia, New England, and the Summer Isles, 1624," in Smith, *Complete Works* 2:776. He wrote of the first New England plantation, "So in the afternoone we went to measure out the grounds, and divided our company into 19 families, alotting to every person a poule in bredth and three in length: and so we cast lots where euery man should lie, which we staked out."

83. Alexander, *Map and Description of New England.*

84. Winsor, *Narrative and Critical History* 3:307.

85. For a description of this process, see W. Keith Kavenagh, ed., *Foundations of Colonial America: A Documentary History,* vol. 1, *Northeastern Colonies* (New York: Chelsea House Publishers and R. R. Bowker Co., 1973), 5–6, which does not, however, mention maps. Independent confirmation of the use of maps in this process is suggested by the map collections of English royalty and statesmen in this period.

86. F. N. Thorpe, ed., *The Federal and State Constitutions, Colonial Charters, and Other Organic Laws of the United States,* 7 vols. (Washington, D.C.: Government Printing Office, 1909), 7:3783, quoted in Sack, *Human Territoriality,* 134.

87. Ibid., 7:3784. For the wider legal background to this doctrine, see Olive Patricia Dickason, "Old World Law, New World Peoples, and Concepts of Sovereignty," in Palmer and Reinhartz, *Essays on the History of North American Discovery and Exploration,* 52–78, note 43.

88. Thorpe, ed., *Federal and State Constitutions,* 7:3783–84.

89. Kavenagh, ed., *Foundations of Colonial America,* 1:40–44.

90. Ibid., 90–92.

91. See especially Benes, *New England Prospect: A Loan Exhibition of Maps.*

92. Richard M. Candee, "Land Surveys of William and John Godsoe of Kittery, Maine: 1689–1769," in Benes, ed., *New England Prospect: Maps, Place Names,* 12.

93. See Viola Barnes, *The Dominion of New England* (New Haven: Yale University Press, 1923). A map associated with this proposal is described by Jeanette Black, *The Blathwayt Atlas,* vol. II, map 12, 86–87.

94. Kavenagh, ed., *Foundations of Colonial America,* 1:96–107.

95. The examples reproduced in Benes, *New England Prospect: A Loan Exhibition of Maps,* bear this out.

SEVEN ◆ *Can There Be a Cartographic Ethics?*

A version of this essay was presented as a seminar in the Department of Geography at Penn State University on 13 March 1991. I am grateful for constructive comments received on that occasion; to David DiBiase for offering to publish it as a contribution to the debate he has initiated; for the observations of my colleague Sona Andrews on

278 ◆ *Notes to Pages 198–203*

an earlier draft; and for help from Ellen Hanlon and Pellervo Kokkonen in preparing the manuscript for publication.

1. "Agency Shows Way for Gulf Forces," *Washington Post,* 2 January 1991.

2. Patrick McHaffie, Sona Andrews, Michael Dobson, and "Two anonymous employees of a federal mapping agency," "Ethical Problems in Cartography: A Roundtable Commentary," *Cartographic Perspectives* 7 (1990): 3–13.

3. Quoted in Martin Wachs, "Introduction," in Martin Wachs, ed., *Ethics in Planning* (Piscataway, N.J.: Rutgers Center for Urban Policy Research Institute, 1985), xiii.

4. McHaffie et al., "Ethical Problems," 4.

5. Mark Monmonier, *How to Lie with Maps* (Chicago: University of Chicago Press, 1991), 1.

6. McHaffie et al., "Ethical Problems," 8.

7. For ways in which aesthetics in general is a socially constructed and historically contingent set of values see Terry Eagleton, *The Ideology of the Aesthetic* (Oxford: Basil Blackwell, 1990).

8. P.J. Stickler, "Invisible Towns: A Case Study in the Cartography of South Africa," *GeoJournal* 22, no. 3 (1990): 329–33.

9. Ibid., 333.

10. Monmonier, *How to Lie With Maps,* 147.

11. Ibid., 154.

12. Arthur H. Robinson, *The Look of Maps: An Examination of Cartographic Design* (Madison: University of Wisconsin Press, 1952), 12.

13. Edward R. Tufte, *The Visual Display of Quantitative Information* (Cheshire, Conn.: Graphics Press, 1983), passim, epitomizes the positivist belief—adhered to by many cartographers—in the power of graphic representation to "tell the truth" with "clarity, precision, and efficiency," and with violations of the rules being measured in such meaningless statistical abstractions (from an ethical point of view) as the "Lie Factor" (57–58).

14. Michael F. Goodchild, "Geographic Information Systems," *Progress in Human Geography* 15, no. 2 (1991): 194–20.

15. Quoted without citation in Gerald Holton, *The Advancement of Science and Its Burdens: The Jefferson Lecture and Other Essays* (Cambridge: Cambridge University Press, 1986), 294.

16. McHaffie et al., "Ethical Problems," 8.

17. The International Cartographic Association, for example, often seems to view the history of map making in these terms: a recent example is Joel Morrison, "The Revolution in Cartography in the 1980s," in *Cartography Past, Present, and Future: A Festschrift for F. J. Ormeling,* ed. D. W. Rhind and D. R. F. Taylor (London: Elsevier for the International Cartographic Association, 1989), 169–85.

18. Duane Marble, Computer Network Conference, *Geography,* 31 January 1991.

19. I have explored this question more fully in a number of recent essays: J. B. Harley, "Silences and Secrecy: The Hidden Agenda of Cartography in Early Modern Europe," *Imago Mundi* 40 (1988): 57–76; J. B. Harley, "Maps, Knowledge, and Power," in Denis Cosgrove and Stephen Daniels, eds., *The Iconography of Landscape* (Cambridge: Cambridge University Press, 1988), 277–312; and J. B. Harley, "Deconstructing the Map," *Cartographica* 26, no. 2 (1989): 1–20.

20. For a discussion of this point, critical of the assumption that the cartographer—as in the traditional communication model—controls the selection of "reality" to be included in the map, see J. S. Keates, *Understanding Maps* (London: Longman, 1982), 101–6.

21. Patrick McHaffie, "The Creation of Public Cartographic Information: 'Penciling in' the Nexus," Paper presented at the Miami meeting of the Association of American Geographers, April 1991.

22. As a subject, cartographic ethics appears to be in a very early stage of what philosophers call "descriptive ethics": for relevant questions see D. T. Goldberg, *Ethical Theory and Social Issues: Historical Texts and Contemporary Readings* (New York: Holt, Rinehard, Winston, 1988).

23. On the problems of the increasing commodification of computer-based geographic and land-information systems see Earl F. Epstein and John D. McLaughlin, "A Discussion on Public Information: Who Owns It? Who Uses It? Should We Limit Access?," ACSM *Bulletin,* October 1990, 33–38.

24. For some examples, see J. B. Harley, "Cartography, Ethics, and Social Theory," *Cartographica* 27, no. 2 (1990): 1–23.

25. The implicit discrimination in maps has now become an ethical issue for educators: see Keith Hodgkinson, "Standing the World on Its Head: A Review of Eurocentrism in Humanities Maps and Atlases," *Teaching History,* 62 (1991): 19–23.

26. Quoted in Andrew Ross, "Techno-Ethics and Tele-Ethics: Three Lives in the Day of Max Headroom" (Milwaukee: University of Wisconsin-Milwaukee, Center for Twentieth Century Studies, Working Paper No. 8, 1988), 4.

27. Denis Wood, "Responses" to "Cartography, Ethics, and Social Theory," *Cartographica* 26, nos. 3 & 4 (1989): 117–19.

28. Ross, "Techno-Ethics," 3.

29. The latter is implied by Dobson in McHaffie et al., "Ethical Problems," 4.

WORKS BY J. B. HARLEY

compiled by Matthew H. Edney

The primary source of this extensive bibliography—comprising approximately 180 publications and two doctoral dissertations, but excluding book reviews—is Brian Harley's own curriculum vitae of July 1991, a copy of which was kindly provided by David Woodward. This has been corrected and updated with Harley's posthumous publications. Richard Oliver and Roger Kain checked some of Harley's essays in English local history journals, and Paul Laxton added further details.

Published Works

1958   "Population Trends and Agricultural Developments from the Warwickshire Hundred Rolls of 1279." *Economic History Review* 11: 8–18. Reprinted, with a new "Supplementary Note," in Alan R. H. Baker, John D. Hamshere, and John Langton, eds., *Geographical Interpretations of Historical Sources: Readings in Historical Geography*, Studies in Historical Geography. London: David & Charles; New York: Barnes & Noble, 1970, 55–68.

1960   "Population and Land-Utilization in the Warwickshire Hundreds of Stoneleigh and Kineton, 1086–1300." Ph.D. diss., University of Birmingham.

1961   "The Hundred Rolls of 1279." *Amateur Historian* 5 (autumn): 9–16.

1962   *Christopher Greenwood, County Map-Maker, and His Worcestershire Map of 1822.* Worcester: Worcestershire Historical Society, viii + 72 pages and folded facsimile.

        Contribution to the discussion of G. R. Crone, E. M. J. Campbell, and R. A. Skelton, "Landmarks in British Cartography." *Geographical Journal* 128: 427–28.

"The One-Inch to the Mile Maps of England and Wales." *Amateur Historian* 5 (autumn): 130–40. Reprinted in *The Historian's Guide to Ordnance Survey Maps* (1964), 7–16 (see below).

1963   "The Maps of England and Wales at the Six Inch and Twenty-Five Inch Scales." *Amateur Historian* 5 (spring): 202–11. Reprinted in *The Historian's Guide to Ordnance Survey Maps* (1964), 17–26 (see below).

"The Society of Arts and the Surveys of English Counties, 1759–1809. (i) The Origin of the Premiums." *Journal of the Royal Society of Arts* 112, no. 5089 (December): 43–46.

"The Town Plans and Small-Scale Maps of England and Wales." *Amateur Historian* 5 (summer): 251–59. Reprinted in *The Historian's Guide to Ordnance Survey Maps* (1964), 27–34 (see below).

1964   "William Yates and Peter Burdett: Their Role in the Mapping of Lancashire and Cheshire During the Late Eighteenth Century." *Transactions of the Historic Society of Lancashire and Cheshire for 1963* 115: 107–31.

"The Evaluation of Historical Evidence on British County Maps." In F. E. Ian Hamilton, ed., *Abstracts of Papers: 20th International Geographical Congress.* London: Thomas Nelson, 7–8.

"Industrial England in the Late Eighteenth Century." In F. E. Ian Hamilton, ed., *Abstracts of Papers: 20th International Geographical Congress.* London: Thomas Nelson, 266–67.

"The Settlement Geography of Early Medieval Warwickshire." *Transactions of the Institute of British Geographers* 34: 115–30.

"The Society of Arts and the Survey of English Counties, 1759–1809. (ii) The Response to the Awards, 1759–1766." *Journal of the Royal Society of Arts* 112, no. 5090 (January): 119–24.

"The Society of Arts and the Survey of English Counties. (iii) The Changes of Policy, 1767–1801." *Journal of the Royal Society of Arts* 112, no. 5092 (March): 269–75.

"The Society of Arts and the Survey of English Counties. (iv) The Society's Place in Cartographical History." *Journal of the Royal Society of Arts* 112, no. 5095 (June): 538–43.

"Introduction," "The Ordnance Survey Maps of Scotland," and "Conclusion." In J. B. Harley and C. W. Phillips, *The Historian's Guide to Ordnance Survey Maps,* 5–6, 42–50, and 51. London: National Council of Social Service for the Standing Conference for Local History, 1964 (see below).

[J. B. Harley and C. W. Phillips]. *The Historian's Guide to Ordnance Survey Maps.* London: National Council of Social Service for the Standing Conference for Local History. (Contains three of Harley's essays originally published in *Amateur Historian* in 1962–63 and some additional material.)

1965   "A Proposed Survey of Lancashire by Francis and Netlam Giles." *Transactions of the Historic Society of Lancashire and Cheshire for 1964* 116: 197–206.

Contribution to the discussion of G. R. Crone, "New Light on the Hereford Map." *Geographical Journal* 131: 460–61.

"The Re-Mapping of England, 1750–1800." *Imago Mundi* 19: 56–67.

1966   "The Bankruptcy of Thomas Jefferys: An Episode in the Economic History of Eighteenth Century Map-Making." *Imago Mundi* 20: 27–48.

"English County Map-Making in the Early Years of the Ordnance Survey: The Map of Surrey by Joseph Lindley and William Crosley." *Geographical Journal* 132: 372–78.

"From Saxton to Speed." *Cheshire Round* 1, no. 6: 174–88.

"John Strachey of Somerset: An Antiquarian Cartographer of the Early-Eighteenth Century." In "Proceedings of the Symposium of the British Cartographic Society, University College Swansea, 17th–19th September 1965," 2–7. *Cartographic Journal* 3, no. 1: separately paginated appendix.

1967   "The American Revolution Maps of William Faden." In *The American Philosophical Society Yearbook for 1966,* 346–49. Philadelphia: American Philosophical Society, 1967.

"Enclosure and Tithe Maps." *Amateur Historian* 7, no. 8: 265–74. Reprinted in *Maps for the Local Historian* (1972), 29–39 (see below).

"Estate Maps." *Amateur Historian* 7, no. 7: 223–31. Reprinted in *Maps for the Local Historian* (1972), 20–28 (see below).

"Maps and Plans of Towns." *Amateur Historian* 7, no. 6: 196–208. Reprinted in *Maps for the Local Historian* (1972), 7–19 (see below).

"Maps of Early Georgian Cheshire." *Cheshire Round* 1, no. 8: 256–69.

"Ogilby and Collins: Cheshire by Road & Sea." *Cheshire Round* 1, no. 7: 210–25.

"Uncultivated Fields in the History of British Cartography." *Cartographic Journal* 4: 7–11.

1968   "Cheshire Maps, 1787–1831." *Cheshire Round* 1, no. 9: 290–305.

"Conference on the History of Cartography, London, September 1967." *Imago Mundi* 22: 9.

"Error and Revision of Early Ordnance Survey Maps." *Cartographic Journal* 5: 115–24.

"The Evaluation of Early Maps: Towards a Methodology." *Imago Mundi* 22: 62–74.

"Maps of Communications." *Local Historian* 8, no. 2: 61–71. Reprinted in *Maps for the Local Historian* (1972), 40–50 (see below).

"Marine Charts." *Local Historian* 8, no. 3: 86–97. Reprinted in *Maps for the Local Historian* (1972), 51–62 (see below).

"Preface," "Introduction," and "A Carto-Bibliographical Note." In William Yates, *A Map of the County of Lancashire, 1786,* 5–22 and 48. Liverpool: Historic Society of Lancashire and Cheshire (with a facsimile of Yates's map).

[editor]. "Papers Presented to the Conference on the History of Cartography, London, September 1967." *Imago Mundi* 22: 10–84.

1969   "Bibliographical Notes." *First Edition of the One-Inch Ordnance Survey of England and Wales.* 97 sheets, each with a substantial bibliographical note. Newton Abbot, Devon: David & Charles, 1969–71.

"County Maps." *Local Historian* 8, no. 5: 167–79. Reprinted in *Maps for the Local Historian* (1972), 63–76 (see below).

"Introduction to the 1969 Edition." In Charles Close, *The Early Years of the Ordnance Survey,* xi–xxxv. Newton Abbot, Devon: David & Charles. Paperback edition, 1971.

"Physical Features of Herefordshire." *Encyclopedia Britannica* 14th ed., 11:427–28.

1970   "Bibliographical Note." In John Ogilby, *Britannia, London 1675,* v–xxxi. Theatrum Orbis Theatrum, Series of Atlases in Facsimile, 5th series, vol. 2. Amsterdam: Theatrum Orbis Terrarum.

"Introduction." In Emmanuel Bowen, *Britannia Depicta or Ogilby Improved by Emmanuel Bowen, 1720, Facsimile Reprint,* 3–16. Newcastle upon Tyne: Frank Graham, Ltd.

"Medieval and Early Modern Liverpool." In J. A. Patmore and A. G. Hodgkiss, eds., *Merseyside in Maps,* 12–13. London: Longman.

[J. B. Harley and Paul Laxton]. "Merseyside in 1800." In J. A. Patmore and A. G. Hodgkiss, eds., *Merseyside in Maps,* 14–15. London: Longman.

[J. B. Harley and Paul Laxton]. "Nineteenth-Century Building Patterns." In J. A. Patmore and A. G. Hodgkiss, eds., *Merseyside in Maps,* 18–19. London: Longman.

1971   "From Manpower to Steam." *Geographical Magazine* 43, no. 6 (March): 417–26 (A revised and expanded version appeared in 1973).

"The Ordnance Survey and the Origins of Official Geological Mapping in Devon and Cornwall." In K. J. Gregory and W. L. D. Ravenhill, eds., *Exeter Essays in Geography in Honour of Arthur Davies,* 105–23. Exeter: University of Exeter Press.

"Place Names on the Early Ordnance Survey Maps of England and Wales." *Cartographic Journal* 8: 91–105.

[J. B. Harley and Donald Hodson]. "Introduction." In Emmanuel Bowen and Thomas Kitchen, *The Royal English Atlas: Eighteenth-Century County Maps of England and Wales.* Newton Abbot, Devon: David & Charles.

[J. B. Harley and William Ravenhill]. "Proposals for County Maps of Cornwall (1699) and Devon (1700)." *Devon and Cornwall Notes and Queries* 32: 33–39.

1972   "Introduction." In *The County Maps from William Camden's Britannia, 1695, by Robert Morden: A Facsimile,* vii–xii. Newton Abbot, Devon: David & Charles.

Maps for the Local Historian: A Guide to the British Sources. London: National Council of Social Service for the Standing Conference for Local History, 86 pages. (Contains Harley's several essays published in *Amateur [Local] Historian* in 1967–69, with a bibliographic postscript.)

"Specifications for Military Surveys in British North America, 1750–75." In W. P. Adams and F. M. Helleiner, eds., *International Geography 1972: Papers Submitted to the 22nd International Geographical Congress,* 1:424–25. 2 vols. Montreal: University of Toronto Press.

1973 "Change in Historical Geography: A Qualitative Impression of Quantitative Methods." *Area* 5: 69–74.

"England circa 1850." In H. C. Darby, ed., *A New Historical Geography of England,* 527–94. Cambridge: Cambridge University Press.

Essay review of *An Exact Survey of the City's of London Westminster ye Borough of Southwark and the Country near Ten Mile Round Begun in 1741 & Ended in 1745 by John Rocque Land Surveyor & Engrau'd by Richard Parr,* edited by Harry Margary (Lympne Castle, Kent: Harry Margary; Chichester, Sussex: Phillimore & Co., ca.1973). *Bulletin of the Society of University Cartographers* 7, no. 2: 8–10.

"From Manpower to Steam" (a revision and expansion of the 1971 essay). In A. R. H. Baker and J. B. Harley, eds., *Man Made the Land: Essays in English Historical Geography,* 167–80 (see below).

[A. R. H. Baker and J. B. Harley, eds.] *Man Made the Land: Essays in English Historical Geography.* Newton Abbot, Devon: David & Charles.

[J. B. Harley and J. C. Harvey] "Introduction." In Thomas Jefferys, *The County of York, Surveyed in MDCCLXVII, VIII, IX, and MDCCLXX.* Lympne Castle, Kent: Harry Margary.

1974 "Changing the Minister's Mind: A Guide to the Ordnance Survey Review." *Area* 6: 211–19.

"Editor's Preface." In R. A. Skelton, *Saxton's Survey of England and Wales, with a Facsimile of Saxton's Wall-Map of 1583,* edited by J. B. Harley, 5. *Imago Mundi* Supplement, 6. Amsterdam: Nico Israel.

[J. B. Harley and Paul Laxton]. "Introduction." In *A Survey of the County Palatine of Chester: P. P. Burdett, 1777* (with a facsimile of Burdett's map).

Historic Society of Lancashire and Cheshire, Occasional Series, 1. Liverpool: Historic Society of Lancashire and Cheshire, 36 pages.

1975   *Ordnance Survey Maps: A Descriptive Manual.* Southampton: Ordnance Survey, xv + 200 pages.

[Susanna Guy and J. B. Harley] "Printed Maps of Devon, 1575–1900: A Survey of Resources Within the County." *The Devon Historian* 11 (October): 12–20.

[J. B. Harley, D. V. Fowkes, and J. C. Harvey]. "P. P. Burdett's Map of Derbyshire, 1791 Edition: An Explanatory Introduction." In *Burdett's Map of Derbyshire, 1791,* fols. 1v–7v. Derby: Derbyshire Archaeological Society. (The essay is located on the verso of the first seven [unnumbered] leaves of the facsimile.)

[J. B. Harley and Yolande O'Donoghue]. "Introductory Notes." In *Kent, Essex, E. Sussex and S. Suffolk,* vol. 1 of *The Old Series Ordnance Survey Maps of England and Wales, Scale: 1 Inch to 1 Mile: A Reproduction of the 110 Sheets of the Survey in Early State,* vii–xxxvi. Lympne Castle, Kent: Harry Margary.

1976   "George Washington Map-Maker." *Geographical Magazine* 48: 588–94.

"Irish Geography and the Early Ordnance Survey: A Review." *Irish Geography* 9: 137–42.

"The Map-User in Eighteenth-Century North America: Some Preliminary Observations." In Brian S. Osborne, ed., *The Settlement of Canada: Origins and Transfer; Proceedings of the 1975 British-Canadian Symposium on Historical Geography,* 47–69. Kingston, Ont.: Department of Geography, Queen's University.

[Audrey Erskine, J. B. Harley, and William Ravenhill]. "A Map of 'the way to Deartmoore Forest, the Comen of Devonshire' made circa 1609." *Devon and Cornwall Notes and Queries* 33: 229–36.

1977   "Evidence for Surveyors." *Geographical Magazine* 49, no. 5 (February): 334–35.

"Atlas Maker for Independent America." *Geographical Magazine* 49: 766–71.

"Harry Thorpe, 1913–1977: A Tribute." *Journal of Historical Geography* 3, no. 3: 307–8.

[J. B. Harley and Yolande O'Donoghue]. "Introductory Notes." In *Devon, Cornwall and West Somerset,* vol. 2 of *The Old Series Ordnance Survey Maps of England and Wales, Scale: 1 Inch to 1 Mile: A Reproduction of the 110 Sheets of the Survey in Early State,* vii–xxxvii. Lympne Castle, Kent: Harry Margary.

[J. B. Harley and Gwyn Walters]. "William Roy's Maps, Mathematical Instruments and Library: The Christie's Sale of 1790." *Imago Mundi* 29: 9–22.

1978   "The Contemporary Mapping of the American Revolutionary War," "The Spread of Cartographical Ideas between the Revolutionary Armies," and "The Map User in the Revolution." In J. B. Harley, Barbara Bartz Petchenik, and Lawrence W. Towner, *Mapping the American Revolutionary War,* 1–110 and 149–67. Chicago: University of Chicago Press.

"The Map Collection of William Cecil, First Baron Burghley, 1520–98." *Map Collector* 3: 12–19.

"Mapping the Great Lakes." *Journal of Historical Geography* 4, no. 2: 228–30 (Conference report).

"William Roy and the Ordnance Survey after 200 Years: An Assessment." *Chartered Surveyor: The Journal of the Royal Institution of Chartered Surveyors* 110: 163–69.

[J. B. Harley and J. B. Manterfield]. "The Ordnance Survey 1:500 Plans of Exeter, 1874–1877." *Devon and Cornwall Notes and Queries* 34: 63–75.

[J. B. Harley and Gwyn Walters]. "English Map Collecting, 1790–1840: A Pilot Survey of the Evidence in Sotheby Sale Catalogues." *Imago Mundi* 30: 31–55.

1979   "Christopher Saxton and the First Atlas of England and Wales, 1579–1979." *Map Collector* 8: 2–11.

The Ordnance Survey and Land-Use Mapping: Parish Books of Reference and the County Series 1:2500 Maps, 1855–1918. Historical Geography Research Group, Research Series, 2. Norwich: Geo Books, 59 pages.

"Packaging the Image: The Philadelphia Map Trade and United States Cartography, 1783–1815." In Ralph D. Vicero, ed., *Proceedings of CUKANZUS '79: Rural, Urban, and Physical Environments in Frontier Transition: An International Conference for Historical Geographers, August 26–September 2, 1979, Los Angeles California*, 33–34.

1980   Contributions to W. A. Seymour, ed., *A History of the Ordnance Survey*. Folkestone, Kent: Dawson: "The Origins of the Ordnance Survey" (1–20); [J. B. Harley and Yolande O'Donoghue] "The Resumption of the Trigonometrical Survey" (21–32); "The Birth of the Topographical Survey" (44–56); "The Ordnance Survey Becomes a Map Publisher, 1801–1820" (67–78); [J. B. Harley and W. A. Seymour] "Place-Names" (60–62, 105–7, 175–76, 326).

"Costing Cartography (A Commentary on the Report of the Ordnance Survey Review Committee, Chaired by Sir David Serpell)." *Area* 12, no. 1: 1–8. Reprinted in *Surveying Technician* 9 (1980): 10–12.

[Michael J. Blakemore and J. B. Harley]. "Concepts in the History of Cartography: A Review and Perspective." Edited by Edward H. Dahl. *Cartographica* 17, no. 4: *Monograph* 26, 120 pages.

[J. B. Harley and Minda C. Phillips]. "Introduction." *The Revolutionary Era*, vol. 1 of *Manuscript Maps Relating to North America and the West Indies . . . in the Public Record Office*. Wakefield: EP Microform (a separate pamphlet accompanying a microfilm).

[J. B. Harley and William Ravenhill]. "The Gift of a Saxton Atlas to the University of Exeter." *Devon and Cornwall Notes and Queries* 34: 194–201.

1981   "Ancient Maps Waiting to be Read." *Geographical Magazine* 53, no. 5 (February): 313–17.

[Michael J. Blakemore and J. B. Harley]. "The Authors Reply." In "Concepts in the History of Cartography: Some Responses, with the Authors' Reply, Especially to Questions of Definition," edited by B. V. Gutsell, 77–96. *Cartographica* 19, no. 1: 66–96.

[J. B. Harley and R. W. Dunning]. "Introduction." In *Somerset Maps: Day and Masters 1782, Greenwood 1822; Introduction by J. B. Harley and R. W. Dunning*, 5–30. Somerset Record Society, vol. 76. Taunton: Somerset Record Society. (Part of a 38-page booklet included within a large portfolio of facsimiles.)

[J. B. Harley and Yolande O'Donoghue]. "Introductory Notes." In *South-Central England,* vol. 3 of *The Old Series Ordnance Survey Maps of England and Wales, Scale: 1 Inch to 1 Mile: A Reproduction of the 110 Sheets of the Survey in Early State,* vii–xxxviii. Lympne Castle, Kent: Harry Margary.

1982   "Historical Geography and its Evidence: Reflections on Modelling Sources." In A. R. H. Baker and Mark Billinge, eds., *Period and Place: Research Methods in Historical Geography,* 261–73 and 354–57. Cambridge Studies in Historical Geography, 1. Cambridge: Cambridge University Press. Reprinted in D. Brooks Green, ed., *Historical Geography: A Methodological Portrayal* (New York: Rowman and Littlefield, 1991), 347–62.

"The Ordnance Survey 1:528 Board of Health Town Plans in Warwickshire, 1848–1854." In T. R. Slater and P. J. Jarvis, eds., *Field and Forest: An Historical Geography of Warwickshire and Worcestershire,* 347–84. Norwich: Geo Books.

[J. B. Harley and Gwyn Walters]. "Welsh Orthography and Ordnance Survey Mapping, 1820–1905." *Archaeologia Cambriensis* 131: 98–135.

1983   "Meaning and Ambiguity in Tudor Cartography." In Sarah Tyacke, ed., *English Map-Making, 1500–1650: Historical Essays,* 22–45. London: The British Library.

[J. B. Harley and E. A. Stuart]. "George Withiell: A West Country Surveyor of the Late-Seventeenth Century." *Devon and Cornwall Notes and Queries* 35: 45–58 and 95–114.

[J. B. Harley and David Woodward]. "The History of Cartography Project: A Note on Its Organization and Assumptions." *Technical Papers of the Annual Meeting of the American Congress on Surveying and Mapping* 43: 580–89.

1984   "Contributions to the History of Cartography and Historical Geography. Studies submitted for the degree of D.Litt. in the University of Birmingham." 4 vols. (degree awarded 1985).

1985   "The Iconology of Early Maps." In Carla C. Marzoli, ed., *Imago et Mensura Mundi: Atti del IX Congresso Internazionale di Storia della Cartografia,* 1:29–38. 2 vols. Rome: Istituto della Enciclopedia Italiana.

"Writing Colonial Cartography: Report on the Seminar in Colonial Cartography at the Eleventh International Conference on the History of Cartography, Ottawa, July, 1985." *Map Collector* 33: 42.

1986   "Imago Mundi: The First Fifty Years and the Next Ten." *Cartographica* 23, no. 3: 1–15.

"Introductory Essay." In *Central England,* volume 4 of *The Old Series Ordnance Survey Maps of England and Wales, Scale: 1 Inch to 1 Mile: A Reproduction of the 110 Sheets of the Survey in Early State,* vii–xxxv. Lympne Castle, Kent: Harry Margary.

"Monarchs, Ministers, and Maps: Report on the Eighth Series of Kenneth Nebenzahl, Jr., Lectures in the History of Cartography, held at the Newberry Library, Chicago, 7–9 November 1985." *Map Collector* 35: 42–43.

1987   "Cartobibliography and the Collector: Review Article." *Imago Mundi* 39: 105–10.

"Innovation, Social Context and the History of Cartography: Review Article." *Cartographica* 24, no. 4: 59–68.

"Introductory Essay." In *Lincolnshire, Rutland and East Anglia,* vol. 5 of *The Old Series Ordnance Survey Maps of England and Wales, Scale: 1 Inch to 1 Mile: A Reproduction of the 110 Sheets of the Survey in Early State,* vii–xxxii. Lympne Castle, Kent: Harry Margary.

"My Favourite Map. The Map as Biography: Thoughts on Ordnance Survey Map, Six-Inch Sheet Devonshire CIX, SE, Newton Abbot." *Map Collector* 41: 18–20. Reprinted without notes in Peter Gould and Antoine Bailly, eds., *Le Pouvoir des Cartes: Brian Harley et la Cartographie,* trans. Philippe de Lavergne, as "La carte en tant que Biographie" (Paris: Anthropos, 1995), 11–18.

[J. B. Harley and David Woodward]. "Preface," "The Map and the Development of the History of Cartography," and "Concluding Remarks." In *Cartography in Prehistoric, Ancient, and Medieval Europe and the Mediterranean,* vol. 1 of J. B. Harley and David Woodward, eds., *The History of Cartography,* xv–xxi, 1–42, and 502–9 (see below).

[J. B. Harley and David Woodward, eds.]. *Cartography in Prehistoric, Ancient, and Medieval Europe and the Mediterranean,* vol. 1 of *The History of Cartography.* Chicago: University of Chicago Press.

1988 "L'Histoire de la Cartographie comme Discours." In Christian Jacob and Hervé Théry, eds., "Dossier: La Cartographie et ses Méthodes," 70–75. *Préfaces. Les Idées et les Sciences dans la Bibliographie de la France* 5 (December 1987–January 1988): 66–114.

"Maps, Knowledge, and Power." In Denis Cosgrove and Stephen Daniels, eds., *The Iconography of Landscape: Essays on the Symbolic Representation, Design and Use of Past Environments,* 277–312. Cambridge Studies in Historical Geography, 9. Cambridge: Cambridge University Press. Reprinted without notes in Peter Gould and Antoine Bailly, eds., *Le Pouvoir des Cartes: Brian Harley et la Cartographie,* trans. Philippe de Lavergne, as "Cartes, savoir et pouvoir" (Paris: Anthropos, 1995), 19–51. Reprinted in the present volume, as originally published.

"Silences and Secrecy: The Hidden Agenda of Cartography in Early Modern Europe." *Imago Mundi* 40: 57–76. Reprinted in facsimile as "Silences and Secrets: The Hidden Agenda of Cartography in Early Modern Europe" in A. J. R. Russell-Wood, ed., *An Expanding World: The European Impact on World History 1450–1800,* vol. 6, William K. Storey, ed., *Scientific Aspects of European Expansion* (Aldershot, Surrey: Ashgate Publishing, 1996), 161–80. (The erroneous title "Silences and Secrets" is the result of typographical error.) Also reprinted in the present volume.

1989 "Deconstructing the Map." *Cartographica* 26, no. 2: 1–20. Reprinted in John Agnew, David N. Livingstone, and Alisdair Rogers, eds., *Human Geography: An Essential Anthology* (Oxford: Blackwell, 1996), 422–43. A modified version appeared in T. J. Barnes and J. S. Duncan, eds., *Writing Worlds: Discourse, Text and Metaphor* (London: Routledge, 1992), 231–47. The original version is reprinted in the present volume.

"Historical Geography and the Cartographic Illusion." *Journal of Historical Geography* 15: 80–91.

[J. B. Harley and R. R. Oliver]. "Introductory Essay." In *North-Central England,* vol. 7 of *The Old Series Ordnance Survey Maps of England and Wales, Scale: 1 Inch to 1 Mile: A Reproduction of the 110 Sheets of the Survey in Early State,* vii–xxviii. Lympne Castle, Kent: Harry Margary.

[J. B. Harley and David Woodward]. "Reviewer's Errors on *The History of Cartography, Vol. 1:* A Factual Rejoinder." *Annals of the Association of American Geographers* 79: 146.

[J. B. Harley and David Woodward]. "Why Cartography Needs Its History." *American Cartographer* 16: 5–15.

1990   "Cartography, Ethics, and Social Theory." *Cartographica* 27, no. 2: 1–23.

"Foreword to the Map." In *The County of Kent in 1801: A Reproduction of the First Published Ordnance Survey Map of Great Britain.* Lympne Castle, Kent: Harry Margary and Kent County Library (four unnumbered pages at the head of the work).

"Guest Editorial." *Map Collector* 50: 2.

"Introduction: Text and Contexts in the Interpretation of Early Maps." In David Buisseret, ed., *From Sea Charts to Satellite Images: Interpreting North American History through Maps,* 3–15. Chicago: University of Chicago Press. Reprinted in the present volume.

Maps and The Columbian Encounter: An Interpretive Guide to the Travelling Exhibition. Assisted by Ellen Hanlon and Mark Warhus. Milwaukee: The Golda Meir Library, University of Wisconsin-Milwaukee.

[Howard Deller and J. B. Harley]. "The World by Lake Michigan." *Map Collector* 50: 2–9.

1991   "Can There Be a Cartographic Ethics?" *Cartographic Perspectives* 10: 9–16. Reprinted without notes in Peter Gould and Antoine Bailly, eds., *Le Pouvoir des Cartes: Brian Harley et la Cartographie,* trans. Philippe de Lavergne, as "Peut-il y avoir une Éthique Cartographique?" (Paris: Anthropos, 1995), 109–20. Also reprinted in the present volume.

"The Map as Mission: Jesuit Cartography as an Art of Persuasion." In Jane ten Brink Goldsmith, J. Patrice Marandel, J. Patrick Donnelly, and J. B. Harley, *Jesuit Art in North American Collections,* 28–30, 67–68. Milwaukee: Haggerty Museum of Art, Marquette University.

"The New History of Cartography." *UNESCO Courier* (June), 10–15.

[J. B. Harley and R. R. Oliver]. "Introductory Essay." In *Northern England,* vol. 8 of *The Old Series Ordnance Survey Maps of England and Wales, Scale: 1 Inch to 1 Mile: A Reproduction of the 110 Sheets of the Survey in Early State,* vii–xxxi. Lympne Castle, Kent: Harry Margary.

[J. B. Harley and David Woodward]. "An Alternative Route to Mapping History." *Americas [English Edition]* 43, nos. 5 and 6: 6–13.

Posthumously Published Works

1992   "Deconstructing the Map" (a modified version of the 1989 paper). In
Trevor J. Barnes and James S. Duncan, eds., *Writing Worlds: Discourse, Text,
and Metaphor in the Representation of Landscape,* 231–47. London: Rout-
ledge. Reprinted without notes in Peter Gould and Antoine Bailly, eds.,
Le Pouvoir des Cartes: Brian Harley et la Cartographie, trans. Philippe de
Lavergne, as "Déconstruire la Carte" (Paris: Anthropos, 1995), 61–85.

"Maps and the Invention of America." Edited by Catherine Delano Smith
and Peter Barber. *Map Collector* 58: 8–12.

"Rereading the Maps of the Columbian Encounter." Edited by Karl W.
Butzer and William M. Denevan. *Annals of the Association of American
Geographers* 82: 522–36. Reprinted without notes in Peter Gould and An-
toine Bailly, eds., *Le Pouvoir des Cartes: Brian Harley et la Cartographie,*
trans. Philippe de Lavergne, as "Relire les Cartes de la Découverte de
Christophe Colomb" (Paris: Anthropos, 1995), 87–107.

[J. B. Harley and R. R. Oliver]. "Introductory Essay." In *Wales,* vol. 6 of
*The Old Series Ordnance Survey Maps of England and Wales, Scale: 1 Inch to
1 Mile: A Reproduction of the 110 Sheets of the Survey in Early State,* vii–
xxviii. Lympne Castle, Kent: Harry Margary.

[J. B. Harley and David W. Tilton]. "Cosa, Juan de la." In Silvio A. Bedini,
ed., *The Christopher Columbus Encyclopedia,* 1:213–15. 2 vols. New York:
Simon and Schuster.

[J. B. Harley and David Woodward, eds.] *Cartography in the Traditional
Islamic and South Asian Societies,* vol. 2.1 of *The History of Cartography.* Chicago: University of Chicago Press. (Includes "Preface," xix–xxiv, and "Concluding Remarks," 510–18, by editors.)

[J. B. Harley and Kees Zandvliet]. "Art, Science, and Power in Sixteenth-
Century Dutch Cartography." *Cartographica* 29, no. 2: 10–19.

1993   "The Culture of the Map in Western History." *Cartographica* 30, no. 1:
Monograph 44, 170.

1994   [J. B. Harley and David Woodward, eds.]. *Cartography in the Traditional
East and Southeast Asian Societies,* vol. 2.2 of *The History of Cartography.*
Chicago: University of Chicago Press.

"New England Cartography and the Native Americans." In Emerson W. Baker, Edwin A. Churchill, Richard D'Abate, Kristine L. Jones, Victor A. Konrad and Harald E. L. Prins, eds., *American Beginnings: Exploration, Culture, and Cartography in the Land of Norumbega*, 287–313. Lincoln: University of Nebraska Press. Reprinted in the present volume.

1997 "Power and Legitimation in the English Geographical Atlases of the Eighteenth Century." In John A. Wolter and Ronald E. Grim, eds., *Images of the World: The Atlas through History*, 161–204. New York: McGraw-Hill for the Library of Congress. Reprinted in the present volume.

Works in Edited Series

Studies in Historical Geography. Series edited by Alan R. H. Baker and J. B. Harley and published by David & Charles, Newton Abbot and London, and by Barnes & Noble, New York.

Alan R. H. Baker, John D. Hamshere, and John Langton, eds. 1970. *Geographical Interpretations of Historical Sources: Readings in Historical Geography.*
J. C. Russell. 1972. *Medieval Regions and Their Cities.*
Alan R. H. Baker, ed. 1972. *Progress in Historical Geography.*
P. J. Perry. 1974. *British Farming in the Great Depression, 1870–1914: An Historical Geography.*

Studies in Historical Geography. Series edited by Alan R. H. Baker and J. B. Harley and published by Dawson, Folkestone (Kent), and by Archon Books, Hamden (Connecticut).

A. J. Christopher. 1976. *Southern Africa.*
Brian K. Roberts. 1977. *Rural Settlement in Britain.*
J. M. Powell. 1977. *Mirrors of the New World: Images and Image Makers in the Settlement Process.*
Michael Jones. 1977. *Finland: Daughter of the Sea.*
M. L. Parry. 1978. *Climatic Change, Agriculture and Settlement.*
J. H. C. Patten. 1978. *English Towns, 1500–1700.*
Robert M. Newcomb. 1979. *Planning the Past: Historical Landscape Resources and Recreation.*
Michael Turner. 1980. *English Parliamentary Enclosure: Its Historical Geography and Economic History.*

Cambridge Studies in Historical Geography. Series edited by Alan R. H. Baker, J. B. Harley, and David Ward and published by Cambridge University Press.

1. A. R. H. Baker and Mark Billinge, eds. 1982. *Period and Place: Research Methods in Historical Geography.*

2. David Turnock. 1982. *The Historical Geography of Scotland Since 1707: Geographical Aspects of Modernisation.*

3. Leonard Guelke. 1982. *Historical Understanding in Geography: An Idealist Approach.*

4. Richard J. Dennis. 1984. *English Industrial Cities of the Nineteenth Century: A Social Geography.*

5. A. R. H. Baker and Derek Gregory, eds. 1984. *Explorations in Historical Geography: Interpretative Essays.*

6. Roger J. P. Kain and Hugh C. Prince. 1985. *The Tithe Surveys of England and Wales.*

7. Robert David Sack. 1986. *Human Territoriality: Its Theory and History.*

8. David Watts. 1987. *The West Indies: Patterns of Development, Culture and Environmental Change Since 1492.*

9. Denis Cosgrove and Stephen Daniels, eds. 1988. *The Iconography of Landscape: Essays on the Symbolic Representation, Design and Use of Past Environments.*

10. Dietrich Denecke and Gareth Shaw, eds. 1988. *Urban Historical Geography: Recent Progress in Britain and Germany.*

11. J. M. Powell. 1988. *An Historical Geography of Modern Australia: The Restive Fringe.*

12. J. H. Galloway. 1989. *The Sugar Cane Industry: An Historical Geography from Its Origins to 1914.*

13. David Ward. 1989. *Poverty, Ethnicity, and the American City, 1840–1925: Changing Conceptions of the Slum and the Ghetto.*

14. M. C. Cleary. 1989. *Peasants, Politicians and Producers: The Organisation of Agriculture in France since 1918.*

15. A. D. M. Philips. 1989. *The Underdraining of Farmland in England During the Nineteenth Century.*

16. David J. Robinson, ed. 1990. *Migration in Colonial Spanish America.*

17. Gerry Kearns and Charles W. J. Withers, eds. 1991. *Urbanising Britain: Essays on Class and Community in the Nineteenth Century.*

18. Alan R. H. Baker and Gideon Biger, eds. 1992. *Ideology and Landscape in Historical Perspective: Essays on the Meanings of Some Places in the Past.*

This is a consolidated bibliography of all citations in the seven essays by J. B. Harley republished in this book, except those of works authored or coauthored by Harley (see the chronological list of his works).

Adams, Percy G. *Travelers and Travel Liars 1660–1800* (New York: Dover Publications, 1980).

Adorno, Rolena. *Guaman Poma: Writing and Resistance in Colonial Peru* (Austin: University of Texas Press, 1986).

Ager, John. "Maps and Propaganda," *Bulletin Society of University Cartographers* 11 (1977): 1–14.

Akerman, James R., and David Buisseret. *Monarchs, Ministers and Maps: A Cartographic Exhibit at the Newberry Library* (Chicago: Newberry Library, 1985).

Akerman, James R. "National Geographical Consciousness and the Structure of Early World Atlases." Paper presented at the Eleventh International Conference on the History of Cartography, Ottawa, Canada, July 1985.

Alexander, William. *The Map and Description of New England* (London, 1624).

Allen, James Egert. *Black History Past and Present* (New York: Exposition Press, 1971).

Almagià, Roberto. *Monumenta Cartographica Vaticana,* vol. 3, *Le Pitture Murali della Galleria delle Carte Geografiche* (Vatican City: Biblioteca Apostolica Vaticana, 1952).

Anderson, P. *Passages from Antiquity to Feudalism* (London: New Left Books, 1974).

Andrews, J. H. *Plantation Acres: An Historical Study of the Irish Land Surveyor and His Maps* (Belfast: Ulster Historical Foundation, 1985).

———. "The Playwright as Historian." This paper was written for a planned festschrift, "Essays for Brian Friel," but that project was abandoned and Professor Andrews's essay, written in 1988, was not published. Its arguments are covered in J. H. Andrews, "The Cartography of Celtic Placenames" *Ulster Local Studies* 14 (1992): 7–21 and Andrews, "Notes for a Future Edition of Brian Friel's *Translations,*" *Irish Review* 13 (1992–93): 93–106.

Andrews, Sona Karentz. Review of *Cartography in the Media* in *American Cartographer* 16 (1989).

Archer, Gabriel. "The Relation of Captaine Gosnols Voyage to the North Part of Virginia . . . 1602," in Samuel Purchas, *Hakluytus Posthumus; or, Purchas His Pilgrimes,* 20 vols. (Glasgow: MacLehose, 1905–7; reprint, New York: AMS Press, 1965), 18:304.

Arnheim, Rudolf. "The Perception of Maps," in Rudolf Arnheim, *New Essays on the Psychology of Art* (Berkeley: University of California Press, 1986), 194–202.

Arte e Scienza per il Disegno del Mondo, catalogue of an exhibition held at the Mole Antonelliana, Turin, June–October 1983 (Milan: Electa, 1983).

Atherton, H. M. *Political Prints in the Age of Hogarth* (Oxford: Clarendon Press, 1974).

Axelsen, Bjørn, and Michael Jones. "Are All Maps Mental Maps?" *Geo Journal* 14, no. 4 (1987): 447–64.

Axtell, James. "Colonial America without the Indians: A Counter-factual Scenario," in Frederick E. Hoxie, ed., *Indians in American History: An Introduction* (Arlington Heights, Ill.: Harlan Davidson, 1988), 47–65.

———. "Europeans, Indians, and the Age of Discovery in the American History Textbooks" *American Historical Review* 92 (1987): 621–32.

Bagrow, Leo. *A History of Russian Cartography Up to 1800,* ed. Henry W. Castner (Wolfe Island, Ontario: Walker Press, 1975).

Bakhtin, M. M. *The Dialogic Imagination: Four Essays,* ed. Michael Holquist, trans. Caryl Emerson and Michael Holquist (Austin: University of Texas Press, 1981).

Balchin, W. G. V. "The Media Map Watch in the United Kingdom," in M. Gauthier, ed., *Cartographie dans les Médias* (Sillery: Presses de l'Université de Québec, 1988), 33–48.

Barbour, Philip I., ed. *The Jamestown Voyages under the First Charter, 1606–1609,* Hakluyt Society, 2d ser. 136–37 (Cambridge: Cambridge University Press for the Hakluyt Society, 1969).

Barker, Francis et al., eds. *Europe and Its Others,* 2 vols. Proceedings of the Essex conference on the sociology of literature, July 1984. (Colchester: University of Essex, 1985).

Barnes, Viola. *The Dominion of New England* (New Haven: Yale University Press, 1923).

Barrell, John. *The Dark Side of Landscape: The Rural Poor in English Painting, 1730–1840* (Cambridge: Cambridge University Press, 1980).

Barthes, Roland. *Mythologies,* selected and trans. by Annette Lavers (London: Paladin, 1973).

———. "The Plates of the *Encyclopédie,*" in *New Critical Essays,* trans. Richard Howard (New York: Hill and Wang, 1980).

Basso, K. H. "To Give Up on Words: Silence in Western Apache Culture," in Pier

Paolo Giglioli, ed., *Language and Social Context: Selected Readings* (Harmonds-worth: Penguin, 1972).

Baxandall, Michael. *Painting and Experience in Fifteenth-Century Italy: A Primer in the Social History of Pictorial Style* (Oxford: Clarendon Press, 1972).

Baxter, J. P., ed. *Documentary History of the State of Maine*, 24 vols., 2d ser. (Portland: various publishers, 1869–1916).

Beckett, J. V. *The Aristocracy in England, 1160–1914* (Oxford: Blackwell, 1986).

Belanger, Terry. "Publishers and Writers in Eighteenth-Century England," in Isabel Rivers, ed., *Books and Their Readers in Eighteenth-Century England* (London: St. Martin's Press, 1982), 5–25.

Bell, Leonard. "Artists and Empire: Victorian Representations of Subject People," *Art History* 5, no. 1 (1982): 73–86.

Benes, Peter. *New England Prospect: A Loan Exhibition of Maps at the Currier Gallery of Art, Manchester, New Hampshire* (Boston: Boston University for the Dublin Seminar for New England Folklife, 1981).

Benvenisti, Meron. *Conflicts and Contradictions* (New York: Villard Books, 1986).

Berkhofer, Robert F., Jr. *The White Man's Indian: Images of the American Indian from Columbus to the Present* (New York: Vintage Books, 1979).

Bertholt, Brecht. *The Life of Galileo*, trans. Howard Brenton (London: Eyre Methuen, 1980).

Bertin, Jacques. *Semiology of Graphics: Diagrams, Networks, Maps*, trans. William J. Berg (Madison: University of Wisconsin Press, 1983).

Best, George. *A True Discourse of the Late Voyage of Discoverie, for Finding a Passage to Cathaya under M. Frobisher, General* (London, 1578).

Black, Jeannette D. "Mapping the English Colonies in North America: The Beginnings," in Norman J. W. Thrower, ed., *The Compleat Plattmaker: Essays on Chart, Map, and Globe Making in England in the Seventeenth and Eighteenth Centuries* (Berkeley: University of California Press, 1978), 101–25.

———. *The Blathwayt Atlas*, vol. 2, *Commentary* (Providence, R.I.: Brown University Press, 1975).

Bloch, Maurice. "Symbols, Song, Dance and Features of Articulation: Is Religion an Extreme form of Traditional Authority?" *European Journal of Sociology* 15 (1974): 79.

Blocker, H. G. *Philosophy and Art* (New York: Charles Scribner's Sons, 1979).

Boelhower, William. *Through a Glass Darkly: Ethnic Semiosis in American Literature* (Venice: Edizioni Helvetia, 1984).

———. "Inventing America: A Model of Cartographic Semiosis," *Word and Image* 4, no. 2 (April–June 1988): 475–97.

———. "Inventing America: The Culture of the Map," *Revue Française d'Etudes Americaines* 36 (1988): 211–24.

Boorstin, Daniel J. *The Discoverers* (New York: Random House, 1983).

Bowen, Margarita. *Empiricism and Geographical Thought from Francis Bacon to Alexander von Humboldt* (Cambridge: Cambridge University Press, 1981).

Bracher, Frederick. "The Maps in Gulliver's Travels," *Huntington Library Quarterly* 8 (1944): 60–64.

Braudel, Fernand. *Civilization and Capitalism 15–18th Century,* vol. 1, *The Structures of Everyday Life: The Limits of the Possible,* trans. Siân Reynolds (London: William Collins, 1981).

Brotherston, Gordon. *The Image of the New World: The American Continent Portrayed in Native Texts,* trans. and prepared in collaboration with Ed Dorn (London: Thames and Hudson, 1979).

Brown, Larissa. *Africans in the New World, 1493–1834: An Exhibition at the John Carter Brown Library* (Providence, R.I.: John Carter Brown Library, 1988).

Brown, Lloyd A. *The Story of Maps* (Boston: Little, Brown, and Co., 1949).

Bucher, Bernadette. *Icon and Conquest: A Structural Analysis of the Illustrations of De Bry's Great Voyages* (Chicago: University of Chicago Press, 1981).

Buisseret, David. "Spanish and French Mapping of the Gulf of Mexico in the Sixteenth and Seventeenth Centuries," in Dennis Reinhartz and Charles C. Colley, eds., *The Mapping of the American Southwest* (College Station: Texas A & M University Press, 1987), 3–17.

Bunge, William. *The Nuclear War Atlas* (Victorianville, Quebec: Society for Human Exploration, 1982; Oxford: Blackwell, 1988).

Burton, Sir Richard. *Personal Narrative of Pilgrimage to Al-Medinah and Meccah,* 2 vols. (New York: Dover Publications, 1964).

Campbell, E. M. J. "The Development of the Characteristic Sheet, 1533–1822," *Proceedings of the 8th General Assembly—17th Congress—of the International Geographical Union* (Washington, D.C.: International Geographical Union, 1952), 426–30.

Campbell, P. N. "Scientific Discourse," *Philosophy and Rhetoric* 6, no. 1 (1973).

Campbell, Tony. "A Descriptive Census of Willem Blaeu's Sixty-Eight Centimetre Globes," *Imago Mundi* 28 (1976): 21–50.

——. "Knowledge and Market Mechanism as Impulses for Map Publishing," in *Abstracts, 13th International Conference on the History of Cartography* (Amsterdam, 1989) 55–56.

Candee, Richard M. "Land Surveys of William and John Godsoe of Kittery, Maine, 1689–1769," in Peter Benes, ed., *New England Prospect: Maps, Place Names, and the Historical Landscape* (Boston: Boston University, Dublin Seminar for New England Folklife, 1980).

Carpenter, Kenneth E., ed. *Books and Society in History Papers of the Association of College and Research Libraries Rare Books and Manuscripts Preconference 24–28 June 1980, Boston, Massachusetts* (New York: R. R. Bowker, 1983).

Carroll, Lewis. "Bellman's Map," *The Hunting of the Snark: An Agony in Eight Fits* (London: Macmillan, 1920).

Cartographic Perspectives: Bulletin of the North American Cartographic Information Society 1, no. 1 (1989).

Castiglione, B. *The Courtier,* trans. George Bull (1528; Harmondsworth: Penguin, 1967)

Certeau, Michel de. *The Practice of Everyday Life,* trans. Steven Rendall (Berkeley: University of California Press, 1984).

Chamberlain, Judge. "Early Map of Eastern Massachusetts," *Massachusetts Historical Society Proceedings,* 2d ser. (1884): 211–14.

Champlain, Samuel de. *The Works of Samuel de Champlain,* ed. H. P. Biggar, 6 vols. (Toronto: Champlain Society, 1922–36) 1:335–36.

Chubb, Thomas. *The Printed Maps in the Atlases of Great Britain and Ireland: A Bibliography, 1579–1870* (London: E. J. Burrow, 1927).

Cirlot, J. E. *A Dictionary of Symbols,* 2d ed., trans. Jack Sage (London: Routledge and Kegan Paul, 1971).

Clanchy, M. T. *From Memory to Written Record: England 1066–1307* (London: Edward Arnold, 1979).

Clarice E. Tyler. "Topographical Terms in the Seventeenth-Century Records of Connecticut and Rhode Island," *New England Quarterly* 2 (1929): 382–401.

Clark, J. C. D. *English Society, 1688–1932: Social Structure and Political Practice during the Ancien Régime* (Cambridge: Cambridge University Press, 1985).

Clarke, G. N. G. "Taking Possession: The Cartouche as Cultural Text in Eighteenth-Century American Maps," *Word and Image* 4, no. 2 (April–June 1988): 455–74.

Coates, Jennifer. *Women, Men and Language: A Sociolinguistic Account of Sex Differences in Language* (London: Longman, 1986).

Collins, Larry, and Dominique Lapierre. *Freedom at Midnight* (London: William Collins, 1982).

Conrad, Joseph. *Heart of Darkness: An Authoritative Text, Backgrounds and Sources, Criticism,* ed. Robert Kimbarough (New York: W. W. Norton and Co., 1971).

Cook, Terry. "A Reconstruction of the World: George R. Parkin's British Empire Map of 1893," *Cartographica* 21, no. 4 (1984): 53–65.

Corbett, Margery, and R. W. Lightbown. *The Comely Frontispiece: The Emblematic Title-Page in England 1550–1600* (London: Routledge and Kegan Paul, 1979).

Cortesão, Armando. *Cartografia a Cartógrafos Portugueses dos Séculos XV et XVI* (Lisbon: Edição da Seara Nova, 1935).

———. *History of Portuguese Cartography,* 2 vols. (Coimbra: Junta de Investigaóes Científicas do Ultramar, 1969–71).

Cortesão, Jaime. "The Pre-Columbian Discovery of America," *Geographical Journal* 89 (1937): 29–42.

Cosgrove, Denis E. *Social Formation and Symbolic Landscape* (London: Croom Helm, 1984).

Crone, G. R., and R. A. Skelton. "Collections of Voyages and Travels, 1625–1846," in E. Lynam, ed., *Richard Hakluyt and His Successors* (London: Hakluyt Society, 1946).

Crone, Gerald R. *Maps and Their Makers: An Introduction to the History of Cartography* (London: Hutchinson, 1953; 5th ed., Folkestone, Kent: Dawson and Hamden, Conn.: Archon Books, 1978).

Cronon, Williams. *Changes in the Land: Indians, Colonists, and the Ecology of New England* (New York: Hill and Wang, 1983).

Cumming, William P. *The Southeast in Early Maps,* rev. ed. (Princeton: Princeton University Press, 1962).

———. *British Maps of Colonial America* (Chicago: University of Chicago Press, 1974).

———. "The Colonial Charting of the Massachusetts Coast," in *Seafaring in Colonial Massachusetts: A Conference Held by the Colonial Society of Massachusetts, November 21 and 22, 1975* (Boston: Colonial Society of Massachusetts, 1980).

———., R. A. Skelton, and D. B. Quinn. *The Discovery of North America* (London: Paul Elek, 1971).

Curley, Thomas M. *Samuel Johnson and the Age of Travel* (Athens: University of Georgia Press, 1976).

Dainville, François de. "Le Signe de 'Justice' dans les Cartes Anciennes" *Revue Historique de Droit Français et Etranger* 4th ser., 34 (1956): 111–14.

———. *Le Langage des Géographes: Termes, Signes, Couleurs des Cartes Anciennes, 1500–1800* (Paris: A. et J. Picard, 1964).

Danforth, Samuel. *A Briefe Recognition of New-England's Errand into the Wilderness* (Boston: S. Green and M. Johnson, 1671).

Darnton, Robert. *The Great Cat Massacre and Other Episodes in French Cultural History* (New York: Basic Books, 1984).

Darwish, Mahmud, Samid al-Qasim, and Adonis. *Victims of a Map,* trans. Abdulla al-Udhari (London: Al Saqi Books, 1984).

Dauenhauer, Bernard P. *Silence: The Phenomenon and Its Ontological Significance* (Bloomington: Indiana University Press, 1980).

Davenport, William. "Marshall Islands Navigational Charts," *Imago Mundi* 15 (1967): 19–26.

Davis, Bruce. "Maps on Postage Stamps as Propaganda," *Cartographic Journal* 22, no. 2 (1985): 125–30.

De Brahm, William Gerard. *Report of the General Survey in the Southern District of North America,* intro. by Louis De Vorsey, Jr. (Columbia: University of South Carolina Press, 1971).

de Bruslans, J. Savary. *The Universal Dictionary of Trade and Commerce, Translated from the French* (London, 1757).

De Vorsey, Louis. "Amerindian Contributions to the Mapping of North America: A Preliminary View," *Imago Mundi* 30 (1978): 71–78.

———. "Maps in Colonial Promotion: James Edward Oglethorpe's Use of Maps in 'Selling' the Georgia Scheme," *Imago Mundi* 38 (1986): 35–45.

Dear, Michael. "The Postmodern Challenge: Reconstructing Human Geography," *Transactions, Institute of British Geographers,* new ser. 13 (1988): 262–74.

A la Découverte de la Terre. Dix Siècles de Cartographie. Tresors du Département des Cartes et Plans, [Exposition] Mai-Juillet 1979 (Paris: Bibliothèque nationale, 1979).

Delano Smith, Catherine. "Cartographic Signs on European Maps and Their Explanation before 1700," *Imago Mundi* 37 (1985): 9–29.

———. "Maps in Bibles in the Sixteenth Century," *Map Collector* 39 (1987): 2–14.

———, and Elizabeth M. Ingram. *Maps in Bibles, 1500–1600: An Illustrated Catalogue* (Geneva: Librarie Droz, 1991).

Dematteis, Giuseppe. *Le Metafore della Terra: La Geografia Umana tra Mito e Scienzia* (Milan: Feltrinelli, 1985).

Derrida, Jacques. *Of Grammatology,* trans. Gayatri Chakratvorty Spivak (Baltimore: Johns Hopkins University Press, 1976).

Destombes, Marcel. *Cartes Hollandaises: La Cartographie de la Compagnie des Indes Orientales, 1593–1743* (Saigon, 1941).

Dickason, Olive Patricia. "Old World Law, New World Peoples, and Concepts of Sovereignty," in Stanley H. Palmer and Dennis Reinhartz, eds., *Essays on the History of North American Discovery and Exploration* (College Station: Texas A & M University Press, 1988).

Diffie, Bailey W. "Foreigners in Portugal and the 'Policy of Silence,'" *Terrae Incognitae* 1 (1969): 23–34.

Dilke, O. A. W. *The Roman Land Surveyors: An Introduction to the Agrimensores* (Newton Abbot: David and Charles, 1971).

———. *Greek and Roman Maps* (London: Thames and Hudson, 1985).

Drabble, Margaret. *For Queen and Country: Britain in the Victorian Age* (London: Deutsch, 1978).

Ducrot, Oswald, and Tzvetan Todorov. *Encyclopedic Dictionary of the Sciences of Language,* trans. Catherine Porter (Oxford: Blackwell, 1981).

Duffy, Christopher. *Siege Warfare: The Fortress in the Early Modern World 1494–1660* (London: Routledge and Kegan Paul, 1979).

———. *Siege Warfare: The Fortress in the Age of Vauban and Frederick the Great 1660–1789* (London: Routledge and Kegan Paul, 1985).

Durkheim, Emile. *The Elementary Forms of the Religious Life,* trans. Joseph Swain (1915; Glencoe: Free Press, 1974).

Eagleton, Terry. *Literary Theory: An Introduction* (Minneapolis: University of Minnesota Press, 1983).

———. *Against the Grain* (London: Verso, 1986).

———. *The Ideology of the Aesthetic* (Oxford: Basil Blackwell, 1990).

Eco, Umberto. *A Theory of Semiotics* (Bloomington: Indiana University Press, 1976).

Edgerton, Samuel Y., Jr. "From Mental Matrix to *Mappamundi* to Christian Empire: The Heritage of Ptolemaic Cartography in the Renaissance," in David Woodward, ed., *Art and Cartography* (Chicago: University of Chicago Press, 1987), 10–50.

Edney, Matthew H. "Politics, Science, and Government Mapping Policy in the United States, 1800–1925," *American Cartographer* 13, no. 4 (1986): 295–306.

Ehrenberg, Ralph E. *Scholars' Guide to Washington D.C. for Cartography and Remote Sensing Imagery* (Washington, D.C.: Smithsonian Institution Press, 1987).

Eisenstein, Elizabeth L. *The Printing Press as an Agent of Change: Communications and Cultural Transformations in Early Modern Europe,* 2 vols. (Cambridge: Cambridge University Press, 1979).

Ekirch, A. Roger. *Bound for America: The Transportation of British Convicts to the Colonies, 1718–1775* (Oxford: Oxford University Press, 1988).

Elyot, Thomas. *The Boke Named the Gouernour,* edited from the 1st ed. of 1531 by H. H. S. Croft, 2 vols. (London, 1880).

Epstein, Earl F., and John D. McLaughlin. "A Discussion on Public Information: Who Owns It? Who Uses It? Should We Limit Access?" *ACSM [American Congress on Surveying and Mapping] Bulletin* (October 1990): 33–38.

Fabian, Johannes. *Language and Colonial Power: The Appropriation of Swahili in the Former Belgian Congo, 1880–1938* (Cambridge: Cambridge University Press, 1986).

Feather, John. "The Provincial Book Trade in Eighteenth-Century England," in *London and the Country* (Cambridge: Cambridge University Press, 1985): 1–11.

Febvre, Lucien, and Martin, Henri-Jean, *L'Apparition du Livre* (Paris: Edition Albin, 1958); English edition, *The Coming of the Book: The Impact of Printing, 1450–1800,* ed. Geoffrey Nowell-Smith and David Wooton, trans. David Gerard (London: NLB, 1976).

Ferraris, Maurizio. "Postmodernism and the Deconstruction of Modernism," *Design Issues* 4, nos. 1 and 2, special issue (1988): 12–24.

Flavel, John. *Husbandry Spiritualized, 10th ed.* (Boston: Nicholas Boone, 1709).

Fordham, H. G. *John Cary: Engraver, Map, Chart and Print-Seller and Globe-Maker 1754 to 1835* (Cambridge: Cambridge University Press, 1925; rpt. Folkestone: Dawson, 1976).

Foucault, Michel. *The Order of Things: An Archaeology of the Human Sciences,* trans. Alan Sheridan-Smith (London, 1966; New York: Vintage Books, 1973).

——. "Résponse au Cercle d'Épistémologie" *Cahiers pour l'Analyse* 9 (summer 1968).

——. *The Archaeology of Knowledge and the Discourse on Language,* trans. A. M. Sheridan-Smith (New York: Pantheon Books, 1972).

——. *Discipline and Punish: The Birth of the Prison,* trans. Alan Sheridan (London: Allen Lane, 1977).

———. *History of Sexuality*, vol. 1, *An Introduction*, trans. Robert Hurley (New York: Random House, 1978).

———. *Power/Knowledge: Selected Interviews and Other Writings 1972–77*, ed. Colin Gordon, trans. Colin Gordon, Leo Marshall, John Mepham, and Kate Sopher (New York: Pantheon Books, 1980).

Fremantle, Anne, ed. *The Papal Encyclicals in Their Historical Context* (New York: Putnam, 1956).

Friel, Brian. *Translations* (London: Faber and Faber, 1981).

Gance, Abel. *Napoleon vu par Abel Gance, Épopée Cinégraphique en Cinq Époques* (Paris: Plon, 1927).

Ganong, W. F. *Crucial Maps in the Early Cartography and Place-Nomenclature of the Atlantic Coast of Canada*, with an introduction, commentary, and map notes by Theodore E. Layng (Toronto: University of Toronto Press, 1964).

Gates, Henry Louis, Jr., ed. *"Race," Writing and Difference* (Chicago: University of Chicago Press, 1986).

Gauthier, M., ed. *Cartographie dans les Médias* (Québec: Presses de l'Université du Québec, 1988).

Geertz, Clifford. "Art as a Cultural System," in *Local Knowledge: Further Essays in Interpretive Anthropology* (New York: Basic Books, 1983), 94–120.

[German Cartographical Society]. "The So-Called Peters' Projection," *Cartographic Journal* 22, no. 2 (1985): 108–10.

Giddens, Anthony. *The Contemporary Critique of Historical Materalism: Power, Property and the State* (London: Macmillan, 1981).

Gilmartin, Patricia. "The Austral Continent on 16th Century Maps; An Iconological Interpretation," *Cartographica* 21, no. 4 (1984): 85–90.

Goffart, Walter. "The Map of the Barbarian Invasions: A Preliminary Report," *Nottingham Medieval Studies* 32 (1988): 49–64.

Goldberg, D. T. *Ethical Theory and Social Issues: Historical Texts and Contemporary Readings* (New York: Holt, Rinehart, Winston, 1988).

Gombrich, Ernst. "Mirror and Map: Theories of Pictorial Representation," *Philosophical Transactions of the Royal Society of London*, ser. B, 270 (1975): 119–49.

———. *The Sense of Order: A Study in the Psychology of Decorative Art* (Ithaca: Cornell University Press, 1979).

Goodchild, Michael F. "Geographic Information Systems," *Progress in Human Geography* 15, no. 2 (1991): 194–220.

Goodman, Nelson. *Languages of Art: An Approach to a Theory of Symbols* (Indianapolis: Bobbs-Merrill, 1968).

Gorges, Ferdinando. *A Briefe Narration of the Original Undertakings of the Advancement of Plantations into the Parts of America* (London: E. Brudenell, 1658).

Gough, Richard. *British Topography*, 2 vols. (London, 1780).

Gould, Peter. *The Geographer at Work* (London: Routledge and Kegan Paul, 1985).

The Great Dictator, dir. Charlie Chaplin (United Artists, 1940).

Gregory, Derek. "Postmodernism and the Politics of Social Theory" *Environment and Planning, D: Society and Space* 5 (1987): 245–48.

Griffiths, Antony. "A Checklist of Catalogues of British Print Publishers, c. 1650–1830," *Print Quarterly* 1 (1984): 4–22.

Guthrie, William. *A New System of Modern Geography* (London: C. Dilly and G. G. and J. Robinson, 1795).

Hakluyt, Richard. *The Principal Navigations Voiages and Discoveries of the English Nation imprinted at London, 1589,* a facsimile edited by David Beers Quinn and Raleigh Ashlin Skelton, with a new index by Alison Quinn (Cambridge: Cambridge University Press for the Hakluyt Society and Peabody Museum, Salem, 1965).

Hale, J. R. *Renaissance Europe 1480–1520* (London: Fontana, 1971).

Hall, James. *Dictionary of Subjects and Symbols in Art* (London: John Murray, 1974).

Harbsmeier, Michael. "On Travel Accounts and Cosmological Strategies: Some Models in Comparative Xenology," *Ethnos* 50, nos. 3–4 (1985): 273–312.

Harrison, John. *The Library of Isaac Newton* (Cambridge: Cambridge University Press, 1978).

Harvey, P. D. A. *The History of Topographical Maps: Symbols, Pictures and Surveys* (London: Thames and Hudson, 1980).

Harvey, R. A. "The Private Library of Henry Cavendish (1731–1810)" *Library,* 6th ser., no. 2 (1980): 281–92.

Head, C. Grant. "The Map as Natural Language: A Paradigm for Understanding," in Christopher Board, ed., "New Insights in Cartographic Communication," Monograph 31, *Cartographica* 21, 1 (1984): 10–32.

Heidenreich, Conrad E. "Mapping the Great Lakes: The Period of Imperial Rivalries, 1700–1760," *Cartographica* 18, no. 3 (1981): 74–109.

Helgerson, R. "The Land Speaks: Cartography, Chorography and Subversion in Renaissance England," *Representations* 16 (1986): 51–85.

Henrikson, Alan K. "The Map as an 'Idea': The Role of Cartographic Imagery during the Second World War," *American Cartographer* 2, no. 1 (1975): 19–53.

Hobsbawm, Eric, and Terence Ranger, eds. *The Invention of Tradition* (Cambridge: Cambridge University Press, 1983).

Hodgkinson, Keith. "Standing the World on Its Head: A Review of Eurocentrism in Humanities Maps and Atlases," *Teaching History* 62 (1991): 19–23.

Hodgkiss, A. G. *Understanding Maps: A Systematic History of Their Use and Development* (Folkestone: Dawson, 1981).

Hodson, Donald. *County Atlases of the British Isles Published After 1703,* vol. 1, *Atlases Published 1704–1742 and Their Subsequent Editions* (Tewin, Hertfordshire: Tewin Press, 1984).

————. *The Printed Maps of Hertfordshire, 1577–1900* (London: Dawson, 1974).

Holtgen, Karl Josef. *Aspects of the Emblem: Studies in the English Emblem Tradition and the European Context* (Kassel: Reichenberger, 1986).

Holton, Gerald. *The Advancement of Science and Its Burdens: The Jefferson Lecture and Other Essays* (Cambridge: Cambridge University Press, 1986).

Honour, Hugh. *The New Golden Land: European Images of America from the Discoveries to the Present Time* (New York: Pantheon Books, 1975).

Hooykaas, R. "The Rise of Modern Science: When and Why?" *British Journal for the History of Science* 20, no. 4 (1987): 453–73.

Hoy, David. "Jacques Derrida," in Quentin Skinner, ed., *The Return of Grand Theory in the Human Sciences* (Cambridge: Cambridge University Press, 1985), 41–64.

Hubbard, William. *The Present State of New-England, Being a Narrative of the Troubles with the Indians 1677* (New York: York Mail-Print, 1972).

Hulme, Peter. *Colonial Encounters: Europe and the Native Caribbean, 1492–1797* (London: Methuen, 1986).

Ihde, Don. *Experimental Phenomenology* (New York: Putnam, 1977).

Imhof, Eduard. *Cartographic Relief Presentation*, ed. H. J. Steward (Berlin: De Gruyter, 1982).

Iser, Wolfgang. "The Reading Process: A Phenomenological Approach," in Jane P. Tompkins, ed., *Reader-Response Criticism: From Formalism to Post-structuralism* (Baltimore: Johns Hopkins University Press, 1980), 50–51.

Jackson Lears, T. J. "The Concept of Cultural Hegemony: Problems and Possibilities," *American Historical Review* 90 (1985): 567–93.

Jaenen, Cornelius J. "Characteristics of French-Amerindian Contact in New France," in Stanley H. Palmer and Dennis Reinhartz, eds., *Essays on the History of North American Discovery and Exploration* (College Station: Texas A & M University Press, 1988), 79–101.

Jager, Eckhard. *Prussia-Karten 1542–1810. Geschichte der Kartographischen Darstellung Ostpreussens vom 16, bis zum 19, Jahrhundert. Entstehung der Karten-Kosten-Vertrieb. Bibliographischer Katalog* (Weissenhorn: A. H. Konrad, 1982).

Janson, H. W. *Apes and Ape Lore in the Middle Ages and the Renaissance* (London: The Warburg Institute and the University of London, 1952).

Jennings, Francis. *The Invasion of America: Indians, Colonialism, and the Cant of Conquest* (New York: W. W. Norton and Co., 1976).

Johnson, Hildegard Binder. *Order upon the Land: The U.S. Rectangular Land Survey and the Upper Mississippi Country* (New York: Oxford University Press, 1976).

Johnson, Samuel. Dedication for George Adams's *Treatise on the Globes* (London, 1766).

Jones, Mary G. *The Charity School Movement: A Study of Eighteenth-Century Puritanism in Action* (Cambridge: Cambridge University Press, 1938).

Jordan, W. K., ed. *The Chronicle and Political Papers of King Edward VI* (London: Allen and Unwin, 1966).

Karrow, R. W. "Carto-bibliography," *AB Bookman's Yearbook* (Clifton, N.J.: AB Bookman, 1976), Part 1, 43–52.

Katzir, Yael. "The Conquests of Jerusalem, 1099 and 1178: Historical Memory and Religious Typology," in Vladimir P. Goss and Christine Verzar Bornstein, eds., *The Meetings of Two Worlds: Cultural Exchange between East and West during the period of the Crusades* (Kalamazoo: Medieval Institute Publications, Western Michigan University, 1986).

Kavenagh, W. Keith, ed. *Foundations of Colonial America: A Documentary History*, vol. 1, *Northeastern Colonies* (New York: Chelsea House Publishers and R. R. Bowker Co., 1973).

Kawashima, Yasu. "Jurisdiction of the Colonial Courts over the Indians in Massachusetts, 1689–1763," *New England Quarterly* 42 (1969): 532–50.

———. "Legal Origins of the Indian Reservation in Colonial Massachusetts," in Bruce A. Glasrud and Alan M. Smith, eds., *Race Relations in British North America, 1607–1783* (Chicago: Nelson-Hall, 1982), 65–83.

Keates, J. S. *Understanding Maps* (London: Longman, 1982).

Kern, Stephen. *The Culture of Time and Space* (London: Weidenfeld and Nicolson, 1983).

Kernan, Alvin. *Printing Technology, Letters and Samuel Johnson* (Princeton: Princeton University Press, 1987)

Kertzer, David I. *Ritual, Politics and Power* (New Haven: Yale University Press, 1988).

Keuning, Johannes. "Isaac Massa, 1586–1643" *Imago Mundi* 10 (1953): 66–67.

Kidron, Michael, and Ronald Segal. *The New State of the World Atlas* (New York: Simon and Schuster, 1984).

Kimble, George, H. T. "Portuguese Policy and Its Influence on Fifteenth Century Cartography" *Geographical Review* 23 (1933): 653–59.

Kinross, Robin. "The Rhetoric of Neutrality," *Design Issues* 2, no. 2 (1985): 18–30.

Knox, Paul L., ed. *The Design Professions and the Built Environment* (London: Croom Helm, 1988).

Kolata, Gina. "Are the Horrors of Cannibalism Fact—or Fiction," *Smithsonian* 17, no. 12 (1978): 150–70.

Konvitz, Josef W. *Cartography in France, 1660–1848: Science, Engineering, and Statecraft* (Chicago: University of Chicago Press, 1987).

Korzybski, Alfred. *Science and Sanity: An Introduction to Non-Aristotelian Systems and General Semantics,* 3d ed., with new preface (Lakeville, Conn.: International Non-Aristotelian Library Publishing Co., 1948).

Krim, Arthur J. "Acculturation of the New England Landscape: Native and English Toponymy of Eastern Massachusetts," in Peter Benes, ed., *New England Prospect:*

Maps, Place Names, and the Historical Landscape (Boston: Boston University, Dublin Seminar for New England Folklife, 1980), 69–88.

Kuhn, Thomas S. *The Structure of Scientific Revolutions* (Chicago: University of Chicago Press, 1962).

Kulikoff, Allan. *Tobacco and Slaves* (Chapel Hill: University of North Carolina Press, 1986).

Kupperman, Karen Ordahl. *Settling with the Indians: The Meeting of English and Indian Cultures in America, 1580–1640* (Totowa, N.J.: Rowmand and Littlefield, 1980).

La Capra, Dominick. *Rethinking Intellectual History: Texts, Contexts, Language* (Ithaca: Cornell University Press, 1983).

Lakatos, Imre, and Alan Musgrave, eds., *Criticism and the Growth of Knowledge* (Cambridge: Cambridge University Press, 1970).

Lamb, Ursula. "Science by Litigation: A Cosmographic Feud," *Terrae Incognitae* 1 (1969): 40–57.

Lambarde, William. *A Perambulation of Kent,* 2d ed. (London, 1596).

Landes, David S. *Clocks and the Making of the Modern World* (Cambridge, Mass.: Harvard University Press, 1983).

Lanman, Jonathan. *On the Origin of Portolan Charts* (Chicago: Hermon Dunlap Smith Center, Newberry Library, 1987).

Laslett, Peter. *The World We Have Lost: Further Explored* (London: Methuen, 1965; 3d ed., 1983).

Laudan, Larry. *Progress and Its Problems: Toward a Theory of Scientific Growth* (Berkeley: University of California Press, 1977).

Laxton, Paul. "The Geodetic and Topographical Evaluation of English County Maps, 1740–1840." *Cartographic Journal* 13, no. 1 (1976): 37–54.

Laxton, Paul. *250 Years of Mapmaking in the County of Hampshire,* introduction to a collection of facsimiles (Lympne Castle, Kent: Harry Margary, 1976)

Le Corbeiller, Clare. "Miss America and Her Sisters: Personifications of the Four Parts of the World," Metropolitan Museum of Art, *Bulletin* 19, new ser. (1961): 209–23.

Lewis, G. Malcolm. "The Indigenous Maps and Mapping of North American Indians," *Map Collector* 9 (1979): 25–32.

———. "Indicators of Unacknowledged Assimilations from Amerindian Maps on Euro-American Maps of North America: Some General Principles Arising from a Study of La Verendrye's Composite Map, 1728–29," *Imago Mundi* 38 (1986): 9–34.

———. "Misinterpretation of Amerindian Information as a Source of Error on Euro-American Maps," *Annals of the Association of American Geographers* 77 (1987): 542–63.

———. "Native North Americans' Cosmological Ideas and Geographical Awareness," in John I. Allen, ed., *North American Exploration* (Lincoln: University of Nebraska Press, 1997), 1:71–126.

Lowance, Mason I., Jr. *The Language of Canaan: Metaphor and Symbol in New England from the Puritans to the Transcendentalists* (Cambridge: Harvard University Press, 1980).

Loxton, John. "The Peters' Phenomenon," *Cartographic Journal* 22, no. 2 (1985): 106–8.

Lupton, Ellen. "Reading Isotope," *Design Issues* 3, no. 2 (1986): 47–58.

Lynam, Edward. "Boazio's Map of Ireland," *British Museum Quarterly* 11 (1937): 92–95.

McCloskey, Donald N. *The Rhetoric of Economics* (Madison: University of Wisconsin Press, 1985).

MacDonald, Gill. "Decorative Maps," *Studio* 128 (1944): 161–69.

McHaffie, Patrick. "The Creation of Public Cartographic Information: 'Penciling in' the Nexus," Paper Presented at the Miami Meeting of the Association of American Geographers, April 1991.

———, Sona Andrews, Michael Dobson, et. al., "Ethical Problems in Cartography: A Roundtable Commentary," *Cartographic Perspectives* 7 (1990): 3–13.

McKenzie, D. F. *Bibliography and the Sociology of Texts,* the Panizzi Lectures (London: British Library, 1986).

McLuhan, Marshall. *The Gutenberg Galaxy: The Making of Typographic Man* (Toronto: University of Toronto Press, 1962).

McNally, Andrew. "You Can't Get There from Here, with Today's Approach to Geography," *Professional Geographer* 39 (November 1987): 389–92.

Machiavelli, Niccolo. *Arte della Guerra e Scritti Politici Minori,* ed. S. Bertelli (1521; Milan: Feltrinelli, 1961).

Mann, Michael. *The Sources of Social Power,* vol. 1, *A History of Power from the Beginning to A.D. 1760* (Cambridge: Cambridge University Press, 1986).

Marble, Duane. "Computer Network Conference," *Geography* (31 January 1991).

Marchant, Hilda. "A 'Memento Mori' or 'Vanitas' Emblem on an Estate Map of 1612," *Mapline* 44 (1986): 1–4.

Marin, Louis. *Portrait of the King,* trans. Martha M. Houle, Theory and History of Literature, no. 57 (Minneapolis: University of Minnesota Press, 1988).

Markham, Beryl. *West with the Night* (New York: North Point Press, 1983).

Marshall, P. J., and Glyndwr Williams. *The Great Map of Mankind: British Perceptions of the World in the Age of Enlightenment* (London: Dent, 1982).

Mazzeo, Joseph Anthony. *Renaissance and Seventeenth-Century Studies* (New York: Columbia University Press, 1964).

Meinig, D. W. *The Shaping of America: A Geographical Perspective on 500 Years of History,* vol. 1, *Atlantic America, 1492–1800* (New Haven: Yale University Press, 1986).

Merquior, J. G. *Foucault* (Berkeley: University of California Press, 1987).

Meynen, E., ed. *Multilingual Dictionary of Technical Terms in Cartography* (Wiesbaden: Franz Steiner Verlag for International Cartographic Association, 1973).

Middleton, Charles Theodore. *A New and Complete System of Geography* (London, 1778).

Miller, Perry. *Errand into the Wilderness* (Cambridge: Harvard University Press, 1964).

Mitchell, R. B., and Phyllis Deane. *Abstract of British Historical Statistics* (Cambridge: Cambridge University Press, 1962).

Mitchell, W. J. T. *Iconology: Image, Text, Ideology* (Chicago: University of Chicago Press, 1986).

——, ed. *The Language of Images* (Chicago: Phoenix Books, 1980).

Monmonier, Mark S. "Cartography, Geographic Information and Public Policy," *Journal of Geography in Higher Education* 6, no. 2 (1982): 99–107.

——. *How to Lie with Maps* (Chicago: University of Chicago Press, 1991).

—— and George A. Schnell. *Map Appreciation* (Englewood Cliffs, N.J.: Prentice-Hall, 1988).

Moodie, D. W. "Science and Reality: Arthur Dobbs and the Eighteenth-Century Geography of Rupert's Land," *Journal of Historical Geography* 2 (1976): 293–309.

More, Thomas. *The Essential Thomas More,* ed. and trans. James J. Greene and John P. Dolan (New York: New American Library, 1967).

Morgan, Victor. "Lasting Image of the Elizabethan Era," *Geographical Magazine* 52 (1980): 401–8.

——. "The Literary Image of Globes and Maps in Early Modern England," in Sarah Tyacke, ed., *English Map Making 1500–1650* (London: British Library, 1983), 46–56.

Morris, J. "The Magic of Maps: The Art of Cartography," M.A. diss., University of Hawaii, 1982.

Morrison, Joel L. "Recommendations for the Classification of the Extent Maps of the Great Lakes." Unpublished report to the Hermon Dunlap Smith Center for History of Cartography (Chicago: Newberry Library, 1975).

——. "The Revolution in Cartography in the 1980s," in D. W. Rhind and D. R. F. Taylor, eds., *Cartography Past, Present and Future: A Festschrift for F. J. Ormeling* (London: Elsevier for the International Cartographic Association, 1989), 169–85.

Morton, Thomas. *The New English Canaan, or New Canaan: Containing an Abstract of New England Composed in Three Books* (Boston: Prince Society, 1883).

Muehrcke, Phillip C. *Map Use: Reading, Analysis and Interpretation* (Madison: J P Publications, 1978, 1986).

Mukerji, Chandra. "Visual Language in Science and the Exercise of Power: The Case of Cartography in Early Modern Europe," *Studies in Visual Communications* 10, no. 3 (1984): 30–45.

——. *From Graven Images: Patterns of Modern Materialism* (New York: Columbia University Press, 1983).

Munby, A. N. L., ed. *Sale Catalogues of Libraries of Eminent Persons,* 12 vols. (London: Mansell with Sotheby Parke-Bernet Publications, 1971–75) vol. 11, *Scientists,* ed. H. A. Fiesenberger (1975).

Neale, R. S. *Class in English History, 1680–1850* (Oxford: Blackwell, 1981).

Nebenzahl, Kenneth. *Maps of the Holy Land: Images of Terra Sancta through Two Millennia* (New York: A. R. Liss, 1986).

Needham, Joseph, and Wang Ling. *Science and Civilization in China,* vol. 3, *Mathematics and the Sciences of the Heavens and the Earth* (Cambridge: Cambridge University Press, 1959).

Nelson, John S., Allan Megill, and Donald N. McCloskey, eds. *The Rhetoric of the Human Sciences: Language and Argument in Scholarship and Public Affairs* (Madison: University of Wisconsin Press, 1987).

Nordenskiöld, A. E. *Facsimile-Atlas to the Early History of Cartography with Reproductions of the Most Important Maps Printed in the XV and XVI Centuries* (Stockholm, 1889; New York: Dover Publications, 1973).

Norris, Christopher. *Deconstruction: Theory and Practice* (London: Methuen, 1982).

———. *Derrida* (Cambridge, Mass.: Harvard University Press, 1987).

Norwich, Oscar I. *Maps of Africa: An Illustrated and Annotated Carto-bibliography* (Johannesburg: Ad. Donker, 1983).

Nowell, Charles E. *The Rose-Coloured Map: Portugal's Attempt to Build an African Empire from the Atlantic to the Indian Ocean* (Lisbon: Junta de Investigaóes Científicas do Ultramar, 1982).

Ong, Walter J. *Orality and Literacy: The Technolgizing of the Word* (London: Methuen, 1982).

Ormeling, F. J., Jr. "Soviet Cartographic Falsifications," *Military Engineer* 62 (1970): 389–91.

———. "Cartographic Consequences of a Planned Economy—50 Years of Soviet Cartography," *American Cartographer* 1, no. 1 (1974): 48–49.

———. *Minority Toponyms on Maps: The Rendering of Linguistic Minority Toponyms on Topographic Maps of Western Europe* (Utrecht: Drukkerij Elinkwijk Bu, 1983).

Panofsky, Erwin. *Meaning in the Visual Arts* (New York: Doubleday, 1955).

Panofsky, Erwin. *Studies in Iconology: Humanistic Themes in the Art of the Renaissance* (Oxford: Oxford University Press, 1939).

Pappas, Peter. "The Superimposition of Vision: Napoleon and the Meaning of Fascist Art," *Cineaste* 9 (1983): 5–13.

Parker, Geoffrey. *The Army of Flanders and the Spanish Road 1567–1659: The Logistics of Spanish Victory and Defeat in the Low Countries' Wars* (Cambridge: Cambridge University Press, 1972).

———. *The Thirty Years' War* (London: Routledge and Kegan Paul, 1984).

Parry, J. H. *The Spanish Seaborne Empire* (London: Hutchinson, 1966).

———. "Old Maps Are Slippery Witnesses," *Harvard Magazine,* April 1976, 32–41.

Patterson, Annabel. *Censorship and Interpretation: The Conditions of Writing and Reading in Early Modern England* (Madison: University of Wisconsin Press, 1984).

Payne, Anne. "Medieval Heraldry," in Jonathan Alexander and Paul Binski, eds., *Age of Chivalry: Art in Plantagenet England, 1200–1400* (London: Royal Academy of Arts in association with Weidenfeld and Nicolson, 1987), 55–59.

Pedley, Mary. "Gentlemen Abroad: Jefferys and Sayer in Paris," *Map Collector* 37 (1986): 20–23.

Penfold, Peter A., ed. *Maps and Plans in the Public Record Office*, vol. 2, *America and West Indies* (London: HMSO, 1974).

———, ed., *Maps and Plans in the Public Record Office*, vol. 3, *Africa* (London: HMSO, 1982).

Perkin, Harold. *The Origins of Modern English Society 1780–1880* (London: Routledge and Kegan Paul; Toronto: University of Toronto Press, 1969).

Peters, Arno. *The New Cartography*, trans. Ward Kaiser, D. G. Smith, and Heinz Wohlers (New York: Friendship Press, 1983).

Phillips, P. L. *A List of Geographical Atlases in the Library of Congress*, vols. 1–4 (Washington, D.C.: Government Printing Office, 1909–1914; rpt., Amsterdam: Theatrum Orbis Terrarum, 1967).

Philp, Mark. "Michel Foucault," in Quentin Skinner, ed., *The Return of Grand Theory in the Human Sciences* (Cambridge: Cambridge University Press, 1985), 65–82.

Picard, Max. *The World of Silence,* trans. Stanley Godman (Chicago: H. Regnery, 1952).

Porter, Phil, and Phil Voxland. "Distortion in Maps: The Peters' Projection and Other Devilments," *Focus* 36 (1986): 22–30.

Porter, Roy. *English Society in the Eighteenth Century* (London: Penguin Books, 1982).

Poster, Mark. "Foucault and History" *Social Research* 49 (1982): 116–42.

———. *Foucault, Marxism and History: Mode of Production versus Mode of Information* (Cambridge: Polity Press, 1984).

Prince, Hugh. "Art and Agrarian Change, 1710–1815," in Denis Cosgrove and Stephen Daniels, eds., *The Iconography of Landscape* (Cambridge: Cambridge University Press, 1988) 98–118.

Pugh, Ralph B. *The Records of the Colonial and Dominions Offices,* Public Record Office Handbook no. 3 (London: HMSO, 1964).

Pyenson, Lewis. "Cultural Imperialism and Exact Science: German Expansion Overseas, 1900–1930," *History of Science* 20 (1982): 1–43.

Quam, Louis O. "The Use of Maps in Propaganda" *Journal of Geography* 42 (1943): 21–32.

Quinn, David B., and Alison M. Quinn, eds. *The English New England Voyages, 1602–1608,* 2d ser., no. 161 (London: Hakluyt Society, 1983).

Rabinow, Paul, ed. *The Foucault Reader* (New York: Pantheon Books 1984).

Raffestin, Claude. *Pour une Géographie du Pouvoir* (Paris: Libraires Techniques, 1980).

Ravetz, Jerome R. *Scientific Knowledge and Its Social Problems* (Oxford: Clarendon Press, 1971).

Rees, R. "Historical Links between Cartography and Art," *Geographical Review* 70 (1980): 60–78.

Reinhartz, Dennis. "Herman Moll, Geographer: An Early-Eighteenth-Century European View of the American Southwest," in Reinhartz and Colley, eds., *The Mapping of the American Southwest,* 18–36.

Reinhartz, Dennis, and Charles C. Colley, eds. *The Mapping of the American Southwest* (College Station: Texas A & M University Press, 1987).

Reitan, E. A. "Expanding Horizons: Maps in the *Gentlemen's Magazine,* 1731–1754," *Imago Mundi* 37 (1985): 54–62.

Richardson, W. A. R. "Jave-la-Grande: A Case Study of Place-Name Corruption," *Globe* 22 (1984): 9–32.

———. "Jave-la-Grande: A Place Name Chart of Its East Coast" *Great Circle* 6, no. 1 (1984): 1–23.

Ristow, Walter. *American Maps and Mapmakers: Commercial Cartography in the Nineteenth Century* (Detroit: Wayne State University Press, 1985).

Robertson, Donald. *Mexican Manuscript Painting of the Early Colonial Period* (New Haven: Yale University Press, 1959).

———. "The Pinturas (Maps) of the Relaciones Geográficas, with a Catalog," in *Handbook of Middle American Indians,* vol. 12, *Guide to Ethnohistorical Sources,* ed. H. F. Cline (Austin: University of Texas Press, 1972), part 1, 243–78.

Robinson, Arthur H. *The Look of Maps: An Examination of Cartographic Design* (Madison: University of Wisconsin Press, 1952).

———. "Arno Peters and His New Cartography" *American Cartographer* 12 (1985): 103–11.

———, and Barbara Bartz Petchenik. *The Nature of Maps: Essays toward Understanding Maps and Mapping* (Chicago: University of Chicago Press, 1976).

———, Randall D. Sale, Joel L. Morrison, and Phillip C. Muehrcke. *Elements of Cartography,* 5th ed. (New York: John Wiley, 1985).

Robinson, Brian S. "Elizabethan Society and Its Named Places," *Geographical Review* 63 (1973): 322–33.

Robinson, F. J. G., and P. J. Wallis. *Book Subscription Lists: A Revised Guide* (Newcastle upon Tyne: Harold Hill and Son for the Book Subscription List Project, 1975).

Rogers, J. E. Thorold. *Six Centuries of Work and Wages: The History of English Labour,* with a new Preface by G. D. H. Cole (London: Allen and Unwin, 1949).

Rorty, Richard. *Philosophy and the Mirror of Nature* (Princeton: Princeton University Press, 1979).

Ross, Andrew. "Techno-Ethics and Tele-Ethics: Three Lives in the Day of Max Headroom," Working Paper no. 8 (Milwaukee: University of Wisconsin-Milwaukee, Center for Twentieth Century Studies, 1998).

Roszak, Theodore. *Where the Wasteland Ends: Politics and Transcendence in Post-industrial Society* (New York: Doubleday, 1972).

Rotberg, Robert I., and Theodore K. Rabb. *Art and History: Images and Their Meaning* (Cambridge: Cambridge University Press, 1988).

Rothrock, George A. "Maps and Models in the Reign of Louis XIV," *Proceedings of the Annual Meeting of the Western Society for French History* 14 (1987): 50.

Rouse, Joseph. *Knowledge and Power: Toward a Political Philosophy of Science* (Ithaca: Cornell University Press, 1987).

Ruggles, R. I. "Governor Samuel Wegg: Intelligent Layman of the Royal Society," *Notes and Records of the Royal Society of London* 32 (1978): 181–99.

Saarinen, Thomas F. *Centering of Mental Maps of the World* (Tucson: Department of Geography and Regional Development, University of Arizona, 1987).

Sack, Robert. *Conceptions of Space in Social Thought: A Geographic Perspective* (London: Macmillan, 1980).

———. "Human Territoriality: A Theory," *Annals of the Association of American Geographers* 73, no. 1 (1983): 55–74.

———. *Human Territoriality: Its Theory and History* (Cambridge: Cambridge University Press, 1986).

Said, Edward W. "The Problem of Textuality: Two Exemplary Positions," *Critical Inquiry* 4, no. 4 (summer 1978): 673–714.

———. *Orientalism* (London: Penguin Books, 1985).

Salisbury, Neal. "Red Puritans: The 'Praying Indians' of Massachusetts Bay and John Eliot," *William and Mary Quarterly* 31 (1974): 27–54.

Sanders, Ronald. *Lost Tribes and Promised Lands: The Origins of American Racism* (Boston: Little, Brown, and Co., 1978).

Sauer, Carl O. "The Education of a Geographer," *Annals of the Association of American Geographers* 46 (1956): 287–99.

Schilder, Gunter. "Organization and Evolution of the Dutch East India Company's Hydrographic Office in the Seventeenth Century," *Imago Mundi* 28 (1976): 61–78.

Schlichtmann, Hansgeorg. "Codes in Map Communication," *Canadian Cartographer* 16 (1979): 81–97.

———. "Discussion" [of article by C. Grant Head], Monograph 31, *Cartographica* 21, no. 1 (1984): 33–36.

———. "Characteristic Traits of the Semiotic System 'Map Symbolism,'" *Cartographic Journal* 22 (1985): 23–30.

Schulz, Juergen. "Jacopo de' Barbari's View of Venice: Map Making, City Views and Moralized Geography before the Year 1500," *Art Bulletin* 60 (1978): 425–74.

———. "The Map Mural Cycles of the Renaissance," in Woodward, ed., *Art and Cartography*, 97–120.

Schwartz, Seymour I., and Ralph E. Ehrenberg. *The Mapping of America* (New York: Harry N. Abrams, 1980).

Seager, Joni, and Ann Olson. *Woman in the World: An International Atlas* (New York: Simon and Schuster, 1986).

Shortridge, Barbara Gimla. *Atlas of American Women* (New York: Macmillan, 1987).

Singer, Charles, et al., eds. *A History of Technology,* 4 vols. (Oxford: Clarendon Press, 1954–78).

Sinnhuber, K. A. "The Representation of Disputed Political Boundaries in General Atlases," *Cartographic Journal,* 1, no. 2 (1964): 20–28.

Skelton, R. A. *Decorative Printed Maps of the 15th to 18th Centuries* (London: Spring Books, 1952).

———. "Raleigh as a Geographer," *Virginia Magazine of History and Biography* 71 (1963): 131–49.

———. *Looking at an Early Map* (Lawrence, Kans.: University of Kansas Libraries, 1965).

———. "The Military Surveyor's Contribution to British Cartography in the 16th Century," *Imago Mundi* 24 (1970): 77–83.

———. *Maps: A Historical Survey of Their Study and Collecting* (Chicago: University of Chicago Press, 1972).

———. *Saxton's Survey of England and Wales. With a facsmile of Saxton's Wall-Map of 1583* (Amsterdam: N. Israel, 1974).

———, ed. *James Cook Surveyor of Newfoundland. Being a Collection of Charts of the Coasts of Newfoundland and Labradore, etc. Drawn from Original Surveys Taken by James Cook and Michael Lane, London, Thomas Jefferys, 1769–1770,* with an introductory essay by R. A. Skelton (San Francisco: David Magee, 1965).

Smith, John. *The Complete Works of Captain John Smith,* ed. Philip I. Barbour, 3 vols. (Chapel Hill: University of North Carolina Press, 1986).

Smith, Mary Elizabeth. *Picture Writing from Ancient Southern Mexico: Mixtec Place Signs and Maps* (Norman: University of Oklahoma Press, 1973).

Snyder, John P. "Social Consciousness and World Maps," *Christian Century,* 24 February 1988, 190–92.

Soja, Edward W. *Postmodern Geographies* (London: Verso, 1989)

Speir, Hans "Magic Geography," *Social Research* 8 (1941): 310–30.

Spence, Jonathan D. *The Memory Palace of Matteo Ricci* (London: 1984).

Stahl, W. H. "Representation of the Earth's Surface as an Artistic Motif," in *Encyclopedia of World Art* (New York: McGraw Hill, 1960), 851–54.

Stengers, J. "King Leopold's Imperialism," in Roger Owen and Bob Sutcliffe, eds., *Studies in the Theory of Imperialism* (London: Longman, 1972), 248–76.

Sterne, Laurence. *The Life and Opinions of Tristram Shandy, Gentleman,* ed. James Aiken Work (New York: Odyssey Press, 1940).

Stevenson, Edward L. "The Geographical Activities of the Casa de la Contratación," *Annals of the Association of American Geographers* 17 (1927): 39–59.

Stickler, P. J. "Invisible Towns: A Case Study in the Cartography of South Africa," *Geo Journal* 22, no. 3 (1990): 329–33.

Stilgoe, John R. *Common Landscape of America, 1580 to 1845* (New Haven: Yale University Press, 1982).

———. "Mapping Indiana: Nineteenth-Century School Book Views," in John R. Stilgoe, Roderick Nash, and Alfred Runte, *Perceptions of the Landscape and Its Preservation* (Indiananapolis: Historical Society, 1983).

Stoddard, D. R., ed. *Geography, Ideology and Social Concern* (Oxford: Blackwell, 1981).

Stone, L., and J. C. F. Stone. *An Open Elite? England, 1540–1880* (Oxford: Clarendon Press; New York: Oxford University Press, 1984).

Swift, Jonathan. *On Poetry: A Rhapsody* (London, 1733).

Szegö, Janos. *Human Cartography: Mapping the World of Man,* trans. Tom Miller (Stockholm: Swedish Council for Building Research, 1987).

Taylor, E. G. R. "John Dee and the Map of North-East Asia," *Imago Mundi* 12 (1955): 103.

———. *The Mathematical Practitioners of Hanoverian England, 1714–1840* (Cambridge: Cambridge University Press, 1966).

Teixeira da Mota. "Some Notes on the Organization of Hydrographical Services in Portugal before the Beginning of the Nineteenth Century," *Imago Mundi* 28 (1976): 51–60.

Therborn, Göran. *The Ideology of Power and the Power of Ideology* (London: New Leaf Books, 1980).

Thomas, Louis B. "Maps as Instruments of Propaganda," *Surveying and Mapping* 9 (1949): 75–81.

Thompson, F. M. L. *Chartered Surveyors: The Growth of a Profession* (London: Routledge and Kegan Paul, 1968).

Thomson, Morris M. *Maps for America: Cartographic Products of the U.S. Geological Survey and Others,* 2d ed. (Reston, Va.: U.S. Department of the Interior, 1981).

Thorpe, F. N., ed. *The Federal and State Constitutions, Colonial Charters, and Other Organic Laws of the United States,* 7 vols. (Washington, D.C.: Government Printing Office, 1909).

Todorov, Tzvetan. *The Conquest of America: The Question of the Other,* trans. Richard Howard (New York: Harper, 1984).

———. *Mikhail Bakhtin: The Dialogical Principle,* trans. Wlad Godzich (Minneapolis: University of Minnesota Press, 1984).

Tompkins, Jane. " 'Indians': Textualism, Morality, and the Problem of History' " *Critical Inquiry* 13 (1986): 101–19.

Tooley, R. V. *Title Pages from 16th to 19th Century* (London: Map Collectors' Circle, 1975).

Tuan, Yi-Fu. *Topophilia: A Study of Environmental Perception, Attitudes, and Values* (Englewood Cliffs, N.J.: Prentice-Hall, 1974).

———. *Landscapes of Fear* (Oxford: Blackwell, 1980).

Tufte, Edward R. *The Visual Display of Quantitative Information* (Cheshire, Conn.: Graphics Press, 1983).

Tyacke, Sarah. *London Map-Sellers, 1660–1720* (Tring, Hertfordshire: Map Collector Publications, 1978).

Valerio, Vladimiro. "The Neapolitan Saxton and His Survey of the Kindom of Naples," *Map Collector* 18 (1982): 14–17.

Van Donzel, E., B. Lewis, and C. Pellat, eds., *Encyclopaedia of Islam* (Leiden: Brill, 1978), vol. 4.

Verner, Coolie. "The First Maps of Virginia, 1590–1673," *Virginia Magazine of History and Biography* 58 (1950): 3–15.

———. "The Identification and Designation of Variants in the Study of Early Printed Maps," *Imago Mundi* 19 (1965): 100–105.

———. "The Fry and Jefferson Map," *Imago Mundi* 21 (1967): 70–94.

———. "Carto-bibliographical Description: The Analysis of Variants in Maps Printed from Copperplates," *American Cartographer* 1, no. 1 (1974): 77–87.

———. "Copperplate Printing," in David Woodward, ed., *Five Centuries of Map Printing*, 51–75.

Wachs, Martin "Introduction," in Martin Wachs, ed., *Ethics in Planning* (Rutgers Center for Urban Policy Research Institute, 1985).

Wahl, François. "Le Désir d'Espace" in Centre de Création Industrielle, *Cartes et Figures de la Terre* (Paris: Centre Georges Pompidou, 1980).

Wallace, Anthony F. C. "Political Organisation and Land Tenure among the Northeastern Indians, 1600–1830," *Southwestern Journal of Anthropology* 13 (1957): 301–21.

Wallerstein, Immanuel. *The Modern World-System*, vol. 1, *Capitalist Agriculture and the Origins of the European World-Economy in the Sixteenth Century* (New York: Academic Press, 1974).

———. *The Modern World-System*, vol. 2, *Mercantilism and the Consolidation of the European World-Economy, 1600–1750* (New York: Academic Press, 1980).

Wallis, Helen. "Globes in England up to 1660," *Geographical Magazine* 35 (1962–63): 267–79.

———. "The Cartography of Drake's Voyage," in J. W. Thrower Norman, ed., *Sir Francis Drake and the Famous Voyage, 1577–1580: Essays Commemorating the Quadricentennial of Drake's Circumnavigation of the Earth* (Berkeley: University of California Press, 1984), 121–63.

———, and Arthur H. Robinson. *Cartographical Innovations: An International Hand-*

book of Mapping Terms to 1900 (Tring, Hertfordshire: Map Collector Publications, 1987).

———, ed. *The Maps and Texts of the Boke of Idrography Presented by Jean Rotz to Henry VIII, Now in the British Library* (Oxford: Roxburghe Club, 1981).

Warner, Deborah J. *The Sky Explored: Celestial Cartography 1500–1800* (New York: A. R. Liss, 1979).

Waselkov, Gregory A. "Indian Maps of the Colonial Southeast," in Peter H. Wood, Gregory A. Waselkow, and M. Thomas Hatley, eds., *Powhatan's Mantle: Indians in the Colonial Southeast* (Lincoln: University of Nebraska Press, 1989), 292–343.

Wheat, C. I. *Mapping in the Transmississippi West, 1540–1861,* 5 vols. (San Francisco: Institute of Historical Cartography, 1957–63).

Whitaker, Arthur P. *The Western Hemisphere Idea: Its Rise and Decline* (Ithaca: Cornell University Press, 1954).

Whittemore Boggs, S. "This Hemisphere," *Department of State Bulletin* 12, no. 306 (Washington, D.C., 6 May 1945): 845–50.

Wieder, Frederick C. *Monumenta Cartographica: Reproductions of Unique and Rare Maps, Plans and Views in the Actual Size of the Originals; Accompanied by Cartographical Monographs,* vol. 5 (The Hague: M. Nijhoff, 1933).

Wilkinson, H. R. *Maps and Politics: A Review of the Ethnographic Cartography of Macedonia* (Liverpool: University of Liverpool Press, 1951).

Williams, Glyndwr. "The Hudson's Bay Company and Its Critics in the Eighteenth Century," *Transactions of the Royal Historical Society,* 5th ser., 20 (1970): 150–51.

Williams, Raymond. *The Country and the City* (London: Chatto and Windus, 1973).

———. *The Sociology of Culture* (New York: Schocken Books, 1982).

Williamson, J. A. *The Voyages of John and Sebastian Cabot* (London: Argonaut Press, 1929).

Winner, Langdon. "Do Artifacts Have Politics?" *Daedalus* 109, no. 1 (1980): 121–36.

Winslow, Edward. "Good Newes from New England . . . ," in Alexander Young, ed., *Chronicles of the Pilgrim Fathers of the Colony of Plymouth from 1602 to 1625* (Boston: C. C. Little and J. Brown, 1841), 361.

Winsor, Justin. "Early Maps of New England," in Winsor, ed., *Narrative and Critical History of America,* 3:381–84.

———. "The Earliest Maps of Massachusetts Bay and Boston Harbour," in Justin Winsor, ed. *Memorial History of Boston,* 4 vols. (Boston: James E. Osgood, 1888).

———, ed. *Narrative and Critical History of America,* 8 vols. (Boston: Houghton, Mifflin, 1884–89).

Winthrop, John, Sr. "General Considerations for the Plantation in New England, with an Answer to Several Objections," *Winthrop Papers,* 6 vols. (Boston: Massachusetts Historical Society, 1863–92), 2:120.

Wolff, Janet. *The Social Production of Art* (London: Macmillan, 1981).

Wolter, John A. "Cartography—An Emerging Discipline," *Canadian Cartographer* 12, no. 2 (1975): 210–16.

———. "The Emerging Discipline of Cartography," Ph.D. diss., University of Minnesota, 1975.

Wood, Denis. *I Don't Want to, but I Will: The Genesis of Geographic Knowledge, a Real-time Developmental Study of Adolescent Images of Novel Environments* (Worcester, Mass.: Clark University Cartographic Laboratory, 1973).

———. "Pleasure in the Idea: The Atlas as Narrative Form," in R. J. B. Carswell, G. J. A. de Leeuw, and N. M. Waters, "Atlases for Schools: Design Principles and Curriculum Perspectives," Monograph 36, *Cartographica* 24, no. 1 (1987): 24–45.

———. "Responses" to "Cartography, Ethics, and Social Theory," *Cartographica* 26, nos. 3 and 4 (1989): 117–19.

———, and John Fels. "Designs on Signs: Myth and Meaning in Maps," *Cartographica* 23, no. 3 (1986): 54–103.

Wood, William. *New England's Prospect* (1634; Boston: Publications of the Prince Society, 1865).

———. *New England's Prospect,* ed. Alden T Vaughan (Amherst: University of Massachusetts Press, 1977).

Woodward, David. "The Study of the History of Cartography: A Suggested Framework" *American Cartographer* 1 (1974): 101–15.

———. "Medieval *Mappaemundi,*" in J. B. Harley and David Woodward, eds., *The History of Cartography,* vol. 1, *Cartography in Prehistoric, Ancient, and Medieval Europe and the Mediterranean* (Chicago: University of Chicago Press, 1987), 286–370.

———, ed. *Five Centuries of Map Printing* (Chicago: University of Chicago Press, 1975).

———, ed. *Art and Cartography* (Chicago: University of Chicago Press, 1987).

Woolgar, Steve. *Science: The Very Idea* (Chichester, Sussex: Ellis Horwood, 1988).

Wright, J. K. "Map Makers Are Human: Comments on the Subjective in Mapping," *Geographical Review* 32 (1942): 527–44.

Yates, F. A. *Astraea: The Imperial Theme in the Sixteenth Century* (London: Routledge and Kegan Paul, 1975).

Young, Alan. *Tudor and Jacobean Tournaments* (New York: Sheridan House, 1987).

Zelinsky, Wilbur. "Some Problems in the Distribution of Generic Terms in the Place-Names of the Northeastern United States," *Annals of the Association of American Geographers* 45 (1955): 319–49.

Maps and Atlases

Bowen, Emanuel. *A Complete Atlas or Distinct View of the Known World, Exhibited in 68 Maps* (London, ca. 1750), map 38, "A New and Accurate Map of Virginia and Maryland."

———, and Thomas Kitchen. *The Royal English Atlas: Being a New and Accurate Set of Maps of All the Counties of South Britain, Drawn from Surveys, and the Best Authorites . . . by Emnuel Bowen, Geographer to His Late Majesty, Thomas Kitchen, Geographer and Others. The Whole Comprised in Forty-Four Sheet Maps* (London, ca. 1763).

Cary, John. *Cary's New and Correct English Atlas, Being a New Set of County Maps from Actual Surveys, etc.* (London, 1787).

D'Anville, Jean Baptiste Bourguignen and Didier Robert de Vaugondy. "A New and Correct Map of North America with the West India Islands," in *A General Atlas Describing the Whole Universe* (London, 1782).

Dunn, Samuel. "A Map of the British Empire in North America," sheet 8 in Thomas Jefferys, *The American Atlas; or, A Geographical Descrition of the Whole Continent of America* (London: Sayer and Bennett, 1776).

England Displayed Being a New, Complete and Accurate Survey and Description of the Kingdom of England, and Principality of Wales . . . by a Society of Gentlemen. . . . Revised, Corrected and Improved by P. Russell, Esq; and . . . Mr Owen Price (London, 1769).

Fry, Joshua, and Peter Jefferson. *A Map of the Most Inhabited Part of Virginia, Containing the Whole Province of Maryland and Part of Pennsylvania, New Jersey and North Carolina* (1751).

Jefferys, Thomas. "North America from the French of Mr. D'Anville," in *The Natural and Civil History of the French Dominions* (London, 1760).

———. "A Map of Pennsylvania Exhibiting not only the Improved Parts of That Province, but also Its Extensive Frontiers: Laid Down from Actual Surveys, and Chiefly from the Late Map of W. Scull Published in 1770," sheet 20 in Jefferys, *The American Atlas.*

Kitchen, Thomas. "A Map of the Whole Continent of America . . . with a Copious Table Fully Showing the Several Possessions of each European Province and State, as Settled by the Definitive Treaty Concluded at Paris, Feby. 19th 1763," and "An Accurate Map of North America Describing and Distinguishing the British and Spanish Dominions on This Great Continent, According to the Definitive Treaty. . . . " in Thomas Kitchin [*sic*], *A General Atlas* (London, 1773–93)

Moll, Herman. *The World Described* (London, 1708–1720).

———. *Atlas Minor* (London, 1729).

Sayer, Robert. *Catalogue of New and Interesting Prints Consisting of Engravings and Metzotintos of Every Size and Price, Likewise Paintings on Glass, Books of Architecture and Oranments, Penmanship, etc. etc. etc.* (London, 1786).

———. *Catalogue of Pilots, Neptunes and Charts, Both General and Particular; for the Navigation of All the Seas and Coasts of the Universe* (London, 1787).

———. *Atlases, Both Ancient and Modern Books of Maps, Surveys and Catalogue of Single Maps of All the Empires, Kingdoms, States, etc. in the Universe* (London, 1788).

——, and Thomas Jefferys. *A General Topography of North America and the West Indies* (London, 1768).

——, and John Bennett. *Catalogue of Prints for 1775* (rpt., London: Holland Press, 1970).

Senex, John. *A New General Atlas, . . . Containing a Geographical and Historical Account of All the Empires, Kingdoms and Other Dominions of the World* (London, 1721).

Velasco, Don Alonso De. Untitled map of the east coast of North America (1611), MS, Estado., Log. 2588, fol. 22 (Archivo General de Simancas, Simancas, Spain).

Newspaper Articles

"Agency Shows Way for Gulf Forces," *Washington Post* 2 January 1991.

Broad, William J. "U.S. Ends Curb on Photographs from Satellites," *New York Times,* 21 January 1988.

"Faked Russian Maps Gave the Germans Fits" *New York Times,* 11 September 1988.

"Gone Missing," *New Statesman,* 27 May 1983, 5.

"National Geo-glasnost?," *Christian Science Monitor,* 12 September 1988.

"NWT Natives Seek to Put Own Stamp on Map of North," *[Toronto] Globe and Mail,* 12 October 1987.

"Soviet Aide Admits Maps Were Faked for 50 Years," *New York Times,* 3 September 1988.

"Soviets Admit Map Paranoia," *Wisconsin State Journal,* 3 September 1988.

"Soviets Caught Mapping!" *Ottawa Citizen,* 3 September 1988.

"A Town with a History, but Whose?" *New York Times International,* 20 April 1991.

"In West Map Makers Hail 'Truth,'" *New York Times,* 3 September 1988.

"What's in a Name? For Indians, Cultural Survival," *New York Times,* 4 August 1988.

J. B. HARLEY was born in Bristol in 1932 and raised in rural Staffordshire. He gained his degrees from the University of Birmingham, which in 1985 also awarded him a D. Litt. He lectured in historical geography at the Universities of Liverpool (1958–69) and Exeter (1970–86) before moving to the University of Wisconsin-Milwaukee. His ideas on the meaning of maps have influenced not just geographers and map historians but students of art history and literature. At Milwaukee he began, with David Woodward, the multivolume *History of Cartography*, the first volume of which was published by the University of Chicago Press in 1987. Brian Harley died in 1991.

PAUL LAXTON was born in Rochdale, Lancashire, and graduated at the University of Durham. He has taught at the University of Liverpool since 1969, where he succeeded J. B. Harley as a lecturer in historical geography. His main academic interests are in eighteenth- and nineteenth-century English cartography, British and American urban history, and historical demography. He is currently working on public health and social development in early Victorian Liverpool and on urban mapping in Britain and the United States.

J. H. ANDREWS was born in London and attended Cambridge University and the London School of Economics. He retired as Professor of Geography at Trinity College Dublin in 1990, after thirty-six years of service. Among his numerous books and articles on map history and historical geography are *A Paper Landscape: The Ordnance Survey in Nineteenth-Century Ireland* (1975) and *Shapes of Ireland* (1997).

MATTHEW H. EDNEY was born in London and studied geography at University College London and the University of Wisconsin-Madison. He is associate professor and faculty scholar in the Osher Map Library, University of Southern Maine, and author of *Mapping an Empire: The Geographical Construction of British India, 1765–1843* (1997). His work explores cartographic cultures of eighteenth-century Britain and North America.

Library of Congress Cataloging-in-Publication Data

Harley, J. B. (John Brian)
The new nature of maps : essays in the history of cartography /
J.B. Harley ; edited by Paul Laxton ; introduction by J.H. Andrews.
p.   cm.
Includes bibliographical references and index.
ISBN 0-8018-6566-2 (alk. paper)
1. Cartography—History.   I. Laxton, Paul.   II. Title.

GA201 .H37 2001
526'.09—dc21   00-047804